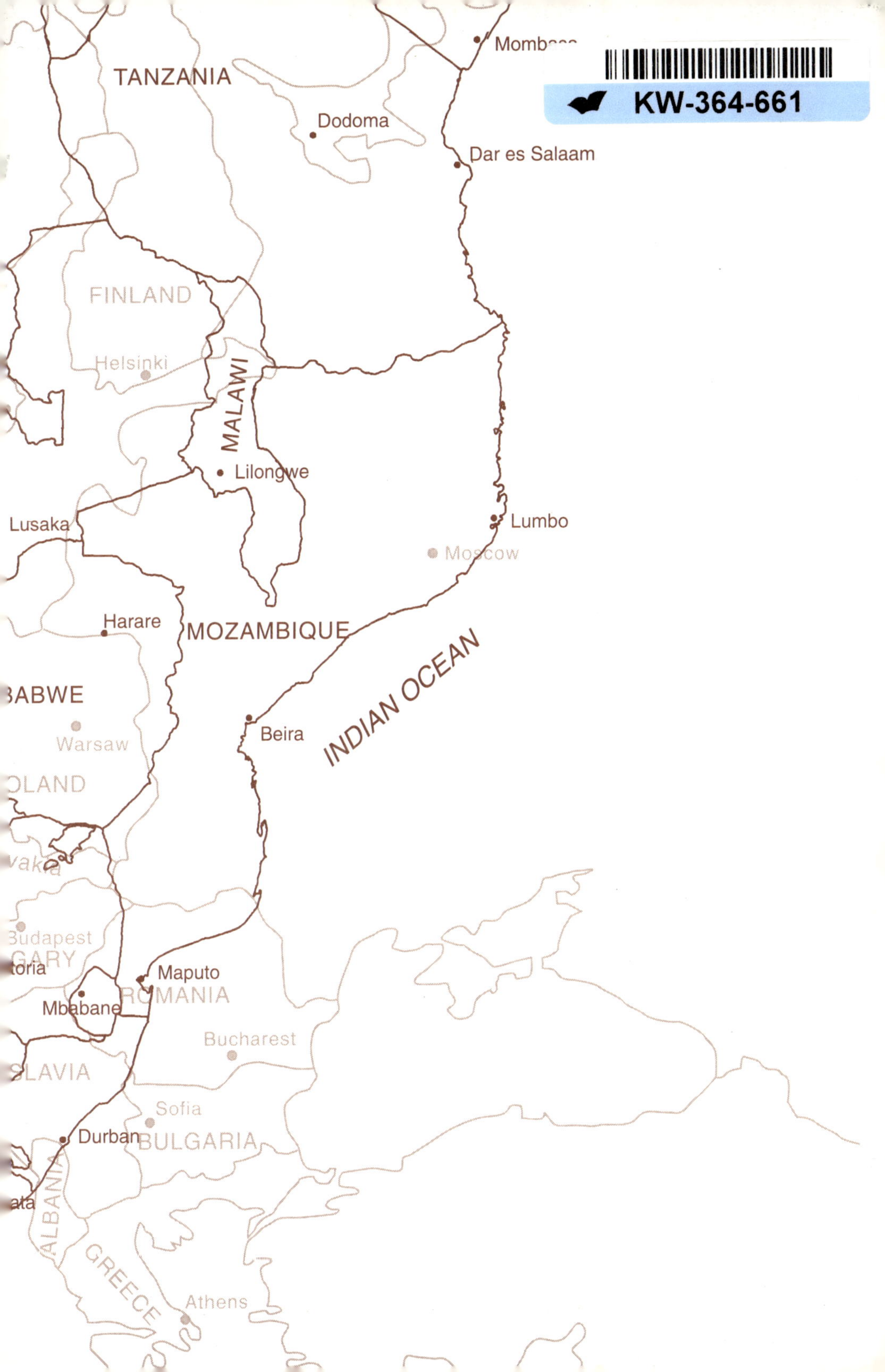
TANZANIA
Mombasa
Dodoma
Dar es Salaam
FINLAND
Helsinki
MALAWI
Lilongwe
Lusaka
Lumbo
Moscow
Harare
MOZAMBIQUE
INDIAN OCEAN
ABWE
Warsaw
Beira
OLAND
vakia
Budapest
GARY
toria
Maputo
Mbabane
ROMANIA
Bucharest
SLAVIA
Sofia
Durban
BULGARIA
ata
ALBANIA
GREECE
Athens

A GENERAL'S STORY

A General's Story

FROM AN ERA OF WAR AND PEACE

JANNIE GELDENHUYS

Jonathan Ball Publishers
Johannesburg

First published in 1995 by
Jonathan Ball Publishers (Pty) Ltd
P O Box 33977
Jeppestown 2043

ISBN 1 86842 020 5

Design by Michael Barnett
Original translation by Annemarié Geldenhuys
Editor and language consultant Madeline Lass
Typesetting and reproduction of text by Book Productions, Pretoria
Set in 11 on 13 Palatino
Reproduction of dust jacket and picture sections by Effective Reproductions
Maps by A1 Graphics, Pretoria. (By courtesy of J. L. van Schaik Publishers, Pretoria.)
Printed and bound by National Book Printers, Goodwood, Cape

CONTENTS

FOREWORD

A leader is a product of his time.

In the Western World the twentieth century, in the real sense, started with the outbreak of war in 1914 and ended with the fall of the Berlin Wall in 1989.

Jannie Geldenhuys is a leader who was created by this period; but he also witnessed the emergence of a new world order.

The course of history is largely determined by the interaction between leaders. This book relates Jannie Geldenhuys's personal experiences and perceptions as a leader in the making, as a leader and as a private individual. It provides a fascinating insight into one of the most incisive periods in South Africa's history.

If we do not know about the past, we cannot understand the present or determine the future. For that reason this book is of the utmost importance for those who are, and will be, part of our future.

M. T. Steyn

Bloemfontein
7 April 1993

PREFACE

I made a decision about sixteen years ago never to write a book of this nature. I therefore kept no papers and made no private notes. But at the end of November 1990 I allowed myself to be talked into putting on ice a book I was writing on aspects of leadership and management and tackling this one instead.

It was not easy. I had to choose between relying on my memory and writing in a popular style or doing serious research and producing a documentary type of book.

I decided on the first option and confirmed only basic facts, names, dates and places by way of various reference documents and authoritative persons.

I have not attempted to write a history of the past few decades, I have written about my personal experiences during this time. And I have tried to do so more or less chronologically.

I completed the final version of the Afrikaans manuscript during February/March 1993. It was an awkward time in which to write because on 2 February 1990 South Africa took a quantum leap from an old political era into an entirely new dispensation.

The situation, the thinking and the attitudes of people changed dramatically overnight. And subsequent political changes advanced more rapidly during weeks and months than during years and decades before this date. I decided, however, not to attempt any major update.

My original intention was always to write only about my life in the military up to my retirement on 1 November 1990; I never intended to give an account of or to comment on up-to-date 'hard news' events (for which a book is not really a suitable medium) especially in an ultrafast-moving environment.

I also found, working through the manuscript in search of sections to be updated, that it was still remarkably 'with it' in terms of its contemporary meaningfulness.

In the original script I did preview certain pointers of patterns and tendencies to come. I concluded that events that took place during the period March 1993 to March 1994, when I completed the English manuscript, tended to confirm such future indications rather than add new dimensions (for example, the continued and increased violence, and the formation of new political parties and groupings).

The book is about life and competition, about togetherness and conflict; about foes and friends – people who paved the route of the story and people who followed it; people who walked the road together and those who did not. It is about big people who are small, and about small people who are great.

Jannie Geldenhuys
Pretoria
April 1994

1

THE END AND THE BEGINNING
The ABC of war and peace – fortune and misfortune

'I warn you, we are on the brink of a devastating war!'

The warning was issued by my Cuban counterpart, Gen Ulises Rosales Del Toro. Seated next to him was his staff officer, who was also acting as interpreter.

At my side were Gen Neels van Tonder and my personal staff officer, Brig Johann Sonnekus.

It was 4 May 1988.

We were sitting in a small, sparsely furnished, private lounge, in Brown's Hotel, London.

The occasion was an informal meeting during the Angola/South West Africa negotiations. We had been attending the first in a long series of drawn out peace-making conferences.

During this conference the leader of our delegation was super diplomat, Neil van Heerden. Other members of the team were Dr Niel Barnard of National Intelligence and Derek Auret of Foreign Affairs.

The leader of the Cuban delegation was Jorge Risquet. (His beard had earned him the nickname of Oom Kaspaas – a character in a South African comic strip.) Among others, his team included Señor Carlos Aldana Escalante and Gen Rosales.

The Angolan team was led by their Minister of Foreign Affairs, Afonso van Dunem, assisted by the Deputy Minister of Defence and Chief of Staff, Gen Antonio dos Santos Franca, better known as Ndalu. However, according to certain observers, such as Fred Bridgland, the Cubans and Angolans were really part of the same delegation.

Chester Crocker, the United States Assistant Secretary of State for Africa, acted as chairman. We suspected that the Russian envoy,

Anatoliy Adamishin, was waiting somewhere in the wings. This later proved to be correct.

On 4 May, at the end of the conference, when we were adjourning, I received a personal message from Rosales: he wanted to talk to me. Privately.

He started our informal meeting in the small lounge by saying that he wasn't threatening me and that he merely wished to warn me. But for almost half an hour, through the interpreter, he told me how they had been mustering a large force comprising their best troops. They were concentrated in the south-west of Angola, just north of the South West (Namibian) border. They were ready for us. Not even the Namibian border would stop them.

In effect he was saying: If you do not use this opportunity to make peace and if you do not fall into line, you are in for a big war – a war that will destroy you.

He was calm, but very serious. He talked without notes, in measured words and sentences. Now and again he would move forward slightly and widen his eyes to accentuate the gravity of his words. He ended in a tone that said: I've had my say, what do you think?

I met his eyes. What did I see – challenge and expectation, hope and ... fear?

It was drizzling outside. A thousand and one thoughts were racing through my mind. He had mentioned war and peace in the same breath as if they went hand in hand. But peace and war are poles apart. However, negative and positive poles will attract one another – the threat of war and the hope of peace. I thought of our troops in Angola and South West; of *Blackmail or war* by Geneviève Tabouis. Was Rosales serious? Would they invade South West Africa? Did Fidel Castro aim to crush the South African Forces decisively and so bring an end to the war? Was it blackmail?

My feeling was that the Cubans were trying to bluff their way out of the defeats that their alliance had suffered on the battlefield and at the same time bluff their way into a strong negotiating position around the conference table. We did not have to allow ourselves to be intimidated. Suddenly the picture of Foreign Minister Pik Botha in action on a particular day about four years ago came into my mind's eye.

I stared intently at Rosales ... and pulled a 'Pik Botha' on him.

***

Minister Pik Botha was the leader of the South African delegation during a round of negotiations between South Africa, Angola and the United States in Lusaka on 13 February 1984. The venue was the Mulungushi Conference Centre, which had been made available to us by Pres Kaunda.

The aim was to negotiate a cessation of hostilities. It was just after the South African Operation Askari in Angola had been completed. We had actually already withdrawn, but had to return, crazy as it may seem, to negotiate our withdrawal. But the negotiations comprised more than that. The talks eventually led to the Mulungushi Declaration and the Lusaka Agreement over which a joint monitoring commission would play watchdog.

Mr Botha, his aides, my accompanying officers and I had met in advance to discuss how we would conduct the discussions in Lusaka. Mr Botha decided upon a certain approach.

The negotiations began. One must remember that Pik Botha is a super diplomat de luxe – the longest serving minister of foreign affairs in the world. He is a man who can think on his feet. He is flexible. He is unpredictable. He comes up with surprises. He often surprises his own side. That day he would once again do so.

Before the formal conference was opened he had had informal talks with the other parties. (This was not an unusual procedure.) His superb insight into the mood of the opposition made him abandon the approach that had been decided upon earlier. I did not know this.

Once the conference had started I sat doodling in my notebook, because I thought I knew what Pik Botha was going to say. But when he took the floor, his deep, resonant voice captivated every person present. He took the entire audience on a journey into the past. His speech was compelling and passionate. He spoke of how the South African republics had resisted the mighty Great Britain, the strongest military power in the world at that time, for three years from 1899 to 1902 …

The rest of the conference is history. An agreement was successfully concluded. I accept part of the blame.

***

It was this episode that came to mind four years later in London.

Then I too spoke to Rosales of the Boer War.

In the process I reminded him that Cuba is a small island, far away from the African continent. Waging a war thousands of kilometres away from home is extremely difficult and expensive. And if they should now dare to set one foot across the border to take us on, on our own turf – we, who for three years had braved the mightiest power in the world – it would be the blackest day in Cuban military history.

Despite his threat, Rosales was not militarily impolite. Neither was I. Waging war and making peace involve the unravelling of many intrigues. One dare not allow oneself to be intimidated or conned. But one should never take reckless risks either. One must remain calm, calculated and responsible. I believed that Rosales felt the same, and that is why I said to him: 'Let's not be unsporting; let's forget about threatening each other, and let's concentrate on the issue at hand.'

And that was what we did from that day on.

That grey London day was the beginning of the end of a long journey.

It was a journey over roads and crossroads that took us through fortune and misfortune, joy and pain, truths and untruths – through an era of storms and quiet. That was the time of the ABC of War and Peace: Angolans, Boers,[1] Cubans. Some of the leading figures were: Aldana, Botha, Crocker. Because the journey takes us through war and peace, I would like to give some thought to those concepts before we go any further.

Peace. As far back as Adam and Eve and the Fall we have not understood it. And even when we thought we did, we did not know how to achieve and safeguard it. We keep studying the causes of war but we remain ignorant of the causes of peace. We learn of love and peace at a tender age, we are taught to cherish love and peace by the church and at school, but generation after generation continue to make peace and war, to love and to hate.

The human race managed to work out how to put a man on the moon, and did so; but we have not yet learnt how to live in peace with our neighbour. We will probably savour everlasting peace only in heaven.

War. A certain exceptional aspect of war is ever present. One does not hear of it often, but if we do not bear it in mind, we may well lose sight of the full meaning of the stumbling blocks that we encountered on the road to war up to 4 May 1988 in London. It is a phenomenon that can decide the outcome of a war. It was formulated in the previous century by a German student of warfare, Carl von Clausewitz, as *friction de guerre* – the stress of war. He said:

> Everything in war is very simple, but the simplest thing is difficult. The difficulties accumulate and end by producing a kind of friction that is inconceivable unless one has experienced war ... countless unforeseeable minor incidents ... combine to lower the general level of performance, so that one always falls far short of the intended goal ...
>
> Friction is the only concept that more or less corresponds to the factors that distinguish real war from war on paper ... None of the (military machine's) components is of one piece: each part is composed of individuals, everyone of whom retains his potential of friction (and) the least important of whom may chance to delay things or somehow make them go wrong ...
>
> This tremendous friction ... brings about effects that cannot be measured, just because they are largely due to chance ...
>
> Action in war is like movement in a resistant element. Just as the simplest and most natural of movements, walking, cannot easily be performed in water, so in war it is difficult for normal efforts to achieve even moderate results.[2]

This is *friction de guerre*, the stress of war.

The accent often falls on 'countless unforeseeable minor incidents' and '... that are largely due to chance'.

There are people who argue that there is no such thing as 'chance'. They say everything is caused by something specific. They are right, of course. But in human terms and for all practical purposes chance is a fact of life.

I do not refer here to acts of God. I believe in those myself.

I can illustrate one kind of chance by using rugby as an example. A rugby ball has an oval shape. A player kicks the ball high into the air. The exact way boot and ball make contact, the effects of air-pressure, wind and temperature when the ball travels through the air, the exact manner in which it makes contact with the ground, and other factors will make it bounce in a certain direction. But the player merely wanted to kick the ball high into the air. He did not intend to make it hop in a specific direction. The ball may bounce in any direction, either to the advantage of one player, or the disadvantage of another – this is chance.

I can illustrate another form of chance by using bridge as an example. Once during a game at Oshivelo in the then South West Africa, Johann Sonnekus was dealt the full suit of thirteen clubs. The odds of this happening are less than one in six hundred thousand million. One's planning would never make provision for something that has such a low probability of happening. He benefited from it. He was fortunate – it was chance.

Johann Sonnekus cannot be praised for the luck that came his way. And in the same way the rugby player cannot be blamed for the ball that bounces the wrong way. But there are times when one holds someone else responsible for a chance happening. However, the degree of culpability is sometimes so small as to make it excusable in human terms.

Take the player for whom the ball bounced the wrong way: An opponent grabs it and scores. Something of this nature can happen to anyone. The more players in the team, the greater the possibility of accidents happening to a number of them. It could result in a weaker team winning a game against a stronger side.

We tend, however, to conveniently identify and tag excusable mishaps when they cause the opponents to score points, but we don't really take notice of those which do not lead to points, and of which the accumulative effect can be just as decisive as the more obvious 'blunders'. Injury to a key player in a strong team, a player skidding on a wet patch, a ball hitting the crossbar and bouncing back, errors of judgement by the referee, all these cases of 'bad luck' often lead to a team losing the advantage.

It is then that we say that we were beaten by the bounce of the ball; that we just had bad luck; that is the way things happen. Or we say we made too many mistakes; the team that makes the least errors is the one that wins; or that the opponents made better use of their opportunities – the team that takes advantage of their chances is the team that wins. However, we should not forget that the element of chance, *friction de guerre*, was also present here.

This is sport. But in war there are other aggravating factors. War is not a game you play on a standard tennis court or rugby field – you may even have to fight for the terrain you selected for battle. The teams do not play with the same standard cricket bat. If you want to use a wider bat, that's your decision. And if your opponent chooses to hurl an iron ball at you, he is free to do so. And people shoot at each other. To kill. To destroy. To conquer.

And when a battalion fights, there are a thousand individuals each of whom can 'slip on a bad patch', who can 'fumble while the ball bounces the wrong way' and who may 'tighten the wrong screw'.

Maybe this is what a British officer meant when he told me in 1960: 'In a future war, I suppose we'll muddle through to victory again!'

There is the chance that anything can go wrong with any one of 3 000 men in a task force. Call it Murphy's Law if you like (if anything can go wrong, it will;) or *friction de guerre*, it doesn't matter; if you and those with you suffer more than your fair share of mishaps caused by chance, you are in danger of losing.

The outcome of a few excusable 'blunders' can be frightening. Jeff Dewar says that 99,9 per cent effectiveness, let's say 0,1 per cent *friction de guerre* in South Africa, could mean two unsafe aircraft landings every week, 1 600 pieces of mail lost by the post office hourly, 2 000 faulty medical prescriptions per year and 1 000 cheques posted against the wrong accounts daily.

One can hardly imagine what might happen in a war with military equipment, weapons, ammunition, explosives – and an enemy.

Everyone whom I have encountered on the road of peace and war, and fortune and misfortune, will confirm this: seniors, equals and juniors; commanders and staffs; warrant officers, non-commissioned officers and troops; men and women in uniform and civvies; black, brown, white and yellow people of the Army, Air Force, Navy, Medical Services and Special Forces; people of South Africa, South West and Angola from all walks of life, who each made a contribution in whatever part of southern Africa or wherever – each with the potential to have been unlucky.

They have had experiences that only those who have had similar experiences will understand. They've learnt what it is that separates real war from the war game. They suffered the strains of all those countless, unforeseen incidents which make the simplest of acts difficult in war.

And now I come to the beginning of the beginning. The story leading up to 4 May 1988 and thereafter.

2

FIRST STEPS TO KNOWLEDGE
Style is good, but it is better to win

This story begins amid threats of war and promises of peace – the 1930s. A time of drought, depression, misery and unemployment. Young people were looking for work, amongst others at the railways and the Ess Ess Bee 'SSB' (1 Special Service Battalion).

I was born on 5 February 1935 on the farm Dansfontein in the Kroonstad district, the second son of Barend Petrus (Ben) and Anna Geldenhuys.

I became aware of the concepts of war and peace early on in my childhood. Old photographs still remind me of how my father and other farmers played soldier-soldier as it were. They were members of the rifle association.

But I was also given the message of peace and love, especially from my mother. She was the finest person I have ever known.

The first few years of my life were peaceful. The worst thing that happened to me was when as a toddler I pushed a .22-cartridge into our car's cigarette lighter socket. It exploded and the sharp edge of the shell stabbed into my right eye. My father was extremely upset. But *friction de guerre* was on my side. I suffered no permanent damage.

The year 1939 saw the release of David O Selznick's film *Gone with the wind*. And in Europe the winds of war were blowing and World War II broke out. South Africa declared war on Germany. My father joined the Union Defence Force and we moved to Pretoria. This was the beginning of a nomad existence, moving around from one place to another.

It was only much later that I learned of the internal political repercussions of South Africa's decision to go to war. Prime Minister J B M

Hertzog and his supporters were against fighting on the side of Great Britain. They wanted the country to remain neutral, but the Prime Minister's adjutant, Gen J C Smuts, opposed him. On 4 September 1939 Smuts won the debate in the House of Assembly by a margin of 13 votes. He took over the reigns and declared war against Germany. My father was a Smuts man, a Sap (South African Party supporter), and those like him who joined up and who were prepared to serve outside the country's borders wore red tabs on the shoulders of their uniforms.

My father initially served in a mounted regiment and later in the South African Instructional Corps. As he was transferred from one place to another until he eventually went 'up North', his family became camp-followers. That is why I never played around in the streets of Pretoria like the other children – we moved to Piet Retief after two months.

The war actually passed me by. However, during that time I learned other truths, like the story of my little friend Rosalie whom I met at Piet Retief. At first I spoke to her in Afrikaans. As she never responded, I gathered that she did not understand Afrikaans. So I tried English. She still did not reply. I wondered whether it was just my kind of English that she didn't understand; but I persevered. However, Rosalie was deaf and dumb. It had never occurred to me that some people could not hear and therefore could not speak.

One of my father's colleagues was a certain Captain Porky van Rensburg. The name probably referred to his size. He was the adjutant of the regiment. One day the commanding officer and Porky were summoned to Defence Headquarters in Pretoria. Everybody wondered why. On the evening that they were expected to return, some of the officers gathered to have a few drinks while waiting for them to arrive. They were obviously keen to hear what new developments had taken place. Then one of the wives appeared and said: 'You don't have to wait any longer, we've just heard over the Zeesen German news broadcast that the Regiment is going to be transferred to Ladysmith.' That was the news everyone was waiting for!

And so we moved from Piet Retief to Ladysmith. Here the mounted regiment was converted to an armoured car regiment. We stayed in a boarding house within the walls of an old fort. Porky's son Herman, known to everyone as Boytjie, and I now played war-war with the other children of the fort.

I started school in Ladysmith. Here, again, I was given the message of love and peace every morning, when we were gathered in the courtyard for scripture-reading. By the end of the year I was singing along with the other children in phonetic Afrikaans:

... la ... la ... la einjils seeheeng
... la ... la ... la and muhseemaail
... la ... la ... la sinnirsrêkonsaail

I did not know what it meant. But it was beautiful and full of goodness. Many years later I realized that it was 'Peace on Earth':

Hark the herald angels sing
Peace on earth and mercy mild
God and sinners reconciled ...

At Ladysmith I participated in athletics for the first time. Seven of us took part in the 75 yards race. For some reason I took off only my shoes but not my socks, and by the end of the race they were flapping around like two sausages. At home I told my mother that I had won seventh.

My father was sent 'up North' and we moved to Frankfort where we stayed with my mother's sister, Aunt Maggie Fröhlich, then the owner of the Good Hope Café. She was married to an English-speaking South African of German descent. Here I continued my school career in all seriousness and passed Sub A.

But once again I did not fish barbel in the Wilge River or play among the hills of Frankfort with the other children for long because we soon moved to Bethlehem. My mother's maiden name was Bruwer, and she had grown up in this district. Most of her family still lived there.

Bethlehem is a picture of dams, streams and weeping willows set against the foot-hills of the Drakensberg range. It is the world of the sun-gazing girdle-tailed lizards, known as *'Ouvolk'*, of the north-eastern Free State, known as the *'riemland'*: a mosaic of farmlands with maize and potatoes in summer and waving wheat-fields in winter – the time when you freeze to death!

By the time I started my second year at school, I had learnt that there were white people and black people; there were people who could talk and people like Rosalie who could not; people who speak but say nothing; people who can hear but do not listen. I had discovered in Frankfort that some people supported the English and some the Germans. And in Bethlehem I relived the trauma of making new friends: Are you for the English or are you for the Germans? And if your answer was unacceptable, you did not fit in. And if you do not fit in you were bullied.

As the son of a red tab I preferred to keep my mouth shut. If I had to, I'd say 'but Jannie Smuts really is quite clever', which seemed to pacify everybody.

I also learned something else: If you are an achiever it does not matter much if you are for the English or for the Germans. I was good at backyard and playground games. With my new-found fleet-footedness, and having got rid of the handicap of flapping socks, I also did well at athletics.

At last I could now walk to school in peace with the other children, play in the streets of the town and go fishing at Loch Athlone and Loch Lomond.

My mother was a teacher at the primary school. In those days of rationing and petrol coupons she probably committed the only crime of her life: she sieved flour to make white bread!

If anybody knocked at the door while this crime was being perpetrated, we'd all scatter hurriedly to hide the evidence. And for all we knew it could have been a neighbour wanting to borrow the sieve.

We spent all our holidays and weekends with my grandfather and grandmother Jan and Annie Bruwer on their farm, Davelsrus. In between, during the schoolterm, we stayed in town. The farm is situated between Clarens and Kestell, on the other side of the Golden Gate mountains, beneath huge ochre and crimson cliffs.

My best friend on the farm was Matjarapan. I was called Motle. I don't know what became of him. I often wonder.

Memories of experiences during the English War (1899–1902) were still smouldering on the farm. I heard from my grandmother how they had lived in the concentration camps.

In 1989, ninety years after the beginning of the Anglo-Boer War, Chaplain Dawie Scheepers, a distant relative, brought me a letter. My great-grandfather had written it to my great-grandmother during the war:

Ladysmith

M M du Plessis 9 November 1899

My dearest and never-forgotten wife and children.

By the Grace of God I am still alive, and I hope you are too.

I have received your letter, which, like a drop of cold water, quenched my thirsting soul. My longing for you is so profound that no words can describe it.

My darling, you must not stop writing to me as long I am still alive, because the thundering of the guns never cease and every moment could be the last.

We hope that our circumstances will improve if we achieve victory at Ladysmith.

Our side have 15 dead and 04 wounded. Tomas is dead. My dearest wife, you write that you are becoming impatient, but you must rather pray.

Jan is also here, and if he goes back I will ask him to hire a man and send him here. Because I cannot be released from my duties here and we do not know when the war will end, you will have to have the sheep sheared.

All our friends are well and there is so much to write that I do not know what to say.

And if you can perhaps find a man to hire to take my place, you must do so and send him here. It would make me very happy because I yearn for you my love. I long for you. If only I could be with you for a few hours, I'd be so happy to see your face again. And my children?

How is Koos?

Now I shall end, but never with my yearning heart.

My deepest regards my dearest wife and children.

W du Plessis
Address
Bester Stasi
Naudé laager

The Boer leaders quickly put a stop to the practice, as mentioned in the letter, of hiring a burgher to take one's place in the commando.

Jan, to whom my great-grandfather refers, was probably my grandfather. Koos was probably Uncle Koos du Toit of Kestell. He used to tell me stories while feeding his lizards on the verandah. He enjoyed reliving the cricket 'test' matches they, the prisoners of war, had played against the English in Ceylon – or was it St Helena?

I also heard about Hans van Rensburg of the Ossewa Brandwag (OB) when the grown-ups whispered about politics. The OBs were secretly planning to sabotage Smut's war policy. I knew very little of all this and understood even less.

But again the song of peace was there. During family prayers my mother used to play the piano and we would all sing. Once I was allowed to choose the hymn, so I suggested that we sing the song about the little car that rides over the mountains. It was 'Oor berge en in dale en overal is God' (over mountains and in valleys and everywhere is God).

With my cousins also visiting the farm during the December holidays, I experienced all the conflict and competitiveness that children normally do. Especially boys. You had to prove that you were a man. A boy does not feel pain, because he is a boy. A boy does not cry, because he is a boy. He must be able to lash a whip; he must have a penknife; must know how to cut riempies (leather strips), milk cows, and shoot. You shoot with a pea-shooter, a catapult, or clay-stick, and if you shoot with a .22 or actually have your own, then you're really a man.

But unfortunately it sometimes goes further. One day at school, during long break, a friend, Kobus Colyn, and I were goaded into having a fight. I still believe the bell saved me that day.

I was often the youngest and the smallest and always had to do the dirty work. But I learned fast: as long as someone is in a position to further his own cause, such as to prove his manliness or to acquire status, he will do just about anything – and then you don't have to do it. I found that if I didn't compete with them, and left them alone, the bigger boys would cut the riempies and milk the cows. In this way they had the opportunity to demonstrate their skills and to prove that they were men.

But there are men and men. My brother, Johan (or Ouboet), three and a half years my senior, reminded me of something I once did: Hans Seubring, the then well-known Dutch artist and adventurer, had arrived on the farm. He hawked his paintings from farm to farm and from school to school. He was a man. He was more than 7 ft tall. Standing in the farm outbuilding one day he told us that he could do something that we could not. We asked him, 'What?' He lifted up his arm and pressed his hand against the ceiling. Taking up the challenge I told him that I could do something that he could not. He asked, 'What?' So I walked through the door, upright.

Those days we used to walk bare-foot. And because of all the playing around without shoes the soles of one's feet became hard and tough; so tough that when one had run across a field full of devil's thorn and reached the other side, one did not sit down to remove the thorns, one just stood and wiped one's feet on the grass. And in winter the skin under one's heels and big-toes cracked. With my country bumpkin feet I was basking in the sun at the municipal swimming bath one day, lying on my stomach on the warm cement next to the pool. A couple of English-speaking girls walked past behind me and I heard one of them say in disgust: 'Gosh, look at that boy's feet!' I was so ashamed of myself that from that day on I always picked a spot on the grass where I could lie with my feet pressed against the perimeter wall.

When I started going to high school and had to participate in sport more regularly, I could not go to the farm so often and became more of a townee.

During some of my school holidays I worked as a petrol attendant doing night-duty at Oom Frans Furstenburg's Central Garage. This service station was in town on the main road to Durban. Here I added a great deal to my knowledge about people and human nature. I always got the jitters when someone told me to 'fill her up', because with the old pumps and cars it was always quite tricky not to spill the last bit of petrol. And if it happened, some of the obviously more well-to-do people would pay me a penny or a tickey short, 'for the petrol you spilt on the ground'. But some of the people who seemed rather on the needy side would in the same situation actually tip me a penny or a tickey.

When the war was over, my father who was then a captain, was stationed at the Demobilization Depot in Pretoria. After a short while he suffered a stroke and died. My mother moved back to Bethlehem with us.

At Bethlehem I got my first glimpse of important people.

In 1947 King George VI, the Queen and the two princesses visited South Africa. Sap newspapers made a fuss of them while Nat newspapers ignored them. They came to Bethlehem too. During their visit they went to the Goble Park sports stadium where everyone could see them. The King appeared at ease, but neat in his suit. My standard 6 teacher, Schalk van Niekerk, was also the mayor. He escorted them in his stately robe, chain of office and all. I was there and so was Emily who worked for us in our house.

Back at home my mother asked Emily what the king looked like. She said, striking. Very nice. She liked the beautiful clothes the king wore – especially the chain!

Johan Steyl, who played rugby for the Free State, taught me mathematics and introduced me to the wonder of music. He was also the commanding officer of our school's cadet detachment, and I was the student sergeant-major. He and Appels Odendaal, who played rugby for Eastern Province and Free State, taught me to play rugby.

Koot Brits was the teacher who taught me the most about Afrikaans with the least effort. Miss Agnes Holtzhausen, who would later become principal of the Afrikaans Girls High School in Pretoria, tried to teach me English. And if I am not a modest person it is not for lack of trying on her part. Only during these days did I find out that 'se-breiter' was not really a proper Afrikaans word. It is actually 'roomafskeier' – separator.

Kiep van Schalkwyk taught me history and I enthusiastically shared the successes of Garibaldi and Napoleon with him.

I had good friends, especially among the sportsmen. I played in the same rugby team as three boys who later became Springboks: the well-known Tom (Karel) van Vollenhoven, the best threequarter I've ever seen on a rugby-field, and Bennie van Niekerk, who toured the British Isles and France with the Springbok rugby team in 1960–1961. The third one was Hannes Botha. He later became a South African shot-put champion, professor in physical education at the University of Pretoria and President of the SA Amateur Athletics Union.

My cousin Antoinette, the daughter of my English-speaking South African uncle of German descent, was married to Alberto Claudio Scopetti, an Italian prisoner of war who made South Africa his new home. They now also lived in Bethlehem. Scopetti boxed and I keenly followed his example. I was most enthusiastic. On 31 May 1950 Viccie Toweel beat Manuel Ortiz of America in fifteen rounds on points. He was now the new bantam weight champion of the world.

To get back to athletics, Tom van Vollenhoven still says that I ran the 220 yards hurdles with style; but that he beat me. When it comes to boxing I can say that whether he had style or not, I beat him. But he was small then. Another chap, Johhny McLaren, hit the living day-lights out of me, but I was small then. Tom taught me that style is good, but that it is better to win.

Amongst the grown-ups of the district there were some big names. Doc Craven of Lindley was already a legend in those years. He was not known only as a Springbok and rugby expert, but was also a highly respected military officer during World War II. Drs Tavi du Preez and James Gilliland would both become Deputy Surgeons General of the Defence Force, and Jakkals Keevey was a rugby Springbok in the team that toured the British Isles and France in 1951/1952.

My earlier contact with military life continued. My brother was in the Citizen Force in the Regiment Louw Wepener, which was headquartered in Bethlehem. The Permanent Force officer at the headquarters was Captain W P Louw. He later became Officer Commanding OFS Command and also Chief of the Army. One of the Permanent Force instructors in the region was Staff Sergeant Umlaut Lötter. (Lötter with an umlaut.) Later, when I was in Windhoek, he was the Commanding Officer at Grootfrontein, South West Africa.

I matriculated in 1952.

Without distinctions.

Without a first class.

With a D in geography.

Bad teacher!

3

MORE STEPS TO KNOWLEDGE
With an open mind, you can even do it with tackies

In 1953, while Bing Crosby's 'Little Boy Lost' and 'Scared Stiff' bleated from juke boxes, I voluntarily began training at the Military Gymnasium at Roberts' Heights, which was already then known as Voortrekkerhoogte, but I still called it Roberts' Heights for a while, as my father had done.

A year in the army would give me time to decide what I wanted to do with my life.

From Bethlehem with its clean air I arrived at the Pretoria station. To me it looked black and grimy. Voortrekkerhoogte looked red and brickish. I felt lost and alone.

The first time out on the parade ground I, the former student sergeant-major, got the fright of my life. When the instructors, Sergeants Eric Pierce and Blackie Swart, formed us up I didn't even realize they were speaking Afrikaans. Their commands were rattled like machine-gun fire. Before I could react to the first burst, the next had been delivered.

A few days later some of us received orders to report at the parade ground. Staff Sergeant A-Jack van Zyl informed us that we had been chosen to be the *'vuurparty'* for a colonel. I gathered that we had been detailed to make the fire at some barbecue.

As had happened before, he drilled us for a while, just as a warming-up exercise before we got to the real task at hand. After quite a few sessions of marking time and about-turns at a bewildering rate I felt that he was overdoing the warming-up somewhat. But suddenly I realized what he was in fact doing. He was putting us through our paces to prepare us to act as the ceremonial platoon which has to fire the salute at the military funeral of a colonel – we were the firing-party!

The one-year course that I was doing also served as the first year of a four-year officers' course. It was murderous. The pace was much like the later three months' 'basics' training at the beginning of a national service term, but right through the year!

We invented 'taxis'. They consisted of two pieces of blanket, one for each boot. One shuffled around on them in the bungalow so as not to scratch the shiny black mirrorlike floors. It cut the daily early morning spit-and-polish ritual by a few minutes.

I must say, however, in later years the troops always told me that 'basics' was the best time of their lives that they would never like to repeat.

During this year we were also required to register for two first-year academic subjects at the University of Pretoria.

I tried to play some rugby too. I made the Northern Transvaal under-nineteen side as replacement for the selected flyhalf who was not available. During the latter part of the season I played for the senior Garrison team (Defence). My first match was against Police. Their team included Fiks van der Merwe, war veteran and Springbok flank forward in 1949, and Hansie Brewis, Springbok flyhalf. I was still under eighteen.

At our passing-out parade at the end of the year, Genl H B Klopper took the salute. During World War II he had been the commander of the South African Forces at Tobruk.

At the end of the year I decided to complete the full course and obtain a degree.

We were a small group who continued our training during 1954 at the Military College. Course 322G. It was an officers' course and we were called cadets. Magnus Malan, later to become Minister of Defence, was then a senior cadet. His group completed the course a few months after our arrival. Constand Viljoen, later to become Chief of the Defence Force, was a year ahead of us.

By this time I had naturally become quite a bit wiser. For the second time I experienced the issuing of equipment. The staff-sergeant read and marked off the items in a book, and the sergeant handed it over the counter. It went like this:

'Braces, left and right – one and one.'

'Bottles, water – one ...'

I just grabbed and packed away. I thought to myself, with the brand new clothes the senior men will tease me by calling me a rookie as I still 'smelled of quartermaster stores'.

'Bottles, water carrier – one.'

'Belts, webbing – one.'

I began to see humour in the quartermaster language and soon found the opportunity to use it. It happened like this: As would-be officers and gentlemen we were also expected to acquire the appropriate civilian clothes. We each had to have a hat, a dress-suit and so forth.

The cadet wing commander decided to conduct a special inspection one Saturday morning. On this occasion he not only wanted to see our military gear, but also our civilian attire. We had to present our gear in a prescribed manner in our rooms. In addition, we were also expected to prepare a list of all our clothes. The list had to be placed at the foot of one's bed, so that your complete inventory could be checked.

The commander, Maj Dawid Schalk Pretorius, was a very imposing man. He was nicknamed 'Pieringoog', (Saucer-eyes), or 'Piering' (Saucer) for short because he had the habit of widening his eyes when addressing one.

And this is where the quartermaster language humour came in. With 'Braces, left and right – one and one' and 'Glasses, looking mirror – one; Glasses, looking mirror, stands – one' still fresh in my mind, I prepared my list:

Shoes, brown leather, civilian, pairs – one
Shoes, black conservative, pair – one
Flannels, long gentlemen's, pairs – one
Jackets, sports sober – one ...

My room was the second door from the entrance. The major and his entourage walked into the first one. The sergeant-major shouted: 'Stand by your beds!'

My friend, Cadet Malcolm Baillie Anderson, was next door. I could hear the loud stamping of his feet as he came to attention. Bombastic questions were asked and feeble answers given. Otherwise it was dead quiet. I suddenly realized that this inspection was bad news. It was a serious affair.

I had certainly gone too far with that list of mine. But it was too late. There was no way that I could re-do it. If I moved they would hear me.

The first room done, the inspection group walked into mine. I was holding my breath.

The major went straight for my list. He picked it up. He studied it. And as was his custom, he turned to the sergeant major: 'Sergeant-major, look at this. Look at what this cadet has written,' and he passed on the list. The sergeant-major stared at it for a long while, marking time. The poor man was probably trying to work out what the major wanted to hear. At long last he muttered: 'Uh ... yes, I see, sir.' I stood dead still.

Then the major widened his eyes at me and declared dramatically: 'This cadet is obviously a born soldier!'

Major Pretorius was quite a character. I think it was Capt Vic Dreyer who nicknamed him 'Pieringoog'. Piering was the SA hammer-throw champion before the war and Vic Dreyer, who captained the Springbok athletics team at the 1954 Empire Games in Vancouver, was the current champion. One couldn't help noticing a continued competitiveness between the two.

There were other interesting people at the Military College too. One was Maj Kuno van der Post. He was a dear man. It is only once you understand war and the military, that you can appreciate how such a gentle man can feel at home in the army. I had the pleasure of meeting other members of his family, such as the writer, Col Laurens van der Post, and his nephew, Tommy Bedford, the Springbok rugby captain.

Our training at the college was very broad: we were instructed in horse-riding at the Police College; we were taught to fence by Maj Harry Schmidt; and we also had to take lessons in judo and dancing.

In our second year we underwent training in weapons and leadership and took three further first-year university courses. After that we became second lieutenants.

There were only eight of us at our passing-out parade. Two other members of our group, Ian Gleeson and Lourens Oosthuizen, would also become generals one day. Later, during my term as Chief of the Defence Force, Gen Gleeson was the number two.

We stayed on at the college for the second half of the four-year course and completed our second- and third-year university courses as full-time students at the University of Pretoria. Our further military training was done on a part-time basis, on Saturdays and during university holidays.

The academic subjects I liked most and which later stood me in good stead were military history, military law, criminal law, law of evidence, international law, geo-politics, political science and economics. What I really learned was, in the words of Benjamin Disraeli: 'To be conscious that you are ignorant is a great step to knowledge.' I became aware of my ignorance and took a few steps towards knowledge.

We were the last group to do our academic training at the University of Pretoria. Thereafter the cadets went to Stellenbosch, which led to the Military Academy at Saldanha being founded.

Various exceptional people at the University of Pretoria made an important contribution to our education, such as At Pelser, F J du Toit Spies and Cmdt (Dr) Cassie Bakkes of the History Department; and Jan Lombard, D G Franszen and Gerhard de Kock of the Economics Department. Franszen and De Kock later became governors of the Reserve Bank.

E F W Gey van Pittius, professor in political science, was an arch democrat. It was said that he would sjambok you until you also became one. But that was not how I was 'democratized'. I was influenced rather more by his younger colleague, Charles Nieuwoudt.

I admired their scientific approach. And I became an enthusiastic freemarketeer.

However, there was no way in which politics could remain an academic endeavour. Party politics was on everybody's lips. The red-tab days were not yet quite forgotten. D F Malan came to power in 1948. He was succeeded by Hans Strijdom. Elections were held in 1953 and 1958. And at the college, reading the newspapers at breakfast was no simple matter. If you read the *Rand Daily Mail,* you were a Sap; if you read the *Transvaler,* you were a Nat – despite the fact that officers were supposed to be non-political.

At Voortrekkerhoogte I once again found myself in a top-class sports community. Staff-sergeant Andy Botes took over from Capt Vic Dreyer as hammer thrower. Retired super-athlete, Snaar Viljoen, was always to be seen on the sidelines. There were other Springboks, such as hurdles athlete, Poena Malan. John Short, the well-known shotput athlete who was later to become an athletic coach and commentator, even played rugby in those days – in the centre position! My friend Thaba (-zimbi) du Plessis became a pentathlon Springbok. He and Maj Harry Schmidt took part in the 1956 Olympic Games in Melbourne.

For two years I played flyhalf for the Northern Transvaal under-ninteen side; and I played club rugby for Garrison during the entire period of my stay. On Saturdays, after games, we were expected to get together at the Garrison clubhouse for a bit of socializing. Dancing was sometimes part of the programme.

Dancing was not one of my strong points. I usually did the rounds and chatted to everybody, which inevitably meant ending up at the bar. The only drink I knew was beer. In those days, if you wanted to be a bit daring you drank a ginger square. But as the men at the club felt that it was a sissy's drink, I stuck to beer.

On one of those evenings, chatting with two of my under-nineteen mates at the bar, I noticed that they certainly weren't holding back on the brandy and coke. I thought to myself: 'These chaps are not serious about rugby. They're only under-nineteen and look at them. They'll never get anywhere.'

They just happened to be Frik du Preez and Ollie Ahlers. Frik was to become one of South Africa's all-time great rugby players.

It was on the rugbyfield that I learnt another important lesson about life – from a soccer player, Sergeant Sheehan-Shepherd.

One day, while we were kicking the ball around, friendly old big-mouth Sheppie sauntered up to us: 'You rugby guys are stupid. You don't play with your brains and you don't even know the basic skills.'

Everybody present wanted to crucify him, but he quickly explained: 'Wait, wait! I'll show you how to kick at goal.'

In those days one would place the ball and walk backwards in a straight line to measure the distance. The approach preceding the kick was also in a straight line to the ball and goalposts. Sheppie took the rugby ball, placed it on the halfway-line, walked a dogleg backwards, looked at the poles, ran up to the ball along a circular path and kicked it well over the crossbar between the uprights – with his tackies! Everybody was astonished and embarrassed. And Sheppie was off again with his big mouth: 'If you have an open mind you can do it with tackies too.'

No rugby player had questioned the accepted style of kicking at the goalposts, yet Sheppie proved that his way could be more effective. Unaccountably, more than a decade passed before it became the internationally recognized technique. Why hadn't I taken the initiative? In those days one did not easily question accepted rules – even more so in a military milieu. Yet, for progress to take place, accepted practices sometimes need to be challenged and replaced, where necessary.

Sport played an important role throughout my military career. I also found sport to be very helpful in studying conflict. (Sport is after all a form of conflict.) And the primary role of the Defence Force is, if it cannot prevent conflict, to win the confrontation.

After the course, Second Lieutenant Geldenhuys and a few others were posted to their first regiments.

As a pipsqueak lieutenant I arrived at Tempe in Bloemfontein in 1956 at the 1 SSB Training Regiment, the well-known SSB. It was my choice.

I received my first shock when I was told that I was to take over as regimental transport officer.

My second shock was finding out that I had one surplus Sherman tank in stock. What does an infantry second lieutenant do with a surplus Sherman tank? Luckily the annual transfers necessitated some reorganization and I became an infantry platoon leader. (The problem of the Sherman tank was therefore solved by somebody else.)

My third shock was that in practice my platoon was well over company strength.

My regimental commander was W R (Bossie) van der Riet, a war veteran. The regiment had a squadron of armour, a battery of field artillery and a company of infantry – B Company, of which I was a member.

I learned a lot about waging war at 1SSB. It was a privilege to train and do military manoeuvres where all the elements of infantry, armour, and artillery were combined in one force.

Of course there was also the normal regimental routine: PT at six o'clock in the morning, parades and so forth, which reminds me of an incident that took place one day while I was in command of the daily early-morning parade with troops of the 1957 national service intake. The parade ground was a green field, which had been mowed the previous day.

At a certain point in the parade I would have to give the command: 'Remove head dress! Let us pray.' Everyone would then take off their caps, bow their heads, and I would read the Lord's Prayer.

However, on this particular morning I said: 'Remove head dress! Let us pray.' And swoosh! My dental plate flew out of my mouth onto the grass. (My denture replaced two teeth: one was removed by a recalcitrant Vickers medium machine gun at Voortrekkerhoogte and the other by an unfriendly boot during a rugby game at Oudtshoorn.)

Luckily for me nobody noticed my discomfort, as their heads were bowed and their eyes closed. I quickly picked up the denture, replaced it, and read the Lord's Prayer.

Unfortunately grass-cuttings from the previous day's mowing, still damp from the morning dew, stuck to the plate. There I stood looking like a goat with stalks of grass protruding from my mouth.

Thereafter I was required to shout: 'Staff!' On this command the staff-sergeant would march up to me and stand at attention while I gave him instructions for the day's training programme. After that I would order him to dismiss the parade.

But this staff-sergeant was no ordinary staff-sergeant. He was Frederick George Crumpton. A Second World War veteran, he was as hard as nails and sported a broomlike moustache.

'Staff!'

Frederick George Crumpton marched towards me with measured tread, pace-stick under his arm. He halted. He fixed his icy gaze on me. He didn't move a muscle. He listened.

I gave him the instructions for the day and commanded: 'Dismiss the parade!'

Frederick George Crumpton replied: 'I will comply with your instructions, Sir, but before I do so, there's something I should like you to know, Sir. I do not mind your reading the Lord's Prayer, Sir, but next time you do so – finish your breakfast first ... Sir!'

Every intake of recruits produces its incidents. The procedure for receiving the new arrivals was as follows: They were transported from the railway station in town to the Gym Hall in Tempe, where they were lined up in two long rows at the entrance. Inside they were individually enlisted at a number of registration tables. This production-line functioned right through the night.

On such a night, while processing the 1958 intake, a group of sloppy chaps arrived there in a jolly mood. They seemed not at all interested in lining up properly; somehow they did not care.

This type of disorderly conduct immediately causes any sergeant-major to spring into action. Sergeant-major Ben Benade shouted them into a state of dead silence and formed them up neatly behind the other two lines.

But when they eventually reached the registration tables, their names did not appear on the lists.

They were incoherent and struggled to identify themselves – obviously the after-effects of celebrating the last day of freedom before going to the army.

Sergeant-majors also have a cure for such problems. 'Never mind, Captain, these scallawags are so plastered we won't get anywhere with them tonight. We'll sort them out tomorrow after they have sobered up. In the meantime I'll put them in the cells for the night,' he said to the company second-in-command.

On being questioned the next morning, they explained that they had taken the municipal bus from the city to the bus stop next to the Tempe parade ground, where the sergeant-major had somehow taken charge of them; they had actually been to see a movie and were simply strolling through the base back to their homes at Toevlug – a settlement next to Tempe in the direction of Kimberley. They were not recruits!

But in those days there was a genuine recruit who was making quite a name for himself elsewhere. He was also part of the 1958 intake and reported on 24 March for basic training. Thereafter he was trained for his mustering in the armored corps, qualifying as a lorry and jeep driver in the Third Armored Division. He was then transferred to Germany: Elvis Presley, blue suede shoes and all. Those were the days of the GIs, and Elvis made the movie, *GI Blues*, which also starred the leggy South African-born dancer, Juliet Prowse.

One thing that I came to know during my military career was that one's army pals may come and go, but that your paths cross again somewhere in the future.

In my company there was a corporal, Herman van Rensburg. He was Boytjie, the son of old Porky van Rensburg of the Ladysmith days with whom I played army-army in the fort. But now he was no longer Boytjie, he was called Large – a sturdy fellow. Among my fellow-officers were also Lieutenants Raymond Holtzhausen, Charles Lloyd, Dirk Marais and Lourens Oosthuizen. All these persons played a role in my small world at 1 SSB, Bloemfontein. I have always regarded 1SSB as a first-class regiment, my mother-unit.

In 1959 a number of personalities who would play important roles in shaping the destiny of southern Africa in the decades to come, shot into the international headlines. On 1 January Batista fled from Cuba and his administration crumbled. Fidel Castro occupied Havana and took over.

In December of that year, having been transferred to Pretoria, I reported at the SA Military College as Officer-instructor. In January 1960 I was promoted to the rank of captain. On 6 February I married Marié Martins.

My tour of duty at the college would last until the end of December 1963. Those would prove to be my toughest, most enjoyable and best years.

Here I once again met up with Capt Dirk Marais who had been at Bloemfontein and was now the college adjutant.

Once during a conference, Dirk saw Col P J Jacobs, former college commanding officer, breaking his own 'holy' rules by smoking a cigarette while walking around outside among the rondavels and the main buildings. The young captain politely addressed the colonel and requested him to refrain from smoking in the built-up area. The older man flew into a rage and caused quite a scene. This episode led to Dirk Marais being accused of lacking tact in some quarters. He did not. He was a decent man who acted according to the rules, regardless of the effect that it would have on his popularity.

Another interesting person who spent some time at the college was Jos Rossouw. He was a unique character.

Initially, during the process of enlisting him, they noticed that he had a B Phys degree. So the Defence Force, in need of people with a knowledge of physics, sent him to Potchefstroom as a new member of the South African Corps of Signals. There he had a few problems with radios and the like. Apparently he once depolarized a whole lot of batteries in one shot.

The army was furious and prohibited him from ever touching army batteries again. However, during this process they also discovered that they had misread his qualification and immediately transferred him to the Physical Training Branch of the Military College where he served under the well-known Major Piering Pretorius. Jos Rossouw's degree was B Educationis Physicae!

Jos and I sometimes worked together at the Infantry Branch of the college. I got to know him well. His lectures often provided a great deal of light entertainment.

When Jos had not prepared a lecture adequately, he employed a certain technique to overcome the problem: He would ask himself a question aloud, and then provide the answer. This technique had its merits, because the answer contained the information that the students needed to know.

In January 1961 I slipped into the back of one of his classes. It was a wood and zinc building, constructed by the British at the beginning of the century as a temporary facility. He was then busy with exactly such a monologue.

Jos asked himself aloud: 'OK then, what kind of weapon do we get in the mortar platoon?'

He answered: 'In the mortar platoon we get the three-inch mortar.'

'What kind of weapon is it?'

'It is an area weapon.'

'What does area weapon mean?'

'It is used for bombing a wide area.'

'What does one shoot with this weapon?'

'One shoots at enemy troops in the open.'

Coming to the antitank platoon he asked: 'And what kind of weapon do we have here?'

'Here we have among others the six-pounder anti-tank gun.'

'And what do we shoot with this gun?'

'Not at people ... Why not ...?'

He hesitated. Realizing that this was a poor question, he quickly answered: 'Because they duck!'

Coming to the medium machine gun platoon: 'Here we have the Vickers medium machine gun. What is the maximum effective range of this weapon?'

'During direct firing it can shoot up to a maximum range of 2 800 yards, and during indirect firing up to 4 500 yards – but then one has to have special ammunition.'

'What kind of ammunition must one use?'

'One must have ... Mark 7Z ammunition.'

He hesitated for a while and then spoke to me at the back of the lecture room: 'Gellie old boy, it is mark 7Z ammunition, isn't it?'

'Well Jos, now that you ask me, it is actually mark 8Z.'

'Oh yes, of course! I had quite forgotten that we're already in the new year. It is 1961 now. Last year we spoke of mark 7Z ammunition; this year we talk about mark 8Z ... and if you return to the college next year we will teach you about mark 9Z ammunition!'

In 1964 Jos moved the Infantry Branch of the College to Oudtshoorn – sans wood and corrugated iron. That was the beginning of the present Infantry School.

During this time I caught impersonal glimpses of a few well-known personalities. On 31 May 1961 I was in command of the streetlining troops in a certain sector along which the first State President Designate of the new Republic of South Africa, C R Swart, would travel for his inauguration.

I was also in command of the guard of honour on 27 January 1960 at Jan Smuts when the minister of Foreign Affairs, Eric Louw, welcomed the British Prime Minister, Harold Macmillan. Accompanying him during the inspection of the guard was the 1937 rugby Springbok, Gen Nic Bierman.

It was during this visit that Macmillan made his Winds of Change speech in parliament.

Though not on a reciprocal basis, I visited his country shortly after his visit to mine. On 1 March 1960 I left for the United Kingdom to attend a series of military courses.

We travelled by South African Air Force IP (Important Persons) Dakota. We refueled in Windhoek, Bamako, Villa Cisneros, Gibraltar and Bordeaux. Our overnight stops were Luanda, Lagos, Dakar and Madrid. We were also scheduled to stay over at Agadir but because of a shattering earthquake we were diverted to Casablanca.

Thanks to a loan of £150 from my mother, my wife could follow me by sea a month later. My first course was at Old Sarum. It was a course in air portability which was also attended by Nato Students. The aircraft with which we worked were the Hastings, Beverley and the Hercules C130.

At first I couldn't make out a word of what was being said in lectures owing to partial deafness caused by flying in a Dakota for a whole week.

While I was on this course, the Sharpeville shootings took place and I felt very far away from home.

I did my second and third courses in air photo-reading and counterintelligence at the British army's intelligence school at Maresfield.

One of our instructors on the counterintelligence course, the jovial, stocky, blond Captain Jones, gave us a challenging theoretical exercise to do. It concerned a building with a special room where certain important conferences were to be held. Each individual student was required to devise a plan to ensure the security and secrecy of the place, the people and the proceedings. It was only later that I found out that this had been where Churchill's war cabinet had met and that our captain had in fact been the responsible security officer.

The person in charge of the air photo-reading course was an unobtrusive little man whose battle-dress bunny jacket was always too big for him. Uninformed as I was, it was only later that I realized that he was *the* Lt Babington-Smith. He and his wife made names for themselves as first-class air-photo interpreters.

Everyone had been looking for the secret German V1 and V2 launching bases, installations which could handle rockets of unusual tonnage. At some stage during the course of the search they studied the first prints to emerge from Merifield's photo reconnaissance flight over Peenemünde airfield.

> Constance Babington-Smith found two identical ramps on the northeast edge of the island, and at the foot of one was a 'Peenemünde 20' which could clearly be seen to have no cockpit … (They) … had found the flying bomb at last …[1]

But as is often the case, South Africans also proved their mettle in this project. The same book mentions various South Africans who participated in the whole effort, *inter alia* Capt Williams and Lt Godden of the South African Air Force in their Mustang IIIs.

> … the prints brought back by the two Mustang pilots were so precise that Bomber Command could see exactly where to place their bombs.

The most important course I did was a long company commanders' course for officers of the United Kingdom and Commonwealth countries at the Infantry School, Warminster.

The Sharpeville and Poqo incidents remained on people's minds and this made being a South African a bit difficult at times. One evening in the mess a British officer, probably out of sympathy, joined me for a beer. He told me that in Korea they were always eager to see which squadron had been designated for close air support. Because, he said, they always hoped it would be the Cheetahs, the South Africans. When they gave close support, he said, you actually heard and saw them. It was heart-warming news.

The course comprised lectures, demonstrations and field exercises about nuclear, conventional and unconventional warfare, and the battle-handling of a battalion group.

In those days I listened in awe as foreign officers with operational experience discussed combat situations over a glass of beer. In years to come, it would be their turn furtively to contact South Africans to learn from our experience.

It was here that I became friendly with a Maj E K Kotoka of Regiment Ghana. Six years later, on 24 February 1966, he was the leader of the coup that toppled the founder-president of Ghana, Kwame Nkrumah. I was back in Pretoria when this happened. I reported to Military Intelligence that I knew him, but they were not really interested. They did not foresee that he would be in power for long. They were right. In April 1967 Lt Gen Kotoka was hanged upside-down in a tree or something to that effect.

I did not have the opportunity of seeing much of the United Kingdom. I didn't get to Wales, Ireland or Scotland. I did, however, see the South African cricket team in action. I was there when Springbok bowler, Geoff Griffin, performed a hat trick only to be no-balled out of test cricket forever for 'chucking'. I also saw parts of the 1960 Olympic Games in Rome on TV. South Africa won one silver and two bronze medals.

My wife and I returned to South Africa in the Cape Town Castle in August-September 1960. My wife travelled second class and I first. I could not travel second class because the South African military adviser at our embassy in London, Col D A du Toit, was on board as well and in those days it was certainly frowned upon for an officer on an official trip to travel second class.

Shortly after my return, the country started gearing up for decimalisation. South Africans woke up to the voice of Lance James singing about Decimal Dan and Daan Desimaal over the radio. On 14 February 1961 the pound became two rand, and twelve pennies ten cents.

The new cent had barely lost its glitter when another star attracted the attention of the world. On 12 April 1961 Maj Yuri Gagarin undertook the first manned space flight.

At this point my fellow officer, André van Deventer, of whom I shall write more later, offered my wife and me the use of his bungalow in the WAAF camp while he attended a year-long course overseas. We were newly married and financially it was a relief to move into that cheap little red brick matchbox with its compressed wood partitionings – much like the homes in Toevlug near Tempe.

During 1963, while still on the staff of the Military College, I did the most advanced military course of my career, the Army's staff duties (SD) course. My brother-officer and life-long friend Ian Gleeson had already done the course the year before and moved on.

On the SD course I learned how to manage pressure, especially time-pressure, and how to plan creatively.

It was general practice to 'bugger the students around', as many of them, some quite senior, described it.

The lecturers would, for example, set assignments due on a specific date and at a specific time. However, the assignments were of such a nature that the students never had quite enough time to complete them in the time allowed.

To increase the pressure the lecturers, or rather the directing staff (DS), would visit all the students pretending to be sincerely interested in their progress and wellbeing. And they would also arrange for a college non-commissioned officer to go around to the students with ostensibly urgent return forms which they were required to complete immediately.

This, of course, was simply a transparent ruse to waste the students' precious time. Many students kept their doors locked, but I recognized the value of these methods.

I understand why some students saw this practice as a means of buggering them around. One such student later became Chief of the Army, Gen W P Louw from my Bethlehem days. He then prescribed more 'enlightened' training methods for the course. His argument was that the students registered for the course to be taught something, not to be harassed.

Years later, when I was Chief of the Army, I issued clear guidelines to return to the old proven technique, with a few adaptations. My argument was that one could teach the student to plan, but this was not good enough; he should also learn to plan under pressure, even if the pressure is created only by limiting the time allocated for assignments.

Later in my career I found that I had less time to solve real problems than I had to solve fictitious problems during training courses when I thought the time was inadequate.

When Cmdt Piering Pretorius was a student on the SD course each student had to do a movement exercise by himself. It was all about moving a division of troops from point A to point B, which meant that one had to move all the vehicles, loads and personnel along determined routes at certain times.

We are now talking about tens of thousands of men, vehicles and tonnes of cargo. It can be quite a complicated logistical problem, and it was especially so in those days before computers. And, with only a few minutes to spare, Cmdt Pretorius still had a few tonnes of 'dog biscuits' that required loading space.

A gunner, one of his impish fellow-students, Major Harry Pierson, said to him: 'Let me have a quick look at your exercise.' He looked at it and said: 'But Dawid, here you have a Rogers tank transporter, quite empty. It can carry 30 tonnes. It can easily accommodate a few tonnes of dog biscuits.'

By now the pressure had taken its toll and there was no more time for thinking. Cmdt Pretorius had time only to say thank you and to finalize his exercise with the Rogers trailer stacked full of biscuits.

After he had submitted his exercise he realized that the biscuits on the trailer stood hundreds of metres into the air!

Every SD course usually produced a fair amount of humour. Whether on course or in reality, one often has to calculate how many of which items must be provided at particular places at set times for certain operations. You have to plan, for example, what types and quantities of ammunition you require and where.

How does one calculate how much toilet paper will be needed when and where? Trust the same Major Harry Pierson to come up with the formula: The length of the paper must be the number of troops times the number of days, times 'one up, one down, one polish'.

In 1963 I concluded my formal training in the Defence Force. It was only much later that the SA Defence College was established, where on the highest level, officers are now trained for top positions in the South African Defence Force. Senior officials of some of the other departments also attend the courses. In the Defence Force itself it provides for joint training of officers of all the branches of the service. It is called the joint staff course (JSC).

From this time onwards one could not become a brigadier if you had not done the JSC. I was nominated for the course in 1972 but never did it because of other official commitments. I was therefore to become an unqualified Chief of the Army and Chief of the Defence Force.

Instead of doing the course I was appointed as the project officer of the Ratel infantry combat vehicle. I regretted not doing the course, but on the other hand the Ratel project stimulated my interest in science, technology, and research and development.

I began to attach great importance to certain elements of the traditional military culture. The formative years at the Military Gymnasium, the Military College, and then as a young officer in my regiment, left a permanent impression. Although I contributed enthusiastically towards an own South African military culture, there were aspects of the British military culture which I continued to support, for example those things which were 'just not done'. It is a disgrace for an officer's cheque to be referred to drawer, and an officer has no right to additional income through business. Some of these concepts clashed with modern ideas and often caused me emotional distress.

Something else I experienced was that one does not really master a subject by merely doing a course in it. It is one thing to know the answers to examination questions, but is a totally different thing to understand the subject with deep insight. You start doing that only when you have to teach it to others.

I also learned later that to understand the contents of a voluminous memorandum thoroughly, one must be able to summarize it in plain language on one page. It forces one to discriminate between the important and the trivial, to discover patterns, and to identify the salient points. There is a certain integrity in simplicity.

I was privileged to have had the opportunity to train students in tactics, battle-handling, joint land-air warfare and so forth. It was possible to apply the knowledge and insight that I gained in this way throughout my career. And I later also experienced the real thing.

I became extremely enthusiastic about the doctrine of science. Political analyst, Dr Jan du Plessis, once explained to me that it is the discipline whereby the assumptions, underlying principles, methods and boundaries of scientific knowledge is explored, and scientific laws and concepts are formulated. In other words, it is the science about science.

I set out to be rational. And I practised it to the extreme – a sure way of becoming a pain in the neck to everyone within earshot.

For example, when I returned to Pretoria, somebody would say to me: 'I like the northern Transvaal climate.' I would ask:

'Why do you say that?'

'I like it here.'

'Yes, but Pretoria is not in the northern Transvaal.'

'Yes it is. Isn't it?'

'Go and have a look at the map. You'll see that Pretoria is in the southern half of the Transvaal.'

This is not the sort of attitude that makes one very popular.

If at a cocktail party someone said: 'It really was a scorcher today, wasn't it?' I would reply:

'How can you say that? The average maximum and minimum temperatures during the past few days was higher than today. You would be more correct to say it was a cool day.'

I soon discovered that this was the quickest way to kill a conversation – a casual social encounter that was probably started in good faith and with good intentions.

If decisions were made without proper consideration of the relevant facts and the necessary application of cold logic, it grieved me no end. This reminds me of my young days on the farm. Once, when I wanted to go for a swim in the farm dam at one o'clock in the afternoon, my grandmother refused:

'No, you may not,' she said, whereupon I wanted to know:

'Why not?'

'You'll get sunstroke.'

'But I'll wear my mother's wide-brimmed sunhat.'

'That's a good idea.'

'So, may I go?'

'No.'

'Why not?'

'You'll get sunburn.'

'Ok, I'll just go for a dip and then go and sit in the shade of the trees.'

'That is a good idea.'

And so she continued to approve every precaution I proposed against sunstroke or sunburn. And after she had okayed everything, I asked:

'So, can I go now?'

'No.'

'Why not?'

'Because why.'

I have become wiser in recent years and hopefully improved my ways a bit.

Now, when somebody says to me:

'We are lucky to live in the northern Transvaal with its wonderful climate,' I say:

'Yes, if you mean Pretoria, I agree. The far northern Transvaal becomes a bit hot.'

Small talk is probably a necessary part of one's social life, but it is not my forte. A serious debate is of course a different story. One should probably learn to accept that logic has its time and place.

Indeed, I have discovered that facts and logic are not the be-all and end-all. There are also other important elements, such as experience and gut feeling. One can try to be clever for a while but then the wisdom of 'because why' teaches you that nine out of ten times something does go wrong when a child goes for a swim in the mid-day sun.

I tried hard to emulate N P van Wyk Louw's ideal: 'Someone who had made it his golden rule in life to approach every issue reasonably, to judge fairly, to condemn hesitantly and to regard his own opinion with a touch of humble self-criticism.'

Armed with only hard facts and cold logic, an inexperienced person could find himself on very thin ice. Fortunately I was also in a position to gain the necessary experience.

My first impression of the army had merely been the worm's-eye view of a student and junior training officer. But soon I would get the opportunity of taking a bird's-eye view from the top – Army Headquarters; and I would also have the privilege of being able to observe conflict closely, and in fact in another country – Angola.

At the beginning of 1964 I was transferred to the Operations and Intelligence staff of Army Headquarters where I learned how to write letters and telexes. One of the interesting people I got to know during this time was the first South African pilot to break through the sound barrier in our country – Capt John Inglesby – in a Sabre 352 on 21 September 1956.

On 11 November 1965, on my way to hospital for a medical check-up, I heard the broadcast of Ian Smith's unilateral declaration of independence in Rhodesia.

On 2 December 1965, having passed the check-up, I succeeded Ben de Wet Roos as Vice-Consul at the South African Consulate-General in Luanda, Angola. By now there were four of us in our family: Marié, Annamarié almost four, Martin just over a year, and I.

In those days Angola was not at all as involved with the South African situation as in later years, and in Angola there was an ongoing revolutionary war. My duty was to study it.

At the time of my arrival Ben had just been serving as liaison officer during the rescue operation involving the South African Air Force Buccaneer that had crashed into the sea during its delivery flight from the United Kingdom to South Africa.

The Buccaneers were brought out at the end of October 1965 under the leadership of two officers who would both later become Chief of the Air Force, Gen Bob Rogers and Gen Mike Muller. Brig Theo de Munnink, who co-ordinated the Oceanos rescue operation in 1991, was Mike Muller's navigator.

Buc 417 piloted by Martin Jooste with navigator Anton de Klerk, was in Mike Muller's formation. They ejected into the sea between Las

Palmas and Ascension. The Portuguese Air Force was involved in this successful rescue operation.

Despite a very small vocabulary and very little concern for grammar, Ben speaks Portuguese more effectively than any foreigner that I know. He was exceptionally skilful in using the word, 'bloody'. Whenever he had any trouble finding the right Portuguese word he would merely substitute 'bloody' for the missing word and carry on. Everybody knew exactly what he meant. The Portuguese used to call him 'Old Bloody Ben'. He features in this story later on.

Mike Malone was our Consul-General. He had attended the South African College School (SACS) in Cape Town and soon thereafter, while on holiday in the British Isles with his family, World War II broke out.

During 1941, when he was 19 years old, he consequently found himself in the Orkney Islands on the northeast coast as a volunteer second lieutenant of the Commonwealth Armed Forces.

He is the only person known to me who claims to have seen a prehistoric animal. He had found it washed up on the beach. According to a book which he consulted at the local Kirkwall Library, it was a Plesiosaurus. It lived 70 million years ago.

He sliced off a piece of its flipper and reported his find to the curator of the museum on the other side of the island. They went over to have a look the next day but the sea had already reclaimed the beast. To this day Mike regrets that he missed out on the honour of having had a Monstrosis Malonii named after him.

In 1961 Mike captained the Springbok pistol-shooting team in Germany, England and Switzerland. In 1962 he became the founder commanding officer of the first English-speaking commando in Pretoria, Hillcrest Commando (later Hillcrest Regiment). He is a remarkable man.

The Portuguese are refined cultured people who take great pride in their long and illustrious history.

The Portuguese officer is a skilful professional with excellent academic grounding and with wide-ranging interests – an outstanding person. Contact with the Portuguese culture opened a new world to me.

If I had not felt so strongly about my own country, I would have said that Angola was the most beautiful country in the world. Such an abundance of large rivers, cascades, mountains and tropical vegetation is hard to equal. I once again realized that despite the beauty to be found on other continents, Africa still remained the only continent for me. I would not feel at home anywhere else.

After my experience at Army Headquarters and in Angola I was ready for the next move: South West Africa.

Now we were five in the family. Bruwer had arrived on 6 April 1968.

4

LAND BETWEEN TWO DESERTS
Until the rains come

I arrived at Headquarters South West Africa Command (HQ SWA Command) in Windhoek during April 1970. This Headquarters was militarily responsible for South West Africa south of the Red Line. (The Red Line was the foot-and-mouth boundary set up to control this feared disease.) In other words, the following northern areas were excluded: Kaokoland, Ovambo, the Kavango, western and eastern Caprivi and Bushmanland.

My new commanding officer was my old friend, Brig André van Deventer. His predecessors included Fritz Loots, Chokkie Coetzer and Magnus Malan. They all subsequently became generals. So did André.

I was the 'Colonel G', that is, the senior staff officer responsible for operations, intelligence, training and so forth. According to the 'first among equals' principle, I was also the second in command. The other senior officer was the 'Colonel, commandos and cadets', responsible for their administration and training. He was my old friend, Col Jos Rossouw.

Jos was a wise man. Clever. A philosopher. Well-spoken. But he was also practical. And he had good experience. I learned a lot from him. But he provided a few lighter moments as well.

Jos, Maj Des Radmore and myself lived in Pioniers Park. To get there from our HQ at the old Eros Airport terminal, we had to take a dirt road with a level-crossing over the Okahandja railway line. Daily I reminded myself on the way home: Remember the railway line, take care.

One evening after a social gathering we left the HQ to go home together. Des Radmore was driving out in front in his Land Rover, followed by Jos in his car and then me in my DKW 3-6 Sonderklasse. Jos was driving a dilapidated old green Mini Austin. It made a terrible noise. It was impossible to hear a thing above its rattles on a dirt road.

Nearing the railway line and looking out for trains as usual, I noticed that a train was in fact approaching. I wondered what Des would do. He suddenly accelerated and crossed the tracks well ahead of the train. Then I watched the Mini. What was Jos going to do? But he drove on at a steady crawling pace – no speeding-up or slowing-down. The train was coming on and Jos was cruising along. The train kept coming and Jos kept cruising. And I held my breath.

I watched Jos cross the track in the nick of time while the train sped past him, right on his tail!

I heaved a sigh of relief and listened: clickety-clack, clickety-clack, clickety-clack. The train's red taillight disappeared into the night. There was no sign of Jos Rossouw across the line.

The next day I said to him: 'Jos, you just made it, hey?'

'Yes, e … e … what do you mean?'

'Last night.'

'Oh.'

'Yes, the train.'

'What train?'

***

André van Deventer was transferred after a few months. Like those before him, he had made his mark in the territory. But the tracks that he left in South West were fifty times more than those left by any of his distinguished predecessors.

Throughout history one finds military officers making names for themselves as researchers of repute. Now, I don't think André considers himself a researcher, but before he left South West Africa he discovered the existence of a creature then still unknown to science – a centipede, later to be named *Cormocephalus Deventeri*. It is still leaving its tracks in Namibia.

André was succeeded by 'Old Bloody Ben', or Brig Ben de Wet Roos. He was an exceptional man. During his school years he spent some time at both the Helpmekaar Hoër Seunskool and Pretoria Boys' High. And during the early 1950s he sported the Second Battalion Transvaal Scottish kilt on a few occasions. In 1953 he obtained a lawyer's diploma through private study. He spoke highbrow English peppered with Latin phrases and Shakespearian quotations, in a Voortrekkerhoogte accent. He had worked his way up through the ranks and excelled as an officer.

Our paths had crossed many times before and would do so again in the future. He was a good judge of human nature and a born leader. He did not acquire his leadership qualities and techniques by studying theory. He was a natural. He spontaneously set the example, motivated people – and got things done. Everyone respected him. He was not interested in popularity. He believed that it was better to have the confidence of his people than to ride high on cheap popularity.

I learned a lot from him about leadership which I applied until the end of my career. He was a winner. He proved to me that what seemed impossible could indeed be achieved – as in the case of the competition for the Chief of the Army's shooting trophy. Ben Roos had decided that we, HQ SWA Command, would win the trophy. Impossible! The competition was too tough. It had always been won by one of the army's many prestige units, not by a small HQ set-up such as ours.

But he willed it. He believed we could win, in the same way that South Africa's Arnold Taylor did on 5 November 1973 in Johannesburg. Taylor got up from the floor and knocked out Romeo Anaya in the fourteenth round to become the new bantam weight boxing champion of the world – because he wanted to win. He did. And so did we. We had a simple plan, worked hard and succeeded.

As the number two I tried my best to serve Ben well. I impressed on the staff that we should be good followers. Our duty was to be honest with our commander. To be honest may be cruel, but it is often also constructive. To be honest behind someone's back is two-faced and is often destructive. I believe in expressing my opinions fearlessly and without ulterior motive, as did that corporal I came across a few years later at Grootfontein:

As I remember the story, the Minister of Defence, Mr P W Botha, visited Grootfontein in 1978. During the customary briefing, Cmdt Wim Heunis, the technical officer, explained that the percentage serviceability of the vehicle fleet was unacceptably low. He blamed it on the non-availability of reserve vehicle components.

After the briefing, as was his custom, the minister walked around the base asking questions, shaking a hand here and making a comment there. Arriving at the workshop, he spoke to a corporal. The corporal told him what his responsibilities were. Mr Botha, typically with his hat in his hand, then asked him: 'Well now, Corporal, what is your position with vehicle components?' The corporal answered crisply and confidently: 'No problem, Minister, no problem at all!'

The entire party felt rather embarrassed on Wimpie Heunis's behalf. He was also there, listening. He quickly chipped in: 'Corporal, tell the minister about the spares.'

'Oh, Minister, spares? No, Minister, we've got f** all!'

After this very clear summary of his position, I leave the corporal to his spares to come back to the characteristics of a good follower. I believe that even if I disagree with my commander, once he has made his decision, it is my duty to support his plan one hundred per cent, as if it were my own. This is easy. However, should the plan fail, it is also my duty to act as if it were my own. This is not so easy.

But it is not only through good leaders and followers that mutual respect and *esprit de corps* are fostered. Cameraderie develops when people go through hard times together. And it was here that I had my first anxious moments with Ben.

The two of us visited Cmdt Nico Retief's Walvisbaai Commando during an exercise. Early that morning, when our Cessna 185 landed in the desert at his camp, the sand was still moist and hard after the previous night's mist. But that afternoon when it was time to take off, the sand, after a full day in the sun, had become loose and the air less dense. We had to take off in the direction of the Kuiseb River. It is one of those dry riverbeds; when the wind blows it sweeps up streams of dust. It is actually just a large donga full of sand, rock and bush.

Flaps down, the pilot started the take-off run at full speed. But full speed in soft sand meant merely crawling along slowly as Jos's old Austin had done over the railway line. There was no sign of acceleration or lift. I had a nasty feeling that we were not going to get into the air that day. We chugged along while the river got closer. We chugged even harder and the river got closer still.

I had often wondered what it would be like to be in an air crash, but now I felt that I wouldn't have to wonder any more; I was going to know, if I survived.

When we reached the riverbank, we were not yet airborne. And then, bang, it happened – we plunged over the edge!

The aircraft landed on a level ledge with a thud, fortunately on its wheels. And suddenly we bounced into the air, with just enough height to scrape over the tree tops.

The Cessna has a spring-loaded undercarriage. The strut to which the wheels are attached is actually a metal spring bent in the shape of an upside down 'V'. this caused the bounce that enabled us to gain height.

Ben Roos immediately looked out of the window to check whether the wheels were intact, because we still had to land back at Windhoek!

I have always called this incident 'The prang that never was'.

In April 1973 the Defence Force took over the responsibility for border protection in South West from the police; and in October 1973 I took over from Ben.

Just as the job of second-in-command had been a learning process for me, the experience as commander on this level stood me in good stead in later years. It was some time since I had held a command post.

My staff and everybody else in Windhoek were wonderfully supportive. Perhaps they had taken my talk on how to be a good follower too literally, because they always seemed to agree with any new suggestions I put forward.

If one does not watch out, one can easily start thinking that everything one does is right. One might forget that by agreeing with their superior, subordinates may only be showing good manners and tact. One might get the idea that one is really as good as some peoplc say one is, and that is extremely dangerous.

To protect myself against this folly, I made a certain routine arrangement with the command sergeant-major. Every Friday morning we had coffee somewhere in Windhoek to talk about current command matters.

He was Sergeant-Major Raymond Marshall. He could be quite obstinate and very straightforward. And that is what I wanted. He would tell me without ceremony that I was making a mess of things if he thought so. If he didn't like a new idea, he would be as precise as that corporal in Grootfontein had been. But he did not go overboard; he was critical but positive. He always presented alternative ways of doing things.

I listened to his proposals very carefully and often abandoned my own plans for his ideas. I would give him credit for his suggestions and get on with the job of implementing them.

However, Raymond Marshall was not the only independent thinker who did not hesitate to speak his mind.

At this time my path once again crossed that of my old acquaintance, Boytjie of Ladysmith's fort, Corporal of Bloemfontein's 1SSB and now Major Large van Rensburg of Windhoek's training wing.

New acquaintances on the cross roads of soldiering were Capt Charlie Hochapfel and Eros. Eros was actually a dog. He was recruited locally and employed as a guard at the HQ. As a rookie he was a semi-official member of the Defence Force, but later he achieved full status with his own identity card, official rations, medical services and all.

Charlie Hochapfel recruited him, trained him and looked after him. He instructed the sentries himself on how Eros had to be handled. He said: 'Guys, when you do guard duty at headquarters you will find a dog there. His name is Eros. Be good to him, make friends. You are going to need him.

'You will also find a nice comfortable chair in the hall. At night you sit in the chair with Eros on your lap. You will fall asleep, of course. So will he. But when the duty-officer arrives on his inspection rounds, Eros will wake up and start investigating the disturbance. And by the time the duty officer gets to you, you will be up and about, a watchful and alert sentry. He will never catch you sleeping on duty!'

Charles was an English-speaking South West African South African of German descent. He was full of fun, but a good soldier. He died on 24 March 1986 after being shot in an ambush.

Charles was killed while his team was evaluating live encounters. South Africa is only one of a very few countries in the world where evaluation teams accompanied troops into battle to critically assess their combat skills.

SWA Command did not only consist of Windhoek and Grootfontein. There was also a military base at Walvis Bay. The main unit there was 2 South African Infantry Battalion Group. The base commander was another old friend, Col Ian Gleeson.

At the time, Walvis Bay was one of the enlisting centres where men reported for national service training. Naturally, during 'intake' the place was a bee-hive of activity. Some recruits arrived by train, others by bus and by car; some were brought by their parents.

One day at the height of the hustle and bustle there was a knock at Col Gleeson's door. The adjutant walked in. 'Colonel, we have another mother with her son wanting to see you.'

'Please show them in.'

They entered rather apprehensively. The adjutant withdrew. Colonel Gleeson turned to the mother: 'Madam, young man, please sit down. What can I do for you?'

The lady sat down timidly on the edge of her chair with her feet together, tightly clutching her handbag on her lap, 'Colonel ... my son, I came to ...'

He immediately tried to put her mind at rest: 'Madam, please do not worry. Leave your son here, I will personally see to it that he gets prompt and proper attention, everything will be fine. By the way, where do you live?'

'Walvis Bay.'

'Fine. Go home now, don't worry. You will hear from us again.' So she went home.

The necessary orders were given and a corporal fetched the recruit. He first had him enlisted and then took him to the quartermaster stores to get his kit. After that, loaded like a pack-donkey with overalls and linen; with braces, left and right – one and one, and belts, webbing – one, he was sent off to his bungalow.

A day or two later the mother was there again wanting to see Col Gleeson. Hesitantly, and with an anxious look on her face, she asked:

'Colonel, where is my son? How long does it take you to register a notification of change of address?'

The poor boy had not gone there to report for national service. As is required by law, he merely wanted to hand in his new address. How embarrassing! Ian Gleeson apologized profusely and had the boy fetched to his office immediately. But when he was told that he could now go home with his mother, the boy vigorously resisted his liberation. He had by then already made friends with the other chaps in his bungalow, he was part of a team and very happy with all the new things happening to him. He was not going to be discharged. He wanted to stay.

I don't know what eventually became of him.

Ian Gleeson is great. He is a level-headed and humble person with a sense of humour; but this time he was red in the face.

Apart from the permanent force members and national service men at Grootfontein and Walvis Bay, there were also 'part-time soldiers'. I devoted most of my time to the men of the citizen force (24 Brigade) and the commando units.

This was a whole new world with extraordinary characters the like of which I've never met again. I could dedicate an entire book to them. But if I start writing about people such as Col Koot Theron, one of the 'wild men' of the Kalahari in his young days; Piet Mostert, who fought a lion with his bare hands; and the daring men of Cmdt Hans Heinrich Otto Denk's 112 Commando Squadron, where would I stop?

Then there were also the people and the country – South West Africa, previously the old Deutsch Süd-West Afrika, and later the new Namibia.

The sun rises over the Kalahari and sets behind the Namib. And the land between these two deserts is a jewel in the hearts of the people who live there – black, brown, white and yellow. One either loves South West or one hates it. One cannot be lukewarm. It's a tough country. And anybody who does not fit in, is rejected.

In the past South West was isolated by distance, vastness and lack of communications, which made it a closed society where the people are tough and proud, but good. When they work, they work hard. And when they play, they play hard. One does not drive 250 km on a Wednesday afternoon for a game of tennis and then just say goodbye and go back home. There is always the *Gemütlichkeit*, a small party, afterwards. It is one big family. It's a big country.

Distance in South West is unimportant. In 1972, all togged up and raring to go, some friends and I waited at Eros airport to fly to Port Elizabeth with Hans Denk for a rugby test against the French. The control tower could not clear our flight for take-off on the first leg to Upington because the weather was too bad. So Max Kessler quickly fetched his car and drove us to Port Elizabeth and back.

South West is pioneer country, a country of sadness and joy. Drought brings sadness and rain brings joy.

The legendary entrepeneur, Sam Cohen, was one of the pioneers. His son, Jackie, and I were friends. He told me that his father had always said: As soon as it rains in South West, all the problems are cut in half. This is a truth that I will never forget.

Around October the people anxiously start raising their eyes skyward, searching for signs of rain. Everything is barren and dry. Man and animal yearn for water. Clouds loaded with promise gather and hopes run high. Then they disappear – without bringing rain. The next day clouds build up again. There is expectation and tension in the air. And then they disappear again. And if this carries on for a few days, and perhaps for a few weeks, the tension increases and people become grumpy.

Then the clouds build up again and they disappear. Without rain. And if, in an unguarded moment, you say something frivolous, you might find that your joke has become an incident.

It serves no purpose to plan citizen force and commando conferences between October and January. One must wait until the rains come, until all the problems are halved, until *Gemültlichkeit* and good cheer return to the hearts of the people, then one can talk to them, they are prepared to talk to you, and you will all work together.

I will always love South West, but as my mother liked to say: 'Too much of a good thing is not good,' and in December 1974 I was transferred to Army HQ, Pretoria. My friend, Brig Dirk Marais, succeeded me.

By now there were six of us. Lollie, or Mariana, was two years old. I told my wife I would never be transferred again; that we would have to settle in Pretoria. Two and a half years later I was back in South West.

In the meantime many things would come to pass; pleasant things, but also war.

5

A NEW ERA OF WAR
Commandant, you don't really understand the situation

For the first time in ten years I was back in South Africa. It needed a lot of adjustment. In Windhoek the pace had been slow and the atmosphere jovial. In contrast Pretoria seemed grim and busy. I got the fright of my life driving down Potgieter Street when suddenly cars were overtaking me on both sides.

In South West you are somebody. If you have a breakdown, the first person to pass will stop. In Pretoria you are one of many nobodies. Strings of cars with straight-faced drivers speed by before someone eventually comes to your rescue.

I was not the only South Wester in Pretoria to find the going tough. One early evening after work I visited a few of my old mates of 112 Commando Squadron who were doing a ground-air co-operation course at the Air Force College. Over a glass of beer I asked Max Kessler's brother, Tikklie, who was from Helmeringhausen's desert country:

'How do you like Pretoria?'

'The first week or so was OK, but now all the green is getting a bit much.'

That day, 29 April 1975, produced its own drama. While we were drinking our beer, the pub radio kept us informed about the activities of a certain David Protter who was using his rifle to terrorise people from a building in Fox Street, Johannesburg.

All of a sudden Piet Gouws, Thys Rall, Horst Kreitz and Tikklie decided that the news flashes were the call of duty summoning them to Johannesburg to oversee the handling of the situation. They got into a car and drove to Fox Street. They proceeded right up to Gen Lang-

Hendrik van den Bergh who was trying to negotiate with Protter over a walkie-talkie.

The next morning the front page picture of a leading newspaper featured a prim and proper Piet Gouws standing right behind Gen van den Bergh in Johannesburg.

They were South Westers!

But for me life in Pretoria was certainly no game. From January 1975 to mid-1977 I hardly touched ground. During this two-and-a-half-year period at Army HQ I had three different jobs, one after the other. I started off as D Int (Director, Intelligence), then took over as D Ops (Director, Operations) and thereafter became C Army S, Ops (Chief of Army Staff, Operations).

If you are a member of a fighting corps, you are supposed to scoff at office work at an HQ, be it a battalion HQ, command HQ, but especially if it is at the Defence Force HQ complex in Pretoria.

This was the traditional attitude, not supposed to be taken seriously. Be that as it may, there was one lone star providing some light amidst the shadows of bureaucratic gloom – Jos Rossouw.

He was transferred from Windhoek to Pretoria a year before me and I landed up in the same building in the office next to his.

On the wall, next to the staircase, we had the usual location board. When you leave the office, you fill in the date and time of departure, your destination and time of return.

Walking past the board I often noticed that Jos had signed out, mostly from 15:00, to be back again at 08:00 the next morning. His destination was usually UPM – a place I had never heard of. A few times when it crossed my mind I asked an officer what UPM was supposed to be. The answer was: 'Hum ... haw ... it is ... Uniform Personnel Management,' or something like that. I suspected that those officers did not know but were reluctant to show their ignorance.

Then one day I remembered to ask Jos himself: 'Jos, what and where is this UPM you went to yesterday?'

'UPM?'

'Yes man, UPM.'

'Oh.'

Where Ben Roos performed miracles with the word 'bloody', Jos used the word 'Oh'. It got him out of a tight spot on many an occasion. But he could not fool me: 'Oh, what?'

'It means Urgent Private Matters!'

'Oh.'

As D Int I had to establish the Army's organization for conducting Communication Operations.

Its aim was to foster harmony between the Army and its units on the one hand and the population on the other. This applied especially to operational areas. It is difficult to operate successfully where the locals are not friendly.

Then the Angolan civil war started. In terms of an agreement signed in January 1975 at the Portuguese town of Alvor, the Portuguese transferred power in Angola to a government of National Unity. This government would rule until the elections and independence on 11 November 1975. The interim government consisted of delegates of Agostinho Neto's Peoples Movement for the Liberation of Angola (MPLA), Holden Roberto's National Front for the Liberation of Angola (FNLA) and Jonas Savimbi's National Union for the Total Independence of Angola (Unita).

Because of internal problems, Portugal could not or would not really exert its influence during the transitional period. The interim government in Angola disintegrated and with the help of Cuban troops the MPLA soon became the sole rulers. Roberto and Savimbi took to the bush from where they declared war on the MPLA. The MPLA's armed forces were called Fapla; those of the FNLA – Elna, and Unita's – Fala.

During those years – the 1960s and 1970s and thereafter — the pattern was for the big powers to take sides and become involved in regional and local conflicts. They also secured the active participation of their allies. America was the leader of the 'West' and Soviet Russia of the 'East'. The involvement of America and its allies and Soviet Russia with theirs in countries on almost every continent is common knowledge: Vietnam and Nicaragua are only two examples. This is the international 'Cold War' background against which the conflicts of that time must be seen.

The Soviet Union, with the support of Cuba, East bloc countries and others, supported Neto and the MPLA. Cuba was the main supplier of troops.

America became involved on the side of Roberto and his FNLA, who in turn formed an alliance with Savimbi and his Unita. And so South Africa, with the war on its doorstep, became part of the anti-Marxist alliance. We code-named the South African participation in the war Operation Savannah.

Although I had been in the Defence Force for 22 years, I was not always conscious of war. For all practical purposes I had lived and worked in peace. With this operation, however, I felt that it was war. But it was an unreal, uncomfortable feeling. The general public out there did not know much and went about their daily lives as usual.

Nevertheless, it was the beginning of a new era of war. Mr John Vorster was Prime Minister, Mr P W Botha Minister of Defence, Admiral H H Bierman Chief of the Defence Force and Gen Magnus Malan Chief of the Army.

During Operation Savannah I was D Ops of the Army. Because of the extremely clandestine nature of the operation, especially during the early stages, only the absolute minimum number of senior staff officers were involved in the operational control in Pretoria, mainly the directors of operations. The nucleus of the group consisted of the DG Ops[1] at the HQ of the Chief of the Defence Force, Gen Constand Viljoen, and his own D Ops, Brig Wally Black, the D Ops at Air Force HQ, Brig Piet Letley, and myself. We met daily.

Brig Dawie Schoeman, commander of 1 Military Area whose responsibility was to protect the northern borders of South West, was in command of the operation. His HQ was at Rundu.

A few things bothered me. The vastness of the combat zone was one. The distance between Bloemfontein and Cela in Angola is 2 386 km (1 205 nautical miles), and the distance to Cassinga (which two years later became the objective of Operation Reindeer) is 1 928 km (1038 nautical miles). When we compare these distances with Europe, we find that Rome is only 1 216 km (654 nautical miles) from Paris. As the crow flies, the distance between Pretoria and Kinshasa, which was a port of call of South African Air Force transport aircraft, is approximately the same as that from London to Moscow.

Another aspect was the exclusivity of the group of staff officers in Pretoria who controlled the operation. During October-November 1975 I argued strongly that we should implement the normal command and control structures for conducting operations, and revert to the more formal procedures. Genl Malan supported me. This led *inter alia* to setting up HQ 101 task force at Rundu. Gen André van Deventer took over from Dawie Schoeman. He would now assume responsibility for Operation Savannah.

This happened more than eighteen years ago. It is a long time. Much has been written and many arguments have taken place about the campaign. A few years ago two authoritative books on the subject were published. One was titled *Operasie Savannah, Angola 1975–1976,* written by my tutor, Prof F J du Toit Spies, and the other, *Avontuur in Angola: Die verhaal van Suid-Afrika se soldate in Angola 1975–1976* was the work of Sophia du Preez.

She says that the aim of Operation Savannah was to ensure 'a well-disposed government in Angola who would not permit Swapo bases and who would govern the country free from communist Cubans'. And the result was '... a tragic success. By means of a blitzkrieg, a favourably disposed neighbour was placed in control of almost half of Angola.'

Sam Nujoma's Swapo, the South West African People's Organization, later 'Swapo of Namibia', campaigned for the independence of South West. Its armed wing was the Peoples Liberation Army of Namibia, or Plan. They infiltrated South West through Angola and Zambia.

Nevertheless, in spite of the many publications on the subject, I would like to share a few opinions and relate a few personal experiences.

On 30 October 1975, during the first stage of the operation, I had to meet with Dr Jonas Malheiro Savimbi, the president of Unita. The meeting was to take place at Silva Porto, the present Kuito. I had met him once before and it was the beginning of a relationship that would last for many years.

Arriving at Silva Porto, I met two of my colleagues and friends, Col Des Harmse and Maj Nic Visser. Dr Savimbi had not yet arrived and Des asked me if I'd like to accompany them on a reconnaissance flight. I did not accept the invitation because I had come to perform a particular task. I said that I would rather wait for Dr Savimbi.

Des and his party returned by midday and we had lunch together. They repeated the invitation to fly with them that afternoon. I was just about to agree, but asked them if it meant that a passenger with some duty to perform would have to give up his seat for me. The answer was yes, but that it would not matter too much. This persuaded me to decline.

Dr Savimbi did not arrive that day and I had to return to Rundu. We took off again at the latest possible time. Before take-off I remarked that Des and the other would have to be back within the next few minutes or else it would be too dark for them to land.

They never landed.

Shortly after landing at Rundu I heard that their aircraft had crashed. All of them were killed, Maj Piet Uys, the pilot, Col Des

Harmse, Maj Nic Visser of 1 Parachute Battalion and Lance Corporal Neville Beechie of 1SSB.

Friction de guerre played a role that day: fatal for some, lucky for me.

The incident shook me. The Harmses were family friends. We had come a long way together in the Defence Force. A few years later his son, Capt Louis Harmse, was killed in action at the battle of Xangongo during Operation Protea.

Like any other career officer I would have liked to be part of the campaign itself. During the first phases I did go to the combat zone on liaison visits, sometimes with Gen Viljoen, sometimes alone, as in the case of the visit to meet Savimbi. Then on 3 January 1976, one of the field commanders, Brig J D Potgieter, died in a helicopter incident in Angola. My ex-commander and friend, Ben Roos, replaced him on 4 January 1976. A day or two later I was appointed to take over from him as Chief of Staff at Rundu. During the same month I had to tell him over the radio that we were going to withdraw and that he had to prepare himself for that event. After a period of deathly silence I called him up again. His response was: '... We will abide by the order.' At that time we were well on the way to victory. It became known only later that the Cubans were already planning their retreat at that stage.

The turning point of the war that led to the withdrawal of the South African troops was the new law passed by the American Congress forbidding military support to any Angolan Party. It was called the Clark Amendment after Senator Dick Clark. It was valid as from December 1975 for one year, but was extended again in 1976. The South African position was that it was not prepared to protect Western interests alone.

This was actually Ben's second withdrawal. The first took place only a few weeks earlier. Before his involvement in the southern half of Angola, he had been serving at Ambriz in the north. He was the leader of the South African Defence Force liaison team with Holden Roberto, president of the FNLA.

I agree with Steenkamp's description of Roberto: '... Roberto insisted on going his own way. In the end his stubbornness sabotaged not only his own future but, to a large extent, that of Operation Savannah as well.'

His ambition was to conquer Luanda before 11 November 1975. This made no sense. His soldiers were inexperienced and his leader group unskilled.

I visited Ben at least once when C130s delivered 140 mm guns to him. His mood was not a happy one. He complained about Roberto. Roberto had no sense of delegation of authority. His people would not allow even a single Land Rover to be moved without his personal permission.

So, Ben told me, he had a serious talk with Roberto and explained to him how one had to identify operational tasks and allocate each one to a responsible subordinate commander. And when he had finished, Roberto said: 'But Brigadier, war is such a serious thing, you can't leave it to the generals.' This was not the first time that I had heard this opinion.

Roberto's ambition did not materialize. He failed. Luanda celebrated its independence on 11 November 1975, exactly 10 years after Rhodesia's unilateral declaration of independence. The full extent of the negative effects of Roberto's failure would be realized only later.

It was after the defeat of the FNLA in the north that Ben and his team, isolated and apparently forgotten, were brought back by sea.

On 28 November 1975 he was picked up at Ambrizete by Capt Ben van der Westhuizen and Sergeant Smit in a Puma from the frigate, SAS President Steyn. Capt Sam Davis took him to Walvis Bay aboard the President Steyn, where on 30 November he disembarked with his people.

My good old friend, Col Blackie Swart, was task force commander during this war. One of his opponents was a formidable man, but in my opinion Blackie had the better of him. He would feature again later in the history of southern Africa and also make the international headline news. He is Comandante Arnaldo Òchoa Sanchez of Cuba. I write more of him in later chapters.

At Army HQ itself I had a hard time, because, as I have mentioned, during the early stages the whole operation was handled by a handful of people – almost in the manner of a special forces operation. It disturbed me that such an operation was controlled in this manner. One would rather conduct war in the open, with the whole Defence Force involved, and with the public's support.

With the wisdom of hindsight and seen purely from a military point of view, it could have been to our advantage if the media had been better informed. But I do not intend to blame the politicans. They have their considerations – and military objectives are always subordinate to the overall political strategy. I did not have to worry about Clark Amendments, or UN and OAU sessions.

The end of World War II ushered in a new era: wars are no longer formally declared and this kind of undeclared and clandestine operation is the norm all over the world. The French intervened in Africa, and America and the Soviets did so elsewhere.

After Operation Savannah, the approach changed somewhat, and largescale operations were often conducted more openly than before. We also benefited from the experience in other respects.

On 27 January 1976, Gen van Deventer said: 'Now is not the time to pat ourselves on the back because of our combat successes in Angola. Our experience must be communicated to those who have not had it. Our leaders have a great task ahead, because we will still be involved in war for a long time to come.'[2]

I organized and conducted the debriefing conferences on the Army's participation in the war. We identified and formulated the lessons we had learnt and planned our follow-up programme of action. We made substantial changes and adjustments, which proved invaluable later on. The improvements affected battle techniques and procedures; hardware projects, such as the one that became the 127 mm multiple rocket-launcher; closer co-operation between different corps of the Army, and between the arms and branches of the service.

I was proud of the way in which all our leaders at the various levels had proved themselves. And I was just as proud of the South African troops. And when I say troops, I do not only refer to army soldiers, I include all the men in the air, those at sea as well as the medics.

Troops are very resourceful. But they can also be mischievous, as this Savannah story from Rundu will clearly illustrate:

The year was 1975. Because of the sudden stepped-up military acctivity, Rundu was bursting at the seams. The sergeant-major had his hands full in his hastily prepared kitchen. He did not yet have a proper pantry and had stacked the tinned food all over the place. Somehow he had forgotten what hungry troops are capable of.

A soldier is always hungry, no matter what. Even if he has just had a proper meal, and even 'seconds', he is never too full to polish a tin of condensed milk. I know. I did the same. I still do.

The sergeant-major's tins started disappearing. So he made a plan. He went to the quartermaster stores and found himself a few trunks, 'boxes, soldier, steel', and locked the tins away in the trunks with locks that he had scrounged somewhere.

But the tins continued to vanish mysteriously into thin air. He made another plan. He went to the local shop and bought extra strong locks. He reported for duty every morning, opened the trunks and left the locks hanging on the staple. He was always around during the day to keep a close watch. Every evening before going off duty, he closed the trunks himself and saw to it that each one was securely locked.

A few days later he arrived at work, unlocked the trunks and opened the lids, only to find that some tins had disappeared again! And the next day. And the next day again. By this time even a sergeant-major would be at his wits' end. How did the rascals do it?

The troops had also bought identical extra strong locks. During the day they needed just enough time to exchange the locks. When the sergeant-major locked the trunks at night, he was snapping shut the substituted locks. The troops came back later, unlocked the trunks, helped themselves, and replaced the sergeant-major's locks. The next morning, the sergeant-major would kindly unlock the trunks for them again!

The troops showed the same resourcefulness during operations. But just as sergeant-majors sometimes found themselves stymied by the troops, so the troops themselves didn't always have all the answers.

At about this time, a routine patrol somewhere in the Kavango, or just north of it, came upon a herd of elephants. The elephants didn't seem to like being disturbed and reacted quite aggressively. But whether they were merely putting up a show of force or meant business was something the troops were not interested in finding out: they took to their heels.

The radio operator decided that his evasive action was being unnecessarily handicapped by the radio he was carrying and therefore got rid of it. It fell to the ground still functioning: shhh! One of the elephants interpreted the irritating hissing as a serious insult and took the action expected from any proud and honourable beast under the circumstances: he trampled the radio until the offensive hissing was silenced.

But there is a tailpiece to this story. In reaction to the formal requisition for a new radio set to replace the damaged one, Pretoria demanded the old one back. The quartermaster at Rundu was not unwilling to comply with the instruction. He returned the radio – in an official envelope!

***

Two new groups of troops made a name for themselves: One was

Daniel Chipenda's FNLA troops, who under the fearless Cmdt Jan Breytenbach became Bravo Group and later 32 Battalion. I developed a special relationship with them which would strengthen during the years to follow.

I also maintained personal contact with the other group, the Bushman soldiers. In the beginning they were called Alpha Group, then 31 Battalion and later 201 Battalion.

As many others do, I found the Bushmen fascinating. Cmdt Delville Linford was their first commanding officer. That was during the middle and late 1970s. Before Operation Savannah got under way, he told me, he assembled them all to inform them of the forthcoming operation.

His speech was translated bit by bit, first into Portuguese and then into the two Bushman dialects. He announced: 'We are going to war.' Interpret, interpret, interpret. They all cheered. He said: 'We are going to fight against the MPLA.' Interpret, interpret, interpret. Again everybody cheered. He continued: 'We are going to make war against the MPLA on the side of the FNLA and Unita.' Interpret, interpret, interpret. Silence. But he went on and finished his talk.

Some time after the briefing a somewhat displeased Bushman delegation asked to see him. They told him: 'Commandant, Commandant does not really understand the situation ...' Then they explained to him they were going to fight the MPLA, that's right – but they were also going to fight the FNLA and Unita!

By 27 March 1976 the last troops of Operation Savannah had already withdrawn from Angola via Ruacana. It became clear later that had Holden Roberto not squandered his advantage and had the Americans kept up their pressure against Russian intervention, the result might easily have been some form of neutral government in Angola. The outcome, however, did not prevent Swapo from using Angola as a springboard for renewed infiltration.

***

Let us now turn to the South West operational area and what was happening there. The Swapo incursions took a new turn. Many military observers consider 27 March 1976 to be the date on which the insurgency war really started in all seriousness. Swapo was now potentially in a stronger military position than before. For the first time they obtained what is more or less a prerequisite for successful insurgent campaigning, namely a border that provided safe refuge.

From Swapo's point of view, the situation also held certain disadvantages. Nujoma's previous ally, Jonas Savimbi, was now his greatest enemy.

This created a problem for Nujoma as they were both operating in southern Angola. The MPLA also required Swapo to make manpower available for their campaign against Savimbi. Savimbi, however, was retreating to the remote expanses of the south-east, and was in fact fighting for the very existence of his movement.

Plan (Swapo's military wing) established an extensive network of training camps and bases in southern Angola, and they stepped up their incursions considerably.

'For the South Africans – short of men, short of equipment, their defence force still struggling to wrench itself free of the decades of neglect that had followed World War II – the situation was immensely worrying.'[3]

The intensity of the border war was still very low, but a series of intermittent contacts, mine incidents and hit-and-run attacks with rockets and mortars, increased the casualty rate.

During December the actions actually intensified. Reliable reports reached Windhoek that four of the 'front-line states', Tanzania, Zambia, Mozambique and Angola, were supporting a new wave of insurgency planned for early 1977.

From early December 1976 Plan set its sights on traditional leaders who were mostly conservative and well disposed towards the administration. On 7 December Deputy Chief Hausiki Enkaile was murdered by a group of six or seven insurgents and Chief Willipard Enkale's son was abducted and taken to Angola.

On 11 December 1976, Sean McBride, the ageing UN commissioner for Namibia, was responsible for some light entertainment when he told newsmen during an interview in Lusaka that South Africa had assembled 50 000 men armed with 'sophisticated' weapons such as helicopters, tanks, field artillery and hundreds of armoured vehicles in forming-up areas in the Caprivi strip ready to be launched into Angola. The allegation was that South Africa would justify such action by arguing that MPLA and Cuban troops had joined up with Plan insurgents.

McBride added to the comedy by claiming that the Rhodesian government had built three new air bases, one of which was in the Caprivi, and suggested that it indicated preparation for a long drawn-out war.

This allegation was obviously ridiculous. In the first place South Africa could not possibly put a force of such proportions into the field without a full-scale and public mobilization – and P W Botha gleefully grabbed at the opportunity to invite McBride to visit the Caprivi and to point out the Rhodesian airfield. McBride wisely declined the challenge.

Late in February 1977 the Caprivi experienced its first incident since July 1975. A Plan group opened fire on a South African patrol base near the borders with Angola and Zambia and wounded three soldiers. Twelve insurgents were killed during the counterattacks before they could cross the Zambian border.

In the meantime the South African Army's communication operations scheme, or 'goodwill campaign' got off the ground. On 22 March seventy-six selected national servicemen were withdrawn from other duties and assigned teaching duties in black schools in the border area.

On 31 March 1977 Mr P W Botha announced in parliament that during the two years since 1 April 1975 altogether 231 insurgents had been killed in Ovambo, Kavango and the eastern Caprivi. During the same time the security forces had lost 33 men and the infiltraters had killed 53 of the local population.[4]

In the meantime the HQ of 101 Task Force was moved from Rundu to Grootfontein and Gen Viljoen succeeded Gen van Deventer as the general officer commanding the force. A while later he was replaced by my old cadet friend, Gen Ian Gleeson.

In approximately May-June 1977 I relieved him at Grootfontein so that he could go on leave.

I had heard how busy they were at the logistics base at Grootfontein. One day a staff officer received a signal from a forward base requesting 250 000 sandbags. He had been working long hours and under great pressure. There was also the problem of the refugees from Angola. They needed tents, food, blankets and various other necessities. But despite the stress he remained calm and meticulous. According to his calculations 250 000 sandbags seemed excessive. So he signalled back: 'What do you want to do with the sandbags?'

The forward base replied promptly: 'We want to fill them with sand!'

While the war raged in Angola and South West, life in South Africa continued undisturbed. South Africa was the venue for the Third World Bowls Tournament from 18 February to 6 March 1976. Sixteen countries participated – the most ever. South Africa won every competition. There were eighty thousand spectators. At home everybody was glued to their TV sets – then a novelty in South Africa. Doug Watson became a national hero and a household name.

Things were happening to me too. In May1976 I was promoted to major general and appointed Chief of Army Staff, Operations. I took over from the Korean veteran, Gen Jack Dutton. Shortly after this the whole command and control structure in South West changed.

The Army's responsibility for the area north of the Red Line (101 Task Force), and the responsibility for the area south of it (SWA Command) were joined together into one large area under a single commanding general, General Officer Commanding (GOC), SWA Command – and I was appointed to fill the post.

6

SOUTH-WESTERS MUST DECIDE FOR THEMSELVES

Brother against brother

After I had stood in for Ian Gleeson at Grootfontein during July 1977, I went back to Pretoria, packed my things and left for Windhoek on transfer.

A move is always disruptive. My wife and children joined me at the end of the year. The following year Annamarié started standard nine in Windhoek Hoërskool. It was her eighth school in three different languages. But there are people who are worse off.

An old friend, Maj Lex Krogh, ushered in my second tour in South West with a story. He was a well-known medical practitioner in Windhoek and a member of the SWA Medical Unit. In his story, which he put on paper for me afterwards, he links me with the past. The story comes from World War I. The scene was Deutsch Süd-West Afrika: the South African Forces were engaging the Germans.

> You are now the first commanding general in South West since Gen Louis Botha. Gen von Trotha of the Herero War was indeed a general, and various German officers who were here since long ago, later became generals. But between Gen Botha and you, there has not been another one.
>
> Col von Heydebrech was the original commander of the German Forces. He died after a mortar, built locally by the Germans, exploded. While the surgeon-general, who had been a spectator, had had the decency to die right away, the colonel had four operations before he came to an end. Col von Heydebrech was replaced by Maj Francke – a veteran who was good, but not in the same class. He lacked the necessary dash. He regarded

Swakopmund as indefensible and decided to move inland to use the desert in his defence plan.

On Christmas Day 1914 Col Skinner of the Union Forces landed at Walvis Bay. On 3 January 1915 he occupied Swakopmund. On 6 February Gen Botha himself arrived and set up his headquarters at Swakopmund.

Transport for baled grass for the horses and rations for the soldiers was a big problem. But at Swakopmund he picked up another problem – severe diarrhoea.

The diarrhoea was probably the well-known gyppo guts. Then there was also gastro-enteritis, mainly among children, treated with egg white. Another disease, of course, was typhoid fever, which was prevented during this war, for the first time in world history, by inoculation. Up to that time more soldiers had died of typhoid than of wounds.

Swakopmund got its name from two Nama words which mean sh*t hole – he who drinks from this water hole will have an upset stomach. We experienced it at school there. Beyond Goanikontes there are many saline springs in the river containing, amongst others, Epsom and Glaubersalts.

The general's medical officer must have diagnosed the general's complaint as gastro-enteritis because he recommended egg white, which was unobtainable.

Gen Botha struggled endlessly to find wagons for transporting provisions and fodder. When the decisive battle began, he had only 40 instead of the 400 wagons for which he had begged umpteen times. Although the battle was successful, the Union Forces continued to be hampered by the shortage of transport. Later they had 50 mule wagons and 30 donkey carts to keep 1 300 men and 1 500 animals alive.

In the meantime the soldiers had eaten all the oxen used for pulling the heavy artillery, but fortunately there was no need for artillery any longer.'

Krogh quoted Collyer as saying that he found it difficult to understand why Defence Headquarters reacted so poorly to Botha's pleas, considering that Gen Botha was the Prime Minister of the Union of South Africa and the commander-in-chief of the forces in German South West Africa.

Lex also related how Gen Botha's gyppo guts was eventually cured:

'A cruiser was sent from Simon's Town with a few cows, 24 hens and – Mrs Botha!'

The medical officer was a man who did not have a deep regard for discipline. He refused to wear a cap, for example, and resigned some time later. He was also known as the paediatrician, poet and gourmet – Maj C Louis Leipoldt.

I did not suffer from gyppo guts. I had no need for cows and chickens, and I did not have undisciplined poets to deal with – I had other problems. We were facing the beginning of a new era for South West, South Africa and the Defence Force: an era of revolutionary war.

Since the incident in which Breedt was shot in the leg near Grootfontein in 1966, and the skirmishes with insurgents at Ogulumbashe in Ovambo and Singalamwe in the Caprivi during the early years of the conflict, its intensity had increased considerably. One has to bear in mind that, especially after operation Savannah, the hostilities were not to be a conventional war. In a conventional war a general can move a whole brigade or division with one command. But this was an insurgency war consisting of a multitude of small-scale encounters in a 'combat' zone stretching from Kaokoland in the west to the eastern Caprivi, a distance of more than 1 500 km, and which is described by many as a corporals and lieutenants war. It was impossible for a general to oversee every incident.

In addition, military action is always subordinate to politics. When I left for South West, Gen Malan gave me specific orders:

- I had to manage the security situation and contain the level of insurgency so that the constitutional process could develop in an atmosphere of stability and peace.
- I had to amalgamate the old SWA Command in the south and 101 Task Force in the north into a new SWA Command with its headquarters in Windhoek.
- I had to establish a defence force for SWA.
- Everything had to be in line with international and internal political developments.

Steenkamp described my new appointment as one '... which quickly became the most sensitive command position in the SA Defence Force'.

I integrated the two military structures and took over from Gen Gleeson in the north, and also from my other cadet friend, Brig

Lourens Oosthuizen, in the south (he had in the meantime taken over from Brig Marais).

Many defence force officers are obsessed with structural and organizational changes. I have had officers who, to put it bluntly, when given an instruction had to reorganize the whole defence force before they could do the job. Wanting to reorganize can jeopardize getting things done.

This anecdote from my friend, Gen Jack Dutton, illustrates my argument: An outgoing general handed over his responsibilities to an incoming general. He also gave him three envelopes, with the instruction to open envelope number 1 on encountering his first serious problem and then follow the enclosed instructions. He should treat subsequent serious problems that may arise in the same way, acting on the instruction contained in envelopes 2 and 3 consecutively.

The incoming general put the envelopes in his safe. But after a while he encountered his first real problem and opened envelope number 1. He found a piece of paper which read: 'Blame your predecessor.'

He blamed his predecessor and got away with it. Everything ran smoothly for a while. Then he once again encountered serious trouble. He opened envelope number 2. It read: 'Reorganize.'

He reorganized. It proved to be a complicated and time-consuming process that stifled every other problem. The intermittant hassles had to wait until after the reorganization. Then came the third big problem. He opened envelope no 3 and read the instructions:

'Prepare three envelopes.'

The tendency to reorganize instead of getting the work done, is an old disease. Just read this:

> 'We trained hard – but it seemed that every time we were beginning to establish proper teams, we would be reorganised. I was to learn later in life that we tend to meet every new situation by reorganizing, and a wonderful method it can be for creating the illusion of progress while producing confusion, inefficiency and demoralization.'

This quote was given to me by the well-known Afrikaans writer and Armscor public relations officer, Bertrand Retief.

Whom did he quote?

Gaius Petronius, 66 AD.

However, structural changes were necessary in South West, *inter alia* to keep in line with the constitutional and political development. Gen Malan had made this clear.

On the political front, the international initiative concerning South West started to manifest itself in more visible ways. In September 1977 there were negotiations in Pretoria between the South African government and delegates of the Big Five Western powers, the United Kingdom, the United States, France, Western Germany and Canada.

Windhoek acquired new political status with the appointment of the first Administrator General. The Turnhalle Conference, which hosted the negotiations between the leaders of all the population groups and would now function under his guidance, was proceeding well. This was the mechanism that would give substance to the South African government's concept of 'South Westers must decide their own future.'

The Free Stater, Justice Marthinus Theunis Steyn, was appointed Administrator General (AG). This event heralded a new constitutional and political era. He took over from Mr Ben van der Walt, the last in a long line of administrators.

The policy that it was up to South Westers to decide their own future was merely a broad political guideline. Mr Justice Steyn had to start a democratic process that would result in free and fair one-person-one-vote elections. At a press conference on his arrival in Windhoek he said:

> I am here to stimulate politics, but not to participate in it. At all times I am neutral as far as that is concerned.

From the army's point of view the new constitutional dispensation and the implementation of a new political process could succeed only if it (the army) could provide the necessary security. And, in order to accomplish this, the military structures had to be adjusted. One integrated structure with its headquarters at Windhoek was essential. The political climate in which we performed our duties nevertheless remained tough and intricate.

The Turnhalle Conference resulted in a Constituent Assembly and later a National Assembly from which a Council of Ministers was constituted.

The reaction of the general public to the political change was very much in line with patterns forecast by the behavioural sciences for such a scenario. And those who had lived through that period of

South West's history could later also predict the reaction of people to the reform process when it started in South Africa.

I know South West is not South Africa. I know there are many differences and I know that one cannot compare the two. However, there are similarities between the human behaviour of different people reacting to the same type of change.

Profound changes always unleash resistance. What comes into play is the so-called RC-factor, Resistance to Change. It creates emotions such as doubt and confusion because one breaks away from the security of the known to encounter the insecurity of the unknown. Uncertainty causes people to fear for their safety. Change causes splits between people, polarization and friction. The friction can be severe enough to lead to violence.

During September 1977 Dirk Mudge walked out of the ruling white National Party's congress, which resulted in a dramatic split inside the party. A H du Plessis remained the leader of the National Party of SWA and Dirk Mudge formed the Republican Party.

In South Africa political changes, which *inter alia* led to the establishment of the three-chamber parliament, had similar results, for example the breakaway of members from the National Party to form the Conservative Party.

Changes normally also lead to alliances and other kinds of group-forming. The Republican Party formed an alliance with parties of the other population groups and called it the Democratic Turnhalle Alliance (DTA). The National Party (NP) of South West also involved black and brown politicians to form an umbrella organization, the Action Front for the Preservation of the Turnhalle Principles (Aktur).

When Andreas Shipanga returned from exile to South West on 24 August 1978 he founded his own party, the Swapo Democrats, which also found a place in an umbrella organization.

He had been one of the founder-members of the Ovamboland People's Organization, which had been formed early in 1958 in Cape Town, and later became the South West African People's Organization (Swapo).

His new party became part of the Namibian National Front (NNF), established in April 1977. It included the South West African National Union (Swanu), Bryan O'Linn's Federal Party and a few more. For some time the NNF was regarded as the largest party left of the DTA on the political spectrum and just right of Swapo.

South Africa experienced the same type of political activity in the early 1990s, although it manifested itself in different ways: some parties split, some grouped and regrouped and some formed new alliances.

Swapo was not a banned organization in South West and its political organization, or so-called internal wing, continued to exist in the new dispensation. Its external wing and its armed organization, Plan, continued to operate from abroad.

Likewise, since 2 February 1990, the African National Congress of South Africa (ANC) is no longer a banned organization.

But the deeper political changes cut, the wider the rifts become. Polarization and friction between parties and groups of parties become more intense. White resistance expressed itself through 'BlankSWA' (WhiteSWA) and the WWB, 'Wit Weerstandsbeweging' (White Resistance Movement). Acts of politically inspired violence were committed by radicals from the left and right extremes of the political spectrum. John Vorster, Theunie Steyn and myself were described in graffiti on buildings in Windhoek as having sold South West out. Bombing incidents occurred.

South Africa had much the same experience in the early 1990s.

Political splits also led to rifts in other fields. The churches and church councils, school advisory boards and agricultural organizations tended to divide along political lines.

The same phenomenon could be observed in South Africa some fifteen years later.

But wherever you meet South Africans and South Westers, you will find them joking, even about serious matters.

Because of Dirk Mudge's walkout of the National Party Congress, many people called him 'the walker'. One day on a flight from J G Strydom (Windhoek) to Jan Smuts, Mr Mudge was given the seat next to mine. When the hostess took orders for drinks, we both asked for whisky. She returned a while later with two small bottles and asked me: 'I have only Johnny Walker and Bell's. Which would you prefer?'

I answered: 'I would like the Bell's. Please give Mr Mudge the Johnny Walker, it's more his style!'

But among the whites there were also strong emotional concerns. It was often a case of brother against brother and father against son. People threatened each other and sometimes followed up their words with action.

Someone once said that the fiercest kind of conflict is the one between brothers. I always remembered this. I also heard once that

America lost more soldiers during the American civil war than in any other armed conflict, including the world wars, in which they were involved.

I mentioned this to a Jewish friend, who remarked: 'Yes, I believe it. This is why the Israeli's and Arabs hate each other so much – they are half-brothers.'

When there is dissent amongst Afrikaners it is often the same.

The emotional friction in South West often caused the real meaning of the new vision and the rapid changes to become blurred. This was to be expected. But a large number of people also remained levelheaded.

In some cases the changes were just too numerous and too rapid for one to keep pace with and to fully comprehend. The manner in which the one-person-one-vote elections scheduled for December 1978 were to be conducted was a considerable departure from generally accepted procedures. During national elections the whites had been used to voting for a particular candidate in a certain constituency; now they had to cast a vote for a party at a polling booth, anywhere. And unfamiliar parties with strange names and symbols had appeared overnight.

Not long before the elections I visited an infantry company at Drimiopsis, north of Gobabis. They were brown soldiers of the new SWA Territory Force (SWATF) that we had established in the area.

That afternoon, while doing field exercises, it started to rain. Everyone ran for shelter. There were a few buildings with tiny roofed verandas where the troops found overhead cover. Crushed together, with me amongst them, I heard one of them saying: 'Separate out a bit you guys, the lightning might strike an innocent person.'

But the story that I really want to tell is about something that happened at the end of the visit, at an informal party.

An elderly man approached me and struck up a conversation: 'I also want to speak, now,' he said, 'But before I speak, I want to say something.' And then he complained that people of all the population groups were enlisted into the SWATF. I answered him as correctly and politely as possible and explained why this was so. His reaction was, 'I'm just saying.'

But in the course of his 'saying' he raised another complaint. Why had one of his white employees been called up again for a month or two for border duty? Once again I responded politely and explained why this was sometimes necessary.

I added that I respected his right to have his own opinion, but that I could not understand how one person could complain about both issues at the same time. Because if you are against the employment of black, brown and yellow soldiers, then you must accept that whites will have to give more of their time for military service.

Anyway, we had a friendly talk and when he had had his 'say', he started to speak. He became quite serious: 'Now, General, these elections in December, since I can't vote for a candidate any more, can I vote for the Defence Force?' Maybe he wasn't serious. Maybe he was pulling my leg.

When change causes confusion, people tend to fall back on traditional values – and they want to be able to rely on the Defence Force.

But even after the elections some people still failed to comprehend the extent of the changes brought about by one-person-one-vote politics. And it was not only the South Westers who had this problem. Even a number of South Africans involved in the South West situation who occasionally visited the territory, people with the benefit of insight and understanding usually brought about by distance, allowed themselves to be trapped by the emotional aspects of the politics of the day.

I listened to many conversations that started with a balanced discussion about the future of South West. But soon two groups would form: those supporting A H du Plessis, Eben van Zijl and Kosie Pretorius of the National Party (NP) on the one hand; and those supporting Dirk Mudge and his colleagues of the Republican Party (RP) on the other.

It was as if Swapo and the other parties did not exist. In other words, they had reverted to the traditional white politics of the past. The new challenges went unseen – independence for the territory with a democratic government.

One-person-one-vote politics in a country where the electorate comprises voters ranging from high intellectuals to bush dwellers across colour lines, has different dynamics than the kind of politics to which the people were familiar with until then. Everyone could vote, the intellectuals and the bush people. Some voters would make informed decisions after listening to speeches and reading newspaper editorials. What counted were the various methods of intellectual persuasion.

Others would be inspired mainly by emotion. Speeches and leader articles would pass them by. Their votes would be the cumulative end-result of emotions such as anger and fear, sentiments, nationalistic urges, tradition, and ethnic values. This facet of politics is vulnerable to sentimental and emotional incitement and intimidation. Intimidation can even play the main role.

I did not find the going easy myself. One has to be strong: in your belief, in your head and in your heart.

But I was not too unfamiliar with these circumstances. During the stormy late 1940s and early 1950s, even the newspaper you read, as I experienced at the Military College, was a serious matter. It could be an indication of whether you were a patriot or a jingo – or something close to it.

In South West I did not dare leave the office with a newspaper under my arm. Because, if it was *Die Suidwester*, the RP supporters would say I was an NP man and an A H du Plessis supporter. Were I to be seen with *Die Republikein*, I would be branded an RP man and Mudge supporter – 'Boem, schluss, finish and klaar!' It was the 1940s and 1950s all over again.

Just as Ouboet and I had had to choose between the Germans and the English at one school after the other, so my children were confronted with: 'Are you for A H du Plessis or are you for Dirk Mudge?'

My younger daughter, Lollie, was in the same class as Barend Spies at the Eros Primary School. He is the son of the well-known academic, farmer, journalist, story teller and DTA man, Jan Spies. Once, at the wrong time and place, little Barend, who was a proud DTA supporter, announced his sympathies. A bloody nose and a swollen lip soon brought it home to him that not everybody shared his sentiments.

Children can be crueller intimidators than adults. But they are not good at resisting when they are being intimidated. I had some understanding of what must have been going on in the minds of our own children. Eventually they learned to say that they did not vote for either A H du Plessis or Dirk Mudge, they voted for their father, Jannie Geldenhuys.

These were merely some of the stresses of white politics in those days. But other population groups also suffered uncertainty, confusion, anger and fear, especially those who were afraid of Ovambo domination, and intimidation in general.

None of this had anything to do with me; but it was under these changing circumstances and in this atmosphere that the Defence Force had to be commanded and managed in such a way as to achieve its mission. And apart from the formal task of the Defence Force there was also an informal role to play – through its general behaviour to contribute towards calming an unsettled society. Friction resulting in violence becomes a security problem.

This meant that the Defence Force had to remain as neutral as humanly possible. It also meant that the less the Defence Force members participated in politics, the better. I formulated a few principles for myself:

Firstly, I stayed out of party politics and expected the same of my colleagues. This was not a problem as the majority of the permanent force members were South Africans and therefore not personally and emotionally involved in the political situation. And then of course, while the permanent force member is a professional soldier 24 hours a day, the official restrictions on political activities are stricter than those imposed on members of the citizen force and commandos.

The problem with citizen force and commando members is that they are full-time citizens of the country and only part-time soldiers. Most of them spent no more than five per cent of their time on military service. They were born South Westers and they loved their country. How was one to keep them out of party politics when they had a right and duty to partake in it?

There is of course the bureaucratic solution: You throw the regulation book at them. There have always been proper guidelines and restrictions governing the behaviour of Defence Force members in respect of party politics. But one cannot command by means of papers. Papers 'talk' only once, they cannot answer questions. People, especially officers and non-commissioned officers, have questions to ask and they want answers. And one cannot deny any person that human right.

So I developed a formula for the part-time officers. I said that it was their right as citizens to participate in politics. I could not and would not take that away from them. But it was also fair of me to expect extreme circumspection from them in times of unrest and suspicion so as not to damage the cohesion and effectiveness of the military machine. As circumspection is a vague term, I elaborated as follows: Should an officer be politically active, it is his duty to behave in such a manner that the men under his command would not have any reason to complain. They should have no reason to say that they can no longer serve under him as his behaviour causes strife and endangers the *esprit de corps*.

I think this is as fair, just and correct as one can be. And whatever the regulations, one cannot find much wrong with such an approach. Furthermore, the responsibility to play watchdog over the officers and non-commissioned officers was passed from my shoulders to theirs. Everyone was now his own watchdog and his norm became the reaction of the men he led and towards whom he had a moral duty.

The second guideline I followed to develop a politically neutral Defence Force was never to address selected audiences, if at all possible. If I addressed a unit, I never separated the South Africans and South Westers, and colour played no part.

With regard to the public, it would probably have been easy to talk about the Defence Force if you had a politically homogeneous audience. It would have been easy to address a purely Herstigte Nasionale Party (HNP) audience, a DTA gathering, or only NNF people. But if I had any say in the matter, I always addressed mixed audiences, because then one had no choice but to be factually correct and objective as well.

I can't think that I ever invited politicians of only one party for visits to the operational area. I invited them together, from the whole spectrum of South West. All briefings were conducted with representatives from all parties together, as were the discussions afterwards.

My door was always open for members of any of the parties who needed to discuss military matters with me. I had discussions with politicians such as Sarel Becker of the HNP, Eben van Zijl of the NP, Chief Riruako of the DTA, Reinhard Rukoro, Dr Ken and Othile Abrahams and her sister Nora Chase of Swanu, and Andreas Shipanga of the Swapo Democrats. I found all their remarks and requests concerning the Defence Force reasonable. I should like to flatter myself that we did not only listen to them as a matter of courtesy or as a gesture of goodwill, but that we seriously attended to their arguments, followed up and reported back.

In the third place I tried to keep all military personnel informed. My term of command coincided with the negotiations between the five Western powers and the UN, which would eventually lead to the settlement plan for South West and the UN Security Council Resolution 435. After each important political development involving the UN, I always organized a formal session to report back. These sessions included feedback on negotiations with the UN's military representatives such as Gen Hannes Philipp and later Prem Chand. I would inform all permanent force, citizen force and commando commanding officers and their key personnel about events, especially where I was personally involved. These included visits to South West and discussions by the Prime Minister, and later State President, Mr P W Botha, and Min Pik Botha, the Minister of Foreign Affairs as from 1 April 1977. I tried to be factual, unbiased, clinical and accurate.

After a few of these conferences the commanding officers enquired regularly about when the next sessions would take place. I thus deduced that they took them seriously. Political leaders and newspapers also reported on the political events I mentioned, but of course, they would do it in a way that promotes their own policies and viewpoints. This meant that conflicting perceptions were created and that the commanders needed more neutral interpretations.

All commanders in turn had to keep the people under their command informed. After a feedback session with his Bushman battalion, Cmdt Linford told me this story: Having listened attentively to the briefing, the Bushmen were confused. In a roundabout way they explained to him that they were happy with the school at Omega and that their children were doing well: they themselves had also learnt quite a bit. They had learnt to count and demonstrated promptly: 1, 2, 3, 4, 5, 6, 7, 8, 9, 10. Now, what they could not understand, was how the commandant could talk about 'Resolution 435?' Surely it should be 'Resolution 345!'

The UN secretary-general at the time was Kurt Waldheim. He had no feeling for Bushman mathematics. His successor, Perez de Cuellar, was more sympathetically inclined. During the run-up to the Gulf War, he and President Bush accommodated the Bushmen with Resolution 678. During 1992 de Cuellar's successor, Boutros Boutros-Ghali, again messed up the figures with his resolution about violence in South Africa – Resolution 765.

At other places similar presentations required just as much patience. An officer in Ovamboland told me about an occasion when a chief and his advisers had come to talk to him. They wanted to know what was happening. He gave them a detailed explanation about the involvement of the UN, the position of the AG, the role of the Defence Force in Ovamboland and all the other things he thought might be of interest to them. And when he had finished, came the first question:

'When will the primary school's broken windows be repaired?'

I have now described South West's political tangle and the attempts we made to prevent the Defence Force from becoming caught up in it. We might have made mistakes, but I doubt if anyone else could have done better under the same circumstances. I believe our approach was largely successful. To illustrate: It happened a few times that infiltrators penetrated the so-called northern white farming area. During such an incursion into the Outjo district, Cmdt Stoffel Rothman's commando was mobilized, including his cavalry platoon. They operated very successfully.

During the operation, Situation Reports, or Sitreps, were submitted by the commando as per standing procedures.

Sitreps are sent at regular intervals by lower headquarters to the next higher headquarters at prescribed times. It is a report that covers a 24-hour period. To keep the sitrep short, index letters are used to indicate paragraph headings. The letter A substitutes for the heading, Enemy Activities. B is used for that part of the report dealing with actions by Own Forces. C indicates Administrative and Logistic matters. D stands for matters of general interest.

My staff showed me one of the Outjo Sitreps:

A: Unchanged
B: NTR[1]
C: Unchanged
D: Aktur, DTA and NNF members all well!

The dividing line between military activities and politics, however, was not always very distinct. It sometimes caused suspicion and strife.

The Defence Force never performs its duties in a vacuum; the environment in which it operates also features political policies and opinions – in this regard it could take an impassive stand. But there are also political structures; and it cannot ignore these. It has to operate within these structures. After all the Defence Force serves the government of the day.

The Defence Force had contact with the South African government through the normal channels to the Minister of Defence. It had to have contact with the South West government. Thus liaison was established with the office of the AG.

The usual three levels of government also existed in South West. Examples of second-tier governments were the Ovambo and Kavango administrations. If, as has happened, there was a military presence in Kavango, the commanding officer would have to liaise with the Chief Minister of Kavango and his cabinet. If these ministers were DTA members it did not necessarily follow that the Defence Force was involved in party politics. However, not everybody always saw it as such.

The Defence Force tried to remain as neutral as possible towards the parties, with the exception of Swapo. Swapo was not a banned organization, but its external armed wing (Plan) did conduct armed activities inside the territory which, from a security point of view, branded them as the enemy.

Part-time members of the Defence Force sometimes tried to persuade me to give them personal opinions and advice on South West party politics. I did, on a few occasions, go so far as to say that one finds politicians who identify political issues and who would give you their viewpoints on them. Then you find politicians who identify political problems and who would offer their solutions to those problems. I said I took the second category of politicians more seriously than the first; solutions count more that mere opinions, and the only real solution to the South West political problem would be one that enjoyed meaningful international support.

It was mainly in the south, in towns such as Windhoek, Swakopmund, Keetmanshoop and Mariental, where people got tangled up in the party political turmoil surrounding them.

The people north of the Red Line at places such as Oshakati, Rundu and Katima Mulilo, on the other hand, were caught up with what was happening on their doorsteps. They were more sensitive to the daily security situation. The doings of the UN, the AG and such matters almost passed them by. Until 1977 it was much the same with the Defence Force members. Those in the north were busy with operations and did not concern themselves with events in Windhoek. They had closer ties with Pretoria and operations were all that mattered. With the integration of 101 Task Force and SWA Command they acquired more balanced perceptions.

The major military effort in South West was focused on Ovamboland. And this was another political nettle. There the Defence Force fought against insurgents, against people who laid mines on public roads, against people who set up ambushes, who abducted school children and who killed traditional chiefs. During a two-year period in about 1978–1979, 23 chiefs and headmen were killed, including the Chief Minister, Captain Filemon Elifas, Minister Toivo Shiyagaya and Minister Shikongo. The situation in South Africa during the early 1990s, especially in Natal, turned out to be much the same.

This climate of hard intimidation had an inhibiting effect on active politics.

The Defence Force always regarded insurgency as a political struggle between the government and the revolutionary movement that made use of terror tactics. The security forces fought the insurgents to maintain order, stability and security so that politics could be conducted free from organized violence and intimidation. But the government had to fight the political struggle.

I often heard complaints in Ovambo that the government did not fulfil its responsibilities in fighting the political struggle. It is of course quite difficult to determine whether a government conducts the struggle as a government or as a political party.

Swapo conducted politics from kraal to kraal, while the government concentrated on administrative functions, but one cannot fight a revolutionary war through administration alone. It is a principle of successful anti-revolutionary warfare that the government of the day must propagate a cause that is more attractive than that of the revolutionaries. And the Ovambo government could possibly have done this because they were not without political ammunition.

Swapo wanted freedom and independence for South West – that was promised them in the new dispensation; independence in the form of a unitary state; plus free and fair elections. The only condition was that they had to lay down their arms, join the new political process as many others did, and contest the elections. This seemed a better way of getting power than to fight for it.

Judge Steyn and his successors did indeed activate a free democratic process. the December 1978 elections were 'indisputably a free, fair election, conducted under the eyes of a number of Western observers'. One can only speculate about what the outcome would have been if Swapo had accepted the invitation to participate.

Be that as it may, I do not want to be drawn into these political arguments and their merits. The point that I want to make is that, whatever the arguments might have been, the Ovambo government failed to capitalize on what had been offered them.

I often got the impression that the second-tier politicians had been trained in public administration, but that they were never really groomed for party politics. Not that there was a total lack of political activity, but it seemed to be conducted through the traditional tribal chiefs and authorities. They were no match for the Swapo political commissars.

Anti-Swapo party politics in Ovambo had a very low profile. I recall seeing a visitor who came to Ovambo to analyse the situation. On completion of his research he had an interview with me. To my amazement I came to realize that he was not yet even aware of the existence of the party headed by Chief Minister, Pastor Ndjoba!

The profile of international politics did not seem to be much higher than Ndjoba's but it did eventually result in an agreement.

On 26 September 1977 the conference of the Western Five with South Africa ended without reaching a settlement. During February 1978, Western negotiators were in Windhoek to confer with the various political parties, including Swapo's 'internal' wing. During the same month Western diplomats held discussions with Pik Botha and Sam Nujoma in New York without any sign of progress.

At the end of the month Nujoma made his well-known statement that Swapo was not interested in majority government but that the aim of his struggle was to seize power in Namibia.

Then, on 25 April 1978, the South African government formally accepted the Western proposals for a settlement in South West Africa which agreement would later achieve formal status through UN Resolution 435.

7

SOUTH WEST – A WINNING APPROACH

Time does not take sides

While talking-politics was in full swing, shooting-politics continued apace. Plan were well established in Angola and their activities increased considerably. During October 1977 a skirmish involving 88 insurgents started 1 km south of the border. It continued for a few days and ended more than 20 km into Angola. This was the closest to a full-scale battle that had taken place in South West since 1915.

Two Plan bases were destroyed and a third was seriously damaged. All in all 61 insurgents were killed. The security forces lost six men.

The customary propaganda claims followed. This was something Swapo could do very well. On 30 October 1977 Peter Katjavivi stated in London that the South African losses amounted to double figures. He claimed that the encounter took place at Ondangwa, 55 km south of the border. Ondangwa was our biggest operational air base in the north. Katjavivi also announced later that Plan had attacked our border base at Eenhana, many South African soldiers were killed and wounded, they had driven us from the base and destroyed a lot of vehicles and communications equipment.

Apart from the fact that the South African Defence Force may not conceal its personnel losses, it is also impossible on a practical level. But how does one refute such allegations? Many people believed them.

However, for once, these wild allegations suited me well and the *friction de guerre* was on my side. Shortly before this incident I had invited a representative group of journalists to tour the border area, which included stops at Ondangwa and Eenhana. After Katjavivi's claims I invited them for a follow-up visit and they were able to confirm that Katjavivi's statement was a lie. A certain journalist wrote later that the only change he observed since his previous visit to Eenhana two months earlier was the chaplain's new signboard indicating the way to the chapel.

My good fortune had not yet run out. During one of the UN's excursions to South West, the delegation stopped at Luanda on their outbound flight. There Swapo told them the same stories. When they arrived in Windhoek, Gen Philipp, the UN Force Commander designate, requested that Ondangwa and Eenhana be included in their itinerary.

Cmdt Anton van Graan was the base commander at Eenhana. When Philipp and his party arrived there, he wanted to know the name of the base. When Anton confirmed that it was Eenhana, an astounded Philipp said: 'But it can't be. Eenhana was destroyed!' He could judge for himself – and he made no enquiries about Ondangwa.

In the meantime the area of armed activity was extended eastwards, as far as the Caprivi. During November 1977 a potentially nasty incident occurred when Zambian soldiers launched a mortar attack at an observation post on the southern bank of the Zambezi and the South Africans retaliated. It resulted in an hour-long battle during which a few Zambian bombs fell inside the town of Katima Mulilo. The residents were not unduly perturbed, as the town had sporadically come under fire since 1974. Slit trenches had been dug and sandbags stacked in front of the houses along the Zambezi. An alarm system had been installed after the occurrence of two similar incidents earlier in 1977.

On 19 February 1978 a group of infiltrators crossed into the Caprivi from Zambia. They set up an ambush between Katima Mulilo and Mpacha and killed three South Africans by hitting their Land Rover with an RPG7 rocket. Cmdt Bill Poole and Maj Dries Els and also Mr de Lange of the Atlas Aircraft Corporation were killed. A fourth passenger, Mr Mollenbeek of Armscor, survived the attack.

On 27 March 1978 extensive violence erupted again starting with the murder of Chief Clemens Kapuuo, leader of the Hereros, chairman of the Democratic Turnhalle Alliance and a fierce enemy of Swapo. He was regarded by many as a possible future president of an independent South West Africa.

This was the security situation. To win this war, we had to develop a strategy based on sound premises. How does one go about it? Many factors and considerations come into play.

We were definitely not ignorant of the nature of the war. We already had the experience of the acts of violence that had been committed in South Africa by the armed wings of the Pan Africanist Congress (PAC) and the African National Congress (ANC). However, the nature and extent of the violence were such that the SA Police could take responsibility for curbing it.

Members of the police also gained experience in counterinsurgency in Rhodesia. In South West the first incidents occurred as far back as 1966, but once again the frequency was so low that the police remained responsible for public safety and internal security.

During 1973 the Defence Force became responsible for counterinsurgency and the protection of South West's borders and took over from the police. It was a conflict of very low intensity which was 'interrupted' to an extent by Operation Savannah, 1975–1976. When insurgency resumed again after the operation, the scene had changed.

It had been a while since we had campaigned on this scale. There was the Second World War, Korea and Operation Savannah. Officers and other ranks with experience of warfare were hard to come by, and every war is, in any case, unique.

Even during the Second World War very few South Africans held command positions, or served as senior staff officers at a level higher than brigade. And only a few were still available. Formations and units of the Union Defence Force (UDF) had generally formed part of divisions, armies and corps of the Allied Forces. The UDF's formations and units fell in with the higher formations' overall planning, fitted into their command and control structures and were served by their logistic systems.

We now had to rely on ourselves to establish the most effective war machine possible, maintained by its own supporting systems. And though we were not in the desert of North Africa or in Europe, we conducted a war from our base area in South Africa to the northern reaches of South West. While operating in Angola, our troops were deployed over a distance equal to that between Cairo and Paris. It is 2 440 km by rail from Bloemfontein to Grootfontein; 669 km by road from Grootfontein to Cassinga; approximately 1 900 km by air from Bloemfontein to Cassinga. (See map on the inside cover.)

In South West itself we operated across vast areas with a poor infrastructure. In the summer, in the early days, it took a convoy from Grootfontein to Katima Mulilo and back three to four weeks along the Golden Highway; later it took ten days along the new road.

I could now capitalize on my years of training. In South Africa training in counterinsurgency started in all seriousness in 1960. My experience as an instructor in counterinsurgency now stood me in good stead.

My knowledge was also complemented by my observations in Angola, and through continuous private study. The Portuguese fought long drawn-out wars overseas in countries far away – Angola, Portuguese Guinea and Mozambique.

However, for the commanding general in South West there was no ready-made manual on how to go about his task.

One person whose work was of great value to me was a previous Chief of the Army, Lt Gen C A (Pop) Fraser. I found that I could use many of his ideas. He had published a study during the early 1960s titled *Lessons learnt from past revolutionary wars.* I identified myself with its contents emotionally and intellectually and made his ideas my own. They were important. I mention a few lessons that I took over from his work.

- A revolutionary war is a political war.
- The aim of both sides in a revolutionary war is to win the support of the population, their approval, sympathy and active participation.
- The government must win the political initiative by propagating a more attractive cause than that offered by the insurgents.
- The danger of complacency (refusal to acknowlege the real situation) must be avoided before and during a revolution.
- The existence of an outstanding intelligence organization is essential.
- In revolutionary warfare, bureaucratic delays are as dangerous as subversion itself.

The best countermeasure to a revolution is – good government.

During the years I also developed my own approaches and concepts.

I could often apply them in practice and they helped me to read intricate situations with understanding and insight. One such concept concerns the nature of conventional and revolutionary warfare.

Conventional warfare is greatly influenced by the exact sciences, technology and military equipment. The commander of the American air force during the Gulf War said that it was a technological war. Insurgency warfare on the other hand is influenced more by aspects related to the social sciences; it is about people, not machines.

In a nutshell, conventional warfare consists of movement and the delivery of fire power. By concentrating fire power on the right places, at the right time, one could cause enough destruction to win crucial battles and force a final decision. In this way the war can be ended in a short time. This kind of warfare lends itself to centralized command and management.

Insurgency warfare, however, consists of a multitude of small battles. One cannot bring such a war to a quick end through military action because the enemy does not present one with a geographic military objective on which to concentrate fire power. Command should therefore be decentralised to a large extent.

This kind of war will end in a victory for the insurgents when:

- the government forces collapse as a result of continual set-backs over a period; or
- the population's will to resist is broken down by attrition.

The government forces will win when:

- the government can persuade the population that its cause is more attractive than that of the revolutionaries; or
- the insurgents, after lengthy periods of relentless operations, do not make progress, lose the support of the population, and negotiations become a more attractive alternative; or
- the insurgents' host country becomes fatigued by its involvement in the war.

If insurgents have access to a safe haven across an international border, a military victory cannot be achieved unless the host country can be convinced, in some way or another, to withdraw its support. Jordan, for example, refused the Palestinian Liberation Organization (PLO) free access to Israel from its territory. The Israelis also tried for a long time to create a situation that would make it impossible for Lebanon to be used any longer as a launching pad for terrorist attacks against them.

But this is theory. Let us move on to the realities. We asked ourselves certain key questions:

- From a security point of view we had to make a contribution which would enable the political process to succeed – an independent South West with a democratic form of government. What did this mean in practice?

- We had to prevent military adventures and violence from becoming a means to seize power, or unduly to influence political decisions. How could we achieve this?

We found the answers. Flowing from our concept of the management style required for the successful waging of anti-revolutionary warfare, the matter of centralization and decentralization of command was amply clarified.

In addition, the Chief of the Army, Gen Viljoen, and his headquarters expected results from us in Windhoek. They too issued directives and even initiated operational actions.

Yet, it was actually the sector and subsector commanders and their captains and sergeants who fought the war.

One may justly ask what function the commanding general and his staff in Windhoek were supposed to perform between these two levels, while the system was based on decentralized command.

There was an important role to play and that we did. In addition to the directives from higher headquarters we also formulated for ourselves what the Defence Force in South West was to achieve. Although we realized that the sector commanders were actually responsible for operations, we could provide invaluable guidance and support.

We realized that every sector was unique. We tried not to issue instructions of a general nature to be followed by all. From the point of view of the overall command level we rather looked at the sectors individually. Each had to have its own design for operations.

Our concept for managing anti-revolutionary warfare had led us to revise the existing directives issued to the sector commanders as well as their directives to their subordinate commanders.

The formulation of the mission-paragraph in the old directives can be summarized as follows: The commander was required to search for and destroy all insurgents in his area of responsibility (within the period of his appointment). If it was possible in practice to accomplish such a mission we would leave it at that.

However, in certain areas of the border it was an impossible task. The infiltrators could always escape into their host countries, Zambia and Angola. Where that was the position, the mission was redefined to the effect that the commander was expected to decrease insurgency in his area to a certain level within a specified time. This could easily be defined by using various parameters.

One could not allow a competent commander who worked hard and effectively and substantially reduced terror in his area, to believe that he had failed in his mission simply because he did not wipe out all the insurgents. This would be highly demotivating. His new mission would be revised periodically and having reached the set goal, the parameters would be scaled up. In this way realistic goals were set.

Some commanders reached their new goals time and again so that in due course it became a realistic mission for them to completely clear their respective areas of all insurgents.

Apart from the matter of directives, and bearing in mind Pop Fraser's lessons, we seriously addressed our intelligence system. Our intelligence staff officer, Cmdt Johann Saaiman, played an important role. My own contribution towards improving the system was to transfer many of the trained junior intelligence officers and non-commissioned officers on my staff in Windhoek to the operational areas. The aim was to increase the quality and quantity of intelligence collected at the action spots. One can process more and a better quality of intelligence from the forward areas with fewer staff in Windhoek, rather than the other way round.

We formulated the command directives more realistically and we set out to improve the intelligence organization. The answer to the question of how to go about preventing armed intimidation from negatively influencing the political decision-making was: Gain and maintain the initiative.

I held strong beliefs about the concept of initiative. Initiative is of vital importance in conflict and was always an important consideration during our planning cycle.

We developed an approach during the planning process, the thrust of which I had not come across anywhere else. One first has to find an honest answer to the question: Who holds the initiative, you or your opponent? The basic truth in an insurgency war is that the insurgent, potentially and often in practice, has the initiative.

Basically, initiative means that when two parties are in conflict and party A takes certain actions which results in reaction by party B, then party A has the initiative.

For example, compare sabotage with crime. A criminal who plans to snatch a lady's handbag is the one who selects the time, place and victim. He has the initiative. The same goes for a person who plants a bomb or sets up an ambush.

In a conflict situation the one who has the initiative seldom loses. Put another way, it seldom happens that the one who does not have the initiative wins. It is therefore imperative that ways and means of obtaining the initiative and keeping it are found. One way to do this is to act first instead of waiting, by taking the battle to the insurgent.

The planning process thus works as follows: if you believe that your opponent has the initiative, you first plan what to do to successfully counter his expected actions. Then you apply your mind to the question as to what else you could do to gain the initiative, if not immediately, then in due course, and incorporate the answer in your plan.

If you believe that you have the initiative, you first have to decide what it is that you want to achieve and how to go about doing so. Then you ask yourself what your opponent could do to counter your intended action. When you have the answer you augment your plan to prevent him from doing so.

During our planning cycles and normal environmental studies, we also identified patterns through which we developed new concepts and modes of operation.

One such pattern was a seasonal phenomenon. The insurgent is less effective during the dry season because water is scarce and he can easily be ambushed at water points. In addition, the winter foliage affords him little cover against observation. Furthermore, the mobility of the security forces is then at its best.

During the rainy season there is enough water and good cover. These advantages were exploited by insurgents for deep infiltration into districts such as the so-called white farming areas. They avoided waterholes and used pylons and roads as navigational aids.

Another pattern that we identified was the greater intensity of activities during the time of the full moon and less during the dark moon.

Statistics may not always seem clearly to reflect these patterns because other factors tend to disturb the picture. The most important of these was the political factor. Insurgent operations are normally planned specifically to precede, or coincide with, political events such as relevant sessions of the General Assembly or the Security Council of the UN, meetings of the Liberation Committee of the OAU and visits by influential persons.

Likewise, our own periodic major cross-border operations also disturbed the general patterns and created their own. North of the border in Angola, the rank and file insurgents were accommodated in detachment bases. They infiltrated from there to operate in areas south of the border adjacent to their respective base areas. However, there were also special groups with bases elsewhere who could take on targets at any place south of the border. They concentrated mainly on sabotage and laying mines.

After our strikes across the border, we found that the dislodged detachment insurgents became inactive for some time. But the special groups were usually not disrupted to any great extent by our operations. One could then expect a constant or higher frequency of mine and bomb related incidents. These were relatively simple operations with high propaganda value.

Another pattern that we observed was that our communication operations, which Willem Steenkamp called 'goodwill programmes' and the troops called 'plough-and-plant' programmes, tended to prevent insurgency from starting in an area but we were less successful in countering it if it had already commenced. However, communication operations did make a valuable contribution in such areas, provided that they were preplanned as a follow-up action to successful fighting operations.

We also found that the Citizen Force men were more successful in this kind of operation than the National Servicemen. A Citizen Force sergeant with a beard proudly presenting a photograph of his wife and four kids made a better impression on the head of a kraal than a brave and fit second lieutenant with down on his chin and a snapshot of his school girlfriend.

The main objective of our strategy was to clean up Kaokoland, Kavango and Caprivi. It may seem to have been an impossible task in the light of the above, but in time we managed to do so. By achieving this aim, we would reduce the vast area that had been infiltrated by insurgents so that only Ovamboland remained. We could then concentrate our efforts there and fight more cost-effectively.

We distributed our available manpower and other resources with this strategy in mind. The men of Sector 10, Ovambo, remarked on the 'high' force levels allotted to other areas, for example to Caprivi, but eventually we were sufficiently successful in Caprivi so that we could reduce our troops there and increase the force levels in Ovambo.

In addition we made a detailed analysis of the numbers of troops we were employing on defensive tasks as opposed to those we used for offensive action.

Defensive tasks would be, for example, guard and escort duties. This type of operational activity does not in itself win a war. It is therefore necessary to limit to the absolute minimum the number of troops deployed for this purpose.

One example of offensive action is 'search-and-destroy' operations. This kind of operation can give you the upper hand. We tried to make more troops available for this purpose. Similarly we tried to allocate an increased number of troops for night operations, even if it meant using fewer for daylight operations.

Likewise, we planned to use more troops in areas just across the border and smaller numbers inside the border – when it was allowed.

Gen Malan clearly demarcated responsibilities with regard to cross-border operations. The decision to cross the border was a political one. The government and the Minister of Defence carried the responsibility for the decision. The successful execution of the operation was the responsibility of the Chief of the Defence Force.

Detailed instructions were always issued. For example, the circumstances under which hot pursuit operations were allowed and the restrictions governing them were clearly laid down. The instructions with regard to Angola, Zambia and Botswana differed. They were also continually amended as the political situation changed. There were times when we were not allowed to operate at all in Angola, or when we could do only non-offensive reconnaissance, subject to certain limitations. Sometimes we were allowed to conduct operations in Angola south of a specified east-west line, provided we did not exceed prescribed force levels.

Indeed, in the last case, if we could 'shift the border northwards' ten kilometers or so, we could have forced contact with cadres inside Angola which would otherwise have happened south of the border. In this way we could have reduced insurgent incidents inside South West Africa.

If we could dominate the area immediately north of the border, fewer troops would be needed for counterinfiltration, border protection and other defensive tasks inside Ovambo. Thus, more troops would be available for offensive operations. One disadvantage of limiting operations to south of the border is that the tracks of insurgents were often detected only after they had committed an undesirable act. Statistics later proved that operations across the border also saved lives.

There were two kinds of cross-border operations: specific operations and general operations. The first kind was a pre-planned operation, in and out, on preselected Plan bases. A pre-emptive operation before a new wave of infiltration is a good example. During such operations we lost, on average, only one man for every hundred insurgents killed.

General operations, on the other hand, were much the same as the area operations we conducted south of the border with the aim of dominating an area and destroying insurgents. In this case we lost an average of one man to every thirty of the enemy.

With internal operations we lost an average of one to every ten or less of the enemy. However, this was not always the case.

Operations in South West and Angola differed substantially from place to place and from time to time. There were many regional variations within the operational area.

The operational area literally stretched from the Atlantic Ocean in the west to Mpalela Island in the east (the point where four countries meet – South West, Botswana, Zambia and Zimbabwe), and from the Red Line in the south (the foot-and-mouth cattle disease area) to an east-west line approximately 45 km north of the border. Map 1 compares the size of the operational area to that of South Africa.

Isolated actions outside this area also took place periodically. Refer to the overlay of maps on the inside cover for a comparison of southern Africa to Europe.

The zone included regions abounding with trees, such as in the Caprivi; while other areas, such as the southern parts of Angola, were covered in African bush. There are areas with large rivers, such as the Kavango, others flat and empty, for example Ovambo, and areas comprising Savannah grasslands. Other regions consisted of high mountains and deep valleys like Kaokoland. And the populations differed from region to region.

There were many reasons why operational designs and techniques needed to be changed from time to time in the same area. For example, every time the insurgents adapted themselves to our initiatives, we had to come up with new tactics and methods to set them running anew, and to keep them on the defence mentally.

We often had mixed success: while progress was being made in the Kaokoveld, problems would arise in the Caprivi. While there was progress in the Caprivi, the situation would be deteriorating in Ovambo. In Kavango it could be peaceful today and ominous to-morrow.

What worked in one place did not necessarily work in another. What worked in 1980 did not necessarily work in 1987.

I was fortunate to have been able to observe the whole picture from the beginning to the end, from the lowest to the highest level. I was involved throughout the whole period of the war, and across the whole extent of the zone. Over time we slowly but surely got the upper hand.

A few specific cross-border operations made headlines: Operation Reindeer on 4 May 1978 and Operation Sceptic, or 'Smokeshell' on 10 June 1980. Both were particularly significant. Each, in turn, had a positive influence on the course of the war.

In time other cross-border operations further strengthened our position. The cumulative result of all these operations was one of the most successful counterinsurgency campaigns since World War II.

Before providing details of Operation Reindeer, I want to make it clear that in the end it was the general ground and air operations that earned us international acclaim. The large-scale specific cross-border operations with the aim of gaining a winning advantage were dramatic and spectacular. Some of these operations, or parts of them, were professional users of war – the subject of books and videos.

However, in my opinion it was the overall effect of the almost unseen but incessant day-to-day general operations that brought us success.

It was our sustained general operations that distinguished this campaign from other counter insurgency wars elsewhere in the world, and it was this that commanded respect. I refer to protection and escort duties, border protection, tracking and follow-up operations, ambushes, search-and-destroy operations, and relentless offensive area patrolling on foot and for long periods at a time, as well as nagging pursuits.

My statement can be illustrated with the following example: After we had terminated our support to Renamo, people remained suspicious and asked me why the Mozambican government forces, while still receiving aircraft, tanks, armoured cars and artillery from the Soviet Union, could not force Renamo to its knees without South African support.

We had good intelligence on the operational patterns and battle techniques of the Mozambican forces, and to me the answer was obvious. I always answered: If we had been expected to use tanks and guns against Plan, we would not have known what to do with them. We used weapons such as aircraft and guns with devastating hitting power on only a few occasions during the bush war. This usually happened during specific cross-border operations when we attacked strongly defended bases, or when we faced the risk of getting involved with Cuban forces and Fapla. If all other factors remained constant, the war against Renamo could not have been won unless patroling was kept up every day, day and night, far and wide, on foot and for long periods at a time. The Mozambican forces did not do it. We did.

Another example: After the Lusaka Accord in 1984, we sent out joint patrols with Fapla. We were amazed to find that the Fapla soldiers had to operate with only one water bottle per soldier per day. How many kilometres can a soldier patrol with one bottle of water?

It was in this respect that our Citizen Force and Commando troops, during the early stages, and after them the national servicemen and Permanent Force soldiers of all branches, made their mark in silent perseverance. This is the South African soldier. The best I know.

They had to show guts and stamina and they did. In this kind of war, short-lived excellence does not mean much. Many people, including some speaking with authority, liked to use the popular cliché that time is on the side of the insurgent. It is not entirely untrue. The motive of the revolutionary strategist is to wear down and exhaust its target country by means of ceaseless multiple actions over a long time. And it works.

But there is another side to this theory.

I believe that time is neutral. Time does not take sides. Time is on the side of those who make the best use of it. Time can be on the side of the one with the best staying power, but sticking-it-out strategies can become destructive to all parties concerned. For them to succeed, from the point of view of the anti-revolutionaries, there should be a national strategy as this line of approach affects the whole population of a country whose support is essential.

Even revolutionary strategists admit that to start a revolution is easy, the problem is to keep it going to the end. That is why they came up with slogans such as *a luta continua* – the struggle continues. This is used in adverse situations to encourage revolutionaries not to give up or lose interest.

Another similar example was *vitoria é certa* – ultimate victory is assured. This was used to motivate fatigued revolutionary forces with promises of guaranteed success.

This phenomenon can also be found in other conflict situations, such as in sport. After the second test match against the Wallabies in 1969, Frik du Preez was dropped in favour of André de Wet. Frik's response was: 'Well, we'll just have to take the bicycle by the handles again and push it over the hill.'

Frik is a serious man and often comes up with words of wisdom. This was his version of 'the struggle continues' – we must hang in there, vasbyt.

During the same season, in the Currie Cup final between Northern Transvaal and Western Province at Loftus Versveld, he persevered. He took the bicycle by the handles and 'dropped, placed and scored' – and regained his place in the 1970 tour to the British Isles.

I believed that we had to persevere on the winning path. In the long run Soviet Russia could not sustain its efforts in Angola and its support of Swapo. The moment that it withdrew from the scene, the scales would radically tip in our favour.

This reminds me of the admonition of the Duke of Wellington to the House of Lords: 'A great country cannot wage a little war.' I stated publicly that Angola would become the Soviet Union's Vietnam. It was reported in the media. I will come back to that later.

Speaking of Soviet Russia and Vietnam, Swapo's affinity for the communist world was clearly demonstrated by its use of codes and nicknames: it had bases called Moscow and Vietnam. This brings me to the first cross-border operation that made headlines – Reindeer.

This operation had its run-up before I took over command in South West. It happened shortly after the amalgamation of 101 Task Force and SWA Command with the new single HQ in Windhoek.

Ian Gleeson, the last commander of 101 Task Force and his fellow-commanders, Col Blackie de Swardt of the Air Force and Col Giep Booysen of Medical Services, were responsible for the planning that led to Operation Reindeer before I took over. It was therefore decided that they should be in command of the operation. The fighting forces were under the command of Col Jan Breytenbach, Cmdt Deon Ferreira and Maj Frank Bestbier.

Reindeer was launched on Ascension Day, 4 May 1978, and consisted of an air and parachute attack on Plan's most important training and supply base, Moscow, which was Swapo's name for Cassinga, 250 km north of the border.

The other part of the operation was a simultaneous ground attack by a mechanized force on various forward transit bases in Angola's border area. This included a stretched out complex, Vietnam, Swapo's name for the bases at Chetaquera, 28 km north of the border.

'Nearly a thousand insurgents were killed in battle and 200 captured while only six members of the security forces fell. Large quantities of equipment and supplies were destroyed and valuable documents seized. The loss of trained personnel and the effect of the intelligence gathered by the security forces were a great setback from which Plan never recovered completely.'[1] Among the casualties was one South African soldier missing in action.

Gen Viljoen joined by helicopter the forces that were still mopping up the Moscow objective. He was to return with the last wave of helicopters. But before they could take off, a Cuban armoured combat team from Techamutete arrived on the scene to aid Plan. However, fighter-aircraft of the South African Air Force attacked them, making it possible for the helicopters to get away in the nick of time.

This was one of the most daring operations of its kind. Not long afterwards, a group of foreign officers paid South Africa a hush-hush visit. They specifically wanted to know how we had planned and executed the attack on the Moscow base. Gen Viljoen and a team briefed them thoroughly and factually. One of them remarked: 'We wouldn't have done it.' When asked why not, he answered: 'It is too risky. Not even the Israelis would in one day have used more than 250 paratroopers and a mobile air reserve of 120 men in an airborne operation on a target 250 kilometres across an international border, and then fly them back in helicopters.'

However, results speak for themselves. It was a jewel of military craftsmanship. And Swapo knew it.

The operation again triggered the normal propaganda claims and counterclaims:

'More than a decade later Cassinga is still being touted in some circles as an infamous massacre of the innocents. Claims and counterclaims aside, the South Africans' insistence that it was indeed a military target is reinforced by unfakeable aerial photographs showing the extensive fortifications and the resistance offered by the defenders, which was so stiff and protracted that the paratroopers stayed much longer than they had planned and had to leave the garrison still holding part of the town.'[2]

It would have been impossible for 250 men to commit mass atrocities without somebody talking about it out of aversion.

Plan sometimes fought very well, especially when they were surprised or cornered.

To retain a true perspective of what was generally happening in South West at the time, one should bear in mind that while operations continued on a daily basis, other meaningful military developments were taking place at the same time.

The SWA Territory Force and the fittest brass band in the world

With my appointment in 1977, one of my assignments was to establish a defence force for South West. It would be known as the SWA Territory Force (SWATF). It was a challenge, and I met with a fair amount of opposition. Some people held the opinion that a local defence force was not desirable, and many others thought it would not work.

The project stirred the emotion-laden political pot. In South Africa many people regarded the insurgency conflict in South West to be a purely South West concern. They demanded that the South Westers make a maximum contribution to the war.

Some argued that members of the SA Defence Force put their lives at stake for the benefit of all population groups in South West and insisted that they, black, white, brown and yellow, also fulfil their obligations. In South West, some regarded the conflict as black versus black.

Many people warned me that it would cause a white revolt if we armed citizens from all population groups. We did, but the revolt never materialized. It may sound ridiculous now, but in those days it was a serious emotional matter.

During the annual Windhoek argicultural show of 1977 Bushman and brown soldiers were scheduled to perform in the arena. I was pertinently warned that if these soldiers walked around Windhoek after hours carrying their rifles, there would be major problems. But we persisted, and in the end everything went without a hitch.

During that show we experienced real life *The Gods Must be Crazy* incidents.

Naturally, it was an exceptional experience for a Bushman to sit in the Kalahari Sands restaurant and be served by whites and Wambos.

While watching them rehearse for their arena drill display I noticed that they did not execute proper 90-degree turns when doing the normal right and left turns, as they were accustomed to do. Instead they veered at such an angle that when they continued marching, their course took them diagonally aross the stadium. I was intrigued and discussed the matter with their commanding officer, Cmdt Delville Linford. In the end the most acceptable explanation I could get was that it was now the first time in their lives they could not see the natural 360-degree horizon. This disturbed their natural sense of direction. Just like city people sometimes become 'bush crazy' and get lost in the bundu, they became slightly 'town crazy'.

I tackled the establishment of the SWATF scientifically. Although I tried to steer a neutral course, the politics of the day did not make it an easy task. We based much of our planning on the principle of decentralization. We took military training to the man instead of the man to the training. We established a number of units at various places right across the territory instead of at only one central training centre. This was particularly valid for those types of units and troops for which there was a big demand – infantry. The exact locations largely depended on where we could find the most suitable and cheapest terrain and facilities.

A principle of this kind of war was to make maximum use of the local population's knowledge of the environment, languages and customs. We needed them mostly in the border areas. That was why we established units in Kaokoland, Ovamboland, the Kavango and in the western and eastern Caprivi.

On the other hand, in the case of those kinds of soldiers for which there was not a big demand, we centralized. An example was the SWATF band. There was only one and it was stationed in Windhoek.

The members of the band were recruited from all regions. Also from the bush. They were more representative of all the population groups of South West than most other organizations that I knew of. They had one common qualification – not one of them had ever produced a single note on an instrument! And even if one of them had perhaps trilled a jew's-harp before, certainly no one had ever read a single note of sheet-music. They performed in public for the first time approximately six weeks after the formation of the band.

A physical training corporal was responsible for their general military training. I think his name was George Moorcroft, and he did it well. The result was that members of the band eventually won cross-country races all over South West. They were probably the fittest brass band in the world!

The SWATF finally received formal status on 1 August 1980. This meant that there was now, to a large extent, separate structures for the SWATF and the SA Forces in South West. Technically speaking I was now wearing two hats: one as General Officer Commanding (GOC) the SWATF and the other as GOC SA Army Forces in SWA. We also placed the SWATF on a separate account for the purposes of stores and financial accounting. However, we continued to fight as an integrated force. In other words, we used SWATF and South African troops in the same combat formations for operations.

In the political environment of the time, some people accused us of applying a policy of segregation while others maintained that we were integrating. Those days these two concepts were always used when analysing events. And we had to face the criticism.

We explained it as follows: forming a unit such as 101 Battalion in Ovamboland, one naturally recruited troops from that area. That is why ninety-nine per cent of the members of the battalion would be Wambos. The same goes for the Kavango, the eastern Caprivi and other places. The composition of a battalion reflected the composition of the population of that area. If someone chose to regard this as forced segregation of ethnic units, then that was his opinion. From our point of view it was the natural outcome of military planning and decentralization.

The critics who welcomed the integration, as they saw it, however, claimed that it was only a smoke-screen and that the black members of SWATF would not become senior non-commissioned officers and officers. These accusations mainly came from foreign visitors. In due course they were proved wrong.

I remember at least one commandant, one major and many junior officers, warrant-officers and non-commissioned officers before independence who were not members of the white population group.

There were also many white South Westers in the SWATF who stayed on in Namibia after independence and were enlisted into the new Namibian defence force.

In retrospect it appears that the formation of the SWATF was not only a wise move, but essential, and that it worked. After independence, during 1990, various South Westers of different population groups told me that it was the best thing we ever could have done. They said there were many troops, non-commissioned officers, warrant officers and officers who could be integrated with Plan.

Many people were comforted by the fact that the new Namibian defence force would consist of both organizations so that the Namibian defence force would not consist of Plan members alone. Plan consisted mainly of Wambos and they had only one political loyalty.

I am convinced that the creation and development of the SWATF before independence was a success story. It may still play an important role in promoting future stability in the country. The SWATF came a long way and was well managed by all who were involved with me and those who came after us.

The territorial force had to be productive. The troops who served in Ovambo during the early years in 1977 and 1978 were mainly Ovambo soldiers and soldiers from South West and South Africa. I regarded it as unproductive to have units such as the company at Otjisondo in Hereroland who did not serve in Ovamboland. My idea to deploy them there was met with a storm of criticism. Knowledgeable and well-meaning advisers were deeply concerned that it would lead to friction between the Ovambo citizens and Herero soldiers.

I decided nevertheless to proceed with the project in a well-organized way. We experienced very few problems. The military culture is one of a kind. It creates bonds across ethnic boundaries. The discipline of the military culture prevents friction that would otherwise arise. I was quite proud of the fact that we succeeded in doing something that even people who could speak with authority thought was not possible. One cannot always blindly accept experts' advice. If the intention, planning and leadership is good, one can make things work. Where there's a will there's a way.

Perhaps it also paved the way for the later deployment of external troops in Ovambo. Some time afterwards it was no longer strange to see troops of different cultures, for example Kavango and Bushman soldiers, in Ovambo.

I am not trying to pretend that we never had problems. Everyone was careful not to say or do something that might cause friction between members of the different population groups. But spontaneity was not to be suppressed and blunders were made.

I can remember one such incident. There was discord in the ranks of Capt Fourie's Herero Company at Otjisondo. It was claimed that white corporals caused dissatisfaction allegedly by addressing Herero recruits in an improper manner. Mr Clemens Kapuuo and I flew to Otjisondo to try to sort out the difficulties. We sat at a table in the front of a hall in which the corporals and troops were gathered. We listened patiently and objectively to the stories of the complainants. We also listened to the corporals' version.

When one of the corporals put his case he, and I accepted it to be a blunder, used these words: 'And then the troop got white.' I'm not sure that everyone grasped the idiomatic pun during those few seconds, as it did not provoke any reaction.

Mr Kapuuo adopted a calm and fatherlike attitude and delivered a sort of closing address. He gave some credit to the corporals but also cautioned them; he gave the troops some credit, but also reprimanded them. He gave some advice and concluded with these words: 'But now you must remember, this man sitting next to me, Capt Fourie, he is the "boss of the farm" – "die baas van die plaas".' These words did not arouse any reaction either.

At a later stage, I heard these troops sing a song, dedicated to 'Mutango (leader) Fourie.'

As some of the Herero troops became corporals, the problems disappeared. The troops received the same treatment from the new corporals, but they no longer grumbled. The same happened at other units.

The SWATF had a lion's share in operations. In 1982, sixty per cent of the manpower in the operational area was already being supplied by the SWATF. In the following years the sixty per cent increased to seventy per cent.[3] During the crossborder operation in August 1981, Protea, approximately forty-one per cent of the soldiers were members of SWATF.[4] Of the South West troops involved more than ninety per cent were yellow, brown and black. With its total manpower of approximately 30 000 men in 1989 (including a small percentage of RSA elements) the SWATF was already stronger than the defence forces of about forty African states.

Ovambo's 101 Battalion earned the honour that was bestowed on them. But I am not taking sides because when I went to the Kavango they would tell me that their battalion, 202, was the best. And in the Caprivi they would naturally tell me that theirs, 701, was the best.

This brings me to the SWA Specialist Unit (Swaspes).

Swaspes was established at Oshivelo and later moved to Otavi. It included a fair number of South Africans. Although they sometimes participated in fighting, they were really a reconnaissance unit. Certain elements of the unit had to locate the enemy and bring other offensive forces into a position to engage them. They were all reconnaissance troops – trackers and scouts. Some were specialist trackers who worked on foot. Others performed their reconnaissance duties on horseback or on motorbikes. Some were dogs with specialist handlers. The troops carried weapons only for their own protection.

Then one day the Chief of the Army, Gen Viljoen, said to me: 'Disband Swaspes! They are not cost-effective.'

I knew Gen Viljoen well. This was his way of finding out whether they were indeed cost-effective. I did not agree with him right away. But if this was indeed the case, then he was right and the unit had to be demobilised. I ordered an investigation, but also went to take a look myself in order to personally establish the facts.

I was aware of certain popular perceptions, some of which supported Gen Viljoen's point of view. I went to Oshivelo and sat down under a tree to talk to the commander, the horsemen, motorcyclists, trackers and the dog handlers, one after the other, individually or in groups.

One allegation was that the dogs could not actually do the work they were supposed to do. I received explanations to these perceptions. Earlier on some of the lower level commanders were somewhat ignorant of the way dogs should be employed. By way of illustration, a dog would be following a trail, and then one of the junior leaders or even the commander would say: 'This dog is not worth a thing, the spoor is there on the other side, and he is working right here, look!' It may sound ridiculous, but initially some chaps did not realize that a dog does not visually follow a track, he follows the scent, which the wind might have moved away from the spoor.

Also, through lack of knowledge and experience, some people expected too much of the dogs. A dog is like a piece of military equipment in the sense that you have to use it with full regard to its capabilities and limitations. A dog cannot work in the hot sun for hours on end. One should use it when, where and for the time that it can work. One does not start shooting on the way to the battlefield. One takes one's weapons to the point where the enemy is and then starts fighting. The same applies to a dog.

This reminds me of a story: During the early 1970s so-called profiles of the different musterings had to be determined so that the allocation of the most suitable national servicemen to the various musterings could be done by computer. A tank driver, for example, had to be under a certain height and must possess a certain degree of co-ordination. Then per chance someone asked what the profile of a dog handler should be. The answer was: The first requirement is that the handler should be more intelligent than the dog ...!

The men told me how many of their reconnaissance operations were successful, in other words, how many of their operations had led to contact with the enemy. I calculated that it was somewhere between sixty and seventy-five per cent. This was a good percentage, because making contact with the enemy was one of our biggest problems. We specifically wanted to seize the initiative by forcing contact with the enemy.

I also briefly visited the sector and subsector commanders. They confirmed the claims of the troops. In most cases it was difficult for them to tell how many of the contacts had been the direct result of reconnaissance by Swaspes elements.

The reason was that the formats for standard operational reports did not necessarily require the information as to how the initial contacts were made. Everyone was more concerned with the battle itself. One commander in Ovamboland, however, estimated Swaspes's contribution in making contact with the enemy at about sixty per cent.

The motorcyclists and mounted elements were very successful in cost-effectively patrolling the so-called cut line border road. Light vehicles and even light aircraft were also used to patrol the road for signs of crossings. But if they detected infiltration, they did not have the same means to follow up as the trackers, horsemen and motorcyclists.

Swaspes was not disbanded.

8

KATIMO MULILO AND NGANA
Days of sorrow and days of joy

Katima Mulilo, 23 August 1978. At twenty minutes past one in the morning a sudden bombardment rocked the town. Plan had launched about thirty 122 mm rockets from accross the border. A little later Zambian 82 and 60 mm mortars, firing high explosive and phosphor bombs, joined the rocket launchers, hitting the village and one of the border bases, Wenela.

It was, ironically, a poor demonstration of gunnery. The shots fell scattered over an area of several square kilometres. Only two of the rockets caused damage. One hit a school in the township of Katima Mulilo and another struck a barrack in the military base. It killed ten soldiers and wounded ten more. It was a 122 mm rocket and one of the very first shots fired.

The counterbombardment began a few minutes later after locating the positions of the launchers and mortars by means of sound and radar equipment.

It was, of course, a frightening experience for the inhabitants. Only people who have experienced a bombardment of this kind can know what it sounds like and what the psychological effects are. This one was a nightmare for the women and children of the village.

When the explosions started, Johnny Henderson of the SABC just happened to be fidgeting with his tape recorder. So he placed it on top of his bomb shelter and recorded the bombardment. I still have a copy of the original with the cry of a fish eagle and the anxious howl of a dog during the brief periods of silence. While all this was happening, Maj Dirk du Toit once again showed his mettle.

Dirk du Toit had previously been a sports officer in the Cape. When he wanted to come back to the Defence Force, I took him on a flight from, as he described it, the blade of the Kaokoland, past the muscle of Ovambo, the upper arm of the Kavango and the front arm of the western Caprivi to the fist of the eastern Caprivi. He could choose where he wanted to be posted. He decided on the eastern Caprivi. He was a bachelor full of wit and wisdom. He was the father figure for many young wives, their children and the troops who all affectionately called him 'Oom Dirk'. During the bombardment he drove through the streets with his little dog, Gamat, in his Ford 250 4x4 while shouting words of advice and encouragement to everyone through a loudhailer.

At first light the sector commander, Brig A K de Jager, launched the first combat team across the border under the command of Lt Harry Holland-Muter. With the support of armed Alouette helicopters they crossed the border into Zambia and aimed at a well-known Plan camp 30 km north of the cut-line. Another team under the command of Lt Flip Genis crossed the Zambian border shortly after seven and engaged the rear elements of the retreating attackers. Within a few hours paratroopers were also flown to Zambia.

In Windhoek I had received a radio message from Katima Mulilo a few hours before the bombardment with information about a proposed attack on the village that night. It was actually delivered to me while I was playing host to the force commander designat of Untag (United Nations Transitionary Assistance Group), Gen Hannes Philipp, at an informal farewell by the poolside of the Safari Motel. He and Mr Martii Ahtisaari, the special representative of the Secretary General of the UN, had completed a fact-finding mission and were about to leave for J G Strijdom Airport on their way to Europe and the US.

I had to think fast. Was I or was I not to inform Gen Philipp of the contents of the message? There were advantages and disadvantages. I decided to tell him, and did so. Then we left for the airport with Mr Ahtisaari, General Philipp and the rest of the delegation, to see them off.

Shortly after I arrived back home, I received the bitter news of the attack.

Early the next morning I departed for Mpacha airfield to learn exactly what had happened at Katima. I considered it my moral duty to be there when such a serious incident had occurred. I tried my best to keep Judge Steyn away from Katima until we knew exactly what the situation was. However, he insisted on going along and approximately two hours later we landed at Mpacha.

The atmosphere at Katima Mulilo was grim when we arrived there. The military personnel and their wives were calm. Yet it was a bitter experience for all of us and I had to look them in the eye, explain and answer questions.

While Brig de Jager was leading the follow-up operations, his staff officers, Maj Koos Muller and Capt Piet de Lange, briefed us in detail. Although the bombardment was scattered, one of the very first shots had hit the entrance of a bungalow. The troops were running for the bomb shelters and trenches, but the rocket exploded inside the bungalow before all of them could get out.

The follow-up operation continued for several days and nights and eventually involved additional ground troops as well as Buccaneer fighter-bombers and Canberra bombers. Katima Mulilo and its Zambian counterpart, Sesheke, again fired at one another twice with artillery and mortars. When the ground operation ended on 27 August, a confirmed minimum of 20 insurgents had been killed.

In terms of casualties inflicted and damage done, our counteraction did not really revenge our losses. However, Steenkamp wrote: 'But it accomplished a greater purpose: for practical purposes it quashed the insurgency in the Caprivi.'

This incident had a wider impact than merely bringing an end to insurgency in the Caprivi; it became apparent later that it had made a major contribution towards turning the tide of the war as a whole.

The decision to inform Gen Philipp was a good one. South Africa had encountered a lot of opposition with regard to its role in South West and one way of getting at it was to criticize the activities of the SA Defence Force in the territory. We had many critics. Many a time I felt that we could do nothing right, and Swapo nothing wrong. We were often portrayed as the bad guys and Swapo as the good guys.

The UN and its agencies were some of our main critics; and others used the UN as a platform for their criticism. We must bear in mind that the General Assembly of the UN regarded Swapo as the sole and authentic representative of the people of Namibia. The outspoken and hostile UN High Commissioner for Namibia, Sean McBride, and his Institute operated on the UN payroll. Swapo was also the UN's most important source of information about South West.

After encounters such as these, the criticism and statements were often as follows:

- It was untrue that Plan committed loathsome acts. It was propaganda. It might also have been somebody else, for example Unita.
- It was untrue that Plan operated from Angola and Zambia. It was propaganda. Plan operated from bases in South West.
- It was untrue that Angola and Zambia participated in Plan armed activities. It was propaganda. The South Africans were making these allegations merely to cook up excuses to perform hot pursuit operations in those countries.
- It was untrue that Plan attacked civilian targets. It was propaganda. They were fighting against the security forces.
- It was untrue that Swapo did not co-operate in the peace initiatives. It was propaganda. It was the security forces who caused incidents to undermine the peace processes.

It was probably once again *friction de guerre* that I just happened to be talking to Gen Philipp exactly at the moment when I received the message, and could inform him of the incident straight away, hours before it occurred. When the information became fact, he knew exactly what had happened and whodunit.

This time there was no doubt that Plan was the aggressor, that Plan had bombarded a whole village with all its civilian inhabitants, and that Plan had been operating from Angola and Zambia. Plan had spoilt the climate for negotiations at the time when Ahtisaari departed to write his report, while the security forces displayed self-restraint throughout.

For once there was no doubt about who were the good guys and who were the bad guys. They knew that it was not a security force trick. At no stage had we tried to wreck any political efforts. And neither were we doing so now. This time it was Plan, notwithstanding the peace initiatives, who was responsible for the badly timed incident.

When we informed the media, I specifically mentioned to them that we had had information about it before it happened.

A problem I had experienced in the past was that when you report to the media about something that has happened and you try to reinforce its credibility by claiming to have known that it was going to happen, but without substantiating evidence, you are not taken seriously.

I can understand it; otherwise one could report just about anything to the media and expect them to believe you. But by first confiding in

LEFT: Troops awaiting demobilisation following a campaign

BELOW: Jannie Geldenhuys takes over from Gen Constand Viljoen as Head of the South African Defence Force — 31 October 1985 (Photo: *Paratus*)

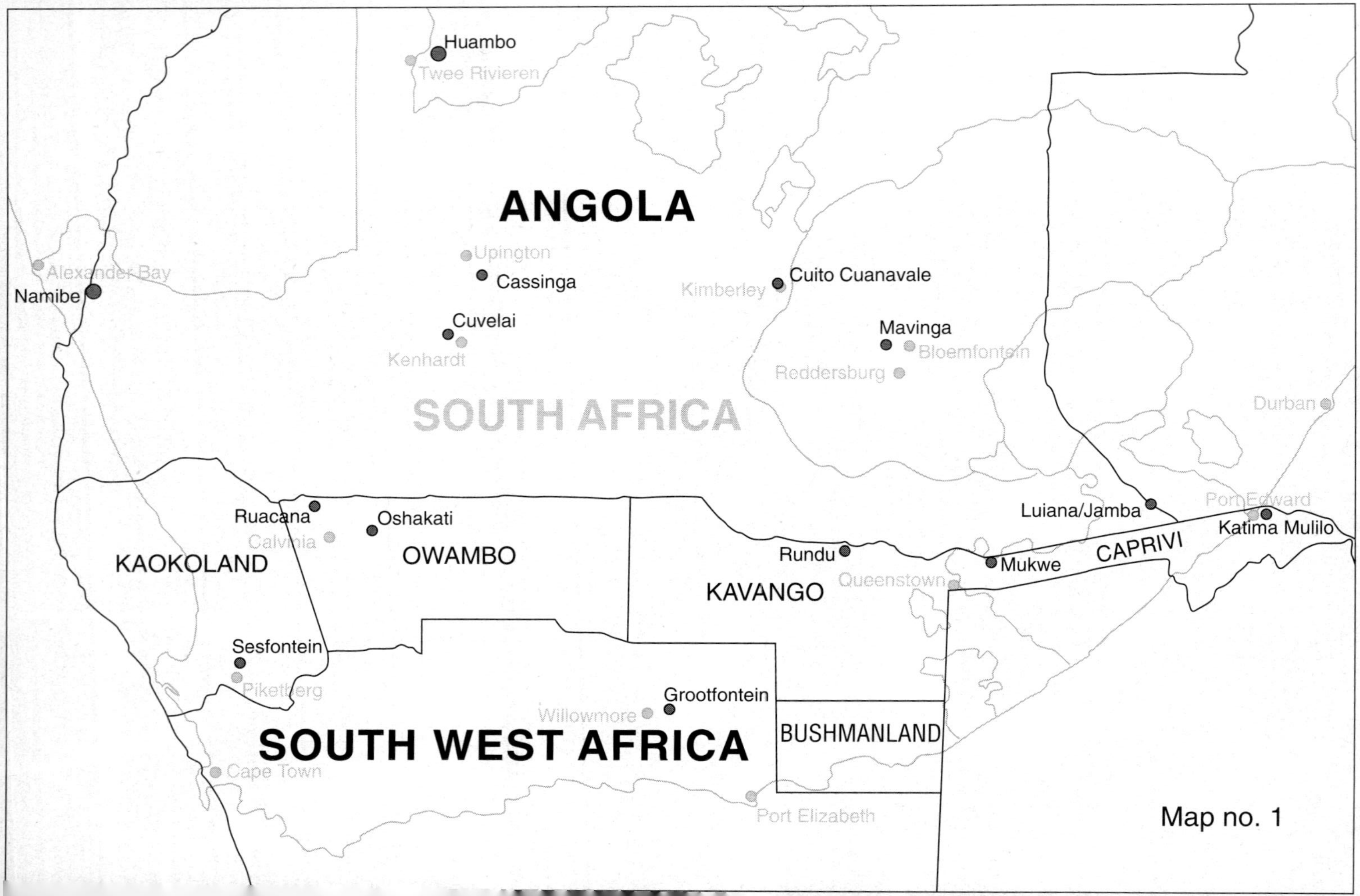
Huambo
Twee Rivieren
ANGOLA
Upington
Cassinga
Alexander Bay
Namibe
Cuito Cuanavale
Kimberley
Cuvelai
Kenhardt
Mavinga
Bloemfontein
Reddersburg
SOUTH AFRICA
Durban
Ruacana
Oshakati
Calvinia
OWAMBO
KAOKOLAND
Luiana/Jamba
Port Edward
Katima Mulilo
CAPRIVI
Rundu
Mukwe
Queenstown
KAVANGO
Sesfontein
Piketberg
Grootfontein
Willowmore
BUSHMANLAND
SOUTH WEST AFRICA
Cape Town
Port Elizabeth
Map no. 1

Map no. 2

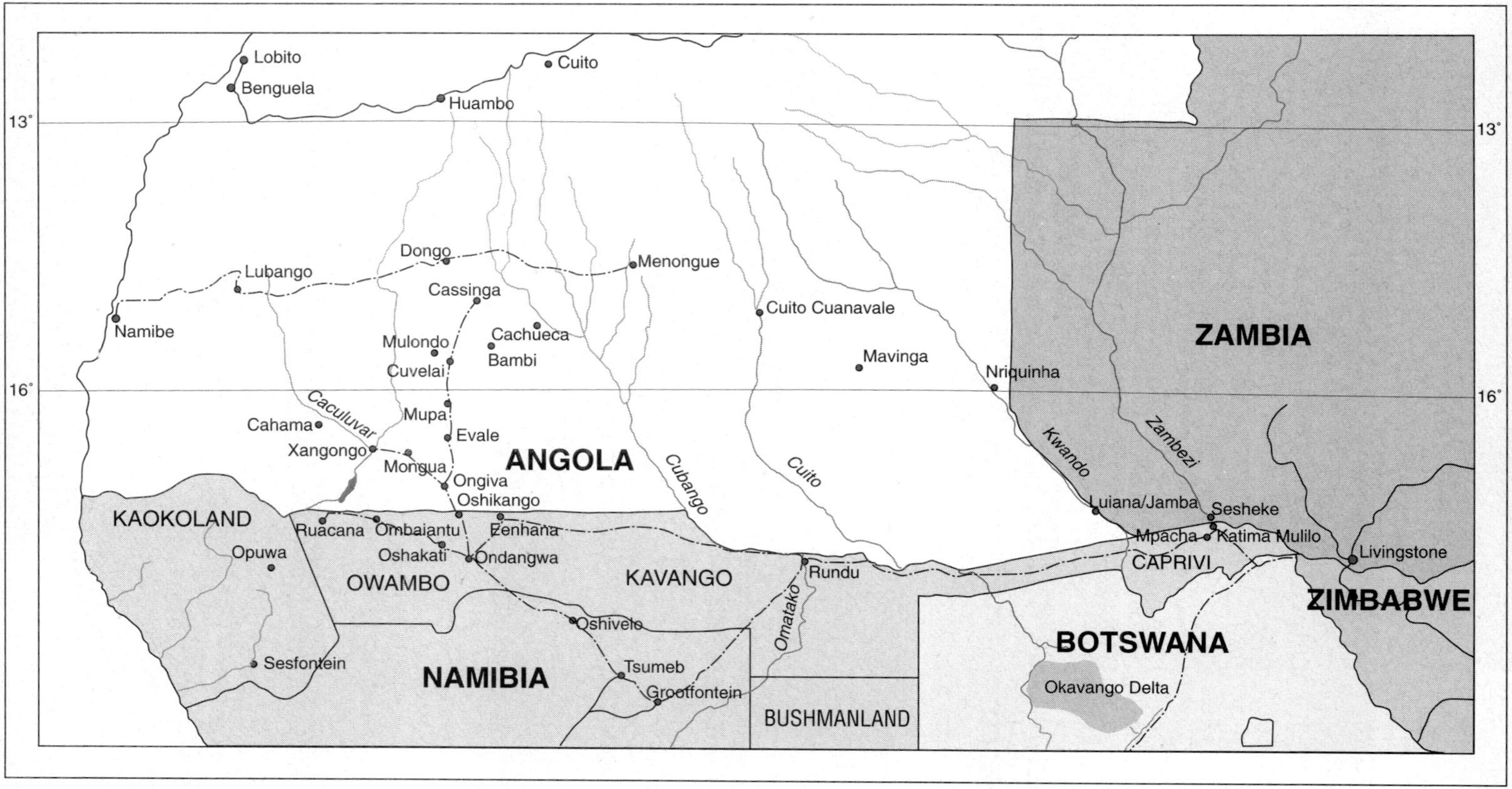
13°
16°
13°
16°
Lobito
Benguela
Cuito
Huambo
Dongo
Lubango
Menongue
Cassinga
Namibe
Cuito Cuanavale
Mulondo
Cachueca
Bambi
Cuvelai
Mavinga
Nriquinha
ZAMBIA
Caculuvar
Mupa
Cahama
Evale
Xangongo
Mongua
ANGOLA
Ongiva
Oshikango
Cubango
Cuito
Kwando
Zambezi
Luiana/Jamba
Sesheke
KAOKOLAND
Ruacana
Ombaiantu
Zenhana
Oshakati
Ondangwa
Opuwa
Mpacha
Katima Mulilo
Livingstone
Rundu
CAPRIVI
OWAMBO
KAVANGO
ZIMBABWE
Omatako
Oshivelo
BOTSWANA
Sesfontein
NAMIBIA
Tsumeb
Grootfontein
Okavango Delta
BUSHMANLAND

RIGHT: Ben and Anna Geldenhuys, Jannie (Kleinboet) and Johan (Ouboet)

BELOW: Davulsrus nestling beneath ochre and crimson cliffs

RIGHT: First rugby team, Voortrekker High School, Bethlehem (1952), with three future Springboks, who attended the school at the same time as Jannie — *from top to bottom:* Hannes Botha, Tom van Vollenhoven and Bennie van Niekerk. "Style is wonderful, but winning is better."

BELOW: Staff Sergeant, Frederick George Crumpton (*left*), and Jannie Geldenhuys

BELOW RIGHT: Brig "O bleddie Ben" De Wet Roos (*left*) and Jannie Geldenhuys (1975–1976)

ABOVE: Administrator General M T Steyn says Goodbye — "Great people are also affected by *Friction de guerre*" (Photo: *Stefan Sonderling*)

RIGHT: The "Winds of Change" visit, 1960. Mr Harold Macmillan, escorted by Capt Jannie Geldenhuys *(front)*, Gen Nic Bierman *(behind left)* and Min Eric Louw *(behind centre)*

LEFT: Mr P W Botha with Gens Ian Gleeson, Magnus Malan, Jannie Geldenhuys and Constand Viljoen (1977–1978)

RIGHT: The SWA Territorial Forces on parade

BELOW: Ministerial visit, Windhoek, 1977–1978. *Left to right back*: Adm Ronnie Edwards, Gen Jannie Geldenhuys, Gen Magnus Malan, Min Pik Botha. *Front*: Judge M T Steyn, Mr John Viall. "Resolution 435 or 345?" (Photo: *André le Roux*)

ABOVE: Key officers: Operation Sceptic. *Left to right, back*: Johan Saaiman, Johan Sonnekus, Ken Snowball, Deon Ferreira, André Kotze, Jorrie Jordaan, Des Radmore, Anton van Graan *Front*: Dippies Dippenaar, Giep Booysen, Witkop Badenhorst, Jannie Geldenhuys, Theo de Munnik, Ollie Holmes, Chris Serfontein (Photo: *Paratus*)

RIGHT: Operation Sceptic: Chris Serfontein, Jannie Geldenhuys and journalist Con Crous

RIGHT: Before the start of an operation (Photo: *Johan Kuus*)

BELOW: "Bottles water four, braces left and right – none!"

BELOW RIGHT: Bush camp, Southern Cross Fund swimming pool (Photo: *Stefan Sonderling*)

ABOVE: The Southern Africa medal, made from metal melted down from a captured Russian tank (*above left*) (Photo: *Paratus*)

LEFT: Sappers: 438 000 km "swept" (Photo: *Stefan Sonderling*)

ABOVE: Gen Prem Chand, the new UNTAG commanding officer, starts his "happenstance" in Windhoek
(Photo: *Stefan Sonderling*)

RIGHT: First UNTAG commanding officer, Austrian Gen Hannes Phillipp "Are we going to drink or are we going to chat?"
(Photo: *Argus Africa News Service*)

LEFT: Lifting mines by hand — nerve-racking

BELOW: Tiffies: "Do what you can, with whatever you have, wherever you are."

a trustworthy person who could confirm it afterwards, you can prove the authenticity of your statement.

This time I could prove it. Gen Philipp would never deny that I had informed him prior to the attack. He was an honest man.

This time the media proved to me that they meant it when they say: if we are fully informed, our reports are accurate; if we are not informed, we have to speculate; and then the manner in which we speculate becomes our business.

It turned out to be one of the few occasions on which all the media agreed with our interpretation of an incident. We also received sympathy from the international political world. And at least, we did not provide those who would prefer not to agree with ammunition to have a go at us as usual.

The way that we handled that incident enabled Mr John Vorster, the prime minister, to state his position in strong language to a sympathetic international community.

Carel Birkby, *To the Point* military correspondent, wrote in the 1 September 1978 issue:

> By this time, no doubt, Lusaka had had time to note the uncompromising stance swiftly adopted by Prime Minister John Vorster, Foreign Minister Pik Botha, and SWA/Namibia Administrator-General Judge Marthinus T. Steyn, towards Swapo's murderous intransigence and Zambia's tolerance, or encouragement, of Nujoma's military bases.
>
> They found swift and unqualified backing by admiral Thomas Moorer, retired American chairman of the joint chiefs of staff committee, and until he retired in 1974 commander-in-chief of the American and Nato naval forces in the Atlantic.
>
> Moorer, who this week is visiting SWA/Namibia, said: 'When anybody attacks you like Swapo did, you are thoroughly and absolutely justified in hitting back and knocking the hell out of 'em.'

In the same issue, John Evert said:

> In terms of the political implications of its attack on Katima Mulilo, Swapo seems to have committed a bad blunder. Its image as a revolutionary force has been dented, the question mark over the willingness to take part in elections has grown, it has embarrassed

> the Zambian government. And, ironically, it has greatly increased the credibility of the South African government, as regards its commitment to the Western plan and its charge that Swapo is the main obstacle to the implementation of the plan.

Not long afterwards I was taken to task for having reported to the media that we had had advance information about the attack. It caused political and psychological embarrassment. People could argue, in the words of John Evert:

> ... why, knowing ... in advance of the impending attack, South African forces did not launch a pre-emptive strike.

It does not happen every day that the Defence Force is criticized for not launching pre-emptive crossborder operations.

It is, of course, a tough question to answer. It was a many-faceted situation, and not all the facets could be controlled. One actually had to have personally experienced the situation at Katima Mulilo and borne the responsibility before one could understand how difficult it is emotionally and intellectually to manage a situation of this nature.

We had a man who was capable of doing so: Brig A K de Jager. This kind of stand-off bombardment can be prevented only by dominating the area across the border or by pre-empting enemy action. But Evert gives the answer to this problem himself:

> South Africa's inaction is justified ... a pre-emptive strike would have resulted in South Africa being branded an aggressor. It would have given Swapo cause to withdraw from the (settlement) plan, into which it had entered with great reluctance anyway.

Over a long time, before this incident occurred, we periodically received information that an attack was possibly going to take place on a certain date. But every time the day arrived, nothing happened. However, in the meantime the men did prepare passive defensive measures. Physical protection was improved, for example bunkers and other forms of bomb shelters were built and alarm systems installed.

One cannot let people live, month after month, over a long time, as if such a bombardment could happen at any moment. We could also not let the soldiers in the town live in safer conditions than the women and children.

In areas plagued by insurgency one must always strive to let daily life continue as normally as possible. Bomb shelters had already been erected at the schools and homes, and if we had forcefully reacted every time we received a bit of alarming information we would have given the impression that we were panicking. The wives and children of some of the officials could possibly have decided to go back to South Africa, which may have resulted in the collapse of the Caprivi administration.

In the meantime, the process of implementing Resolution 435 and the negotiated settlement plan had indeed reached an impasse. It was consequently decided to call free and fair elections in South West for December 1978 in order to establish a multiracial constituent assembly.

Swapo decided not to participate and publicly announced that it was going to launch a plan to wreck the elections. In view of the current wide-spread violence, this threat placed an even heavier burden on the security forces. Many people believed that we would not be able to guarantee the degree of security required for an election in the remote areas of the territory. The fact that Plan's operations to interfere with the elections were successfully foiled was an exceptional achievement and a feather in the cap of the security forces.

Security-related incidents, however, dragged on. On 13 February 1979, 250 insurgents attacked our Nkongo base 15 km south of the border in Ovambo. It was a farce. On 26 February the Elundu base was the target of another bombardment, but all the shots went astray. Swapo declared in London that over a period of three months they had killed more than 300 South African soldiers, destroyed two military bases, shot down two reconnaissance aircraft, damaged forty military vehicles and seized large quantities of weapons and ammunition.

If a quarter of these allegations were true, it would have been regarded as a national disaster in South Africa. However, even the little bit which was true inspired one to react – and the opportunity was now there.

The stand-off bombardment of Katima Mulilo activated the political green light to cross the border. We used the opportunity systematically.

We continued to give intelligence matters much of our attention. Since our withdrawal from Angola in 1976 up to the time of Operation

Reindeer in 1978 we had good intelligence, but only about specific potential targets, such as certain Plan bases and headquarters. Such intelligence, in fact, enabled us to execute Operation Reindeer. On the other hand, our general combat intelligence of Plan's activities, smaller bases, transit bases and infiltration routes, was inadequate. To make things even more difficult, Reindeer's attacks on Moscow and Vietnam stirred up a hornet's nest. After the fluttering and scattering, the cadres made many adjustments to their system of bases and changed their patterns. This totally disturbed the intelligence picture we had had up to that time.

But Johann Saaiman and his people worked hard. Even though certain limitations on our actions remained, we could greatly improve our intelligence by means of crossborder operations. We therefore launched Operation Rekstok and Safraan.

Both these operations kicked off on 7 March 1979. They were really only one operation conducted over an extended area. That part of it which took place in Angola was called Operation Rekstok and that in Zambia, Safraan.

I would like to share this story from those days. It concerns Cmdt Piet Hall. He was the commander of the Bushman battalion, which had their home-base at Omega in the western Caprivi. But they participated in operations everywhere, including Zambia, north of the Caprivi.

Towards the end of 1978 I arrived at Katima Mulilo. This was shortly after lucky-draw type Defence Bonus Bonds had come into circulation.

At that time one of the Bushman companies was somewhere out in the bundu in Zambia, and Piet Hall was also acting as company commander. On this particular day he was expecting to be picked up the next day by helicopter so that he could return to Omega before going on leave with his family.

However, there was a delay. The new company commander who was scheduled to replace him had not yet arrived. But Piet did not know this. I told A K de Jager that Piet would have to stay there until he was properly relieved. I could just imagine how he would feel when he received A K's signal.

The next morning A K de Jager showed me Piet's daily cryptic Situation Report on the previous 24 hours. It read:

A. Unchanged

B. NTR
C. Unchanged
D. THERE'S A BONUS IN YOUR FUTURE.

Under pressure and in difficult circumstances, Piet had retained his sense of humour.

Plan bases were simultaneously attacked in Angola during Rekstok and in Zambia during Safraan. During an air attack in Angola a Canberra light bomber crashed, presumably after it had been hit by ground fire, killing the crew.

Neither of the operations achieved much material success mainly because the cadres had evacuated their bases before they were attacked, some long before the time, others in the nick of time. One reason for our attacking empty bases was, as I have mentioned, that our intelligence had lost track of some of Swapo's bases that had been moved after Reindeer.

The commanders and operations staff officers made full use of the opportunity to take a dig at the intelligence staff officers.

The Dave Roux incident accurately reflects the climate and spirit that existed among them. Col J H Vorster recalls:

> Mid-1979, during Brig Kat Liebenberg's team of duty as commander of Sector 10, an important crossborder operation was launched from Ovambo against Plan targets in the south of Angola.
>
> After a few days it became clear that the operation seemed not to be very successful because it appeared as if all the Plan bases had been evacuated by the time they were assaulted. It almost seemed as if Plan had received early warning of the operation.
>
> Because of this perception, Brig Liebenberg temporarily suspended the operation and summoned the commanders to Sector 10 Headquarters.
>
> At 11:00 the atmosphere in the conference hall was tense. Because of the failures everyone expected some straight talking from the boss. All became quiet when Brig Liebenberg got to his feet, briefly welcomed his commanders and staff officers, and then instructed his intelligence officer, Cmdt Dave Roux, to 'tell us where Swapo is'.
>
> Dave Roux positioned himself next to the map with facial expression and body language saying; 'Yes, yes, always blame intelligence when things go wrong.'

> 'Good morning gentlemen,' he began. Using a pointer he indicated an area in western Ovambo on the map: 'Swapo was here at Ongulumbashe during 1966 and when Gen Dillon of the South African Police attacked them on 26 August 1966, they scattered. From that day they started to spread throughout the whole area ... and to this day nobody knows where they are.'
>
> There was dead silence. Everyone anxiously awaited Brig Liebenberg's reaction.
>
> After a long silence the Brigadier broke the silence: 'Open the bar!'
>
> The tension disappeared like mist before the sun and after a beer or two the commanders returned to their units to continue the operation. The next day the first reports of successes started to come in and in the end the South African Defence Force had concluded another effective crossborder operation in Angola.[1]

Everyone was disappointed. Even today I often hear colleagues, officers and non-commissioned officers who participated in these operations describing them as failures. I can understand why they think that way. But this is the perception at the lower level, and of the commanders and fighters who tackle operations with enthusiasm and professionalism and who like to show results. And so it should be.

However, from my point of view these operations, and the incident of 23 August 1978, were two of the most important turning points in the war. The long-term statistics also showed afterwards that as from July 1979 we started to gain on the insurgents while their position worsened. We began to take the initiative.

Priorities are laid down for every operation. Should one shoot insurgents or capture them? Is this the important thing? Should you destroy enemy equipment, or seize it? Should you rather destroy the enemy's military structures? What are your priorities on the ground while you are there? There is seldom time for everything.

I laid down the priorities for Rekstok and Safraan myself. Priority number one was to gather operational information and everything else associated with combat intelligence.

One usually collects information in order to plan operations, but sometimes you have to execute operations in order to gather information. Information obtained from these operations enabled us to clear up the enemy picture and to devise new plans for collecting intelligence. We began to ignore supposed enemy positions which we had been researching for a long time, while we started to focus our intelligence gathering efforts on places which had never before drawn our attention. If these operations had not taken place, we would have remained ignorant for a long time. But with our new intelligence we could operate much more effectively.

The statistics that I have mentioned, were also released to the media from time to time. During the official opening of the third session of the first Volksraad (Legislative Council) of Rehoboth, I said that Plan had lost approximately 13 men per month before April 1979; afterwards the figure increased to almost 90 per month; this average was sustained for a number of years. Plan lost 156 during November 1979 and 134 during February 1980.

The number of combat contacts with insurgents increased by one hundred per cent from 1978 to 1979. Of these, eighty-five per cent were initiated and forced by the security forces. The security forces suffered three casualties to every hundred insurgents.

However, I am not trying to dress up disappointments as successes by performing tricks with figures. Although I was mentally satisfied with Rekstok and Safraan, I too had hoped for better concrete results. But there was another good reason why I was quietly content with the outcome. It revolved around the concept of initiative.

I had propagated earlier that commanders and staffs should brainstorm collectively to find ways of seizing the initiative. The pattern used to be that the insurgent would strike somewhere, and we would react. He would then move away and strike elsewhere, and again we would react.

What we wanted was to take action that would make the insurgents react. Even if we should win a skirmish here today, and one there tomorrow and next month at another place, with every incident we would only gain the initiative locally and temporarily. This was not good enough.

We wanted plans and patterns that could be forced on our opponent and which would compel him, over a wide area, to react according to our terms. One can achieve it in conventional warfare by the concentration of forces at the right time and place, but in this kind of warfare it is impossible. It would serve no purpose to concentrate a large force on one of Plan's many small bases. However, concentration of force as a principle of war can still be applied. Instead of concentrating troops at one particular place, they could all be activated at one particular time. Our forces now took the initiative by engaging in many small battles at the same time with the enemy; in other words, they simultaneously attacked a number of bases. This is what we did during Rekstok and Safraan.

We had the insurgents abandoning bases from the Cunene province of Angola in the west to Zambia in the east. They all had to react. Every one of them took to his heels. They scattered. With the added help of other plans, which I will mention later, we started to gain and maintain the initiative.

Just before the start of one of the operations in Zambia, I went to draw a few pieces of equipment for myself. One of the young medics there asked me: 'But aren't you a general?' And when I nodded, he said: 'Gee whiz, I didn't know you guys also go on ops!'

We have often been criticized for doing so. But then at least we know what is going on. Besides, the enthusiastic reaction of this soldier is more important than the criticism.

The flight engineer of the helicopter to which I had been allocated, watched me board the aircraft and then faced the front again to continue the take-off procedure. I found an extra headset, put it on, and listened to a conversation that went more or less like this:

'I see we have a Pongo general on board.'

'... wonder what the bugger is doing here.'

'Why doesn't he leave the fighting to the troops?'

'... probably wants to show how tough he is.' And so forth.

By the way, when we reached the objective, it turned out to be a lemon – it was empty.

Years later, in 1987, after WP Defence Force had won the Toyota Rugby Club Championships, I told this story to our team manager, Cmdt Os de Waal.

'Yes General, I know ... I was the pilot.'

Those operations caused some embarrassment to other people too. Cmdt L A Anderson relates:

> It was during operation Safraan, when our combat team of Eland armoured cars and Buffel troop carriers were hot on the heels of the fleeing cadres. We were keen to make contact. Suddenly the whole force came to a standstill at a place where we were definitely not supposed to stop.
>
> I listened but heard no shots. I heard no explosions either, only incomprehensibly foul words coming over the radio from the leading Eland.

The turrets and gunbarrels of the Elands were swung to the sides, while men jumped down from the Buffels and disappeared to either side of the road.

Fine, I said to myself, the drills are working. But there were still no shots – only the unmilitary language over the radio. Something was wrong – very wrong.

I hurried up the dirt road along the convoy of armoured vehicles. We had reached the Zambezi.

Reaching the front of the convoy, I was met by a scene that could take place only in Africa. My troop commander, a lieutenant, was standing in front of his towering Ratel with its huge 90 mm barrel practically resting on his shoulder. He was a very unhappy man.

Standing in front of him was a grey-haired Zambian dressed in khaki shirt and shorts, clutching a clip-board and pen. At his side was a small boy holding one of those old tin Flit pumps. Remember them – they were hardly larger than a bicycle pump.

'I don't care who you are,' said the dignified old man, 'this is a Ngana (sleeping sickness) pest control point and you cannot proceed until all the regulations have been complied with.'

He seemed impervious to the fact that he and the little boy had brought the combat team of the SA Defence Force to a halt.

To prevent my lieutenant from having a heart attack I indicated to him that I would continue the negotiations.

'Look here, I've got orders to take this town of Sela and the ferry crossing, and if you do not get out of the way, the armoured cars will drive over you.'

'What town, what ferry?' asked the old man.

In front of me I could see only reeds and a few huts.

'Isn't this place called Sela?'

'Yes, this is Sela,' he confirmed.

Then I realized, for the umpteenth time in my military career, that a map of Africa could well indicate a 'town', but that Africa's cartographers are the most optimistic people in the world.

'Before you go anywhere, Sir, I must insist on carrying out my duties. I shall now spray your vehicles.'

I then realized that the crews of the armoured cars were having themselves a ball watching the show. Grinning faces all over were peeping through the hatches and following our discussions with intense interest.

With the clip-board in his hand the old grey gentleman

positioned himself in front of the first armoured car and started to write down its registration number. At the same time his young assistant started to do his bit. He swiftly scrambled up the first vehicle. Reaching the top, he flashed the crew a friendly smile and pushing the spray-nozzle down the hatch, he started to jerk the handle to and fro – pumping with gusto.

With a 'Thank you, Sah' he nimbly climbed down again. The next moment the sneezing men were scrambling through the hatches and landing on the dust road shouting and screaming, eyes tear-filled and gasping for breath.

Without looking back once, the hygiene duo of the Ngana Pest Control not only forced the South African armoured combat team to a standstill, but with the power of justice and order, health regulations and bureaucracy, left every tough and trained armour troop in the convoy standing in the dirt road, coughing and sneezing and wiping tears from their eyes.

The old man had done with the last Buffel and walked back to the front slowly with his little assistant.

He stopped and fixed a questioning gaze on me:

'What nationality are you, please?'

When, open-mouthed and more dumbfounded than security conscious, I failed to respond, he formally announced: 'In any case, you are now free of Ngana and may proceed, but ...' addressing me and the lieutenant, 'won't you join me for a cup of tea?'[2]

And he meant it!

On this English note of high tea in Africa I must mention an international political event which would later have a great influence on southern Africa. On 4 May 1979 Margaret Thatcher became the British Prime Minister.

In the meantime we had worked hard at one of our most important operational objectives, which was to clean up all areas that had been infiltrated by insurgents, until only Ovamboland remained.

We gradually managed to do so. In fact, the cleaning-up process had already begun before 23 August 1978, even if it was not then being done specifically as part of a bigger plan.

At that stage small-scale clandestine operations were conducted against Plan hide-outs inside Zambia, east of the Zambezi. They were done very quietly, but ironically demonstrated for the first time the effect of crossborder operations. The resultant complaints of the population in that area became an embarrassment to Kuanda to such an extent that he forbade Plan from operating from Zambia except from the area west of the Zambezi. This was in itself a breakthrough, but infiltration from the area west of the river was still increasing.

Then the incident of 23 August 1978 occurred. This showed Kaunda in a bad light and put him under great pressure. The overt operations following the incident, in addition to Operation Safraan, increased the embarrassment and the pressure and resulted in his forbidding Plan from operating against the eastern Caprivi from anywhere in Zambia. This was the great breakthrough. It was the end of insurgency in the eastern Caprivi.

This incident was the turning point for the realization of our plan. North of the Kavango and the western Caprivi, in the Cuando-Cubango Province of Angola, Savimbi survived, got back on his feet, was able to build up his forces and began to control the area. Unita and Swapo were now arch enemies. All this resulted in the termination of infiltration from Angola to the Kavango and the western Caprivi.

At a later stage three groups infiltrated into the Kavango, mainly via Ovambo, and stayed there for some time. They were located and dealt with.

There was only sporadic infiltration from Angola into Kaokoland. All these efforts were either rejected, subdued, or resisted and the perpetrators killed. Thus we managed in a relatively short space of time to attain our objective of restricting insurgency to Ovamboland. It all started in the eastern Caprivi on 23 August 1978.

The Caprivians were not lost. The tide had turned and developed its own momentum. Canu (Caprivian African National Union), which used to be an integrated part of the Swapo organization, broke away, abandoned the insurgency struggle, returned to the eastern Caprivi and started to practise normal politics. Their leader, Mishake Muyongo, who was a vice-president of Swapo, became the president of the DTA.

While all this was happening we continued to search for new ideas of how to force Plan to react to our initiatives and to keep them reacting.

We stimulated commanders on all levels to think creatively and innovatively. But innovation must be properly managed. The operational plans resulting from this scheme we called 'fox operations'. To obtain total initiative one had to out-fox your opponents all over and everywhere at the same time. For this reason, innovation had to make its impact over a wide area simultaneously. Every quarter we presented a trophy to initiators and leaders of successful fox operations reflecting wit and fighting spirit in combat.

Before we launched this programme, some of the commanders had already been practising 'fox operations' as a natural consequence of their own ingenuity and enterprise. The first recipients of the trophy were Cmdt Deon Ferreira, then commander of 32 Battalion, and Maj Mossie Basson of the Air Force.

They had established a tactical headquarters at Eenhana from where they conducted operations in Angola in the border area just north of their position.

Troops were placed at a selected place north of the border where they stacked waste oil rags and old tyres. Smoke grenades were attached to an Alouette III helicopter, which would then fly high above the selected area. After a while the helicopter would dive towards the ground while the grenade released smoke. As soon as the helicopter reached the pile, it would return to base on the deck, out of sight of the enemy.

In the meantime the troops would set the pile alight, sending a column of smoke into the sky. The cadres would then go to investigate the helicopter 'crash' and clash with the troops on terrain which they had selected and prepared.

We analysed the technique. The first requirement was to create a visible presence. Secondly one had to create an incident that would force the cadres to investigate; and finally one had to be in a dominant position to start the fire-fight. We encouraged the application of this technique throughout the whole operational area.

It worked. In Zambia Cmdt A K de Jager and his air force counterpart, Maj Vink Hattingh, used two Impala aircraft instead of Alouettes, because one can spot them from much further away, and performed the same sequence. One of the Imps would simulate a crash by diving down to the ground and flying back home at tree-top level. The other Imp would circle over the area of the 'accident' a few times and then fly back home. It sometimes took the cadres a bit longer to reach the spot, but the result was always the same.

The number of South African aircraft Zambia and Swapo reported to have shot down totalled more than the whole SA Air Force aircraft inventory.

However, fox operations also produced results of dubious merit. To create the impression of our presence, and to cause incidents which would demand investigation by the enemy, we decided to use the orchard cannons used in the Boland to scare off birds from orchards or vineyards. They are set to go off at regular intervals.

They were ordered and a while later I enquired whether HQ Sector 10 (Oshakati-Ovamboland) had received the cannons. They had not. The Air Force would not transport the carbide with which they function because it was a safety risk. I therefore had them sent by train. But when I enquired a second time, Sector 10 had still not begun their orchard cannon operations.

I established that the cannons and carbide had indeed arrived at Oshakati. Cmdt Chris Serfontein had himself received the cargo, but he was not fully in the picture. So, after a quick glance at the labels he ordered: 'Give these anti-monster and pestillence devices to the hygiene section!'

Later they set up the cannons along the water pipeline which ends at Eenhana base. The insurgents regularly sabotaged the pipeline so that for long periods not a drop of water reached the base. But the periodic bangs of the cannons, instead of drawing them to investigate, deterred the insurgents to such an extent that the troops could now again for many months swim in their Southern Cross Fund pool.

As all these operations occurred over the whole of the operational area at the same time, I believe that they made some contribution towards giving us the initiative.

I cannot conclude the Caprivi story without coming back to Gen Hannes Philipp. He is a man of indisputable integrity, a dedicated professional soldier of the greatest stature. But he is also a man with a sense of humour.

He had a vast repertoire of anecdotes, which he told in a unique way in his delightful Austrian accent. He told many stories about the eastern European and Scandinavian countries, such as this one:

> Two elderly Finns are sitting drinking at an inn. One of them fills his mate's glass and his own from a bottle of aquavit. He lifts his glass and says, 'Skol'. And they drink in silence. After a while he reaches for the bottle again and refills their glasses. He lifts his and says, 'Skol'. And they drink. Silence.
>
> After yet another while he fills the glasses again. He lifts his glass, looks at his mate and says, 'Skol'.
>
> All of a sudden his friend slams his glass on the table and says:

'Let's get this straight now, do we drink or do we talk?'

I had the impression that Hannes Philipp often found the going tough. He stuck to the codes, the principles and the rules, even when his popularity was at stake. As the force commander designate of Untag, he was probably thought to be too neutral, too objective and too impartial.

One should not forget that to have been regarded as a decent human being in the international community during the late 1970s, you had to condemn South Africa and praise its opponents. If you did so, you were normal, but if you did not, you were partial to the wrong side.

This brings me to the eve of the most dramatic operation since Operation Savannah five years earlier – Smokeshell.

9

SMOKESHELL
Tiffies and pigeons

Operation Smokeshell took place in June 1980. During the period leading up to the operation some events attracted attention. On 11 September 1979 I told correspondents that although the war was far from over, in my opinion the tide of the security situation in South West had turned; but the statistics of the following six months did not really seem to support my statement.

Also on 11 September 1979 the Angolan President, Agostinho Neto, visited Moscow and died there, apparently under questionable circumstances.

On 1 October 1979 a new round of negotiations began when a revised Independence Plan for South West, formulated by the Western countries, was submitted to Riaan Eksteen, the South African ambassador at the UN. It contained the concept of the so-called DMZ, demilitarized zone, along the border.

While politics seesawed, security-related incidents continued to occur. The frequency of Plan's personnel losses maintained its upward tendency. Of the 6 000–8 000 insurgents in Angola and the 1 000–2 000 in Zambia, 500 had died between May and 18 October 1979.

The permanent representative of Swapo at the UN, Theo-Ben Gurirab, rejected these figures and declared that Swapo was busy restructuring its forces to intensify the armed struggle.

The intensification did not materialize, but one skirmish after another occurred. The insurgents continued to escape across the border to Angola. The pattern did not change.

1980 (Maps no 1 and 2). The new year began with a revival of Plan activities which were clearly meant to coincide with a visit of the new Untag commander designate, Gen Prem Chand, to Lusaka. He was there to discuss the proposed DMZ.

During February 1980 a Plan group ventured into South West far south of the normal operational area, infiltrating the Tsumeb-Grootfontein-Otavi triangle and killing two white civilians. The security forces tracked them down and killed nineteen, losing two men, one of whom was a Bushman tracker.

The pursuit continued and by the last week of March one more soldier had been killed, and eleven insurgents, three of which by the local inhabitants. Two of them were shot by the fifteen-year-old daughter of one of their victims. The group then changed course in the direction of Ovamboland.

After the incursion a quiet period followed until May. The border war then intensified dramatically. During one contact the security forces lost five men and Plan 81. The Ondangwa airforce base was the target of a brief mortar attack that caused little damage.[1]

This brings me to Operation Sceptic, better known as Smokeshell.

> Operation Sceptic began with a blitz attack on a Plan base in southern Angola, but developed into an extended operation as more and more Plan caches were discovered in the area. Operation Sceptic brought about the first serious clashes with the Angolan forces, Fapla. Also for the first time contact was made with mechanized elements of Plan. Plan lost its forward base facilities and 380 insurgents died. The security forces seized several hundred tonnes of equipment and supplies, as well as many vehicles. Seventeen members of the South African strike force fell in battle.[2]

It was the biggest South African mechanized infantry operation since World War II. The aim was to destroy Plan's command and control centre at Chifufua, 180 km north of the border (260 km by road).

Brig Witkop Badenhorst, the commander of Sector 10 (Kaokoland and Ovamboland), was in command of the operation. Cmdt Anton van Graan first secured an area across the border. Then, on 9 June, the task force consisting of three mechanized battle groups crossed the border. Cmdt Chris Serfontein was in command of battle group 10, Cmdt J M (Dippies) Dippenaar in command of battle group 61 and Cmdt Jorrie Jordaan commanded battle group 53.

At 14:30 on 10 June 1980, after an air strike and preliminary artillery bombardment, the assault force, Chris Serfontein and Dippies, struck the enemy base area of Chifufua, codenamed Smokeshell.

Sceptic was supposed to end on 16 June but as a result of information found at the scene, it was extended to bases west of Smokeshell and thus ended only on 30 June.

I was at the tactical headquarters on D-day, 10 June. Witkop Badenhorst gave me a radio receiver so that I could follow the progress of the battle from H-hour onwards. It was here that I experienced some of the most anxious moments of my life: all because of Gen Viljoen. I heard his radio going off the air and from the rest of the signals traffic on the net I gathered that something had happened to his Ratel. The seconds and minutes dragged by. I was told later that his Ratel had detonated a set of twin-coupled mines. The explosion tossed him right out of the hatch.

A pattern developed during Sceptic which would be repeated in time to come. It can be compared with an ant hill when it is kicked open and the ants scatter. Then you search for the ants around the nest, and they lead you to other nests.

Smokeshell was the ants' nest. Most of the cadres scattered to find safety at their other 'nests', or bases, if you like. Then a combination of area operations, follow-up, and search-and-destroy operations were launched to locate and destroy them.

Battle Group 10 under the command of Cmdt Chris Serfontein continued with the mopping up of Plan bases in the Mulola area, 50 km west of Smokeshell. There were quite a few stray groups of cadres among the various bases. Furthermore, tonnes of ammunition and war material had to be located and destroyed or backloaded.

On 11 June I joined Chris Serfontein. I spent many days with him and his battle group. On Saturday, 14 June 1980, the men were going to work through certain enemy bases and caches. Chris Serfontein tells the story:

> The troops were visibly put out when I told them that the starting time of the mopping-up operation would be 15:00. That was when the Springboks' rugby test match against the British Lions in Bloemfontein was scheduled to start. As Gen Geldenhuys was with us we dared not postpone the operation. We had to make a plan. Bobby Keller, the signals officer, told me that provided we could use the command vehicle's rear link radio, he could guarantee that

old Gerhard Viviers's commentary would be heard loud and clear, and the men could be kept informed of the battle of Bloemfontein on the command net.

The problem was that we had to have somebody with some knowledge of the game to man the rear link. What was wrong with the GOC of Southwest himself? The nominee agreed and so the mopping-up and the test match could take place at the same time. This is more or less how it sounded on the command net: 'Two zero, this is nine, you guys must mop up those trenches properly, just now a terro shoots one of you ... the big number nine (Gen Geldenhuys) says old Gysie has just scored under the posts ... over,' which was followed by an applause equivalent to that of the open stand at the Free State stadium. So it happened that the men reconciled war and rugby.

I went to see Gerhard Viviers in 1991 shortly after his vocal cords had been removed and told him the story. He could not yet talk, but he responded by scribbling on a piece of paper: 'A chap once told me, "Thanks for the commentary in my vehicle, sir."'

In addition to sports commentary, the news media played an important role in our operations. A large contingent was present during the first battle, Smokeshell. Then, around 12–13 June, shortly after I had joined Serfie and his battle group, I heard someone say that they had all left. I got onto the radio and enquired what had happened to them.

Maj Marius Kleynhans, the media liaison officer of SWA Command, told me that the journalists had said they had got a good story at Smokeshell which they wanted to file; they also had bosses and couldn't just drive around in the bush hoping and waiting for the next scrap to happen.

I then urgently and seriously ordered him to ask the media corps in Windhoek to send back at least three journalists – one from radio, one from TV and one from a news agency. And so it happened that Con Crous from SAPA, Johan Brits from SWA-Radio and Ossie Gibson from RSA-TV returned to the bush.

During later years journalists often asked me why we would not allow them to accompany us on operations. This was a valid question, but I could not resist telling them about the above incidents, which proved that we are not as averse to the idea as many people tended to think. Some freelance journalists spent much time with the forces in the bush during operations. Al J Venter was a good example. This man was truly prepared to go anywhere and everywhere, regardless of danger and discomfort.

I left Serfie and his men for a while and flew to Ondangwa with Crow Stannard who was ferrying material seized in combat back to base.

I rejoined Battle Group 10 on 22 June 1980. The end of Operation Sceptic was in sight when we received information that Plan's mechanized force, which included BTR armoured vehicles and field artillery, were to be found at a place called Tanga Nova. Chris Serfontein decided to attack them with two companies and with the support of Capt Budgie Burgers's Impala aircraft.

We moved in for the attack. I saw the first mortar bombs fall. I was uncertain whether they were ours or theirs, but I had no time to find out because something strange diverted my attention.

A cadre suddenly walked out of the bushes straight towards our command vehicle – a Buffel, which is an open vehicle. And we were actually moving between two companies of troops. I did not instantly register what was happening. All I saw was Sterf grabbing his rifle, jumping up and pointing it, shouting: 'Drop your rifle, drop your rifle!' If he had done that to me, I would have had the fright of my life. After all the time in the bush and the sun, his face had become deeply tanned. One saw only two large white eyes with white teeth showing under his black bristle moustache. Only then did I notice the cadre next to our vehicle.

Looking back, the moment was probably not that dangerous, but it was dramatic enough. Serf was standing there, face to face with an insurgent three metres away from him, both hanging on to their rifles. The cadre did not seem to know what he was expected to do with his rifle under the circumstances; but Serfie's was pointed right at the man's chest. Then the Ovambo Staff Sergeant jumped down and relieved the poor man of his weapon. The tension eased.

This was also a fight that never was. The enemy had been occupying a temporary respite area and had made a hasty break just before we got there. We had only slight contact with the last of their rear parties.

To my knowledge this was our first contact with Plan's mechanized force. We seized a lot of military equipment, including 76 mm field guns, and a stack of documents (which came in handy nearly ten years later, as I shall relate in Chapter 18). And that one young man was caught – by the command vehicle! His name was Smokey. We grew quite fond of him.

We were not always a hundred per cent geared to backload the tonnes of seized equipment, but we tried our best. On this occasion, after we had destroyed some of the equipment, we hooked up the guns behind our Buffels, using the command Buffel as well, and started towing them away.

Before we left the general area of the objective and with the Imps still overhead, I happened to listen to the ground-air radio when I suddenly heard one of the pilots say to another: 'I see the 'Swaps' are towing back their guns, let's take a final run and "rev" them a bit.'

I grabbed the radio: 'Stop, stop! There is no enemy here any longer. All the guns you see are now ours!'

Plan's mechanized force attracted international attention many years later. I will come back to that.

By this time there were not many more bases and cadres to be traced. On 23 June 1980 the settlement negotiations got going again. Min Pik Botha made certain proposals.

One night, towards the end of June, a helicopter came to pick me up to take me back to Ondangwa and Windhoek. The next day at Ondangwa, as I was on the point of departing for Windhoek and everyone was clearing out after the operation, I suddenly saw the 'sharp-nose' men scrambling – Cmdt Mac van der Merwe's Mirage F1 pilots. And off they went.

What had happened was that Serfie and his Battle Group 10 were on their way back south and just about to cross the tarred road from Ongiva to Xangongo, when an Angolan force surprised and attacked them.

It was a tough battle. Serfie contacted Maj Bob King, the leader of Battle Group 10's MAOT (mobile air operations team) on the radio with: 'Bob, help!' But it wasn't even necessary for Bob to request close air support from the air command post at Ondangwa, because Col Theo de Munnink, Commander of Western Air Command, and Cmdt Ollie Holmes, the Air Force Commander of Sector 10, were listening in to the 'long conversation' between Serf and Bob and reacted immediately before Bob could even ask.

The ensuing attack of the sharp noses on the Angolans with 1 000 pound bombs enabled Serf to make a clean break. He completed his withdrawal by 17:30 on 29 June 1980. Rifleman de Kock was later awarded the Honoris Crux decoration for his courageous conduct during this encounter; WO2 Schutte, the sergeant-major of the battle group, received the Pro Merito Medal. He had kept wounded soldiers alive by direct blood transfusion while in danger. The Ovambo guide said: 'The Lord looked after us today.'

Not only Sergeant-Major Schutte and Rifleman De Kock performed excellently. Everyone pulled his weight. One should still bear in mind that everything is more difficult in war, that everyone has the potential to slip, and as I have said, 'to turn the wrong screw'.

During Sceptic I learned how the men who had to 'turn the screws' knew what they were doing when it came to the nuts and bolts.

During the preparation phase of the operation, Brig Witkop Badenhorst suddenly instructed Lt Jenkins, Commander of the Sector 10 Light Workshop Troop, to repair eight Buffels needed for the operation. It was already late afternoon and the Tiffies[3] were tired after a long day's hard work; but by first light the next morning the Buffels were repaired, sprayed and ready. They had worked through the night only to hear in the morning that they were to join the operation. Six of the men who had worked non-stop through the night packed their kit and set off. They returned two weeks after their 24-month national service term had expired. They kept the wheels turning. They did not moan.

The wheels had started to turn for me too. During the operation it was announced that I would be transferred to Pretoria.

During my tour of duty in South West Africa there had been heavy military activity and I was also dragged into the domestic and international political scene. I was away from Windhoek at least four days per week; but there was time for recreation too.

I was called away once to attend a conference in Pretoria. It was to take place on a Friday. The next day a rugby test match or Currie Cup final was to be played at Loftus Versveld. I hasten to assure you that it was pure coincidence. Some friends and I arranged to go and watch the game.

We met at the Culemborg Hotel. We had arranged to go together from there by microbus. The hotel was full of people. Jam-packed. They stood around in the bar lounges, in other lounges, in the passages, everywhere. They were warming up for the game, exchanging views, speculating over the chances of the two sides. They were standing around in clusters, drinking beer.

I noticed that a group of rugby enthusiasts standing nearby were whispering among themselves and looking at me. Again they whispered and looked at me. I gathered that they were talking about me. It made me feel good.

One of them detached himself from the group, and with the air of a man with a mission he steered himself past the other people, and headed straight for me.

He came up to me, beer in hand: 'Excuse me, Sir, I don't want to intrude in your privacy, but we're having an argument ...'

I was enjoying the situation. 'You're not bothering me at all. Please carry on.'

'We were arguing about whether you're ... perhaps ...'

'Yes ... Yes?'

'Are you perhaps – Doug Watson?!'

My time in South West was running out and a trip to Ovambo was one of my last obligations before leaving the territory.

I had been asked to make a speech at a social gathering during the opening of the Air Force Club at Ondangwa. I used the opportunity to make an important announcement – a new military unit was to be established in South West. By way of introduction I told the audience how seemingly outdated technology had suddenly become useful again in the bush war. And considering all the problems we had experienced with telecommunications, we might as well equally effectively use carrier pigeons and other birds as messengers. Everyone present politely concealed their amazement at this radical statement, but they were nevertheless curious to know which branch of the service, Army or Air force, would get the responsibility for the bird unit. So I explained as follows: everything that moves on the ground comes under the command of the Army, and everything that moves in the air falls under the Air Force; so this new winged unit would be an Air Force operation.

I continued by announcing that I had already liaised with the Chief of the Air Force and recommended that the key officers to run the new unit were to be Budgie Burgers, Crow Stannard, Mossie (Sparrow) Basson and Vink (Finch) Hattingh.

Some observers diligently searched for the story behind my transfer. There was none. Gen Malan had become the Minister of Defence on 7 October 1980 following an earlier announcement; Gen Viljoen suceeded him as the Chief of the Defence Force and I had to take over from him as Chief of the Army on 1 November 1980. My headquarters would obviously be Pretoria.

My service in South West enriched me. I am thankful for that.

I often come across people who tell me that I have been very lucky in my career. I was lucky to have been transferred to South West in 1970, because that is where everything began; I was lucky to have been given command in South West again in 1977, during the amalgamation of SWA Command and 101 Task Force, because quite a few military operations took place during that time which provided the opportunity to show one's worth.

I was lucky.

But that is not the whole story. It all really started in 1962 at the Loftus Versveld D-field. I played full-back for Defence against Tukkies. I broke my leg just above the ankle and decided to give up rugby. In future I would follow the game as a spectator.

I then calculated how many hours per month I used to spend on rugby and resolved to put this time to a particular use. I thought about it carefully and first decided, for my own pleasure, to write a book. I started at it straight away, but it took me twenty years to have two booklets published. No big deal.

Secondly, I wanted to learn another language. I decided on Portuguese, as it was the language spoken in our neighbouring territories, Angola and Mozambique, and might come in useful sometime. I made a start, attended a private class now and then, but mainly concentrated on records and grammar books.

In 1965 I read in a departmental circular that the post of vice-consul in Luanda was vacant. I applied and was appointed, perhaps because I had taken initiative to learn Portuguese. My term there was extended for one year. But when the possibility of a second extension was raised, I requested to be considered for the annual supplementary transfer list of March-April 1970. In due course, I was told that I would be transferred to Pretoria.

In the meantime, towards the end of 1969, two Second World War veteran officers in succession were transferred to Windhoek as Colonel G, but both made representations not to go. The outcome was that, even before I could move to Pretoria, the Chief of the Army had sent me directly to Windhoek probably because I was available and my experience in Angola could come in handy.

I would say that my first tour in South West was certainly a factor which contributed to the decision to send me there once again during 1977.

I do not think that all was luck. But who can tell? *Friction de guerre* is ever present.

Like my first term in South West, my second was also the end of a chapter for me, but not the end of a book.

The Windhoek I said goodbye to was well described by many artists, including poets, also those who focused on the war. In his volume *Sungong*, Roy Allen describes the Windhoek of those days in his poem 'Bistro' as follows:

Like a sidewalk of some Paris street,
Gay with bright sunshades,
Coffee-sippers, plastic chairs,
People
Watching
People
Pass –

A dumpy old lady, grey, sits, bejewelled,
Painfully
Penning a
Postcard
To some Munich friend.

The beggar from Ovamboland, wizened and watery-eyed
From too many years of the sun
Is shuffling past

Jo'burg pressmen, beer-fat and pale-faced
Say confidential things into microphone cups –
(Perhaps tomorrow's headlines) –

The divorcee, triumphant, ponders her alimony here –
A table away from the Swapo-D man entertaining
New York guests –
Heinrich, ex-Wehrmacht, ex-Stalingrad, Ritterkreuz
And still erect goes marching past
As Novicki, the Warsaw architect talks of Vivaldi
With Aviva – soprano from the opera Don Pascale –

Sarel of security sits there alone
Unreading *Die Republikein* – detachedly carefully,

Watching –
People
Passing –
Coffe-sippers
Plastic chairs.

(Scene at a Windhoek outdoor café off Kaiser Street, '79)

The 1979/1980 yearbook of the Institute for the Study of Conflict in London describes South Africa's military action in SWA-Namibia as: 'An outstanding example of a successful counterinsurgency offensive taken at an early stage of the conflict.'

10

CORRESPONDENTS AND SPIES
Fish eagles and crocodiles

When I left South West I keenly missed my days in the natural wilderness, along with words like Buffalo, Okavango, Liambezi Lake, Mariënfluss and Kunenemund; also fish eagles, storks, lion, crocodile and hippopotamus. Those were the symbols of the wild and the free, and to have lived among them was a magnificent experience.

When I came to South West in 1970, I hunted. When I left in 1980, I no longer hunted but I did enjoy (and still do) biltong, dried sausage and barbequed rib, as well as 'puff-adder' – large intestine stuffed with liver. However, I was still quite willing to tag along on a hunting trip; preferably to advise, beer in hand, during the skinning and cutting up of the meat. I have found that I can no longer look an animal in the eye and cut its throat.

Then again, facing an animal is one thing; facing war is another; but the single most difficult duty for me was facing a media conference.

The world of correspondents and spies represented one of the interesting phenomena that played a significant role during the period 1977–1980. This phenomenon may not have been part of the chronological factual story, nor of the milestones on the route; it was more like surges of the sea while a captain steers his vessel on its course, or like the behaviour of the weather when a safari continues on its way to its destination.

With the media I always followed three guidelines: If I released information on my own initiative, I gave it to the media as a whole – to all. However, if a journalist were to approach me for information and it is no problem to release it, I would give it to that journalist – only to him. Whenever I released information, I tried to give all the facts. It was not always easy – classified information was usually involved.

There were other problems too. Some of them had no solutions. One had to live with them. A story from those days illustrates the nature of the kind of problems the news media had with me:

The media corps was quite extensive for a sparsely populated territory such as South West: there were representatives from the South West press consisting of morning and afternoon papers and one Saturday paper; the RSA press, consisting of morning and afternoon papers, Sunday papers and magazines; overseas media correspondents; SWA radio, and SABC TV.

I used to present regular weekly media conferences. If there was not enough news to justify a conference on that day, I only issued a press statement. Then the morning papers started to complain that we issued the press releases and held the conferences at times that favoured the afternoon press; when we changed that, the afternoon papers complained; all the papers moaned that the radio was always the first to use our information; the weekend papers again, especially the Saturday paper, groaned that we never gave them the chance to be the first to publish security information; the South West press expressed dissatisfaction to the effect that we favoured the RSA media, and vice versa.

Every complaint, on its own, had merit. So I brought about changes to try to accommodate them all. I alternated the conferences, handling them on different days of the week and different times of the day. Embargos ensured that radio and TV news could not jump the gun. But the complaints kept coming in.

By way of illustration, the well-known editor, Hannes Smith, wrote in his paper of 12 July 1980: 'The Windhoek Observer often violently clashed with the General, particularly because we sometimes suspected him of favouring the South African newsmen and neglecting the local newsmen.'[1]

One day I convened a special media conference and said: Come now, elect yourselves a chairman. Decide jointly on which days of the week and on what hours of the day I should arrange my press conferences. If you cannot reach agreement on a fixed day of the week, decide on specific predetermined dates. I undertake to do exactly whatever you decide.'

They agreed and I left them to their conference. It was a rather rash concession because one forfeits all initiative, but a promise is a promise.

They selected Con Crous of Sapa as chairman. He was an experienced journalist and respected by all, and as he was employed by a news agency, he was not a controversial figure.

It surprised me that I did not receive a speedy recommendation. In fact, I had to make enquiries. There was such a clash of interests among themselves that they could not reach an agreement. Carry on as before, he told me.

I learnt an important lesson: there is no such thing as 'the press'. There are different TV and radio stations and specific papers and magazines. But the problem had been eased, if not solved.

There were other difficulties too. Hannes Smith said in the same article mentioned above: '... in fact, at one particular military briefing a London spy sat in the ranks of the press, and the General knew it. He concealed his knowledge and only later did seasoned reporters learn why. For this spy was neatly led by the nose and conveyed the wrong information to sources in London.'

It is true that we had good reasons from time to time to strongly suspect certain persons of playing obscure roles, but I cannot now remember any particular incident where I had taken such a course of action. It would seem to be improbable and impratical. However, many years later I did land up in similar a situation. I will describe it in a later chapter.

Hannes Smith was by any possible comparison absolutely special and unique. A fascinating book could well be written about him. Some people jokingly called him 'crazy Smith', but if he was, then he was wiser in his madness than most of his critics in their state of uncrazy equilibrium. He gave the Defence Force hell.

One of his colleagues reminded me many years later of a special confidential briefing to which I had invited the editors and senior reporters. In his next edition Smith reported on the briefing as follows: 'During a strictly off-the-record briefing yesterday, Gen Geldenhuys said that ...'

I took it philosophically. In one respect Hannes was like Jos Rossouw; they could both just about get away with murder.

In general I have great respect for the media. They were professional and responsible. I always tried my best to treat them fairly and keep them satisfied. I would like to flatter myself that I succeeded to a reasonable degree, but there were favourable factors which made it possible for me.

In respect of liaison with the media in South West and making general press statements, Gen Malan delegated the same authority to me as he did to the Chief of the SA Army. This was very different from the situation of my counterparts in territorial commands in South Africa. In respect of the release of information specifically concerning operations, I had the same powers in my area of responsibility as the Chief of the Defence Force with regard to operations elsewhere. With the appointment of the AG and the isolation of South West politics from South African politics, Pretoria imposed few restrictions on me regarding the media and politics. It meant that I could deal with the media independently.

This brings me to some aspects of the relationship between the military and politics. One should not deduce from the above that there is a firm line between the two. On the contrary, I don't believe one always realizes how totally interwoven war and politics became at all levels of society.

In days gone by peace and war had clear-cut boundaries. During peace-time peoples and states arranged their relations with others by means of politics and diplomacy. They talked to one another.

If relations could not be settled in this manner, the parties agreed to differ. To break a deadlock one or both of the parties might have resorted to violence and declared war. They shot at each other. One overpowered the other or they destroyed one another. Then they started talking again and peace was concluded.

Nowadays peace-time and war-time do not follow in such neat time phases. Wars are not declared and violence and diplomatic politics are conducted at the same time. They talk while they shoot and vice versa.

It has changed the nature of warfare.

During ancient times the two sides agreed that each would appoint a warrior; the two warriors would fight and the side whose warrior emerged victorious had won the battle. The duel between David and Goliath is an excellent example. This trend continued for some time. Dr Cas Bakkes told me that during the eighteenth century opponents on the field of battle could not always agree as to who would fire the first salvo and armies sometimes left the battlefield with no contact having been made.

He told me the story of the Battle of Fontenoy: on 11 May 1745 Lord Charles Hay, lieutenant of the first guards battalion, before the English and French lines could start firing at each other, rushed forward and took off his hat to the advancing French. He bowed deeply and drank a toast from his hip flask.

He ordered his troops to applaud the enemy with three cheers. After the French had returned the salute and applause, the English officer requested them to fire first. The French refused and passed the honour back to the English. The result was that the burst which followed from the English side caused serious casualties in the French ranks.

Customs and traditions have gradually changed. As early as the beginning of the nineteenth century Napoleon very improperly, unsportingly and without ceremony attacked his opponents from the rear.

But it has changed still more. The formalities have disappeared completely. War is no longer formally declared. In other words there is peace, and politics is being practised, but in the meantime fighting is taking place. The politicians know it, but feign ignorance. Politicians are even hesitant to admit that a situation of armed hostilities has developed, because the first one to announce it is accused of having started it all. One party may try to keep its armed actions quiet and then accuse the other of making war while the other party will deny it and throw the accusation back at his opponent.

This is the propaganda of the 'good guys' and the 'bad guys'. It is a very unmilitary kind of conduct, but it is politically acceptable. In the old days people declared war openly and drank toasts, now they make war in the dark and sling mud at each other in public.

This is what happened in many countries during the past three decades and it does not seem entirely uncharacteristic of the early 1990s in South Africa.

In practice, from my perspective, it worked like this: The Soviet Department of Foreign Affairs, for example, would talk politics and peace while the Communist Party and KGB incited war. The top people who perform in public would seem to propagate peace while instructions had been issued for subversion and inciting violence. The politicians are the masters and integrate the action as a whole.

There are political commissars on all levels, even on the lowest, throughout the communist military system. Revolutionary organizations supported by the Soviets likewise had political commissars over the whole spectrum from top to bottom. In Angola, for example, Swapo had political commissars right down to regional and detachment level.

We followed the Western system. The Defence Force had only one connecting point with politics and that was at Minister of Defence level.

I experienced the situation during this period especially with regard to propaganda. There is no doubt that in recent decades South Africa convincingly won its military conflicts although propagandists and those who allowed themselves to be dragged along by their propaganda will, of course, deny it.

Be that as it may, one war which we did lose was the propaganda war.

In 1991 I came upon an old British pamphlet from which I quote: 'Psychological warfare will be conducted after the outbreak of war by the use of all available means ...'[2]

Until the present this policy has always been upheld by totalitarian states and the movements supported by them, with one difference – to them it did not matter whether war had been declared or not.

In Western countries, however, 'outbreak of war' means a formally declared war. But wars are no longer formally declared. Governments therefore never arrive at a point where they enter the propaganda arena.

It is partly because of this difference in approach that the dividing lines between war and peace have become blurred.

With the discussions that later resulted in the 1984 Lusaka Agreement, there were talks about peace while the war was in full swing. The last series of negotiations on a peace settlement in 1988, which resulted in the Cuban troops' withdrawal from Angola and the implementation of Resolution 435 in South West Africa, likewise began long before the war ended.

It could also happen that during one and the same conflict, one of the parties would use propaganda, because they consider themselves to be in a position of war, while the other will maintain normal politics, because they think there is peace.

Swapo and the MPLA regarded propaganda as a dimension of their struggle, and the propaganda organization as just another weapon system. We regarded propaganda as a distasteful word and concept which have no place in democratic politics.

The Swapo propaganda embraced certain themes which they used successfully over a very long time before they were turned upside down, some of them only very recently. To illustrate:

- *Plan was fighting from bases inside South West.* No such base could ever be pointed out to anybody. With the implementation of Resolution 435 during 1988–1989 not a single UN monitoring officer ever saw a Plan base inside South West. But their claims had been believed for many many years.
- *Swapo had about 80 000 refugees in its care.* Over the years we had described this figure as ridiculous. It was only with the implementation of Resolution 435 that our counterclaim was accepted. It caused Swapo great embarrassment when, under UN supervision, only about 30 000 refugees presented themselves. It is easy to understand. If it was the international year of the aged, Swapo had a large number of old people in its care; if it was the year of the children, Swapo had a lot of children; if it is the year of the refugee, they had a lot of refugees. In this way they claimed a lot of aid funds from various sources.
- *The security forces murdered and plundered the local population and looted their towns.* If one or two such cases contained some truth, the other ten or twenty allegations were also believed. Any useful theme was repeated without interruption until it became accepted as a general perception.

On the other hand, in my experience, all our claims were rejected as untrue:

- Although we knew that there were advisers of the Soviet Union and its allies present amongst the Angolan and Swapo forces, we were seldom believed. Analysts insisted on concrete evidence. During Operation Reindeer Cmdt Frank Bestbier found a Russian's suitcase containing uniform, documents and all, at Plan's Vietnam base. Some of these items were displayed to the media. They merely said that we might just as well have planted them. Later, during Operation Protea in 1981, two Soviets were killed and one taken prisoner. Maj Ywvgenii Victorovich Kireev, chief artillery adviser, and Col Joseph Lamonovich, adviser to the political commissar, were killed and Warrant Officer Nilolai Pestretsof was captured. Only then did they believe us – with a shrug of the shoulders.
- Plan abducted people from South West. Few people believed us. But a few days before Operation Reindeer, insurgents hijacked a bus, kidnapped the passengers and took them to Angola. It happened at Olindamba, north of Olushandja in the vicinity of Beacon

6 1/2. The bus got stuck 1,5 km north of the border. The information we released about this incident was received sceptically. But the kidnapped passengers were found at the Vietnam base after the battle. Two of them told their story to the media the following day. Even then many people still would not believe the story. They told me that we had brainwashed them. Later during the implementation of the Lusaka agreement I experienced similar frustrations. We had reported that members of Plan were still infiltrating across the border into South West from the area in dispute in contravention of the agreement. We were not believed. Once we took such a captured infiltrator to the next meeting of the Joint Monitoring Commission and made him available to the Angolans and Cubans for debriefing. Again they refused. They would not even talk to him merely to control their own information or to ascertain if he was not in fact a *bona fide* captured insurgent. They simply said he was brainwashed and that was that.

- We found proof that Cubans, Angolans and Plan occupied bases jointly and that Plan members were wearing Angolan uniforms. Many would not believe us. But after an operation, on the spur of the moment, I asked the intelligence officer to fetch one of the Plan prisoners so that the news media who were waiting for a press conference to start, could talk to him. I didn't know who or what kind of a person he would be and what he would say. A foreign journalist questioned him. The Plan man spoke freely. He complained that Plan discriminated against him. In reply to a question he explained that he was a Damara and he and the other Damaras were given second rate rifles, Simonovs (SKSs), while the Wambos got the better AK 47s. The same journalist then asked him:

  'What is that jacket you are wearing?'

  He replied: 'It is a Fapla jacket.'

  'Why are you wearing a Fapla jacket?'

  'Because Fapla say if we are together with them at the same place we must wear Fapla uniforms, not Plan uniforms; because then the South African forces will attack them.'

  During an operation called Protea we seized a Soviet operational map of the Xangongo base and surroundings. On it was annotated in detail the integrated Cuban, Fapla and Plan artillery fireplan. This contributed towards convincing some people of their mutual co-operation.

- Swapo always denied that they ill-treated their members in detention, or those assembled for 're-education', as they called it. However, when Swapo returned to South West in terms of Resolution 435, the stories of torture caused a public outrage.

One cannot always blame the media, because in conflict situations the air is so thick with propaganda that even I did not always know what was real and what was propaganda. Was any information based on fact, emanating from reliable and credible sources? Or was everything part of a psychological warfare scheme aiming to scare or to influence decision-making?

However, there was one report which did not leave me with any doubts. The well-known military correspondent, Carel Birkby, reported as follows on a piece of information:

> It could have been planted by Moscow. It could have been based on false premises. It could even have been a view sincerely held in some quarters. But whatever its source, a story of an impending invasion of South West Africa by East German paratroopers from Angola was quickly denied last week by defence specialists.[3]

I was one of the so-called defence specialists. But this was not just a wild allegation. Many places, names and facts had been given, some of which were correct, to provide authenticity.

Birkby said:

> The reports were neatly patterned. Word was dropped that 'eleven senior generals' from the eastern side of the Berlin wall had arrived in Luanda. It is correct that a number of officers of general rank were now in Angola as advisers and as observers studying the intermittent activities in an 'interesting' civil war. But a leak to the German newspaper, *Die Welt*, made these professionals sound more ominous. The French intelligence sources cited that five were named and positioned. General Jakanowitz is described as the mastermind planning an invasion. His headquarters are placed in Henrique de Carvalho ...
>
> Vasili Ivanovitz Petrov, described as 'first deputy commander' of the Soviet ground forces who reportedly advised the Ethiopians and their Cuban aids how to defeat Somalia this year, is reported to have been in Angola. It would be logical for him to take a look at another African scene where internal warfare is going on. Top man

in Luanda, where he is close to Pres Agostinho Neto, is Karpov.

Other Soviet officers were also mentioned – at Lubango: Shredin, at Bié: Churopov, and at Roçades (Xangongo): Gobin.

Some people were anxious but I rejected this information.

However, there are also other forms of propaganda used in revolutionary warfare. General Jack Dutton talked of a multidimensional war, of which semantics was one of the dimensions – the skilful use of words to create perceptions. Swapo was very good at it. In certain areas of southern Angola, east of the Kunene River, Plan had its normal detachments, but they gave them other names, 'Ground Forces', 'Air Forces' and 'Naval Forces'.

It paid good dividends. Swapo regularly staged media conferences and issued press releases. One of their well-known spokesmen was Peter Katjavivi in London. He used to tell of incidents on the border and then reported that their 'Air Forces' and 'Naval Forces' had done this and that and the other.

This naturally created the perception that they had a navy and an air force. Many believed them. It seems crazy, but one can be surprised at how stupid intelligent people can be, or prefer to be, if it suits them.

Swapo furthermore divided the south of Angola into so-called 'fronts', among others the 'northern front' and 'north-eastern front'.[4] They also used these designations during press conferences. This again naturally created the impression that they had bases in north and north-eastern SWA.

In the same article in the *Windhoek Observer* which I mentioned above, Smith said:

> In a major military briefing some three years ago, Geldenhuys agreed that it was acceptable to him that a Swapo fighter could be called a guerrilla or an insurgent if he fights the security forces, but a terrorist when he attacks a civilian.

This aspect is another example of the role played by semantics. Some people, because it suited them, used the word terrorists, while the majority referred to 'freedom fighters' and 'guerrillas' because it suited them.

I was always disappointed if acts of terror had been committed and those who were responsible were being called freedom fighters and similarly glorifying names. A recent example is the attack on a golf club at King William's Town on 28 November 1992 when four people were killed and seventeen wounded.

I formulated an approach and discussed it with the media: people who commit deeds of terror, such as the murder of Clemens Kapuuo, the planting of the mine on the garage path of the Ovambo Minister of Health, Mr Toivo Shiyagaya, the murder of Mr David Shikongo, as well as the killing of council members and about twenty-four chiefs during a period of twenty-four months in Ovamboland – they should have been called terrorists. In all other cases where skirmishes took place between armed people and the security forces they could be called guerrilla fighters, if so wished.

Many journalists came back and told me that their editors had advised them that it was against their editorial policy and that they could not go along with this formula. Some of them even reported back apologetically, because they agreed that it was a fair policy. The *Rand Daily Mail* was one of the papers that did accept it.

I made one mistake with the news media. I naively expected accurate and 'positive' reporting and comment. It is unrealistic. Unthinkingly I forgot that different elements of the media also try, each in its own manner, to influence political policy. It is their right. One therefore has to accept 'negative' reporting. But if one is honest with the media, the chances are good that one could also get 'positive' coverage together with the 'negative' coverage.

You have to take the punch. You cannot blame the media. And they cannot be blamed if they report negative statements made by other people. My opinion of the media is described fairly well by Peter Samuel in the *International Freedom Review*:

> Government should try to take the initiative with the media and think positively about it. If the government does not give it a story, it will look elsewhere. Therefore, government should provide spokesmen, keep restrictions to a minimum, and provide all the information it can …
>
> The media may be rotten messengers at times, but they are not the enemy.

When I reflect on those days, the name Theunie Steyn always comes to mind, for what he was and how he too got stumped by semantics.

I had always heard of the tremendous respect people had had for the President of the Orange Free State of bygone times, Marthinus Theunis Steyn. His son, Colin, had also enjoyed a widespread reputation as an intellectual colossus. And when I got to know Justice M T Steyn, I could better understand everything that I had heard about his father and grandfather. Greatness must run in their blood.

I once attended a function to promote the aims of the Society for the Protection of Endangered Species. Justice Steyn was the main speaker.

I was seated next to Prof Fritz Eloff, professor of zoology, rugby man and nature lover. Justice Steyn, as I have seen him do before, took out a scrap of paper about the size of a bus ticket and from the notes on that strip of paper spoke for about an hour and a half.

He began in space, beyond the furthermost solar systems and expanses. He spoke about what was happening there and worked systematically through all the layers of magnetospheres, ionospheres, stratospheres and tropospheres until he reached the crust of the earth. His address penetrated it and ended in the hot, melting masses in the innermost depths of the earth.

But even before he could get there, Prof Eloff admiringly sighed: 'What a man!'

When Justice Steyn and I arrived at Katimo Mulilo from Mpacha on 23 August 1978 by helicopter, it was fired upon by anti-aircraft guns from Sesheke in Zambia. I joined Justice Steyn in a bomb shelter. Our own counterbombardment had begun and with the sound of artillery field guns in his ears he looked at me and said: 'Just listen to the music of battle.' He is a romantic and veteran of the Second World War. 'It feels like Monte Casino all over again,' he added.

The Capetonian Piet Voges told me of a visit he paid ex-Minister Frank Waring and his wife Joyce in Bantry Bay towards the end of 1977. The then Prime Minister John Vorster was also there. He was sitting calmly on a swing seat on the veranda.

Among the guests were acquaintances of mine, Jack and Olga Levinson of Windhoek. Olga was a well-known writer.

They expressed their appreciation to John Vorster of the wonderful person he sent them as Administrator General – Theunie Steyn. He was an exceptionally competent man, Jack said.

After John Vorster had listened patiently, he responded drily and in measured words: 'Yes, his father put me in jail.'

This had happened during the Second World War. Under the emergency regulations people could be interned without trial and without interference from the courts. Theunie's father, Colin, was the Minister of Justice in the Smuts cabinet and Vorster was interned at Koffiefontein for his outspoken anti-government attitude regarding the war.

When Justice Steyn arrived in Windhoek, the Swapo supporters liked to call him the puppet of this and that, puppet of the Pretoria regime, and so forth.

After a successful two years in office, his appointment had expired. His departure from the Eros Airport was official and accompanied by all the prescribed formalities. When he entered the VIP departure hall, his radiant magnetism again rippled through the crowd of well-wishers.

He tapped dignified men on the shoulder and kissed entranced ladies' hands. The moment to say goodbye had arrived and he walked the red carpet to the guard of honour. He returned the salute and inspected the guard. He walked the length of red carpet to the Merlin aircraft which was ready and waiting. At the top of the steps he turned round, removed his hat and waved a last goodbye to the crowd.

The newly formed SWA Territory Force Band struck up and played him a farewell song:

'Puppet on a string'.

Friction de Guerre also strikes great people.

11

THE BEGINNING OF A NEW DECADE 'The South African government has been shocked'

On 1 November 1980 I took over from Gen Constand Viljoen as the Chief of the Army. I was to learn fast.

Shortly after my arrival in Pretoria I attended a party. A woman walked up to me and said: 'Oh, are you General Geldenhuys?'

I nodded.

'How nice, I have seen you on TV, but shame, I didn't know you were such a tiny little man!'

A few months later I invited sports commentator Gerhard Viviers with his wife, Maryna, and rugby heroes Morné du Plessis and Frik du Preez for a visit to the operational area in South West. The troops liked to see these people, to shake hands with them and have a chat. Morné and Frik were also going to do a bit of coaching at Grootfontein, Rundu and Oshakati.

They were to arrive in Pretoria on a Sunday and depart early on the Monday morning. I was to be their host at dinner on the Sunday evening to say a few words of welcome.

I had arranged with my public relations officer that he and I would now and again during the normal course of a day's work, stop any soldier and ask him if he knew Frik and Morné and if he would say something about them. Troops usually come up with good stories and with their contributions I hoped to be able to make a little informal speech with personal and human touches.

On my way to work one morning I arrived at the main gate of Defence Headquarters. For some reason I was dressed in civilian clothes that day. The guard stopped me, which is normal routine. Suddenly I thought of the rugby people and our random research and I asked the soldier: 'Do you know who Frik du Preez is and can you tell me something about him ...?

He interrupted me firmly: 'Mister, before you go any further, you tell me first, who the hell do you think you are?'

So I told him: 'Doug Watson ...'

By this time I had learnt many similar lessons about humility. Anton Rupert, one of the greatest South Africans of our times, said that one should be able to look into the mirror and laugh at yourself; modesty and a sense of humour are useful leadership qualities. But I cannot stand the false humility that some people seem so proud of. One does not brag about being modest. And to be truly humble, you must have self-confidence.

However, we were all small fry. During 1981 big fish Ronald Reagan took over from Jimmy Carter as President of the United States. During the decade of the 1980s he was to play a major role in the new directions that southern Africa would follow.

It is against this background of new American diplomatic initiatives, soon to be unfolded, that I will now continue the operational story in South West and Angola. My successors as GOC, SWA Command were first Gen Charles Lloyd (until the end of 1983) and then Gen Georg Meiring (until the beginning of 1987). Both were good generals – and Free Staters.

I shall describe their most important crossborder operations first and then my personal experiences and perceptions. The first series took place under the overall command of Charles Lloyd. Operations Carnation and Protea, July and August 1981, followed on Operation Sceptic (1980) and resulted in a second confrontation with Fapla. As a result of its setbacks experienced during Sceptic, Plan had moved its bases further north, close to and even among those of Fapla, to discourage attacks by the security forces. Plan's logistic systems also became completely interwoven with those of Fapla.

By mid-1981 the security situation in the northern border area of South West took a serious turn. The sustained delivery of Soviet arms, continued Cuban support and stock-piling of vast quantities of weaponry, and the build-up of Fapla and Plan in southern Angola, posed a real threat. Various skirmishes with Plan took place during July 1981.

Gen Lloyd announced on 6 July that 52 insurgents had been killed during clashes with the security forces over a period of only four days.

This sharp increase in the frequency of skirmishes gave rise to the security forces' launch Operation Carnation. Although 225 cadres were killed during the operation, it was only partially successful. The security forces operation did not extend further than 25 km north of the border, while the bigger Plan bases were situated still further north. But it did create a favourable situation for Operation Protea which was to succeed Carnation.

At this stage Fapla and Swapo were co-operating. Fapla's air defence system posed a real threat to our Air Force's support to our ground forces.

During Operation Protea Gen Lloyd attacked and destroyed several Plan bases and command posts in the area of Xangongo and Ongiva with three task forces. D-day, 23 August 1981, started with an air attack on a Fapla radar station and keypoints of the Angolan air defence system. On 24 August the ground forces began their advance on Xangongo along three different approaches. (See Map no 2.)

It was clear from later information that our intentions were interpreted as wanting to invade Angola itself; that we had long-range objectives in mind; and that Plan was merely a secondary consideration. Long afterwards Cuban and Fapla officers confirmed this to me.

A mechanized force attacked the bases near the town which also accommodated the regional headquarters of Plan's 'North-Western Front'. Simultaneously other elements destroyed Plan bases south and southeast of the town. The combined Plan-Fapla protection force which were well settled in and around the town was driven off after a brief attack on their tanks and infantry. The main force then moved south and eastwards pushing the Fapla force at Mongua out of its way.

The attack on Ongiva took place on 26 August 1981. The town was taken on 28 August after another combined Plan-Fapla force, entrenched in and around the town, had been defeated. Several Soviet officers were killed during this battle and one warrant officer taken prisoner. Plan facilities in and around Ongiva were destroyed and the operation ended on 10 September 1981.

Operation Protea was the biggest mechanized operation by the SA Army since World War II. The security forces lost ten men to the more than 1 000 casualties suffered by Plan and Fapla. Among the approximate 4 000 tonnes of seized equipment were several tanks and armoured cars, a large quantity of anti-tank guns and about 200 logistic vehicles.

Charles Lloyd launched his next big operation, Daisy, on 1 November 1981. Just as Operation Protea was a result of the information collected during the preceding operations, Protea in its turn provided the information that gave rise to Daisy.

A mechanized force penetrated to the deepest point reached since the Angolan civil war. Objectives were attacked at Bambi and Chetaquera. Although no clashes took place with Fapla's ground forces a number of MiG 21 fighter aircraft had encounters with the South African Air Force. A MiG was shot down. The operation ended on 20 November 1981.

At the beginning of 1982 it became clear that Plan was preparing to open a new front in the Kaokoland. Operation Super was launched as a countermeasure. Reconnaissance elements of 32 Battalion were sent in to locate Plan cadres who were ready to infiltrate the area. About 250 cadres were found at an assembly area near the town of Iona, in the south-west of Angola, whence the infiltration was scheduled to begin. A force consisting of seventy-five troops were flown there to launch a blitz attack. Of these, a force of thirty troops was deployed as stopper groups while the remaining main force of forty-five men executed the attack. In spite of enjoying overwhelming numerical superiority, the enemy was completely surprised and overpowered; altogether 201 were killed while only two men of 32 Battalion were lightly wounded. A large quantity of ammunition and weapons was seized.

From a professional point of view this operation delivered proof of the excellent combat capabilities of the lower level commanders and troops. Capt Jan Hougaard was in command.

The next operation, Meebos, was executed during July and August 1982 and consisted of a number of air and ground attacks on Plan's command and control structures. Of the enemy forces 345 were killed and Plan's so-called 'east front' headquarters at Mupa was destroyed before it could be moved. The security forces lost 29 men, 15 of whom died when a Puma helicopter was shot down.

His last operation, Phoenix, in February 1983, was actually Charles Lloyd's internal counteraction against a Plan crossborder operation into South West.

During the first half of February Plan started a new deliberate wave of infiltration. On 13 February a special unit of about 1 700 Plan members, who were divided into different companies, began its infiltration into Ovambo. The first important confrontation took place on 15 February and 15 cadres were killed. Gen Lloyd's counteraction (Phoenix) was extremely successful and when it ended on 13 April

1983 the enemy had lost 309 men and the security forces 27.[1]

In terms of military science and for this type of war, Phoenix was, in my opinion, an excellent performance. A counterinsurgency defensive operation such as this one is usually much more difficult than offensive operations. And in this case we were concerned with a preplanned infiltration of insurgents. It happened over a vast area as flat as a table top and covered in thick African bush. The enemy were trained infiltrators experienced in guerrilla tactics and techniques; and they knew the terrain. To have stopped and contained them, and then sent them off with heavy losses was an exceptional achievement. It required professional knowledge, ingenuity, guts and willpower.

At this time my son, Martin, was doing his national service. He was at the Infantry School at Oudtshoorn during 1983, and a member of 32 Battalion in South West during 1984. He had in the meantime joined the Permanent Force.

I now come to my personal experiences and impressions.

During Operation Protea I joined the fighting forces on D-day minus one, in August 1981. One of my experiences was to watch the first operational firing of the new 127 mm multiple rocket launchers (MRL's) from their launching positions. I had a personal interest in this new artillery acquisition as I had also observed experimental firing of the weapon during the project stage a few years earlier. Armscor had researched and developed this system and made it available to the SA Army in double-quick time to counteract the Soviet BM-21 122 mm MRL (Stalin organ), that we had encountered for the first time in Operation Savannah. Now we had a weapon system that was better than its Soviet counterpart.

I spent the night at tactical headquarters. The next morning I arrived at Xangongo after the mopping-up phase of the battle had almost been completed. Smoke was still curling skywards. The knocked-out Russian tanks drew my attention. They made me think of the enemy guns that the English had seized during the Crimean War. The metal from those guns was used in the minting of the well-known decoration for bravery, the Victoria Cross.

I immediately radioed Brig Witkop Badenhorst and told him to have one of the tanks recovered to Oshakati. I would tell him why later. He was commander of Sector 10 and an outstanding example of the military tradition that we still find in the SA Defence Force. He is the kind of man who says: 'If my captain says make smoke, I make smoke' and 'The commander's wish is my command.' His actions on that winter's day in 1981 made possible the minting of a new South African medal ten years later. Copper from the T34/85 tank, which was shot out at Xangongo, formed a small part of the content of the new *Southern Africa Medal.* It gives recognition to those members of the South African Defence Force and auxiliary services who participated in operations outside the borders of the RSA from 1 April 1976 and who during such service were in danger of being killed, wounded or taken prisoner.

After that I made a quick visit to a place with the name of Peu-Peu to find out first hand what had happened during the fighting there. The commander of the responsible battle group was my old friend from the Sceptic days, Cmdt Chris Serfontein.

During the helicopter flight to Peu-Peu I saw a soccer stadium in Xangongo. It reminded me of the officer commanding 32 Battalion, Cmdt Deon Ferreira. In the period preceding Operation Protea, he had conducted long drawn-out area operations with his troops against Plan in the region immediately north of the border near Ongiva. Over a distance, in some strange way or another, he established a sort of understanding with the Fapla commander in the town. He actually wrote him a letter or two. This personal interaction prevented unintentional clashes between their forces.

At the time I once or twice told Deon to arrange a soccer game against them. We were not really out to pick a fight with the Angolans and if Gen Maritz and Maj Edwards could have negotiated a cease-fire in 1902 at O'Kiep during the Anglo-Boer war to play a game of rugby, why couldn't Deon Ferreira play a game of soccer at Ongiva? He thought I was joking and I left it at that.

Back to the stadium at Xangongo. Returning from Peu-Peu I told the commander of the garrison force, Cmdt Roland de Vries, to arrange a soccer game between the South African troops and the locals at the stadium. This would contribute towards normalizing the situation and eliminating unnecessary suspicion.

In the beginning, when they were establishing themselves at Xangongo, Roland de Vries struggled to make proper contact on an organized basis with the local population. Just before the fighting in the town, pamphlets were dropped in which the locals were requested to evacuate the area so as to escape injury. However, they hesitated to return, because they did not realize that the fighting was completely over.

We spent the night in a house which was used by the Soviets as an office block. It was decorated with posters of the Soviet political structure and photographs of its leaders. The previous occupants also left behind some vodka and other Russian drinks. Roland de Vries had to leave early the next morning to do his bit in the next phase of the operation and handed over to Maj Dawid Mentz. My personal staff officer, Col Peter Gagiano, and I likewise had to join Cmdt Eddie Viljoen's battle group on its way to Mongua and Mupa. So Dawid Mentz was assigned the job of improving relations with the locals and to organize the soccer game. The next morning the town's inhabitants began to return.

Little did I know where all this would lead. I was told much later that Xangongo just happened to be the champions of Angola's Kunene Province. They accepted the challenge with enthusiasm. What our men thought was going to be an informal social game turned out to be a proper match with Xangongo in full club colours. As far as I can remember Xangongo beat them 1-0.

This was, for the time being, one of those typical make-war-but-don't-say-a-thing-operations, which I described in a previous chapter. But at a certain stage a media contingent had been invited to visit the operational scene. It included a sightseeing tour of Xangongo and environs. By this time I was already far away.

On their way back to the aircraft to depart for their next port of call, the journalists happened to pass by the stadium while the game was in full swing. One or two of them caught a glimpse of the activity at the stadium and requested to be taken there to have a look. That was not a problem.

Afterwards, when the news of the operation broke for the first time in the public media, a photograph of this soccer game was given a place of prominence in a number of newspapers.

Now, as happens all over the world during times of war, it is always the other side that shoots first, fights an unjust war, bombards hospitals and schools and mistreats the local civilian population. And this was no exception, especially during the Security Council meeting of 29 August 1981. The South African Ambassador to the UN, Mr Riaan Eksteen, refuted accusations of brutality.

On 10 September 1981 the Minister of Foreign Affairs and Information, Mr Pik Botha, reported on this matter by way of a circular. Part of it read as follows:

> Mention was also made (by the South African Ambassador) of the

fact that during the recent actions against Swapo terrorists South Africa gave assistance to the local population of Angola in various fields. In this respect the reports of four journalists who had been taken to the operational theatre by the SA Defence Force made a major contribution to confirm the facts given in Ambassador Eksteen's address. Two of the biggest television networks, for example, during their new programmes later in the evening, screened films of the soccer game between a defence side and members of the local Angolan population. Precisely this fact was mentioned that afternoon by Ambassador Eksteen in his address.

In the meantime I had arrived at the tactical headquarters at Mupa. Around 27 August 1981 Deon Ferreira, Eddie Viljoen, Cmdt Vos Benade, Maj Smiley van Zyl, the leader of the mobile air operations team, and I were listening to radio conversations, *inter alia* between Lt Thinus van Staden and a Telstar. The Telstar was a Bosbok aircraft used as a radio relay station. Its pilot was Lt Hattingh, younger brother of Maj Vink Hattingh. Some of the radio messages had us all guessing.

At this stage Chris Serfontein and his battle group had already attacked Ongiva. Cmdt James Hills was north of Ongiva with three 32 Battalion companies. They served as stopper groups. Lt van Staden was in command of one of these groups.

Around this time, vehicles and people were moving in Thinus's direction. At this point there was confusion over precisely who and what they were. We discussed it among ourselves. There were reports to the effect that they were intelligence personnel who were towing seized vehicles out of Ongiva, and others that they were people who had reacted on the warning that non-military persons were to evacuate Ongiva to avoid getting involved in the fighting. We were trying to make sense of this information.

The 23-year-old Lt van Staden gets full marks for calm courage and battle discipline throughout the confusion. What followed was a number of exceptional person-to-person contacts with Faplas during which one or both parties did not know who the other was. Thinus was also involved here. This included unorthodox close-range skirmishes in which hardware such as Soviet BM 21s, PT 76 tanks and BRDM armoured vehicles were used.

The details are as follows: Thinus and his men heard the noise of approaching vehicles. He reported the information to Telstar and received the reply that they were seized vehicles being brought out of Ongiva by our intelligence personnel. His mind was put to rest when he saw two Land Rovers, one white and one blue, followed by heavy logistic vehicles. But he noticed that the people in the Land Rovers and the other vehicles were all wearing camouflage dress, not the South African browns. He conveyed this information to the Bosbok but was told not to worry. He related the story as follows. 'Hills told me, "Just show them where to park." As he had to have a better picture of the situation than me, I walked into the middle of the road, and pointed to the left. The Land Rovers stopped, the passengers got out and began directing the rest of the vehicles to pull off and stop under the trees.'

At this stage his sergeant eased up to him inconspicuously and hissed:

'They're Fapla's!'

Thinus realized that the Angolans had mistaken his black troops in camouflage dress for their own troops and Cuban Officers. He walked over to the radio as nonchalantly as possible and told the Bosbok: 'Hey, we've got a problem here ...' Then he received the order to withdraw from the situation. A while later something happened that would strike the headlines all over the world. In 1992 Thinus van Staden described the event in a manuscript as follows:

> I took one platoon, and when we found the tracks I knew they were too narrow for a tank. We were running along the tracks when we came on a Russian-made Jeep. It was very clean, and I reckoned it was a Fapla commander's vehicle. I left one section to guard it and continued on the tracks with two sections. We kept finding more and more abandoned vehicles, and I kept leaving troops. We were down to one section when we ran into an ambush from our right. We attacked immediately. We shot three people there. Four others ran north. We shot three more, and the fourth escaped.
>
> The second body I checked was wearing brand-new Fapla camo, and had a new AK 47. When I turned him over I was stunned to see that it was a white man, and I instinctively knew that he was a Russian. I left six more troops there and, with Lt Leon Naudé and two troops, carried on running down the tracks in the dark. Then we saw the two tanks – they were actually PT 76's – and I climbed on one with a grenade and listened for anyone inside, but it was

> deserted. I radioed back to where I'd left the two platoons and told them to come up and guard the tanks.
>
> Lt Naudé, the two troops and I headed back to the RV (rendezvous – predetermined meeting place) to bring a section up. On the way we passed a kraal and detoured slightly out of the way of some bushes next to it. I was leading, followed by Naudé and the two troops. We were about two or three metres from the bushes when we drew fire. We immediately returned fire, advanced and found two bodies. One of them was white, and he turned out to be the Russian colonel in charge of Ongiva.
>
> I was kneeling, examining the body, when Lt Naudé shouted at someone not to move. I jumped up and looked over the kraal fence to see three bodies in Fapla uniforms, one still moving. I jumped over the fence and took the weapon away from him, then saw to my horror that the other two were women, both of them dead. The man, a warrant officer mechanic, was uninjured ...

The man was Sgt-Maj Nikolai Pestretsov who was then taken prisoner. Brig Ben Roos looked after him for four or five months. He was later exchanged for Sapper Johan van der Mescht, a South African POW held by the Angolans.

Up to this time, most political commentators had doubted our allegations that there were Russian military personnel in remote parts of Angola together with Fapla and Plan.

The manuscript to which I refer above may possibly be published as a book about Pestretsov's and Thinus's life stories and how their paths eventually converged.

Before Operation Daisy started, I had decided to accompany the force from the beginning, and if at all possible, to the end.

At the beginning of November 1981 I joined the battle group when they started their northward movement. I was surprised to bump into freelance journalist, Al J Venter. This supports my contention that, if a journalist has the time, the Defence Force is open to the possibility of letting him tag along, even during operations, and crossborder operations at that.

This was one of the less successful operations. Seen from a professional point of view it was very well executed in terms of doctrine, drills and procedures but few results were produced as the cadres had mostly evacuated their bases before we could reach them. Some enemy war material was seized.

However, disappointing success or successful disappointment, this operation also produced its drama and humour.

I travelled in Cmdt Roland de Vries's command Ratel. The journey was wearisome. The bush was thick, the sand was loose with dust hanging thick in the air on the long road to the north. The movement was executed in 'legs' from halting place to halting place. Each Ratel carried three key persons: the driver, the gunner and the vehicle commander. Sometimes the Ratel crew members swopped places to break the monotony. The driver would become the gunner, the gunner the vehicle commander, etc. Everyone performs certain duties. The vehicle commander, for example, directs the driver over the intercom. The sort of language he would use, was: 'No, go left, man! Pass to the left of that tree! No, now right! Watch out for that bloody donga!' or the language may even have been stronger.

At one of the halts Maj Charl Naudé, who was travelling in the Ratel right behind ours, came over to say that he had just had an extremely difficult leg. The chaplain had been travelling in his vehicle.

Charl explained to me that when they changed round before the previous leg he became the vehicle commander and the chaplain became the driver. And then he asked with a weary smile. 'General, do you know how difficult it is to explain to a chaplain exactly how he should really drive?'

I still owe him an answer. By the time we arrived at the area of the objective, I had told Roland a few times quietly just between the two of us that in my judgment the Ratels were packed too closely. They should spread out more, especially during stops.

There was always a tendency to bunch up and to park in straight lines. This made a large number of vehicles a good target especially from the air. My main worry was not that we were deviating from textbook doctrine; there was a real danger as we were beginning to move out of our own radar cover. In other words we could not really expect our own air force to operate against enemy aircraft in that area. At the same time we were moving in under the Angolan radar cover which made us more vulnerable to the MiGs.

Drama. Something happened that drew the attention of the international media. It became clear that my cautioning had not been unfounded. The day after I left the battle group to return to South West, Maj Johan Rankin with his Mirage F1CZ no 213 shot down a MiG 21 in that area. Eleven months later Johan again aroused the envy of his mates, the other fighter pilots, by shooting down another MiG. It happened in the same general area. On this occasion he was flying as an escort in his F1CZ no 203 when he was attacked by MiGs.

The shooting down of the MiG was not the only piece of drama.

In the meantime our forces had eventually reached their objective and engaged the enemy. In fact there was no real fighting, but mopping up the area to collect all the enemy equipment was a tiresome activity, as usual.

While this was in progress Al Venter, Maj Anderson, of Ngana Pest control fame, and I were talking together. A Buffel stacked with enemy ammunition stood about twenty metres away. Some of the ammunition looked the worse for wear to me. And in the way that thoughts go through one's mind, I asked myself, what would I do if this unstable pile of ammunition suddenly started to explode after all the bumps, heat and friction?

One would surely have to get the vehicle away from its position as there were so many of our own people moving around in its vicinity, including ourselves. I was in fact thinking, yes, Geldenhuys, what an embarrassment it would be if you had to drive the vehicle but couldn't remember how to start it up. But it was only one of those many flashes that goes through one's head.

We were still talking when a loud bang shook the air, immediately followed by others. As I was still concerned about whether we were sufficiently spread out against air attack, I thought instantly, there you have it, probably something coming from a MiG. When I did not immediately hear aircraft or see bombs or rockets falling around us, I realized that it had to be something else.

And indeed, it was something else. Rockets and other ammunition lying on that Buffel had spontaneously started to explode one after the other. In spite of having visualized myself taking action in such a situation, Andy had already jumped up and was running to the vehicle. He started it and drove off with great speed while the different types of ammunition produced red flames and black and white smoke. He parked it far away from everybody.

Andy could think on his feet. And he did not scare easily. He was awarded the Honoris Crux for this deed of bravery. He had put his own life in danger for the safety of others.

The next transborder operation took place in 1983 when George Meiring had just taken over from Charles Lloyd: Operation Askari. Towards the end of 1983 it became apparant that Plan was preparing for a large-scale infiltration early in 1984. The new GOC launched Operation Askari on 6 December 1983 with a number of ground and air attacks aimed mainly at disrupting Plan's logistic infrastructure. Although the attacks were concentrated on Plan, the Fapla forces also got involved in the fighting.

Four mechanized battle groups of 500 men each attacked specific targets, while small infantry groups executed area operations in the border region.

The biggest clash with Fapla took place on 3 January 1984: its eleventh brigade and two Cuban battalions came to Plan's assistance when its headquarters and base five kilometres from Cuvelai were being attacked. But this force was beaten off after they had lost 324 men; most of the security force's 24 losses during Operation Askari fell during this encounter.

The officer commanding 32 Battalion at this stage was Cmdt Eddie Viljoen. His call-sign, neither very original nor good for radio security, was EV, Echo Victor. His people called him Big Daddy. He tells many stories. I was not involved in this Operation Askari saga, but would like to tell it because it is one of his best:

Our forces attacked Cuvelai in January 1984 and hundreds of Faplas scattered in groups, heading for the safety of Techamutete. The town was occupied by a Fapla battalion. One rainy evening, at about 20:00, a Fapla lieutenant and his sergeant, looking for shelter, reported to the sentries at Techamutete. The sentries took them to the commander at his headquarters.

He was a sturdy man of medium height. His stern expression was emphasized by an equally formidable moustache. Other people were also standing around, among whom a tall chap with a drooping Mexican moustache.

The new arrivals sat down and relaxed, each with a mug of warm coffee. They were feeling quite happy and safe now that they were back with their comrades. In silence the comrades stared at the two, drinking coffee and smoking their cigarettes. Eventually the sergeant became somewhat fidgety. He whispered something to his lieutenant every now and again. The lieutenant coughed and asked the comrades which Fapla unit they belonged to. When they were told that they were not with Fapla, their eyes met for a brief moment.

The lieutenant cleared his throat again and asked if the comrades were Cubans. At the negative reply the two sat up, still holding the mugs of coffee.

Again they conferred in whispers and then the clearly worried lieutenant asked in a high-pitched voice whether their hosts were perhaps Russian. No, came the reply. The hosts were staring at them. Only the falling rain broke the silence. Now they were obviously puzzled and deeply afraid.

The lieutenant came with a last, half-pleading enquiry: 'Well, if you are not Fapla and if you are neither Cubans nor Russians, are you Germans then?' With open mouths and fear in their eyes they waited for the reply. Silence. The atmosphere was tense. The one with the droopy moustache, Koos Krokodil,[2] could no longer control himself. He loudly told the two that their hosts were South Africans.

Big Daddy himself recalls:

> 32 Battalion was assigned to occupy the area north of Cuvelai from an easterly direction. We had to launch area operations against Plan bases. The aim was to prevent large scale infiltrations from this area to the south.
>
> We had instructions to avoid contact with Fapla at Techamutete. But in the early hours of 23 December 1983 we sent troops to set up an ambush on the road between Cuvelai and Techamutete. When the ambush troops moved in they heard talking and the clanging of equipment. A skirmish followed and we heard a noise that sounded like elephant breaking through bush.
>
> Then the mystery was cleared up, we hadn't had a brush with elephants or a stray group of Fapla soldiers. We had, in fact, run into an entire Fapla battalion which was occupying their main defensive position in that area. The whole Fapla battalion, including its troops in Techamutete, had taken flight and left all their equipment behind. By 09:00 we had three of our 32 Battalion companies, an 81 mm mortar section, and all the seized Fapla weaponry, deployed in and around Techamutete.
>
> This is how it came about that literally hundreds of Faplas who fled to Techamutete, were welcomed by the black Portuguese-speaking 32 Battalion troops dressed in their traditional camouflage. The Faplas realized only later, to their surprise, that the men of 32 who now occupied Techamutete were not fellow Faplas or Plan members.
>
> Now to return to our headquarters at Techamutete and our two guests: The sound of two tin coffee mugs falling and the two men getting to their feet was all that disturbed the silence. The two halfheartedly looked at their weapons leaning against the wall, but

I could see that they were not very keen to make a grab for them at that moment.

The lieutenant then removed the binoculars hanging around his neck and meekly handed them over to me. The scene resembled a ceremony concluding a peace treaty.

Everyone joined in the laughter which reached a crescendo when the two were escorted to the 'cells'.

It would appear that the Fapla discipline was not of a high standard, because the Fapla sergeant accused his lieutenant in the strongest words that his powers of judgment left much to be desired!

Eddie had them properly disarmed and debriefed, saw to their needs and told them they could go.

For once *friction de guerre* was not on Fapla's side, the joke was on them.

Operation Askari was the last operation of its kind and ended on 3 January 1984. Although it was not the intention, the operation convinced Angola to engage in discussions with South Africa over a cessation of hostilities in southern Angola. Some analysts regarded this as the most important result of the operation. The talks in which I was involved were held in Lusaka and culminated in the signing of the Lusaka Agreement during February 1984 in terms of which, *inter alia*, the South African troops still in Angola after the operation had to be withdrawn.

It was during these discussions that Pik Botha delivered his well-known 'Boer War' address. Angola undertook to ensure that no Swapo insurgents, Cuban forces or conventional weapons, such as tanks and guns, would be allowed in the area evacuated by our forces. This was the so-called area in question or area in dispute. A joint monitoring commission (JMC) would monitor the execution of the operative terms of the agreement.

The area was systematically cleared by zones – first the northernmost part of the area, thereafter the zone immediately south of it and then the zone still further south, and so on, until the border was reached. The next zone was tackled only after the JMC had satisfied itself that the previous zone had been cleared in terms of the agreement. The evacuation was completed in toto only during April 1985.

What is not well known is that the South African troops, as we had announced, had already been south of the border for quite a while before the agreement was signed. But it appeared that the parties concerned refused to believe us; we actually had to send troops back into Angola so that we could visibly withdraw them in terms of the agreement!

In many respects the execution of the Lusaka Agreement was, for me, one big frustration. The signing of the Nkomati Accord a short while afterwards, in which I was not involved, and the signing of the Lusaka Agreement were *per se* political successes. It caused South Africa to be seen in a more positive light internationally. It also contributed towards enabling the State President, Mr P W Botha, to visit Europe and personally put South Africa's case to other presidents and premiers. But inasmuch as it affected the actual security situation in South West and Angola, it was like any other agreement – only a piece of paper.

Whatever is agreed to on paper and duly signed must still be made to work in practice. I had a key role to play in making the Lusaka agreement succeed and for that I needed patience, tolerance and steadfastness. But history has proved that the agreement made little or no difference to the war and peace situation in Angola.

Sometimes we had intelligence of Swapo activities in the forbidden area in contravention of the agreement. But Swapo could not, technically speaking, violate the Lusaka Agreement as it was not a signatory. It was the Angolan government who undertook to see to it that Swapo did not enter into the area in dispute. We therefore had to address such information to the Angolan government for action. In practice it meant that we first had to submit it to the Angolan component at the JMC. However, they and others always found one or other argument for simply ignoring the irregularities.

Sometimes, for example, they would allege that our information lacked credibility. If we then presented confirmed and irrebuttable information of, let us say, Swapo members in the area moving north, we would hear at the JMC that it was unnecessary to make a fuss as they were moving north and they were trying to get out of the area, and surely there could be nothing wrong with that.

Afterwards we would come up with confirmed information that Swapo was moving south in the forbidden area; then we would hear again that if they were moving south, they were on their way to Namibia; of course, you wouldn't want to complain about that!

If we got information, for argument's sake, of twenty Swapo members moving east or west, the excuse would be, look, there are only twenty, do you really want to make a big issue over a measly twenty men?

If we gave them information about a hundred Swapo soldiers in the area, then they would say, yes but those men have not yet received the message; or, even more irritatingly, they would find some argument to the effect that we were really to blame for everything, and that they saw it in a very serious light.

In South Africa towards August-September 1992, I was once again reminded of this type of situation. It was when everybody was praying for peace, preaching against violence, pleading for tolerance and begging for mutual understanding when the ANC-SACP-Cosatu-alliance (African National Congress, SA Communist Party, Congress of South African Trade Unions) announced in harsh language that they were going to march on Bisho in the Ciskei to occupy it and to insist on the removal of the president. They were publicly advised from a variety of sources not to go ahead with their operation; it was not in the spirit of the time, it could seriously harm the negotiation process and it could create a climate for violence. But on 7 September they did it. It led to violence. About 23 people or more got killed and 188 or more were injured.

Now, as in 1984–85, the immediate reaction of spokesmen of the alliance was that the incident once again demonstrated that the government of South Africa was not seriously applying itself to creating a favourable climate for negotiations.

At the JMC, too, we continued to wrestle; not that our patience wasn't taxed to the extreme. I must say that they did agree that certain incidents constituted definite violations of the agreement. These were then registered, but that did not mean that something would be done about it.

Our reports of irregularities were not intended to embarrass anybody; we did not do it to wreck the agreement or cause delays; and we did not try to play the good-guy/bad-guy game. We merely followed conventional practices and used the mechanisms and procedures established in terms of the Lusaka Agreement – with the purpose of making it work. According to the agreement the area in dispute had to be demilitarized as prescribed. If successfully done, it would have created a vast war-free zone.

During July 1984 we had confirmed intelligence of the presence of troops and specific military hardware such as anti-aircraft guns, anti-aircraft missile systems (SAMs), radar systems and T55 tanks at

Techamutete in contravention of the Lusaka Agreement.

We reported it to the JMC in the prescribed manner and requested it to be officially and formally registered as a violation of the agreement; also that it should be investigated so that corrective action could be taken. Special provision had been made in the agreement for joint investigation by SA Defence Force-Fapla patrols in such eventualities.

Once again our information was not accepted and we could not persuade the committee to investigate the matter. As a last resort we flew a photo reconnaissance mission over the area concerned on 12 August, went back to the JMC, and substantiated our allegations with air photos. It could not be, and was not, disputed. Then came the turnaround propaganda twist again, which would land us in trouble because the photo reconnaissance flight was a transgression of the agreement!

This caused me no end of frustration. Our information about the weapon systems was rejected. We provided evidence and proved our claims. And now we were in trouble about the way in which we did it – and our complaint was shoved into the background!

The other parties made such a fuss over the flight that it became virtually the main point on the agenda of a meeting between Minister Pik Botha and Minister Rodrigues of Angola.

Pik Botha stated South Africa's case as follows:

> The South African action was necessary to investigate reports obtained from Swapo prisoners of substantial Swapo activities in the area in question as well as information that the MPLA was in the process of building up its forces in contravention of the spirit of the Lusaka Agreement and the assurances which the United States gave South Africa in January 1984, that Angola would not take advantage of the disengagement process to the detriment of the security of South West Africa. Because of the importance of these allegations for mutual confidence and the continuation of the Lusaka Agreement, it was considered imperative to investigate these reports.
>
> The South African Government has been shocked to learn that Angola has indeed deployed modern armaments in the area which cannot possibly be used against Unita and which must therefore be construed as encouragement of and protection for Swapo's designs to increase its violence against South West Africa and to return to Angola with impunity. South Africa has also learned to its dismay

that a major southward movement of Swapo terrorists through the area in question is at present under way.

The Angolan accusations kicked up so much dust and created such sinister perceptions that the facts disappeared among the clouds of propaganda. The truth was that they were the culprits: by the end of August they were responsible for as many as 63 violations of the agreement, jointly and formally registered by the two parties of the JMC, while only three breaches by South Africa were recorded in the same fashion, including the flight which confirmed a serious Angolan violation.

Our frustrations will perhaps be better understood if I draw comparisons with more recent events. While we were being branded as the bad guys during 1984, we appealed: but what about the 63-3 points on the scoreboard?! Nothing. In the South Africa of the early 1990s we had a similar scoreboard of breaches of the National Peace Accord; now one could ask again, what about that? Perhaps the Peace Secretariat should publicise their successes more often.

I personally pleaded that we should form the JMC into a permanent institution and that the area in question should become a peace zone; but the Angolans would not accept it.

To conclude the JMC saga: after the withdrawal of the South African forces from Angola during April 1985, Plan exploited the situation and started anew to operate across the border from their bases in Angola.

This time the joke was on us.

The security forces were left no option but to resume their operations.

During one of the sessions of the JMC I unexpectedly ran into my son Martin. He was involved in the joint South African-Angolan patrol. He participated in other operations too.

Probably one of the most fearless soldiers South Africa ever produced, Col Jan Breytenbach, relates an incident during such an operation:

> At one time a company conducting operations up the Cubango River, took Klepper kayaks with them to assist in the evacuation of the wounded or sick. The theory, at least, was that the wounded or sick would be canoed downstream, with a paddler plus a doctor per craft.
>
> The problem was that movement on the tracks and landing sites

up and down the river had become dicey, because the whole area had been indiscriminately booby trapped by both Unita and Fapla.

The theory was fine, but as the saying goes, the proof of the pudding is always in the eating.

The company was operating upstream at maximum range, when both Lieutenant Martin Geldenhuys ... and a black sergeant became very ill, requiring evacuation. As planned for in such an eventuality a Klepper was assembled and prepared to take the patients downstream that night.

At the last moment a slightly more than just eccentric Lebanese sergeant, an inveterate collector of snakes, handed them a rucksack containing a selection of live ones to take back to Cachueca.

They pulled away from the bank and began paddling, the going, at first, being good. What they didn't realize, though, was that there were violent rapids downstream. Now, shooting rapids in kayaks by daylight can be terrifying enough, but to unexpectedly run into them in pitch darkness is petrifying, and an unfailing recipe for disaster.

When they did hit the rapids, all they could do was to hope that they would not be smashed against the rocks, against which they were cannoning like snooker balls. The inevitable happened, the Klepper overturned and was smashed by the raging waters. The occupants, two of them very sick men, found themselves struggling for their lives to get ashore, their rifles, food, medicine and the radio having sunk to the bottom, while the remains of the canoe had disappeared downstream along with the snakes – much to the later disgust of their Lebanese owner. After much buffeting by the turbulent waters, they finally dragged themselves ashore in the calmer shallows below the rapids. All they were left with was the clothes they stood up in and their World War II style haversacks.

With the radio gone they could not ask for assistance, so they had no option but to painfully bundu bash their way towards Cachueca, avoiding the river bank because of mines.

Eventually their boots gave in, forcing them to bind their feet with tree bark as a protection against thorns, sharp twigs and branches. After many days of nightmare marching they finally staggered, starving and on their last legs, into Cachueca, clothes falling off their backs and their feet cut to ribbons.[3]

After the Lusaka Agreement, as I have said, we had to continue with our operations just as before.

During Operation Boswilger which started on 29 June 1985 and ended 48 hours later, we followed Plan cadres' tracks right to their bases in three different parts of Angola. On the first day 43 were killed and one captured in 23 separate contacts; on the second day 14 fell and four were taken prisoner during 13 skirmishes. Thereafter the security forces withdrew across the border.

To conclude my story of this period of the border war, I go back briefly to the Lusaka Agreement. If one did not crack a joke or two along the JMC road, weaving through one frustration after the other, you would probably have fallen by the wayside.

Col Dippies Dippenaar of Smokeshell fame was the first South African co-chairman of the JMC. He was relieved during April 1984 at Ongiva, the site of the JMC at that stage, by Col Piet Hall, the ex-commanding officer of the Bushman battalion in the western Caprivi.

There was little signals traffic to Ongiva for a couple of weeks because continuous high level discussions were taking place which affected the position of the JMC. Finality had not been reached yet and we were all waiting to hear what would be decided. Only then could we send Piet Hall new instructions.

Piet in the meantime was feeling very lonely and forgotten, and sent a signal to Army Headquarters asking for guidelines. So Army Headquarters explained the situation to him and told him to wait.

Another week or two went by. Piet remained intensely frustrated. I could understand his impatience. I had had a good taste of it myself. He complained that Plan members who had been killed in the area in dispute had been wearing Fapla uniforms. Then the Angolans replied that they came from the pre-JMC period. Then, when Swapo soldiers with brand-new Fapla uniforms got killed, the Angolans accused us of 'bad form' as it is 'not in good taste' to examine such clothing; 'not in the true spirit of the agreement'; and then they complained that our troops tortured the local population and damaged their property. He complained that when joint RSA-Angolan patrols investigated alleged breaches of the agreement, the Angolans ran out of fuel, rations and water before they got to the place to be examined and could not go any further.

To keep occupied, Piet carved Makalani palm twigs with his Southern Cross Fund pocket knife. He was really down in the dumps. Fed up.

The next time he sent his signal directly to me and begged me to tell him what to do. I replied by signal HLeër (D OPS) 309/1 OP SCLERA

DD 1 JUN 84. I told him again that I understood his frustrations, that he must hang in there; we were still waiting for the results of negotiations ourselves. He should do as he saw fit; as soon as I knew more I would inform him and send new instructions.

I ended the message with:

'Don't be too obstinate. Maintain good relations.

THERE'S A BONUS IN YOUR FUTURE!'

12

INFORMATION AND DISINFORMATION
'The massacred village'

The crossborder operations up to 1985 were neccessary and well executed. I still believe, though, that the accumulated effect of relentless day to day operations south of the border was vital for our overall success. These operations continued and I wanted to know first-hand what was going on.

Because Kaokoland was one of the regions we always wanted to keep free of insurgency, and as there were definite indications that it was going to be infiltrated, I wanted to get into the picture at an early stage. But that you cannot do if you remain stuck in your office in Pretoria.

So I left for the operational area early in 1982. Whenever I went on such trips, I informed the GOC SWA Command in detail well in advance. The GOC himself or his representative would then accompany me. I never gave direct instructions to the GOC's subordinate commanders.

On this occasion, my personal staff officer could not accompany me and I took Col Johann Sonnekus with me, a senior operational staff officer of Army Headquarters.

Cmdt Chris Bouwer was the commander in the Kaokoland. He briefed me on the current situation in his area and the region across the border. He explained what the insurgents were up to and what his men were doing about it. He also described what had happened during an enemy ambush shortly before my visit.

I made further enquiries. He explained to me that the infiltrators were doing this and that which they planned to counter by doing so and so. Then I asked him: 'Where do they come from?' He answered.

My next question was: 'Who is their commander?' That he did not know off-hand. But his intelligence officer, Capt Dave Drew, did. Let us say Dave said his name was Jimmy. What is the significance of knowing the enemy commander as a person?

Well, before I continue, I must first sound a warning, one that I myself should heed: one must always guard against textbook wisdom and clever notions developed theoretically from a distance. But I nevertheless said to him:

> One cannot merely study enemy doctrines and techniques and then adjust your own. Then you make the war a competition between rivals who try to outdo one another at developing better doctrines and techniques. And this is not all that matters. One cannot merely say that insurgents do this and that, because they have a commander and a political commissar who consider objectives, targets and actions, and lay down priorities. It is Jimmy who sent infiltrators into that region, Jimmy who possibly even ordered the ambush and who specified approximately where it should be laid. It is not normally the insurgents themselves who decide. The word insurgents is a vague collective concept. It is the man, Jimmy, who makes the decisions.

I asked him to start thinking about what Jimmy would do next.

I am not mentioning this reasoning because Chris needed the coaching. He is a highly competent officer. I am doing so to provide a background for stories I will soon come to.

The next important point of discussion which cropped up between Chris and me, was the confirmed presence of enemy at a base across the border, near Iona. I asked him why he had not, despite all the information available to him, attacked the base (or requested authorization to do so in the absence of delegated powers) or had it attacked by other own-forces if they themselves lacked the force levels.

His answer, which had merit, came down to this: the enemy at that base come and go. Chris and his men had decided to wait for the right moment when the largest possible number of enemy would be there.

I then gave him a personal opinion, but it was based on a fair amount of experience: it is difficult to determine when that moment will come and often you only hear of it when it has come and gone. And in addition, your information sometimes dries up for a while, or something unforseen happens which disturbs the intelligence picture and then you have to start all over again. If you are sure of you intelligence now, do it now.

A number of days after my visit the operation was launched under the command of the experienced bush fighter, Capt Jan Hougaard of 32 Battalion. It was Operation Super – a resounding success.

I heard perchance afterwards what had happened during the time between our visit and the day of the operation. Back in Pretoria, as befits a good staff officer, Johann Sonnekus followed up and enquired from HQ SWA Command what was being done about the enemy base at Iona.

I do not mind if lower level commanders do not accept my advice; their immediate commanders may not like it either, and in any case, one should not try to fight a commandant's war from Pretoria. But when your advice is not accepted, at least you want the assurance that it had been well considered and that there were more or less good reasons why they had decided otherwise.

Sonnie's enquiry and the exchange of signals that followed apparently contributed towards finally deciding to launch the operation.

This story illustrates that the degree of influence a commander exerts depends much on the efficiency of his staff officers. As a result of this and other operational incidents I later appointed Johann Sonnekus as my personal staff officer.

A year or so later I found myself in Kaokoland again. The commander there now was my old friend of Ngana Pest Control and Operation Daisy, Cmdt Anderson, and the pattern of my previous visit virtually repeated itself.

This time again I emphasized that an operational commander should make it his personal aim intellectually to outwit his opposing commander. I called it the 'personalization of operations'. And just as Operation Super had been launched a year earlier, after my visit to Chris Bouwer, Andy also soon afterwards conducted a successful operation against an enemy base.

Insurgents managed only occasionally and for brief periods to infiltrate the Kaokoland.

My visits to the Kaokoland were followed by similar visits to the Kavango a few times during 1984 and 1985.

Col Deon Ferreira was now the commander of Sector 20, the Kavango and Bushmanland. At one time there were three groups of insurgents in the Kavango. Their presence was not in line with our strategy, as we aimed to confine insurgency to Ovambo only. They had to be removed. But it took time. I went there a few times so that the GOC, Deon and I could put our heads together. We decided to apply the personalisation of war concept.

This concept brings me back to the ideas that I had discussed with Chris Bouwer and Andy in the Kaokoland. I had told them that if the name of the commander of the infiltrators operating against them was Jimmy, I expected them to outwit Jimmy.

I familiarised many commanders with this line of approach. It means that you as commander, if in any way possible, should know who your opposing commander or commanders are. And you must personalize the conflict by asking yourself, is he going to outwit me, or am I going to outwit him?

In this way one stimulates the commander to think competitively. You get him in the right frame of mind to beat his opponent by out-thinking him. It becomes a greater challenge when one realizes that you have to use your intellectual capabilities to beat your opponent.

Many years later, in 1991, I found that the same old British textbook from which I quoted earlier, *Conduct of war*, supported this concept: 'Battle is a struggle between the wills of opposing commanders. Victory will therefore be dependent upon the personality of the commander, who must be equipped with the right mental and moral qualities to achieve it.'

The discussions on personalization inspired Deon to adjust his plans for the Kavango. He appointed three commanders. To each of the three he allocated a specific enemy commander and his group as opponent. They were known to us by name.

Every commander was then given the maximum freedom to choose his subordinate commanders and troops and to forge them into an organization. The challenge was that each had to out-think his opposing commander. I even promised them a free stay at the Army Foundation's holiday lodges at Umhloti if they were successful within the prescribed time.

That was the end of the insurgents' presence in the Kavango. The Kavango was already clean by 28 May 1985, seven months before the target date of 31 December 1985.

The commanders deserved their holiday by the sea at Umhloti.

The modest Deon Ferreira still says that the one thing I can lay claim to is my contribution towards cleaning up the Kavango.

Another incursion by 26 infiltrators took place on 1 June 1985, but by 16 June they were all accounted for and the Kavango was clean again.

In times of conflict one can never get rid of the multi-faceted propaganda. During all these transborder and internal operations it continued full blast. One of the propaganda disputes was: was there a Plan cadre presence in Botswana, as we alleged, or not?

We had released information from time to time of cadres operating in Botswana. Towards the end of 1983 and the beginning of 1984 we specifically stated that their purpose was to open another 'front' against South West Africa from that country. As usual, most political commentators would not accept our word.

I speculated that our critics questioned our intelligence; or they suspected us of trying to justify a future crossborder operation in advance, in this case over the Botswana border; or they thought we wanted to thwart some political incentive or other through military action.

It is of course impossible to do a crossborder operation without political authorisation.

Then, between 22 February and 2 March 1984, three groups of cadres crossed the Botswana border, two in the vicinity of the farm Wilskrag and a third at De Hoek. The operation had been organized in Luanda with the aim of launching armed propaganda in Hereroland East and to mobilise the population there. Some elements were earmarked to infiltrate as far as Windhoek. The district commandant of the Police, Col Klopper, and the military sector commander launched a joint SADF-SAP counteroperation. The Army's elements included local clerks, storemen, chefs and others who were needed in a combat capacity. They had been trained and organized on a contingency basis specifically for such an eventuality. They were remarkably successful. Trackers also played a key role.

Some of the infiltrators were shot, two were taken prisoner and the rest pushed back into Botswana.

The sector commander was my old friend, Col Large van Rensburg. Through their actions they confirmed the credibility of our intelligence and *bona fide's* regarding the question of Plan's presence in Botswana.

The dispute over Plan's activities in Botswana in yet another example of what I have said before: in a conflict situation it is very difficult to distinguish between truth on the one hand and propaganda and various forms of deception on the other.

Apart from using information in this way, it is also used as a tactical tool during negotiations to influence the negotiators. Such information could be true, untrue or half true. I have experienced it several times.

The American Assistent Secretary of State for Africa, Chester Crocker, once told me quite seriously that he had noticed that we were again building up forces to attack Plan in Angola. He warned me that such an operation at that particular point in time would have seriously detrimental effects. I told him unequivocally that his information was not correct.

He replied that it would serve no purpose to hide the truth, because they knew what was going on. I reassured him that it was not the case. After all I was in a position to know that his information was inaccurate. He remained sceptical and warned me that I should realize that they have the capability of knowing these things, and I should not try to conceal it. I inferred that he was hinting that their intelligence services had picked up the so-called build-up on satellite photographs.

But I knew that his assertions were not true.

I have much respect for Chester Crocker. I also have respect for his negotiating talents. And if he had never played little tricks with information and words, he would have been the exception to the rule. To this day I still do not know if he had received such information that he mentioned and believed it to be true; possibly he did believe it and was sincerely worried. This is how I experienced situations of this kind: one is never sure. It might also have been an attempt to provoke me in order to confirm or negate a suspicion. If that was the case, he achieved his purpose and it did not worry me. Or perhaps it was just his way of discouraging crossborder operations.

Ninety per cent of the troops we used for transborder operations were troops who happened to be serving in the area at that time. It was mainly only the air force which was significantly and noticeably reinforced before such operations. In any case, on the odd occasion when we did step up our air capacity it was not done exclusively with the view to future offensive operations, it could also have been done as a deterrent and for defensive purposes.

The information that Crocker had, might have been constructed from inferences the Americans had drawn from bits of information. Quite often we replaced troops and weapon systems with others which, if observed during the actual change, could create the impression of a build up. I cannot blame them for that. Or their air-photo interpretation might not have been accurate.

One is never sure. Just before Operation Moduler during 1987, which I will be getting to soon, we received 'reliable' information that the advancing Cuban-Fapla forces were not using tanks. However, Unita and our forces knocked out just under a hundred tanks during the operation.

Examples of the manipulation of information for the purpose of good-guy/bad-guy propaganda were the allegations of military atrocities. When I became the GOC in South West I was bombarded with accusations of this kind. When Gen Lloyd succeeded me, the same happened to him. About one or two per cent of these were true. They were investigated and the odd one resulted in litigation. The problem is that suspicion about the other 98 per cent always remained.

One of the most incredible cases of disinformation became public only on publication of Andreas Shipanga's book, *In search of freedom*, in 1989. Shipanga was a founder member of Swapo.

During 1970 he became Swapo's Secretary of Information and from 1972 he operated from his office in Lusaka. In the chapter, 'Information and Disinformation', he writes:

> It so happened that about the same time, Dimo Hamaambo, who became the field commander of Plan after Hainyeko's death, was in town, and he said to me one day: 'You know, on our last incursion into Caprivi we went a bit out of our way and came across a village that had been completely wiped out by the Portuguese. There were skulls and bones and spent cartridges and things all round.'
>
> He showed me some cartridges he had picked up off the ground and an idea struck me. 'Dimo,' I said, 'If I found some journalists, could you take them back to that village saying you were in Namibia?' 'Sure,' he answered.
>
> It was 1972 and I was off on a mission to the Scandinavian countries. In Stockholm I met Per Sanden, a television cameraman, and I said to him: 'Would you like to see a village in Namibia where there's been a massacre?' His eyes widened. 'Is it true?' he asked. 'Of course,' I said, and he jumped at the idea. I told him that when I returned to Zambia, I would seek permission for him to come to Lusaka to talk to us. I told Sam and company of my plan and cabled to Per that he was welcome to come any time.
>
> He and his crew arrived soon afterwards, and we set off for the

Caprivi. It was March, and the rains were heavy. Our Russian lorries struggled through the mud towards the front, but at last we made it. Dimo calculated that the massacred village lay about sixteen kilometers inside Angola. As we reached the sensitive zone and prepared to cross the border, I said to the camera team: 'Look, my friends, you're about to go into enemy territory, and for your own security you must take off your wrist watches and give them to the commanders for safe-keeping. And hand over all maps too.'

My main worry was that one of them might have a compass or something that would tell them they were not in Caprivi but in Angola. 'Otherwise, you don't need to worry. The guerrillas will protect you,' I said reassuringly. The crew obediently removed their watches and set off with Dimo and the armed soldiers. I had bad stomach trouble and waited behind at the border for them.

In due course Dimo and his charges returned. They had found the village and taken reels and reels of film of skulls, skeletons and gutted houses. We went back to Lusaka, where I produced the old man, whose name was Haingula, saying he was the only survivor of the massacre. Per spoke to him through an interpreter, and Haingula played his part wonderfully. 'Oh yes, that was my village,' he said as he displayed his wounds. (The 'old man' was somebody who was wounded in South West Africa some time before.)

Next day I called a press conference at which I presented my evidence – the Swedish television film – and got my 'witness', Haingula, to repeat his story. The journalists packed into the conference and the story of the Namibian village 'wiped out by the Boers' spread rapidly across the world.

Of course I expected some response from the South Africans. Pik Botha was minister of information at the time, and he was furious. Later the press came back to me and said: 'Pik Botha says it isn't true.' I replied defiantly: 'Listen, if Pik Botha denies it, ask him and his regime to allow us to take the press to Caprivi under UN protection! I'll be there, and the old man will be there.' It was a gamble. I was afraid that the South Africans might take up my challenge. And what could we show journalists inside Namibia?

In 1987 I discovered how close I had come to being found out. I was in Cape Town; Gen Jannie Geldenhuys and Pik Botha were there too, and I was sitting with them. I had previously told Geldenhuys the story, and he said: 'Mr Shipanga, tell the minister

> about that massacred village.' As I told Pik the story he got more and more indignant. Then he said: 'You bastard, Shipanga. You know, the whole international press was on to me, and I said I would take them to the Caprivi!'
>
> Apparently when the story first came out Pik immediately questioned the military, who said there was no truth in it. So he flew a pack of journalists to Namibia and loaded them into a Puma helicopter and took them himself to the Caprivi. On the way there, he told me, he suddenly got cold feet: 'I thought to myself, God, these military men can't always be trusted. It just might be true that they have wiped out the village. Then what would I tell these people?' Pik told the helicopter pilot to land somewhere in the bush and say there was technical trouble and they could go no further. 'It scared the hell out of me that we might find such a village, so I aborted the trip!' he said. We all laughed.[1]

The *friction de guerre* had smiled on Swapo. Andreas Shipanga had bamboozled everybody. They were good at this type of thing.

One wonders how many such hoaxes are still being played in the early 1990s in South Africa.

Something by Sun Tzu that I read many years ago, assisted me to find explanations for many things. Years later during a conversation with the commander in chief of the American Forces in Vietnam, Gen William C Westmoreland, I learned that he had also found answers to his questions in the same writings. He quotes Sun Tzu in his book, *A soldier reports*:

> Twenty-five centuries ago, Sun Tzu wrote that fighting was the crudest form of warfare. He advised instead:
>
> 'Break the will of the enemy to fight, and you accomplish the true objective of war. Cover with ridicule the enemy's tradition. Exploit and aggravate the inherent frictions within the enemy country. Agitate the young against the old. Prevail if possible without armed conflict. The supreme excellence is not to win a hundred victories in a hundred battles. The supreme excellence is to defeat the armies of your enemies without ever having to fight them.'

I identified many actions that our opponents took against us in Sun Tzu's doctrine.

We have a typical Western approach to propaganda and semantical trickery and it differs quite a lot from that of the communist-orientated countries and those who received their revolutionary education there.

To illustrate: at a meeting of the JMC, Angolan Vice-Minister Venançio de Moura delivered a long rhetorical address, for which he was known, in overworked propagandistic clichés. He talked about the 'Pretoria régime' which has to shoulder the blame for everything and the 'Unita puppets' which only committed thuggery, and so forth.

So I pleaded, for the sake of better mutual respect and confidence, that we should refrain from using offensive language. His reply was: 'General, we might have agreed at Lusaka to stop shooting, but we have not yet signed an agreement to moderate our language.'

Just as one has to agree to cease using firearms, you have to reach agreement to cease using offensive words when you deal with people who use propaganda of the word as a weapon.

13

PROBLEMS AND CHALLENGES
Peace talks and rockets

While Charles Lloyd and Georg Meiring were steering the operational story through South West and Angola, I took up the reigns in South Africa to lead the Army.

My new term started with a bang but then abruptly and by fits and starts changed course into different directions. With a wider field of responsibility and more involvement with a greater variety of activity I struggled to find my bearings. It was frustrating, because I was keen to tackle the new job, especially since I had a handicap to overcome: I had to get into the picture from scratch as I had spent, with the exception of two and a half years, thirteen years outside the country, in Angola and South West; in addition, my predecessors, Gen Malan and Gen Viljoen in the meantime had brought about many changes in the SA Army.

The bang was like that of a starter's pistol – firing a blank cartridge. And it was a false start, because instead of crossing the starting line, finding my feet and bearings in my new job, I landed up on a side-track *en route* to Geneva.

I was a member of the South African delegation that went to Geneva at the start of the new year, 1981, to attend a conference under the auspices of the UN, with the internal parties of South West and Swapo, the Western Contact Group and the BAMTZZ states.[1] The purpose was to compile a timetable for South West to follow in the process to independence. We did not succeed, but for the first time in my life I had the pleasure of having the Organization of African Unity who were also represented, pay for my cocktails. This time, just for the fun of it, I did not try to spare the budget.

Back at Army headquarters and not much further across the startingline I found myself caught up in an unexpected crossfire. It seemed that whenever I was not chasing peace, I was dispatched to war. When I went to Angola, there was war. When I went to South West Africa, there too was war. And when I was not after war then, war was after me.

On the evening of 12 August 1981 I was driving to Voortrekkerhoogte. Along the way I passed Adm Bert Bekker travelling in the same direction. I gathered that he was on his way home. (He was later the number two of the Defence Force.) I was on my way to the Defence sports grounds where Defence was going to play a rugby match against Harlequins. I was president of the Defence Force Rugby Club. After the game I hosted a social for the president of Quins, Jannie Bezuidenhout, their coach, Kitch Christie, and other officials of their club. We gathered in the club house at exactly the same spot where I once enjoyed drinks with Frik du Preez and Ollie Ahlers 25 years ago – I had a beer and they were having brandy and coke.

Amid the conversation and tinkling of ice cubes I heard an unusual sound. Nobody reacted to it. I walked away from the noise and quickly peeped into the hall next door. This was the gym hall where dances were held long ago. Were any gymnasts in there now thumping around on their mats?

The hall was empty. Then I heard it again. Suddenly I realized that I had heard that sound before. I walked to the club's office to make a call while asking somebody to go and apologize to my guests for my absence. After the call I went home to change because there was work to do.

Back to Bert Bekker; around 22:00 he heard noises caused by a field exercise in progress somewhere on the outskirts of Voortrekkerhoogte. He made up his mind to talk to the Officer Commanding Northern Transvaal Command the next morning about this lack of discretion in doing disturbing military exercises at that time of the night near a residential area.

Another noisy object, however, shot through his garage, just missing his car, hitting the room of his housekeeper, Elsie. The roof lifted, letting out a column of flames. The fourth projectile struck the house and destroyed the dressing room next to the main bedroom.

While Bert was stumbling through his dressing room, the last projectile penetrated the roof of the house, ricocheted off the ground in the garden and landed on the terrain of the Army College.

It turned out to be Russian 122 mm rockets fired from a single-barrel launcher.

The house burst into flames. Bert decided not to wait until the next morning and immediately left for the command's ops room to report his discomfort. His two sons, Martin and Shane, took their mother and sister outside and told them to lie on the lawn, and rushed to Elsie's rescue.

Having arrived home and having made a few more telephone calls, I drove straight out to Bert Bekker's place.

If the rockets had struck a little closer this way or a little further that way we could have been faced with a terrible tragedy. But they had just missed and it was almost a joke. Fortune and misfortune were millimetres apart; like joy and pain. This time the *friction de guerre* was on our side.

This incident was a rocket attack on Voortrekkerhoogte by *Umkhonto we Sizwe* (MK), the armed wing of the ANC. Over a period of time they also had a go at Sasol and Koeberg, and Air Force Headquarters in the city centre of Pretoria.

When peace and peace talks were not demanding my attention, war and rockets did. But if there was one issue that did not disturb my stride doing my duties as the Chief of the Army it was rumour that my military career could change to follow a political course.

In South West the Administrator-General, Justice Steyn, was succeeded by Dr Gerrit Viljoen. He was in turn followed by Mr Danie Hough. Rumours then started to circulate that I was a candidate to take over from him: 'General Geldenhuys, who is an old South Wester, is being tipped to succeed Mr Danie Hough.'[2]

I was flattered that I was regarded as a South Wester. Many people thought I was one, probably because I had spent virtually a decade in South West.

Gen Viljoen once enquired circumspectly if I would accept, if I were to be asked to go to South West as Administrator-General. But politics was not for me. I would never take a step that would land me in party politics. It simply is not in my nature.

To be a politician you need guts more than a sense of fair play. In any event, the little advice I can remember getting from my father, was: stay out of politics. So my answer to Gen Viljoen was, please, no. It would mean choosing between soldiering and a political career. I would very much have liked to go to South West, because I love the country and its people. But I could not consider leaving the Defence

Force after thirty years for something such as that. In any case I still do not even know if there was really such a possibility.

Amid peace talks, rockets and political speculation, I began to find my bearings.

Initially there may have been a degree of confusion among the members of the Army's top management, the General Staff, when I took over from Gen Viljoen. They had become used to his style, and the pace at which he did things during his last two years. In that period he was probably anxious to get things done in the little time he had left to do it.

When I arrived at Army Headquarters I would ask the General Staff: What is the problem? And then we would identify and formulate the problem together. After that I would ask: Well now, if that is our problem, what are we going to do about it? And then we would continue to sort it out.

They probably said: 'What the heck is wrong with this Geldenhuys, he doesn't know what the problem is, and he hasn't even got solutions.' But as time went by we got to know each other well and, in my opinion, produced good quality teamwork.

I believed that when embarking on a venture, you should at least found your approach on a practical philosophical base. In the search of such bases I always tried to identify the 'basic truths'. I developed this tendency after I had read this line: 'The study of complex problems usually produces simple truths.' The insight gained from these basic truths means more to me than mere book knowledge. They have seen me through many difficult situations.

If a meaningful military aspect appeared on the agenda about which the General Staff still had no sound elementary philosophy, we developed it.

Thus it happened, for example, that we developed a concept of the nature and characteristics of future Southern African operations. At a later stage we based the Army's Force Development Plan on this concept which concluded, *inter alia,* that firepower, tactical and strategic mobility, and optimal night fighting capability would promote success in current and future conflict. This in turn was later accepted by Armscor as guidelines for their Technology Development Plan for the SA Army. Complicated problems produce basic truths.

One aspect of the overall strategic approach that I propagated at the General Staff was that the communists' socialist system would collapse. This Dr Wim de Villiers had already forecast to me on a few occasions. I did not have his knowledge but I believed him. His explanation made sense. I said that the Soviet Union would eventually have to scale down its military involvement in Angola. In the long term it would not be able to maintain its interventions all over the world far outside its normal sphere of influence.

I propagated our approach quite often. Once during a conference, which I was chairing, I noticed that Dieter Gerhard was also present. At this stage somebody had already warned me that there was a suspicion that he was a spy. This placed me in much the same position as the one I mentioned in an earlier chapter. But then it had been at a press conference and it was a journalist who was alleged to have been a spy.

This time I said to myself, okay, if it is true, I will give him something to report. So I predicted again that a Vietnam was waiting for the Soviets in Angola.

Gerhard was later found guilty of spying for the Soviet Union.

I also expressed these views to correspondents and overseas visitors. The occasional reaction was that it was impossible because the Soviet Union was so powerful! My reply was simply that the US was just as powerful when it withdrew from Vietnam.

In the meantime I had requested military intelligence to determine whether the Soviets had begun to show anxiety over the possibility of Angola becoming a problem for them. They reported back later and their answer was positive. Many years later Prof Willie Breytenbach of Stellenbosch told me that Soviet-Africa experts openly acknowledged at Woodlands Park, London, in 1988, that the signing of the Nkomati Accord (1984) was a big embarrassment for the Soviets. This seems to be in line with military intelligence's opinion that the Soviet Union was worried about its seemingly fruitless and prolonged involvement in Africa – and losing her grip.

But philosophies, however pracctical, and overall strategic guidelines, however clever, *per se* do not win you a war. Actual problems required real attention. We had to adjust the army's organizational structure to be better equipped to meet current and future demands.

We made certain rationalization studies. It was not forced rationalization with a view to cut on human resources and money. Although we had ourselves undertaken not to increase expenditure and create more posts, our intention was focused on improved effectiveness.

We grouped certain logistic elements together in one structure under one commander, the SA Army's Logistics Command. We created the Engineers and Signals Formation in the same way.

Northern Transvaal Command in the meantime had become unmanageable. The span of command became too wide; it was geographically a very large area and the frequency of activities became too high. I got the impression that, faced with this problem, there was a tendency to continue to make its headquarters at Voortekkerhoogte in Pretoria bigger and bigger.

However, we arrived at the conclusion that we should rather decentralize. We divided the command into three commands, the two new ones being Far Northern Command and Eastern Transvaal Command. This division of the area incidentally corresponded with the lay-out of the national physical development regions announced by the government. These changes were completed a few years later when Northern Cape Command was established. This was also in line with the national plan.

Soon after these two new Transvaal commands had been established, floods caused havoc in the eastern Transvaal and Swaziland. The GOC Eastern Transvaal Command was already geared to perform emergency relief tasks. During the same time he was also instructed to prepare the venue for the signing of the Nkomati Accord.

Infiltration, mine incidents and attacks on farms in those areas of the Transvaal also began to occur. Both commands could immediately take the necessary action.

Our forecast of future developments turned out to be correct. Although initially the implementation of the structural changes and territorial divisions did not happen without criticism, many people afterwards told me they could not imagine how it could ever have been otherwise.

But the Army does not consist of philosophies and structures. One has to know the Army.

Although the Air Force is totally dependent upon the dedication and skills of its people in blue, it tends to be characterized by its strong involvement with the natural sciences, high technology and modern armaments.

And although the Navy is equally dependent on its people in white, with their own unique capabilities and human problems, it also relies heavily on high-tech and modern armament systems.

The Medical Services deliver indispensable operational service, but they are by comparison more professionally, humanely and service orientated.

The Army, on the other hand, while also using weapon systems with a high degree of advanced technology content, is really people-intensive. It accommodates the bulk of the military personnel.

For us in the Army it was all about people; people with whose help you had to produce results.

At this high level one cannot command troops directly. It is difficult to motivate so many people in such a big organization on a person-to-person basis.

First you have to know what you want to achieve, or have to, and how it is going to be done. You must have vision and set ideals, and you must have clarity on the objectives that you want to attain. You have to ensure that your people know all these things and that they are mentally and emotionally reconciled to them. Everyone should know what the goals and basic elements of your plan and your policy are.

Secondly, the organization should have a culture that embraces certain values. In a nutshell, one has to create an atmosphere in which you and your people will be stimulated to achieve those ideals and objectives.

If there is not enough time, you have to consider and plan these things yourself. But it is better to formulate it by way of a team effort with your commanders, or at the very least, with your staff.

I am not saying that such a climate was not already in existence, but you have to work at it continuously. There is no continuity in the army, especially at the lower levels. One has to continually motivate consecutive intakes of national servicemen as well as induct new permanent force members.

The Army General Staff and I formulated four objectives in four main fields. They were: The primary responsibility of the Army to win the land battle; the morale of the Army; the image of the Army; and cost-effective management, or productivity.

We also formulated the required atmosphere and culture that the Army should have, as we saw it, which we marketed to its members.

General Malan also made important contributions towards creating culture in the Army in particular, and in the Defence Force in general.

He said that problems did not exist, only challenges did. 'Replace the word problem with the word challenge.'

It had a good effect. Quite often, previously, when I visited units I would hear, for example, a commander say: 'Yes, we have a problem with our vehicles. The serviceability is not even 70 per cent,' or: 'Our problem with this intake of national servicemen is that we have over five per cent absence without leave (Awol).' After the new approach one would arrive at a unit and hear the commander saying things such as: 'We have a few challenges, the first one is to push up our vehicle serviceability figure to over 80 per cent. And the second challenge is to push the Awol figure down to under one per cent and keep it there.'

This approach may sound as if we were playing around with semantics. It is not so. A truly new and positive spirit was being promoted.

But in spite of a positive spirit my time as the Chief of the Army was running out. We were proud of our successes, but for me there were also disappointments.

One of the biggest disappointments was that in five years I had not managed to visit all the commanders and troops. It was an unattainable ideal right from the beginning. I should have known. There were more than 250 Commando units, more than 150 Citizen Force units and more than 100 Permanent Force/National Service units spread over 11 territorial commands in a variety of home bases, operational bases and training bases.

But it is a good thing not to have enough time because it forces you to identify your real priorities. And sometimes you are surprised at the eventual outcome. I decided to give low-profile groups a high priority as far as visits were concerned.

I gave a name to these people that one is inclined to overlook, the Neglected Groups, or 'neglects'. I went out of my way to identify such groups and to satisfy myself about their wellbeing.

Big and well-known organizations can easily take care of themselves. Small and unknown organizations are vulnerable.

A large group, especially if there is a degree of cohesion, develops an inherent force that ensures the survival of the organization. And also units which have acquired public acclaim, and possibly boast a long and proud record, are inspired by the name they have to uphold. Traditions, values and culture keep units going, such as the Parachute Battalion, The Cape Town Highlanders and Regiment President Steyn. They can take the knocks and the bumps. There are also relatively small units with built-in strength, because they are independent and have acquired élite status, such as the Reconnaissance Regiments.

But then, by way of illustration, at a territorial command headquarters you will find a small bunch of military policemen, a handful of signallers and somewhere else a few chefs and clerks. They are usually sections or groups which have been detached from their main functional group and attached to other headquarters and units. For example, at the parachute battalion one finds hundreds of paratroopers together sharing common interests. But you never find a hundred chefs together. They are split up and posted in small sections to other bigger units where they have to perform their service. All the chefs so farmed out have a functional manager somewhere in Pretoria, but where they work they may have an artillery commander who knows nothing of the culinary arts.

'Neglects' may have a feeling of functional togetherness and pride among themselves but they are not always bound to the others by virtue of a common tradition and culture or *esprit de corps*, and are often dominated by them. But it is really so that the efficient functioning of many organizations usually depends on those who work quietly, unseen and unheard behind the scenes – the chefs, clerks, signallers, mechanics and telephonists. It is they who often find the going tough but who have to continue on their own steam. They often perform splendidly without much recognition. They are the vulnerable ones.

It is when you neglect these good people that *friction de guerre* may turn against you. Of course, you do not miss the chef until there is no food. Of course, you do not think about your signaller until the radio does not want to talk. One forgets about the mechanic until your car refuses to go. And then it is too late. One finds them, the 'neglects', on all levels of your organization. They need your attention.

I have mentioned two corps for Excellent Service in Army Orders (Mentioned in Dispatches). They were the Technical Service Corps and the South African Engineer Corps, especially in respect of technicians, or Tiffies, who rendered operational duties, and the Sappers – those men who detect and lift mines by hand. The Tiffies' citation reads as follows:

> Members of the Technical Service Corps of the SA Army demonstrated, during operations, unquestionable expertise of which they can be justifiably proud. Their contribution towards assuring the mobility and fire-power of the forces was indispensable. They recovered and repaired combat equipment

whenever it was necessary, sometimes under the most adverse conditions and even under fire; often with little resources but good cheer and inventiveness as tools.

They proved that mountains can be moved with the right attitude, courage and by doing what you can, with what you have, where you are. For this exceptional quality of the fighting spirit of the Technical Service Corps, their leaders and especially private soldiers in the field, I pay tribute.

I will not quote the Engineer Corps' citation, but consider this: From 1974 until the withdrawal of the South African forces from Namibia in 1989 the engineers lifted and disarmed a total of 1 743 landmines.

To put it into perspective I should mention that we are not now talking about conventional warfare where one finds identified minefields with a high density of mines in a confined geographical area. In that situation one can render hundreds of mines harmless in one effort. What we are talking about now is insurgent mines which are often singly laid and concealed anywhere in a vast area.

If this task was done less successfully, the projected repair costs to vehicles that might have been damaged, could have amounted to R97,44 million. This is important in itself, but the price of lives saved and injuries prevented is of course incalculable.

The Sappers on the ground were fantastic. From 1979 to 1989 they 'spooked' 1,13 million kilometres in Sector 10 (mainly Ovambo). This means that a road is cleared of mines by means of a mine detecting vehicle or mine detonating vehicle or by a sapper on a motorbike who inspects the road for disturbances of the surface.

Over the same period they 'swept' 438 000 kilometres. Sappers make a road or a route safe by walking on foot with a mine detector. Every alarm signal of the detector is investigated by hand. It is exhausting. Detected mines must then be destroyed. This can be nervewracking. Dangerous. They did the same in Sector 20 (Kavango) and Sector 70 (Eastern Caprivi). They were good.

It may be that members of the so-called neglected groups reading this book may be surprised to note my interest in them because it is quite possible that they never saw me. My greatest disappointment was that I did not get to all the places I wanted to. To manage my time was always one of my biggest problems.

On 1 November 1985, a little more than two months after Zola Budd set a new world record in the 5 000 metres for women with a time of 14 minutes 48,07 seconds, I stopped taking malaria tablets after 20 years and prepared myself for the last lap in my career. A tough lap – the appointment as Chief of the Defence Force.

14

THE END OF A DECADE
Sampie Panics Closer to the Problem

On 1 November 1985, as the new Chief of the Defence Force, I had every intention of devoting myself, body and soul, to the Defence Force, as had been the case five years earlier when I had become Chief of the Army. I do not mean that I wanted actively to represent the Defence Force in the world at large. I wanted to give my best inside the Defence Force. I wanted to make as much contact as possible with Defence Force units and people. But it would not work out quite like that and I still regret the fact that circumstances made such contact impossible. Many other important matters demanded too much of my time. A few of those were:

- When I took over command, the wave of unrest lasting through 1984, 1985 and 1986 was already in full swing. It demanded much of my time.
- The unrest had hardly calmed down when South Africa was involved in a big war in southern Angola. To visit the combat zone I often had to travel by aircraft, including helicopters, as well as do cross-country trips by ground transport.
- The war had not even ended when negotiations regarding the withdrawal of Cubans from Angola and the independence of South West started. Once again I had to travel a lot, this time overseas. I stopped counting when I had been away nine times in eight months – and this did not include the Brazzaville-shuttle.
- Cross-border operations against MK-targets in countries other than Angola also took place during this period. Operations in South West and Angola continued.

- The negotiations led to the implementation of UN Security Council Resolution 435, the withdrawal of the SA Defence Force from South West and eventually the territory's independence.
- Under a new government, during the new post-war era, the scaling down of the Defence Force began. Armament projects had to be cancelled. People had to be retrenched.
- During 1990 the new wave of unrest began.

All these things demanded my attention and through it all I also had to perform my normal duties as Chief of the Defence Force.

The result was that I could not achieve the self-imposed goal of giving more attention to the people in the force.

I am talking not only of the 'neglects'; I did not even see as much as I should have of the big and active branches of the service and their units. It was, and still is, a painful admission to make. I still regret that I could not visit the Navy more often.

The biggest omission, however, is being too busy to do one's real job – to think. If you can't think for an hour a day, you are not of much use to society.

But two factors made everything possible. The first was the Gleeson factor. Lt Gen Ian Rimbault Gleeson was my right-hand man – my Chief of Staff. I could not have had a better one. When he retired early in 1990 Niel Knobel, the Surgeon General, described him accurately by quoting Martina Navratilova:

> There are winners and there are losers. And if you choose to be one of the former, the journey through life can be a little lonely. When you're a winner, you have to set the standard for excellence wherever you go. You have to battle against the fatigue, the intimidation, the human tendency to want to take things a little easier. You have to be able to come up with, time and again, one consistently great performance after another. It is gruelling. I don't know how many people are willing to make the effort. But those few true professionals you meet along the way help make the journey just a little easier to manage.

The second was the Holliday factor. Sgt Maj John James Clarke ('Jan') Holliday was not a regimental sergeant-major or a brigade sergeant-major, he was the sergeant-major of the Defence Force. He joined the Defence Force in 1944 when he was 16 years old. He kept me up to date about what was happening in the Defence Force amongst our people from the top sergeant-major down to the last private soldier. This international athletics starter walked with me and together we arrived at the end of the road – another true professional.

Be that as it may – I will start at the beginning. In regard to the internal violence I first have to draw a distinction between terror and politically motivated unrest that includes violence. By terror I refer to, for example, infiltrators who lay mines, set other types of explosive devices and commit political murders. By unrest I mean the burning down of schools and administrative buildings, the barricading of streets, unlawful riotous assemblies and mass syndromes which result in violence such as necklace killings.

As far as terror is concerned: A new pattern of geographical infiltration routes and acts of terror developed after the signing of the Nkomati Accord. The infiltration of insurgents from Mozambique into the eastern Transvaal came to a standstill. New infiltration routes replaced the old ones. One was through Swaziland, which created unique problems, and the other was through Botswana, which resulted in acts of violence in the western Transvaal border area and elsewhere.

Many people, including the Director General of Foreign Affairs, Mr Neil van Heerden, and myself, tried our best to persuade Botswana to join us in establishing some form of joint security committee. To no avail.

In the meantime the western and eastern Cape, the Rand, and Natal experienced unrest incidents, simultaneously or consecutively.

Unrest-related violence goes hand in hand with political change. The referendum on a tricameral parliament in November 1983 and its actual inception in September 1984 marked such a change. Even though everyone may not necessarily agree, it created, in my opinion, a major change in the political dispensation that had existed for decades prior to this era. And political change always brings confusion and conflict. It fanned the emotions of people towards the right of the political spectrum and it unsettled black people, who felt themselves left out in the cold. I do not think it was mere coincidence that we experienced a spell of unrest immediately thereafter during 1984, 1985 and 1986.

This wave of unrest was politically motivated and aimed at the governing authorities and the administration. Stone throwing was not merely the work of unruly schoolkids; barricading of streets was not only a sign of juvenile delinquency. There was a more significant meaning behind it. Revolutionary committees were established, such as the so-called political and military regional committees, and street committees. Street and block commanders were appointed. Forms of 'alternative' structures were organized. Local alternative committees were gradually placed under regional committees and regional committees under national committees. The objective of these actions was to make the country ungovernable and to replace the official administrative structures with alternative structures from the lower levels upwards.

It was a serious situation. The ANC started to spread the word that a black Christmas was going to hit the country in 1986, and that the administration would crumble. One heard this everywhere, from politicians and officials of African countries and from those overseas who get their information about South Africa from the ANC. The application of emergency regulations and the actions of the security forces prevented this.

In the meantime the negotiations, the propaganda and the armed conflict in South West and Angola continued. I will mention only a few events to illustrate the atmosphere in those days.

Early during 1986 the RSA government had to cope with a barrage of protests about its actions in southern Africa; from allegations of forcing strict border control on Lesotho to complaints that the security forces had launched an attack on an infiltrators' base at Maseru on 20 December 1985.

In turn South Africa warned Botswana not to harbour MK insurgents. Pres Quett Masire rejected the allegation.

Security forces shot four insurgents during a hot pursuit operation in Angola. This happened during a follow-up of an attack by a Plan group on Ovambo civilians near Nkongo during which one was killed and another wounded.

A spokesman for the MPLA joined the never-ending war of words on 9 January 1986 with the allegation that a South African force had penetrated 150 km into Angola.

On the same day Chester Crocker arrived in Luanda for continued discussions.

And so on and so on and so forth. One just cannot mention everything. On 4 March 1986 Mr P W Botha proposed in parliament that Resolution 435 could be implemented by 1 August 1986, provided a firm and satisfactory agreement could be reached on the withdrawal of Cubans from Angola before that date.

Crocker grabbed the opportunity and swiftly arranged discussions with his Soviet counterpart in Geneva to tackle the question of Cuban presence in Angola. This session did not immediately deliver concrete results.

In this atmosphere of propaganda and negotiations, with the clouds of unrest still in the air, a new and big storm started to brew in Angola; it would erupt into a thundering outburst of violence only a year later. The preparations of the Angolans and their allies for a new offensive against Unita began to get off the ground. It took place under the leadership of the Soviet general, Konstantin Kurochkin, a veteran of the Afghanistan war, who arrived in Angola in December 1985.

Large quantities of modern Russian weapon systems were being brought into Angola, including aircraft which formed part of its strategic reserve for conflict in Europe (later Cuba would also send to Angola part of its strategic reserves intended for conflict in their part of the world). Moscow sent a thousand Soviet troops to take up training and command posts, and 2 000 East Germans to boost Fapla's intelligence and telecommunication services. Approximately 20 000 Faplas, 7 000 Swapos and 900 MK (ANC) members assembled at Luena and Cuito Cuanavale.

On 9 and 10 August 1986 4 000 Unita troops with possibly a couple of hundred South African gunners attacked Cuito Cuanavale. South African long-range artillery caused considerable damage. The Angolan troops and their Allies received orders to retreat to Lucusse, Munhango and Menongue.

During August-September 1986 I was once more taking malaria tablets and on my way to look at precisely what was happening. One day a few of us found ourselves just east of the Cuito River on the other side of Cuito Cuanavale. Regular bombardments were aimed at targets outside the town to disrupt the combined Fapla forces so as to prevent them from completing their build-up.

During daytime one had to lie low. One tended to get bored: you couldn't sleep all day. It was the typical African bush scene all over again: miles and miles of bloody Africa. Although it is still winter in August it gets warm enough during the day. You have to wipe the perspiration from your face every now and again. Dust, bluebottles, flies and other insects abound. People get irritated with each other.

So I told the fellows that what I wanted was an ice-cream; not just any ice-cream; it had to be a decent one, like those one used to get at the Esplanade in Durban; I did not want an icy ice-cream, it had to be a creamy ice-cream, served in a parfait glass.

I could see that some of the chaps were becoming quite irritated with me. But, I suppose because they could not do much about it, they listened with grim expressions on their faces. I pretended to be unaware of the irritation I was causing and continued to fantasise, swiping and swotting at the flies.

'You have to pour flavouring over the ice-cream. Special flavouring: red raspberry syrup. It runs down the inside of the glass and some of it mixes with the ice-cream. You must not be stingy with the syrup. And to make it all look attractive you put a red cherry glazed with sugar on top of it. Condensed drops of water form on the outside of the glass and run down through the mistiness leaving trails on the glass like rivers on a map. While you feast on this, the ice-cream melts and sinks to the bottom of the glass mixing pink with the syrup. And then you drink the last bit – bottoms up.'

Later that day, Staff Sergeant Sampie van der Westhuizen, the chef, arrived. And I have always wanted him to write down the story of that afternoon for me. Luckily I ran into him again on a visit to Pomfret during 1991. He was then a Sergeant-Major, and I asked him to put the story about the ice-cream, which he later described as a float, on paper. He was in a great hurry and scribbled it in no time with a stub of pencil:

> Gee wiz, I was stunned!
>
> There I was, on my own and in the middle of nowhere, trying my very best to get a fire going to make some coffee for the general and the others. I was trying to blow some life into it when I heard somebody saying: 'Staff, what's so difficult about getting a stupid little fire going?' I thought by myself, bugger you, you haven't got a clue.
>
> I looked up, and yes, there was no mistake – it was the general. I jumped up but, still trying to find my feet, he told me: 'As you were, please carry on.' With a sigh of relief, I thought by myself fortunately he's also a human being. He knows what it's like to try to get a fire started with nothing.
>
> A few other people were hanging around there as well. The water was on the point of boiling when I heard the general say: 'Today I

want an ice-cream float ...' And he started to explain exactly what it should be like.

I was shocked out of my wits. 'Yes General, very well General, I'll do it, General,' I said to myself in silent response.

After I had served the coffee I thought: Okay, there you have it, 'do what you can with what you have where you are'. Here you are, van der Westhuizen, someplace in the nowheres, but nobody will get you down; you know what you are and what you can do.

Alone once more, I asked myself, was the General only joking or was he serious? But the General had spoken. To hell with it! I grabbed a box of ratpax[1] and looked through the contents. I thought to myself, General, I'll show you! I'm going to do what you ask, no matter what.

'Then I saw light. I created my own recipe, the recipe is as follows:

Ingredients
– instant milkshake
– jelly powder
– instant pudding
– water
– jam

Method
Shake jelly powder, water, jam, instant pudding in bag. Place in hole under tree and cover up with sand. Pour water every ten minutes. (After a while it sets, icy cold.)

I opened the bag and tasted. It had worked, it tasted just like ice-cream!

I poured a tin of lemonade into a glass with the mixture on top.

I walked over to him proudly and served him. 'General, here is the ice-cream float you asked for.'

I could see that the General was very surprised ...

What Sampie forgot to mention was that he had found a red cherry, probably in a tin of mixed fruit, which he put on top the the ice-cream – this is one example of the ingenuity, the sense of humour and the sense of duty of the South African soldier.

I leave the build-up of the offensive against Unita and Sampie's ice-cream at that for the time being.

In the meantime I had to fulfil my other duties as Chief of the Defence Force. But for me, as had happened before, the old year did not really end and the new year did not really begin. I did not feel that an old era had come to an end, there was no pause, no new era dawned. I merely had to press on straight from one year right into the next. The office work continued without a break. People kept sending me letters and I had to answer them.

My good friend and colleague, the diplomat, Jackets, or André Jaquet,[2] if you like, once quoted to me a letter from Gen Wellington to Lord Bradford:

> If I attempted to answer the mass of futile correspondence that surrounds me, I should be disbarred from all serious business of campaigning.
>
> I must remind your Lordship that I shall see to it that no officer under my command is debarred by attending to the futile drivelling of mere quill-driving in your Lordship's office, from attending to his first duty which is and has always been so to train the private men in his command that they may, without question, beat any force opposed to them in the field.

I need not say that I absolutely agreed with Wellington. But it is so, unfortunately, that there is other work that simply has to be done – work which is also important.

The Nkomati Accord, or perhaps I should say, accusations that the Defence Force violated clauses of the accord, was one of the matters which now clogged my 'In' tray, just like Wellington's. As this issue previously fell outside the scope of my responsibilities, I had to study it from scratch.

It is now something of the past, but let me state immediately that when the Defence Force was authorized to do so, Renamo was supported, and when it was forbidden, such support was stopped.

For me the allegations were a serious matter. I gave it as much of my personal attention as humanly possible. After I had perused the mass of information and consulted with many people, I was absolutely convinced that no irregularities had been committed. And nothing happened afterwards that indicated that my finding was wrong. Indeed, the possibility that I might have created the impression among my staff that I mistrusted them over irregularities, cause me intense grief.

The accusations persisted for a long time after the assistance to Renamo had ceased. I must take my hat off to the Mozambicans. They are very good at this sort of thing, very good. If you get as many people as possible to repeat the allegations continuously for long enough, they eventually sound like generally accepted truths.

They applied the principle which I propagate myself for one in a conflict situation: Take the initiative, if you can.

The way in which Mozambique applied the principle was to accuse its opponent and to keep him under pressure with continued accusations. The opponent then had to use all available time to react to the charges. In the good-guy bad-guy competition there is rarely enough time for the opponent to effectively disclose the other party's irregular conduct. You cannot shoot if you have to keep ducking all the time. (Might this not be what is happening in South Africa during the early 1990s?)

Mozambique was guilty of irregularities. It had unilaterally withdrawn from the joint security commission and ignored the clause of the Nkomati Accord that the parties should moderate their language.

I did get the opportunity once or twice to express dismay over Mozambique's accusations to some of its people in authority. Their reaction more or less came down to this: 'Oh well, we don't believe all of it ourselves, and you know what the radio and press are like. And we have no control over them. Don't take it too seriously, that's how things go in politics.' And the allegations continued.

Even some South African civil servants would not believe that we had ceased to support Renamo. What sometimes happened was that they were also included in delegations which visited Mozambique for discussions in other fields. Their counterparts, which often included politicians, would then protest against the 'South African Defence Force's continued assistance to Renamo'. They elaborated on the grief it caused and how it was the source of everything that damaged the relations between the two countries.

Our officials, however, found themselves in unfamiliar political terrain, without reliable security information that would allow them to accurately interpret the charges. It was frustrating, to say the least.

Even before I became the Chief of the Defence Force, we offered to set up radar stations to be manned jointly with the Mozambicans to monitor the airspace for violations. They did not accept the offer, but continued their allegations that we were undertaking clandestine flights to Mozambique.

At one stage, after we had insisted that they submit examples of the activities of which they accused us, they came up with reams of invented stories. One was that we had dug a tunnel, from the eastern Transvaal to the other side, by means of which we were replenishing Renamo. But that was one of the mistakes they made. Even people who were staunch supporters of Mozambique rejected this charge as fantasy. And yet the allegations continued.

There was something else besides the 'In' tray and propaganda that tended to keep me in my office. My new appointment brought me into contact with a world I did not know at all – parliament. While it was in session I had to work from my office in Cape Town.

I was not a regular visitor to parliament. Although I have nothing against parliament, I went there only when I had to. The parliamentary system is a good one. And one should not make the mistake of thinking that the debates are what it is all about. As a layman I would say that more work is done by committees and study groups in conference rooms than in the assembly hall itself, but it is indispensible.

Inevitably I would meet interesting personalities in the ambit of parliament. One such was MP, Mr Koos van der Merwe.

He told me that he had to attend a luncheon on the first day after he was elected to parliament. It was a gathering mainly of English speaking people. For various reasons he had not slept and he was completely exhausted by all the work and excitement. Suddenly, but vaguely, he heard the Master of Ceremonies asking: 'Will ... fahn duh Murwie please say grace?' He started to get to his feet, pressing on the table with the palms of his hands to support the effort, trying to recall the old English Bible words like thy, thou, and kingdom cometh, when to his surprise and relief he heard somebody else beginning to say grace.

The Master of Ceremonies had actually said: 'Will Father Murphy please say grace?'

Another interesting person I got to know better was Mr Vause Raw, the well-known former member of parliament for Durban Point. He used to be a member of the United Party which became the New Republic Party. I had met him before. He was a veteran of World War II and usually his party's spokesman on defence matters. He was an invaluable ombudsman for members of the Citizen Force, Commandos, National Servicemen, and their families. He knew what it was all about. He wrote a collection of poems during 1940–1945 while on military service. His 'Again' reads as follows:

He had been home,
One word
Spelling a lifetime
in the endlessness of war,
And now he was going again,
Away ...
To war ...
Would he return?
... No matter now ...
Brave noble soldier.
For he was going away
To war ...
Again.

It was in the operational area that I met Mr Raw for the first time. He was on a visit there with other parliamentarians. I flew with them from Rundu to Omega in a Hercules transport aircraft. Four of us wanted to play bridge. He was one of the instigators and rapidly produced two decks of cards: one pinkish and the other one light blue. On the back of the cards was a circular emblem with the words: United Party, Verenigde Party.

Now, before a game starts, I usually check that the jokers have been removed, and I therefore said: 'Mr Raw, please make sure there are no jokers in those United Party packs.'

He replied: 'Don't worry, they all long ago went to the Progressive Federal Party.'

However, the new world did not consist of parliamentarians only. I was also directly involved with people like Cmdt Piet Marais, the chairman of Armscor.

Piet Marais is a character. He looked like the chairman of a big company, and he was one. He also looked like a Karoo farmer, because he was a Karoo farmer. He looked prim and proper, but he was an imp. However, he could also be a wise man if you were wise enough to notice it.

He could be serious as well. He earned international acclaim for South Africa as chairman of Armscor. He was awarded the Hertzog Prize during 1988. At the ceremony he said: 'A South African doesn't scare away from a problem; he panics closer to the problem.'

That was indeed how it happened. When the UN Security Council Resolution 418, setting up an arms embargo against South Africa, was passed, Armscor did not scare away from the problem. It panicked closer to it – and with stunning results. It produced the G5 and G6 long-range field gun – the best in the world, the Rooikat armoured car and a variety of sophisticated naval and air force equipment.

The Commandant once told me the following story: He was flying from D F Malan airport to Jan Smuts. The only parking he could find was far away from the terminal building and those were the days before the advent of airport trolleys. His suitcase was huge and heavy – the kind my mother would have called a portmanteau. When a porter approached him, Piet asked: 'How much will you charge to carry this for me?'

'You can pay me what you think it is worth,' the porter replied. Piet gave him a R2-note and they embarked on the long trek across the parking area to the terminal. But when they reached the halfway mark the porter put the suitcase down and said, 'Mister, this suitcase has now become far too heavy for two rand!' They both had a sense of humour.

There was another matter keeping the Chief of the Defence Force tied to his desk in Cape Town. As was the case with all the other Directors General he has to appear annually before the parliamentary Joint Committee on Public Accounts (JCPA). During such an appearance one had to give evidence in the form of answers to any questions the committee cared to ask. The questions usually concerned the Auditor General's annual report on one's department.

The JCPA as a democratic parliamentary institution and watchdog over the spending of the taxpayers' money is essential. But one would not volunteer to appear before it for pleasure.

Democratic procedures are often frustrating. Should the democratic processes be scientifically evaluated for their effectiveness in problem solving and decision making, they will probably score very low. But there are other considerations too and I subscribe to Chruchill's statement: Democracy is the worst form of government – except all the others.

Likewise, the JCPA produced its frustrations. Sometimes when I appeared before the committee it felt as if I were the accused in a criminal court of law. On other occasions I felt as if I were the humble servant being admonished by my master, appointed by the voters. This is quite close to the truth, of course. One has to accept it, and I am not complaining. Although they did not exactly approach me with kid gloves, few of the members on the committee were uncivil.

The committee generally consisted of learned people such as lawyers and accountants, well versed in the matters submitted to them for investigation. The common factor was that they were all politicians. And I suppose it is unavoidable, if not always easily noticeable, that party politics play a role in the proceedings of the committee.

It never really worried me. But the political style and techniques that members used to unsettle each other in parliament, were also used against any person appearing before the committee – to a lesser extent, fortunately. However, for somebody like me, who was not used to this kind of fighting, it was bad enough. One feels a bit like being bullied, because it is not possible to retaliate in the same fashion that they do in parliament. I tended to take everything very personally, because as DG I was the official responsible for my department's spending and I had to accept accountability myself. This was something I could not delegate.

Still, I should not complain. I was prepared to accept the task of being Chief of the Defence Force and facing the waves of the JCPA was an occupational hazard.

There are, however, more meaningful frustrations: When the Auditor General's report appears, it is an open document. The political commentators seize upon it immediately to make shocking revelations about the mismanagement of the taxpayers' money. But the rules and conventions do not permit the responsible Director General to comment publicly on such matters until he has appeared before the committee. This ruling was confirmed by a Speaker's decision on 21 February 1979. Although it makes sense to me, it is not pleasant. I was being criticized along with my organisation in public, but I had no right to reply.

Even so, the JCPA should never lose its watchdog function. In spite of the uncomfortable flak, it remains an indispensible institution. Any person who has to appear before that committee has all my sympathy, but he has to sweat it out and face the consequences; there is no other way.

However, one aspect needs further attention. I could often find no other explanation, by way of example, for mistakes in the handling of stores and monies, than the lack of sufficient qualified and experienced personnel. Unfortunately my predecessor and those before him probably found exactly the same problems and offered the same excuses. One of the veterans of the JCPA, Mr Harry Schwartz, in fact told me in the committee that he was tired of hearing that excuse, as he had to listen to it year after year. He was probably quite right.

The causes of the shortage of qualified and experienced personnel follow a pattern. As soon as the personnel concerned are given training and experience, they are bought by the private sector – lured away from us by means of better compensation.

The personnel retained by the Defence Force do excellent work. The force does not consist only of people who were 'bought' on the manpower market; there are also those who are motivated by service to their country. They stay, but there are not enough of them.

I know the generally accepted principle is that people in the employ of the state may not be on par, as far as remuneration goes, with their counterparts in the private sector. For example, an accountant and stores supervisor in the private sector will always be better rewarded financially than the accountant and stores supervisor in the public sector. The same goes for other categories of personnel.

Has the time not come to waive this 'principle'? Or do we want to leave the taxpayer's money in the hands of people who are left on the manpower market after the private sector has skimmed off most of the cream?

Now that we find ourselves in an era where holy cows are being buried, and where old existing concepts are being questioned, and where new ideas are being judged on merit and accepted, we should seriously consider this question: Why can the state as employer not compete with other employers on the same terms when it comes to offering remuneration? And if there is nothing wrong with it, then we should change the system to eliminate the disparity – should any disparity exist.

A prerequisite to this end would of necessity entail a relook at the auditing system. We have already made important changes under Auditors General Joop de Loor and Peter Wronsley by moving away from mere accounting and regularity audits in the direction of performance audit and objectives audit. If it is eventually going to lead to a real productivity audit, we will have reached the point where the civil servant also has 'to produce'. And those who don't, will go the same way as those in the private sector who don't.

I will not argue with those who do not agree with me on this point, but then they should stop complaining that the civil service is not to their liking.

However, whether I was at the office or not, be it in Pretoria or Cape

Town, one activity that always required attention was operations. And this brings me to a sensitive subject: operations across the border. The Defence Force sporadically had to do cross border operations against Umkhonto (MK) targets during the eighties. It was usually done successfully by the Special Forces. It took place in countries such as Mozambique, Zambia, Botswana and Zimbabwe.

These operations were blitz attacks, in an out; sometimes they were pure and simple air attacks such as the Israelis quite often had to do.

During earlier years MK had isolated bases of the same kind as Swapo, with the possible exception that the MK bases accommodated smaller numbers.

As a direct result of previous attacks on their bases, MK changed to a new scheme of hiding places. Instead of a base in the bush, or a camp outside a town, they divided themselves into small groups and dispersed themselves in apartments and houses in cities and towns.

These were good tactics which hampered military actions against them considerably. It was no longer possible to engage them in a single attack as a concentrated group in one location. Besides, they now enjoyed the 'protection' of the civilian community around them. One could forecast that attacks on such targets would result in propaganda to the effect that we had bombed or raided civilians. This made action against them even more difficult.

However, they did not cease their actions against targets in South Africa. On the contrary, these actions increased in frequency and in intensity. Seen from a security point of view, operations against MK had to be continued to prevent an escalation of attacks on farms, and the use of mines and explosive devices.

The crossborder attacks attracted a lot of criticism. Over the years various visitors to the country during interviews tried to pressure me into admitting that we had launched these operations with the specific aim of wrecking political initiatives and negotiations. I categorically denied it then as now.

They pointed out, especially in the case of Angola, that operations took place just before or after international negotiations, and wanted to know why these operations took place at this particular time. Should one look carefully at a political chronology, such as I produce later in this book, a continuous record of conferences, meetings and discussions, like those of the General Assembly and Security Council of the UN and visits such as by the Big Western Five, special envoys and a lot more will become quite clear. It would have been almost impossible to have executed an operation which would not have taken place just before or after some political event or other.

Certain practical considerations have a big influence on the timing of an operation. A farmer will understand that if he does not get his seed in the ground at the right time, he may well have to wait until the next year. It is a matter of natural rhythm of life which will not be denied.

In South West and Angola we actually had to have a dry and a wet season design for operations. Certain operations could be done only during full-moon periods, others during the time when the moon was dark. If you missed out on the right moon, you had to wait 28 days. But your enemy was not going to wait for you. MK activities increased and they had no fear of international political condemnation.

I knew that crossborder operations could hamper negotiations but that was never the motive. We made our recommendations from a security point of view and after having considered the operational factors. The political risks were always judged by the politicians.

I am not hiding behind anybody's political skirts. The Minister of Defence never told me to execute an operation with the intention of wrecking political manoeuvres.

I must also add that, to initiate an operation was not the exclusive right of the military. I mention this as it is my view that it might help to clear the air if this matter is seen in its true perspective.

All the overused and stereotyped expressions like the SADF has done this and that, and the SADF's policy on this and that, created the impression that the Defence Force had its own independent policy and acted highhandedly. We did not! And as the Defence Force is most definitely going to play its appointed role in the future of our country, one should bear this in mind.

Our Defence Force, like any other, is an instrument of the state and acts within the current structures and policies of the state.

One can think this out for oneself: If farms had been attacked, mines had been driven over and detonated, bombs had gone off in busy commercial centres and there was loss of life, then pressure will be exerted on a government to take drastic action against the perpetrators of the violence.

We experienced this kind of situation towards the end of 1992 and at the beginning of 1993. After a series of incidents in the eastern Cape and the eastern Free State, the inhabitants of those areas urged the government in the strongest terms to act against Apla in the Transkei, or they would take the law into their own hands. In one such incident four people were murdered and seventeen wounded when five men attacked the King William's Town Golf Club on 28 November 1992 with hand grenades, rifles and petrol bombs. The armed wing of the PAC, Apla, accepted responsibility. If any counteroperation had in fact been launched at the time, as the government was urged to do, the propagandists would undoubtedly have claimed that it was done with the intention of wrecking peace politics.

Some of the attacks were aimed at farms, for example: A chicken farm near Bosbokrand was attacked on 14 October 1985 with AK 47s, and on 13 February 1988 five infiltrators from Zimbabwe laid mines and attacked Mr Fisher's farm, Rivers, 10 km west of Beit Bridge, with AK 47s, hand grenades and RPG-7 rocket launchers, and then returned to Zimbabwe.

Landmines were often laid by infiltrators from across the border: Four children and two adults were killed, and two children and three adults injured on 15 December 1985 when their bakkie detonated a mine on the farm, Chatsworth, 45 km west of Messina. Two black men were killed and eight injured in a mine incident near Davel on 25 May 1986. On the fourth of January 1986 Mr Hubert de Beer and his daughter-in-law, Elize, were killed and Mr Deon de Beer and Mr Danie Venter injured when their vehicle detonated a mine at Stockpoort, Ellisras.

Bombs and limpet mines were used, for example: On 20 May 1983 a powerful bomb exploded in front of the Nedbank Plaza Building in Church Street, Pretoria, killing 20 people and wounding 199. Two days before Christmas 1985 a bomb exploded in a refuge bin at the Amanzimtoti Sanlam Centre killing three women and two boys and wounding 61 people. On 30 July 1988 a mine exploded at a Benoni Plaza Wimpy Bar injuring 55 people. One woman died of her injuries.

Another major point of criticism against crossborder operations was that South Africa destabilized its neighbours by means of the Defence Force.

I have, however, already mentioned cases such as Jordan, adjacent to Israel, and Zambia, bordering the eastern Caprivi, where these host countries forbade infiltration from their country to the target country as they did not wish to bear the brunt of the retaliatory actions taken against infiltrators in their countries. Now, whether one calls the actions of the target country against infiltrators in the host country destabilization or whatever, the results for the target country, from a security point of view, were good. In the case of Zambia the end result was the cessation of insurgency in the eastern Caprivi.

A seasoned political analyst, normally critical of the administration, recently commented that, whether you call it destabilization or not, crossborder operations had its advantages. His argument was that crossborder operations against MK were a thorn in the flesh of the countries that harboured them. This was one of Kaunda's main considerations motivating him to urge the ANC to enter into negotiations with the SA government.

To see his comment in the right context, we have to look at other chains of events that happened in the same period. Going back to the wave of unrest during 1984–1986, we know that the crumbling of the administrative structures forecast for 1986 was thwarted by means of the emergency regulations and the security forces.

The ANC came to the conclusion that the security forces could not be beaten, and they said so.

During this period until shortly after December 1986 the so-called front-line states, in anticipation of an ANC take-over, came up with their most aggressive speeches ever against South Africa. When the take-over did not occur, they had to reconsider their strategies. One experience they did not want to relive was the continuation of crossborder operations in their countries. That inspired them, especially Zambia, to exert pressure on the ANC to use the opportunities of starting discussions with the SA government.

The effect of the crossborder operations and the failure of the attempts to bring the administration to its knees through unrest therefore played an important part in promoting negotiations and settlement politics.

Talking about allegations regarding crossborder operations, I would like to move on to the next instalment in the serial about accusations of violations of the Nkomati Accord.

As I have already said, the charges that South Africa continued to support Renamo just would not stop. However, one could detect a slow but sure turning of the tide.

Influential Americans and Europeans visiting South Africa often requested interviews with me. Most of them were very critical of South Africa, but some of them, after a trip to Mozambique and having heard of more 'underground supply lines to Renamo' told me they did not believe the Mozambican stories any longer. They asked me why we did not deny the allegations. I replied that my minister had done so on several occasions. They then insisted that we find other ways of proving our innocence. But how does one prove that you had not done something which you had not done?

But, okay, cowboys don't cry. I told them the following story which a German friend had told me:

> A man in a restaurant ordered soup. The waiter served it. He started eating and when he had almost finished, summoned the waiter and disgustedly showed him a fly in his soup. The waiter apologized, removed the bowl and brought him a fresh bowl of soup. The man tucked in with relish and when the soup was nearly finished, he called the waiter and again showed him a fly in it. The waiter apologized, the man said okay, he would not complain any longer if the waiter brought him another bowl of soup.
>
> At the adjoining table another man was watching the whole sequence. He then tapped the soup eater on the shoulder, 'Listen, pal, when you have finished, can I borrow your fly, please?'

As long as you have a fly to put into the soup, you get more food. I began to believe that, as long as Mozambique could complain that South Africa was the fly in the ointment, it would have the sympathy and support of the whole world. Mozambique could not afford to rid itself of the South African fly as long as she wanted more soup.

During the early 1990s Mozambique stopped directing her accusations at the government and the Defence Force, and turned to the private sector.

Moving across southern Africa, to the western theatre: Other events also played a role during this period. The war that had already started to brew in Angola exploded during 1987. It was this war which would lead to real negotiations about Cuban troop withdrawal from Angola and the implementation of Resolution 435 in South West.

I now take up the story on the spot where ice-cream floats were being served by Sampie and the Angolan alliance was driven from Cuito Cuanavale by Unita. The latter encounter was not the end of the campaign against Unita, it was the beginning.

The offensives against Savimbi over the years followed a pattern. There was an annual attempt to drive him out of his base area at Jamba with the ultimate aim of destroying him completely. It failed every year.

Over the years I had often forecast that the day would come when they would fail for the last time – when they would have to choose between total defeat or negotiations with Savimbi.

It is general knowledge that Crocker became frustrated from time to time. Every time he thought the MPLA would be prepared seriously to talk peace concerning South West and the Cubans the Soviet-supported hardliners in the MPLA wanted just one more chance to destroy Savimbi militarily. Only then, they said, would they be prepared to talk. And the next year, after another unsuccessful effort, they came with the same story. And so it went on.

I told Crocker I didn't believe their arguments. If the MPLA were to be successful and Unita ceased to be a factor, why would they want to negotiate? I am sure he didn't believe it himself. On the other hand, if the MPLA really faced military defeat they should be willing to negotiate so as to bargain for the most favourable settlement. But Crocker stuck to his assignment. He persisted patiently with his diplomacy. I take my hat off to him.

I had already initiated limited operational assistance to Unita during July 1987. We had ample confirmed information that the Soviets and Cubans were busy with an enormous build-up for a big war. Never-ending waves of Soviet transport aircraft with tonnes and tonnes of war material landed at Luanda, Lubango, Menongue and Cuito Cuanavale. *The Times* of London reporter said that it reminded him of Afghanistan.

Crocker was continuing with his merry-go-round diplomacy. During middle July 1987 he conducted discussions with the MPLA in Lusaka and departed full of hope.

But not only the SA Defence Force was to be accused of destroying peace talks through military operations. It was now the Soviet's turn. Within a week after the Lusaka discussions the Soviet-inspired Cuban-Fapla advance through Cuito Cuanavale and other places started. On 22 July 1987 a dismayed Crocker said the hope of a breakthrough in South West and Angola had been shattered. He was wrong. The events that now followed would bring about the breakthrough – the breakthrough from mock negotiations to real negotiations.

The big war started. Fred Bridgland called it *The war for Africa – Twelve months that transformed a continent.*

But, however important any matter might be, one seldom has only one special overriding priority to which one can give all one's attention. Dealing with the training of senior officers in chapter 3, I men tioned expressly that one should be able to work under pressure without isolating oneself to the extent that there is no time for other important matters. Here is a good example:

After the advance had already crossed the starting line, life elsewhere still took its normal course and I had to divert my attention to other matters. General Neels van Tonder of military intelligence came to see me one day. He wanted us to go to Paris. I did not like the idea and told him impatiently that he had to persuade me that the trip would be cost-effective. So he mentioned about a dozen things that we had to go and do. I was more stubborn than usual and told him that under such circumstances I was not prepared to go. If a person gives me too many reasons I become suspicious; if he had given me only one good reason, I would have been more agreeable. He was justifiably upset.

A few days later he was back at the office. This time he listed three things. The very first one persuaded me – the possibility that we could arrange the release of Major Wynand du Toit, who had been captured during an operation in Cabinda and evacuated to Luanda as a prisoner of war.

I immediately contacted my friend and colleague, Neil van Heerden, the Director General of Foreign Affairs. Would he have any objections if I concerned myself with the issue? He was naturally affable and even excited about the idea. 'I will welcome any effort by anybody who has a chance to get him out. We must try everything.'

Sometime in July, Neels van Tonder, Johann Sonnekus and I left for Paris. We wanted to persuade a major power, France, to play a role.

France looked promising for a number of reasons. A Frenchman, Albertini, was being held in detention by Ciskei. The French sought his release. The Premier, Jacques Chirac, and the presidential couple, especially Mrs Danielle Mitterrand, all for their own reasons, dearly wished to bring it about. An acquaintance, Mr Ollivier, had access to the Chirac government. We could assist them in trying to secure Albertini's freedom if they could arrange Wynand du Toit's release.

However, there were two problems. First, Neil van Heerden wanted to persuade Pres Lennox Sebe of Ciskei to free Albertini in an attempt to facilitate the acceptance of the accreditation of my namesake, Mr Hennie Geldenhuys, as the new South African ambassador to France. This was the least of the two problems.

The second problem became apparent as we discussed the matter over dinner with Mr Ollivier at his apartment in the 16th arrondissement. He was co-operative and enthusiastic when I explained the idea which offered them an opportunity to get Albertini out. His problem was, how could he approach the Angolans to set Wynand free? It would create the impression of blatant interference in their domestic affairs.

Fortunately for us there were favourable factors too. Pres José Eduardo dos Santos of Angola had planned to visit France towards the end of September 1987. So he would be keen to create a favourable climate for his visit. The government of the Netherlands also brought pressure to bear on Luanda as the release of Wynand du Toit could mean the release of their Klaas de Jonge being detained in South Africa. This was a current point of discussion between our Department of Foreign Affairs and the Dutch administration.

I asked Ollivier if he could not present the case along these lines: He did not want to interfere in Angola's domestic affairs, but discuss a French concern. The detention of Albertini was a matter of great importance to the French. He should not be taken amiss if he explored all avenues to get Albertini back. South Africa is of no concern to him, but if the release of du Toit could assist him to solve French problems, he had to try all options. From his point of view Albertini was all that mattered and he would appreciate Angola's assistance. I got the impression that he found my approach to be quite reasonable. We enjoyed the dinner.

That is how it goes. With a few exceptions, if you want to talk business, you arrange a meal. The follow-up meeting the next day took place over breakfast, also at Ollivier's apartment.

Between the previous night's dinner and this breakfast I had phoned Neil van Heerden from my hotel and reported to him. I asked him if he could temporarily shelve his negotiations concerning Albertini to give me the chance to fully exploit the possibilities of reciprocating action by the French government. He agreed. So, I could confirm to Ollivier that South Africa would untertake to go all out to have Albertini freed if they would do the same in respect of du Toit.

On a happy Friday, two days later, I could tell Gen van Tonder to categorically inform Mr Roussin, the Chef de Cabinet of Chirac, that Albertini could be set free – if du Toit could be released.

But it would take a long time and many discussions before this story came to an end. In the meantime we went back to Pretoria. And to war.

15

TWELVE MONTHS THAT TRANSFORMED A CONTINENT
Cuito Cuanavale – the myth

Five decades have passed since the first day I opened my eyes. More than three of them were spent in the Defence Force. I saw trends come and go.

I did not see much of the Charleston and jazz. That was before my time, rather more in the days of our grandfathers and grandmothers. My mother spoke of crooners and ballroom dancing.

I came into this world in the swing era. Not that Kroonstad was what one would call a swinging town. But Cole Porter's 'Anything goes' was the musical of the decade.

I went through the Second Great War listening to the radio and apart from the propaganda broadcasts, there was Vera Lynn's 'I'll pray for you'. In South Africa a little girl, Eve Boswell, comforted our sick soldiers with 'I'll get by'. The Germans and English quarrelled over whose song Lale Andersen's 'Lily Marlene' really was. But Glen Miller stayed 'In the mood'.

After the war, bikinis decorated the beaches. The juke boxes began to shake, rattle and roll with Bill Haley and his Comets' 'Rock around the clock'.

And so on.

But there were also people such as Beniamino Gigli singing 'O sole mio'.

In the mid 1950s the Teddy Boys, with their long combed-back oily hair, introduced the sharp-pointed shoe fashion and everybody wiggled the hoola-hoop. Women wore pony tails. Then blue jeans and poloneck shirts filled shop windows. The 1950s ended with women wearing the sack.

When Mary Quant made her appearance in 1960 everybody wore what they liked; an approach that went well with the twist mania. I stuck to flannels conservative, blazers gentlemen and ties sober. Twiggy was the rage. The most attractive style of them all hit the fashion stage in 1965 – the mini.

The decade belonged to the Beatles, who inspired men to wear even longer hair, but it was James Bond who thrilled women with *Dr No* and *From Russia with love*. John Kennedy said: 'Ich bin ein Berliner.' Cliff Richard sang 'Thirty days', which later became 'Forty days'.

Fashion reached an all-time low towards the end of the 1960s with unisex clothes.

During the 1970s Simon and Garfunkel, Elton John and Kenny Rogers appeared on the scene. Everybody danced disco. At the home bases in South West I listened to Neil Diamond – 'What a beautiful noise'.

And so on.

But there were also people such as Pavarotti singing 'O sole mio'.

More people, fashions and styles came and went. The era of the old guard came to an end, De Gaulle, Franco, Salazar, Meir, Adenauer, D F Malan. Others took over. And others from them.

There was a time for dictators and one-party states. Cold wars came and went. It was peaceful co-existence and *détente*.

The third world became independent.

Africa became independent.

The oil crisis came and went. Other crises too.

South Africa became isolated.

Thatcher and Reagan appeared on the international front. The Soviet leaders followed each other in quick succession. Gorbachev rose.

And this brings us to the event that would change the course of southern Africa; an event which would echo in Moscow, Washington, Havana, Pretoria and in the assembly halls of the UN in New York – the war in Angola, 1987–1988.

We called it Operation Moduler, then Hooper and then Packer. The names are misleading. It did not in the least signify strategic or tactical phases of the campaign. The names were allocated merely to indicate the three main periods in which units and personnel performed operational duty. They were continually assembled for, and released from, operational service. Timewise, some participated only in the first part,

Moduler, others only in the second, Hooper, and so on. Other than that, the codenames had no significance.

Actual operational phases overlapped these periods rather than coinciding with them. Commentators analysing the campaign in these three 'duty roster shifts' could come to false conclusions. For me and others, including the Air Force, and officers, non-commissioned officers and troops who were not relieved according to these time schedules, it was one ongoing campaign.

During the operation I regularly conferred with commanders and senior officers in the field. These discussions usually took place after they had briefed me on the course of operations in the preceding period, what the current situation was, and on their planning for the times ahead. I also addressed the troops when outgoing units were relieved by fresh troops, or demobilized.

On these occasions, towards the end of the campaign and during the period immediately thereafter, I committed myself to a firm promise. But one would only comprehend the full meaning of the promise once I have told the story of the war:

South Africa had its own interests to defend. An eastern European major world power, USSR, and a Marxist dictatorship from the Carribean sphere, Cuba, got themselves heavily involved in southern Africa. These foreign powers joined forces with the MPLA, on a scale like never before, to destroy Unita in the Jamba area, once and for all. Should they succeed and establish military control in the south of Angola, our operations against Plan would once again extend from the mouth of the Cunene River in Kaokoland in the west, to Mpalela Island in the eastern Caprivi in the east.

The positive results for which South Africa had sacrificed men and money for fourteen years would then become undone. The peace which South Africa had maintained in South West would again be seriously threatened.

There were also MK camps in northern Angola. They would probably have been transferred to the south-east of Angola if Cuban-MPLA forces controlled it. That would bring them right up to the area where the borders of Zambia, Zimbabwe and Botswana converge, which had been used as an infiltration route to South Africa.

South Africa also had interests in common with Unita. It was no secret. The Minister of Defence stated this in parliament on more than one occasion.

South Africa thus became involved. We undertook to supply armaments and troops which would put Unita in a more equable position *vis-à-vis* the advancing forces of the Fapla alliance. Savimbi did not have an air force and such weapon systems and troops which could effectively resist tanks and other types of sophisticated armoured vehicles, and artillery including rockets and missiles.

I will describe the campaign briefly, concentrating on my own observations, feelings and perceptions about which other people cannot write. I cannot tell it as if I were a neutral spectator on the sidelines. I tell the story from the point of view of South Africa's participation and my own involvement.

When you have read the whole story right up to the end of the campaign, you may ask: What about Savimbi and Unita? What did they do? A lot. One hell of a lot. But naturally I am not writing about this war as seen from Savimbi's point of view. And I shall not go out of my way to highlight their actions. So one must bear in mind where I use words like 'ours', 'the RSA', 'the SA Defence Force', 'our commanders and troops', it would have been more correct if I had used the term RSA-Unita alliance throughout. It must be interpreted in this light. The top leadership of Unita and its troops achieved successes that will one day probably figure prominently in military annals.

The Russian-Cuban-Fapla alliance launched two offensives, from different directions. The offensive on the northern front from Lucusse started during April 1987. It was meant to divert the attention from the build-up of forces on the Cuito Cuanavale front which was supposed to have been happening unseen. The Cuito Cuanavale offensive was to have been the main thrust aimed at conquering Unita's general base area and headquarters' complex at Jamba. (See Map 3.)

Unita fiercely countered the northern offensive with mobile, heavily armed regular forces, semi-regular and guerrilla forces. They tackled the enemy from the front, from the sides and from the rear, disrupted their supply lines, and beat them off. After that the Cuban-supported Fapla formations retreated to Lucusse and ceased to be a factor.

The South African participation in these operations only involved preparations and training during 1986 in anticipation of the offensive and brief assistance of two medical orderlies. Unita defeated the offensive in a solo effort and with few losses.

I will now concentrate on the southern offensive, the main advance along the general line of approach from Cuito Cuanavale to Jamba.

The Cuban-MPLA forces started their advance with 16, 21, 47 and

59 Brigades in all seriousness on 14 August 1987. Their 25 Brigade had been moved into the area previously.

The aim of the first phase of their operation was to capture Mavinga. In order to do so, they had to get to the south of the Lomba River. One route was followed by 16 and 21 Brigades and 47 and 59 took another.

The second phase would aim to destroy Jamba.

Initially the SA Army's force levels comprised only one battery 127 mm multiple rocket launchers (MRLs) and one battery 120 mm mortars, each with an infantry company of 32 Battalion for their protection. There were also elements of Special Forces for specific tasks such as tankhunting, clandestine reconnaissance and artillery fire control.

The ground forces were called 20 Brigade and placed under the command of Col Jock Harris. Col Deon Ferreira succeeded him on 5 September 1987. His next higher commander was the new GOC of SWA who had taken over from Georg Meiring, another Free Stater, Gen Willie Meyer. Unita was assisted by 20 Brigade in breaking up the offensive.

The Fapla advance progressed very slowly at an average rate of approximately 4 km per day. They avoided the open veld preferring to move through the thick bush. They dug themselves into well-camouflaged positions every day at about 16:00. They protected the advance with armoured fighting vehicles and anti-aircraft batteries. They were also equipped with Soviet SAM 8 and other ground-to-air missiles. During August 1987 we decided to increase our support to Savimbi. We reinforced 20 Brigade with 61 Mechanized Battalion Group, two infantry companies of 101 Battalion in Casspirs, one battery each of G5 155 mm field artillery and 120 mm mortars. Unita provided the overwhelming majority of the infantry force for the campaign.

The RSA-SWA contingent never exceeded 3 000 men.

During early September 1987 a team of the SA Special Forces partially destroyed a bridge over the Cuito River behind the forward enemy brigades.

It was a special operation such as one sees in film and TV dramas. They wove through and around the enemy up to the river with the aid of Unita guides. They worked downstream and placed their charges behind the enemy troops. During their escape downstream one of our men was attacked by a crocodile. It left him with permanent scars. His knife saved him. If I remember correctly he stabbed the crocodile in the eye.

I got hold of the knife, had it mounted on a plaque with apt engravings and presented it to him at a later opportunity.

As a result of this operation the enemy was forced to take their supplies across the river from west to east by helicopter, and later with pontoons.

With a policy of aggressive defence the Unita-RSA forces successfully attacked the offensive enemy forces. Tough battles took place.

During the end of August and early September 1987, 47 Brigade and a Tactical Group moved westward around the source of the Lomba River and turned eastward in the general direction of Mavinga. On 4 September 1987 we stopped these manoeuvres mainly by means of artillery – G5s and MRLs. The enemy started to experience a shortage of supplies as a result of the damage to the bridge.

As the offensive was being brought to a standstill, we were coming to the final act of a previous drama.

Two years after Maj Wynand du Toit was captured in Cabinda, he was set free at Maputo on 7 September 1987. He was exchanged for 133 Angolan soldiers released by Savimbi and two Dutch citizens charged with terrorism, Klaas de Jonge and Helena Pastoors. It happened, ironically, at the same time that South Africa and Unita forces and Angolan-Cuban forces were clashing at the Lomba River, and while Pres Dos Santos was preparing himself for a visit to Paris.

The exchange was an extensive undertaking. There were small wheels within big wheels and riddles that were solved by means of mirrors. It had become bigger and more complex. There were many intrigues. A lot of people worked hard, cleverly and together to set it all up. Gen Neels van Tonder was a key man. I played only a very small part.

It is an unreal world. Over *nouvelle cuisine* in Paris, city of culture, you discuss the fate of people from different parts of the world who for different reasons find themselves in detention in different parts of southern Africa. Then you go to Pretoria where the jacaranda trees are showering the city with purple blossoms. You struggle with the annual transfers and promotions in the Defence Force, stock-taking and colour parades. You rush off to Jamba to see your ally, the leader of a resistance movement, in the bush. You eat *Caldeirada de Cabrito com Chindungo*[1] and swipe at the flies. His opponent, Pres Dos Santos, makes his personal Gulfstream aircraft available to ferry your fellow-officer back to his own country. At home wasps kill two of your parakeets. And then Northern Transvaal wins the Currie Cup at Ellis Park.

Back to the south-east of Angola. Here the operations of the Fapla forces were characterised by repeated efforts to cross the Lomba River. The first real purposeful attempt was that of 21 Brigade on 10 September 1987, but it was beaten off with tremendous losses in the Fapla ranks. One whole battalion was destroyed.

Two interesting events occurred during these battles. Late one afternoon two MiGs released two bombs over the area. They exploded at a considerable height above the ground causing a thick column of smoke slowly sinking down to the ground. Fearing that it could be chemical dust, Deon Ferreira ordered his troops in the area to clear out. He dispatched a team to test the area for chemical agencies. The result was negative. So the troops re-occupied their positions just in time the following day at first light to thwart the determined effort by 21 Brigade to cross the Lomba. This was the first indication of the possible use of chemical weapons which we knew they had. Some time after, Unita troops were in fact treated for disorders caused by chemicals.

Secondly, the new ZT3 anti-tank missile was successfully used for the first time in operations by Maj Hannes Nortmann and his men in resisting 21 Brigade. As a result of these types of operations South African armaments started gaining an international reputation for being reliable as a result of the fact that they were battle-proven.

The second big attempt of the enemy to cross the Lomba took place on 12–13 September 1987. Elements of 59 Brigade crossed the river and joined up with 47 Brigade. After being attacked on the 13th and suffering very heavy losses, the remainder of 59 Brigade retreated to north of the Lomba. The elements of 47 Brigade and the Tactical Group which were involved withdrew westward. We lost two Casspirs and a Ratel.

The third attempt and a few others which followed took place from 14 to 23 September. Every day 21 Brigade tried to cross the Lomba. They were unsuccessful every time and suffered heavy losses.

In the beginning I could not understand how they could even think to try and cross the river time after time in the same fashion and at the same place; it looked like suicide missions. An explanation was found later which I shall relate in the next chapter.

During these river-crossing attempts Deon received a ministerial visit at his tactical headquarters. Among the visitors were Ministers F W de Klerk, Pik Botha, Magnus Malan and Barend du Plessis; Mr Dave Steward, the DG of the Bureau of Information accompanied them.

They gathered round Deon's radio to listen in on one of 21 Brigade's dramatic attempts at crossing the Lomba. The flamboyant Pik Botha with his ever-intense involvement was all ears. He had insisted on being allowed to try on an anti-chemical warfare suit earlier in the afternoon. But it was Barend du Plessis that caught my eye that day.

Shortly after their arrival, a couple of Deon's men went to show each of them where he was to sleep. But, more important, they showed each one where his foxhole had been dug. That is where you scramble to for cover and safety if the alarm signals a possible bombardment of the tactical headquarters.

So they showed Minister Barend his hole. In fact they showed him three holes. The first was a shallow little hole that barely reached up to the knees. The next one was a little deeper, hip-deep. The third was a proper foxhole, deep enough to make one feel quite safe. He was told to choose one. But they had not made it easy for him to make up his mind.

Behind every hole had been placed a stick with a sort of do-it-yourself signboard. Written on them, from shallow to deep, appeared the following numbers: 10, 20 and 30. When he asked them what they meant, they said it was easy, if he gave the Defence Force an increase of 10% he could use the shallow hole, 20% merited the second one, and so one.

He chose the 30% hole and the Defence Force is still waiting for its 30% increase.

A few weeks later, before a meeting of the state security council, Dave Steward recalled the visit and said: 'What impressed me most was this: Col Ferreira right in the middle of a serious battle and you, the Chief of the Defence Force, are sitting fifty metres away. And what do you do? You leave it all in the hands of the Colonel and you talk to the visitors. Your command culture interests me. It was an experience.' (Of course, neither Deon Ferreira nor I did the fighting.)

The most decisive battle of the whole campaign took place on 3 October 1987. 'Although I did not physically take part in the battle, it was the best conventional attack in which I was ever involved.' Deon told me.

> It was an attack on the whole of the 47th Brigade and the Tactical Group. They had air support, fire support from 59 Brigade and tanks. We didn't have close air support and no tanks and they outnumbered us four to one.

> I must take my hat off to Cmdt Bok Smit and his men of 61 Mech Battalion who handled the attack, along with the gunners with their G5s and MRLs.
>
> Our better equipment and soldiers apart, it was our timing that made the day. I have never seen such timing before: 47 Brigade wanted to cross the Lomba from south to north to join up with 59 Brigade. We knew it beforehand and engaged them on the way. We caught them in the open. They were totally destroyed – by any definition.

That was the turning point. Two hundred and fifty Fapla soldiers were killed. It was the end of 47 Brigade. Among the large number of weapons and equipment destroyed or captured were eighteen tanks, three anti-aircraft batteries, two ground-to-air SAM-8 anti-aircraft missile systems (one system consists of three vehicles) and two SAM-9 systems, in addition to a variety of armoured personnel carriers and reconnaissance vehicles, infantry fighting vehicles, artillery field guns, a Flatface-radar vehicle and one hundred and twenty logistic vehicles.

It was the first time that a SAM-8 ground-to-air missile system had fallen into the hands of anybody not supposed to have it. Although it did not receive much media coverage, it was big news in military circles around the world.

Let us put this stage of the story of war and peace in southern Africa in a broader perspective. A multitude of countries around the world suffered ehtnic, religious and ideological friction, terrorism and different forms of internal conflict. Emergency regulations were being applied in about twenty states (in many countries this was not necessary as their normal laws were stringent enough). In *Beeld* of 30 October 1987, no less than 26 countries where war was being waged in some form or other were listed: Chad, Ethiopia, Nigeria, Sudan, Somalia, South West Africa, Uganda, Zimbabwe, Corsica, Cyprus, Northern Ireland, Spain, Yugoslavia, Burma, India, Iran, Iraq, Israel, Lebanon, New Caledonia, Pakistan, the Philippines, Sri Lanka, Syria, Turkey and Angola. Angola, where the Cuban-Fapla forces abandoned their offensive in the *terras do fim do mundo* – lands of the end of the earth.

All their brigades, minus hundreds of fallen troops and huge quantities of destroyed war material, started the long but generally orderly withdrawal. They eventually landed up close to their original starting

ABOVE: Captured tanks (Photo: *Gert van Niekerk*)

LEFT: Captured anti-aircraft artillery (Photo: *Gert van Niekerk*)

BELOW LEFT: Captured heavy military vehicles. Operation Protea (Photo: *Citizen*)

OPPOSITE PAGE
ABOVE: The Puma: the work-horse of the airforce, over Ovambo — flat as a table (Photo: *Stefan Sonderling*)

BELOW: Swaspes. "Clever dogs" (Photo: *Stefan Sonderling*)

PREVIOUS PAGE: Gen Jannie Geldenhuys wearing a general's beret displaying the crossed sword and baton emblem and the Infantry Corps insignia

RIGHT: Soccer: Xangongo
(Photo: *Sunday Times*)

BELOW: SWASPES.
"Excellent trackers"

RIGHT: Kaokoland: "Cliffs, ravines and the Kunene" (Photo: *Stefan Sonderling*)

BELOW: Ovambo: "Makalini palms" (Photo *Stefan Sonderling*)

BELOW RIGHT: Caprivi: Baobab world (Photo: *Stefan Sonderling*)

BOTTOM: Kavango: "Fish eagles and crocodiles" (Photo: *Stefan Sonderling*)

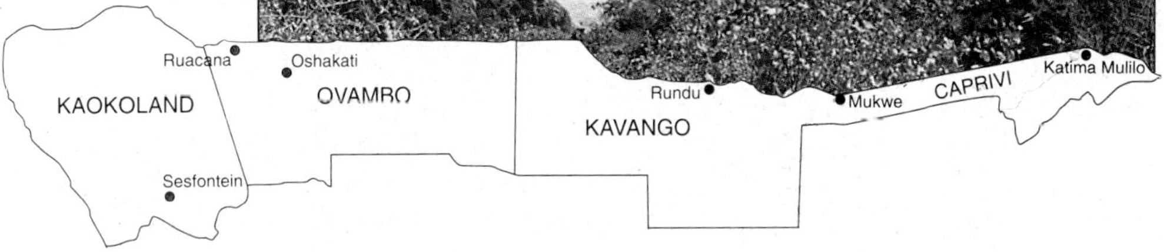

ABOVE: "And who do you think you are?..." Doug Watson *(top)*, South African bowls champion, who bears a striking resemblance to Jannie Geldenhuys *(below)* (Photo: *Beeld*)

ABOVE RIGHT: Martin Geldenhuys becomes Second-lieutenant (1983) (Photo: *The Argus*)

RIGHT: Heliopolous cemetry, Cairo. At the grave of a Geldenhuys (Photo: *The Argus*)

RIGHT: Derek Auret, Neels van Tonder, Johann Sonnekus and Jannie Geldenhuys playing bridge on the pyramids

BELOW INSET: Chester Crocker: "bloody conservative" and "dangerous liberal"

BELOW: The Russian SAM8 missile system that unintentionally landed in foreign hands (Photo: *SA Defence Force*)

LEFT: Gifted diplomat Neil van Heerden. "Nuances and finesse."

BELOW: *Left to right*: Dr Niel Barnard, Jannie Geldenhuys, Gen Magnus Malan, Min Pik Botha, Neil van Heerden and Derek Auret. "Cairo — front row seats at the ring of intellectual violence" (Photo: *The Argus*)

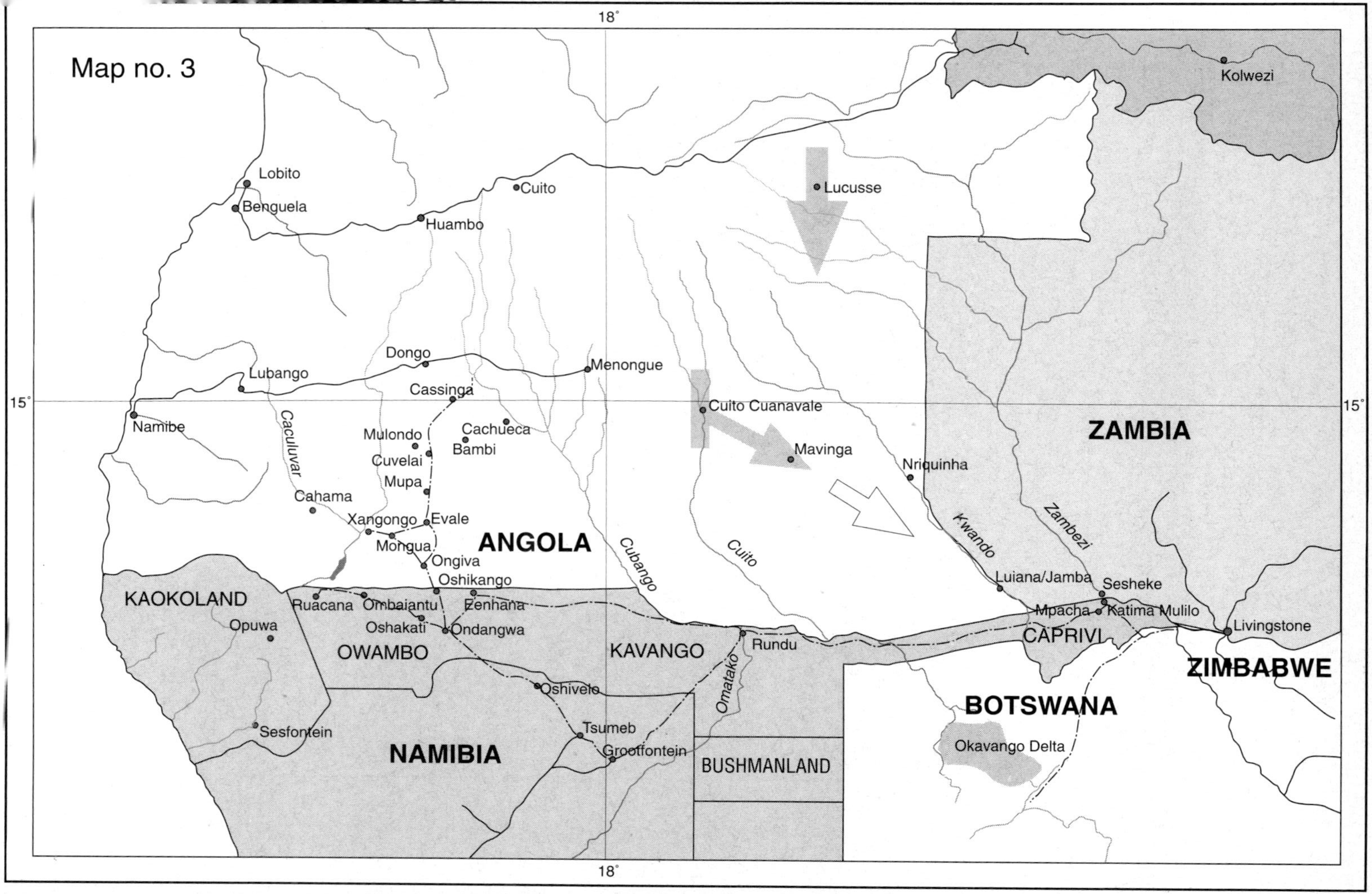
18°
15°
Lobito
Benguela
Huambo
Cuito
Lucusse
Kolwezi
Dongo
Lubango
Menongue
Cassinga
Namibe
Caculuvar
Mulondo
Cuvelai
Mupa
Cachueca
Bambi
Cahama
Xangongo
Evale
Mongua
Ongiva
Oshikango
ANGOLA
Cubango
Cuito Cuanavale
Mavinga
Cuito
Nriquinha
Kwando
Zambezi
ZAMBIA
KAOKOLAND
Opuwa
Ruacana
Ombalantu
Enhana
Oshakati
Ondangwa
OWAMBO
KAVANGO
Rundu
Omatako
Oshivelo
Tsumeb
Grootfontein
Sesfontein
NAMIBIA
BUSHMANLAND
Luiana/Jamba
Sesheke
Mpacha
Katima Mulilo
CAPRIVI
Livingstone
ZIMBABWE
BOTSWANA
Okavango Delta
Map no. 3

Map no. 4

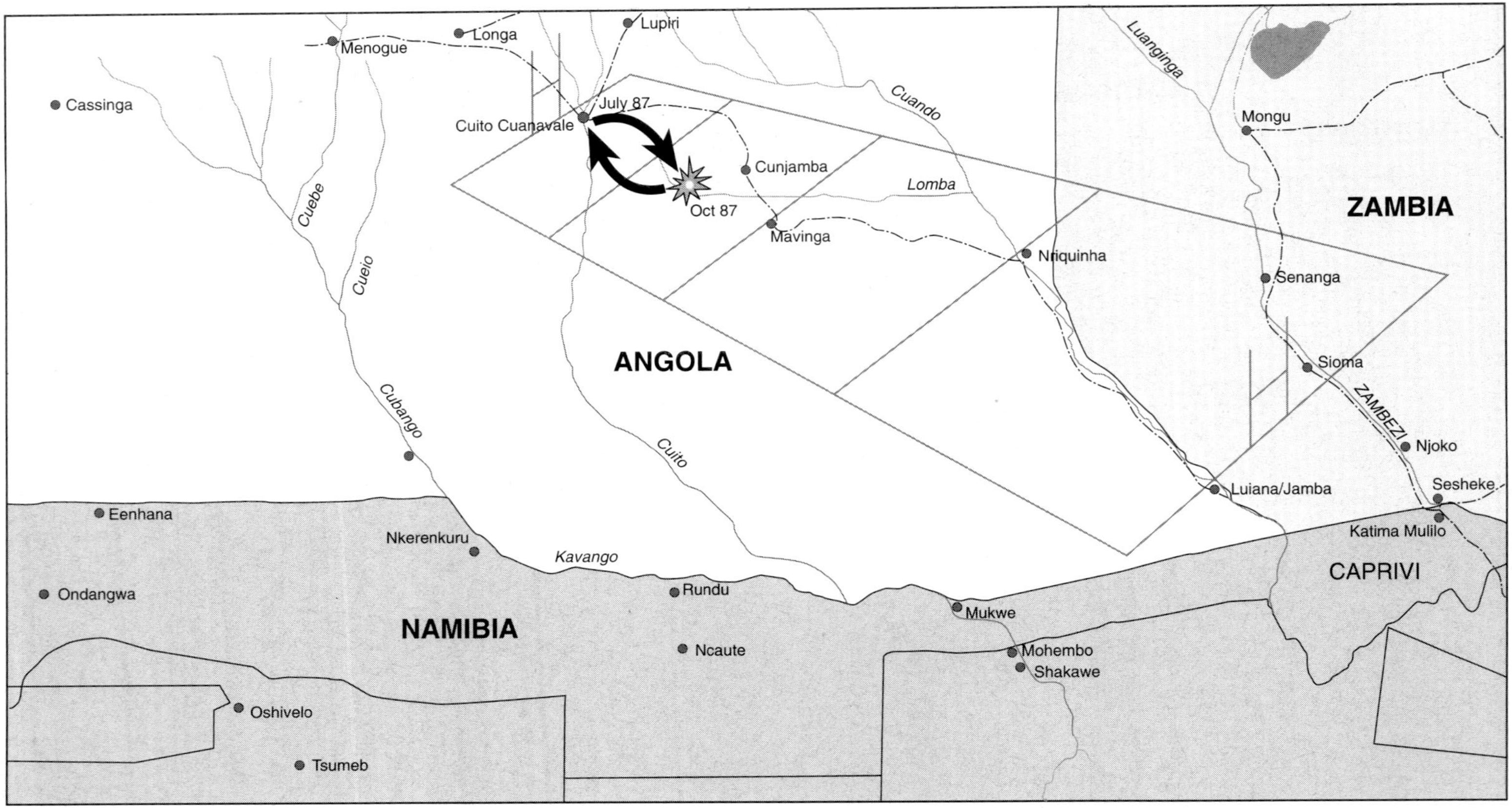

ZAMBIA
ANGOLA
NAMIBIA
CAPRIVI
Cassinga
Menogue
Longa
Lupiri
July 87
Cuito Cuanavale
Oct 87
Cunjamba
Mavinga
Lomba
Cuando
Nriquinha
Mongu
Luanginga
Senanga
Sioma
ZAMBEZI
Njoko
Sesheke
Katima Mulilo
Luiana/Jamba
Cuebe
Cueio
Cubango
Cuito
Kavango
Eenhana
Nkerenkuru
Ondangwa
Rundu
Ncaute
Mukwe
Mohembo
Shakawe
Oshivelo
Tsumeb

Map no. 5

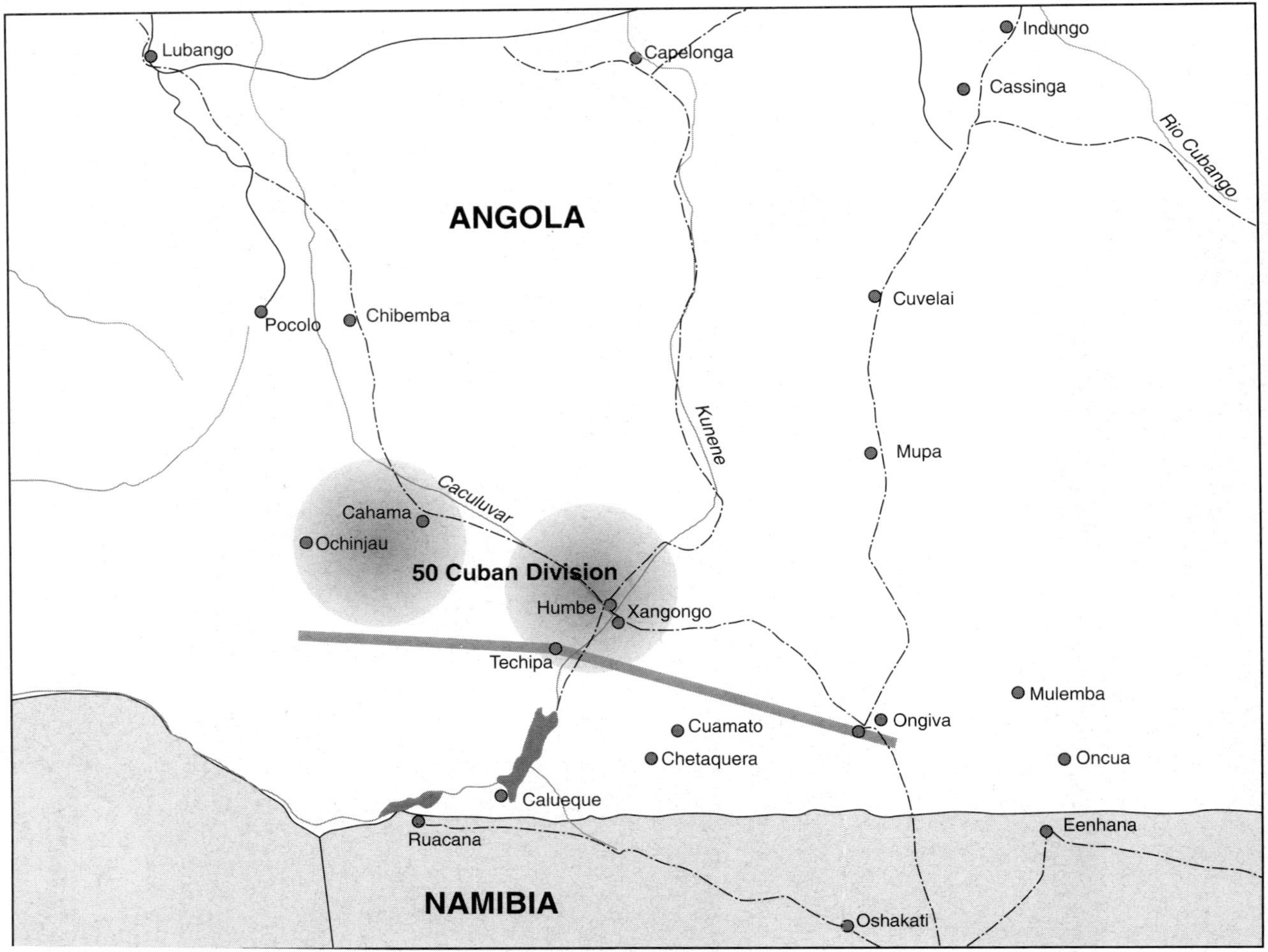
Lubango
Capelonga
Indungo
Cassinga
Rio Cubango
ANGOLA
Pocolo
Chibemba
Cuvelai
Kunene
Mupa
Caculuvar
Cahama
Ochinjau
50 Cuban Division
Humbe
Xangongo
Techipa
Mulemba
Ongiva
Cuamato
Chetaquera
Oncua
Calueque
Ruacana
Eenhana
NAMIBIA
Oshakati

LEFT: Angolan Ndalu, Boer Geldenhuys and Cuban Rosalees — "The ABC of War and Peace"

BELOW: Joint Commission, Havana. Mediator Crocker (*left*), host Castro (*right*)

RIGHT: Senor Aldana, Gen Prem Chand and Gen Ndalu

BELOW: Gen Arnaldo Óchoa Sanchez

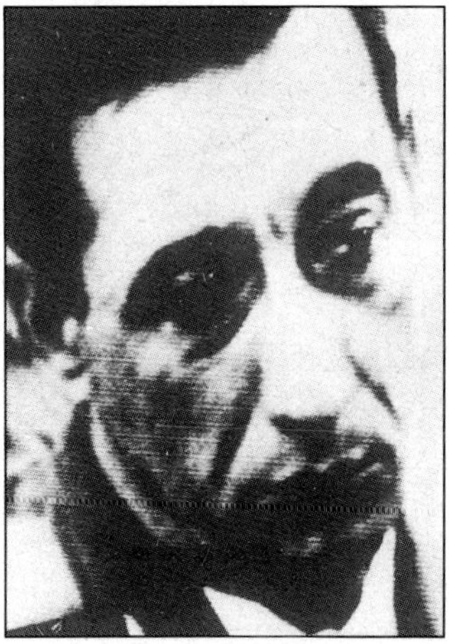

LEFT: John James Clarke "Jan" Holliday with ex-colleagues from 1 SSB

BELOW: "Oom Kaspaas" Resquet (Photo: *The Argus*)

RIGHT: Gen Geldenhuys's "Forty Days Party" organised by his drivers, 1985–1990 *Back*: Bertus, Hein, Garth, Lieb, Michael, Westley, Brent, Kestell, Manie *Front*: Spencer, Johan and Johan (Photo: *Paratus*)

BELOW RIGHT: After retirement. Pres F W de Klerk (Photo: *Paratus*)

RIGHT: Martin, Mariana, Jannie, Marié, Annamarié and Bruwer (Photo: *Paratus*)

BELOW: Stepping-out parade: 1 SDB colour party (Photo: *Paratus*)

point. We used the opportunity to regroup, change troops and service equipment.

From this point onwards I had only one consideration. We had already completed our mission. We had totally broken up the enemy offensive. But we could not immediately leave the battle area. In the short term we had to ensure that the new situation that we had created would not be undone. We had to consolidate our gains and prevent the enemy from regrouping and resuming their offensive.

But we could not assume permanent responsibility for maintaining the advantageous situation that we had established. In the longer term we had to leave the situation arranged in such a manner that Unita itself could take care of its defence in the event of another 'annual offensive'. That is what we wanted to do. No more, no less.

This is classic doctrine. After a successful battle, one consolidates; you secure the captured area and clear it up to a determined 'line of exploitation'; you take the necessary precautions to deal with a possible counteroffensive, and if you leave the area, other forces take over from you to take care of its defence. In this case the line of exploitation was the Cuito River, and the forces earmarked to take over from us the responsibility for the defence of the area was Unita.

During this campaign, as before, we had to take into consideration an established pattern. In every crossborder operation we planned to accomplish our objectives as quickly as possible. The danger always existed that international political pressure could bring a forced end to the operation before we could achieve our objectives. With political pressure I mean resolutions of the UN Security Council and international conferences.

It has also happened, however, as with Operation Sceptic, Protea and Askari, that the political pressure did not materialize as quickly as we had assumed it would in our planning. We then had more time than we had anticipated initially. And as we had no permanent presence in Angola, we had to use this 'borrowed time' as best we could to create the most advantageous security situation possible while we were there.

Political events can be unpredictable, but indications were that 'borrowed time', or as we say in rugby, 'injury time' had started. We could not know how much more time we had. To leave the area in such a situation as described above, we had to pursue the enemy up to the Cuito River and to reinforce it as an obstacle on which Unita could base its future defence of the area. For the defence to be successful, we regarded it as imperative, together with Savimbi, to form a tank force for Unita by utilizing the serviceable enemy tanks captured from Fapla. We had to do all this during the consolidation phase of unknown duration.

During this phase the South African forces were reinforced with elements of 4 SA Infantry Battalion, extra 127 mm MRLs, a squadron of Olifant tanks, and a number of G6 guns. It was the first time since World War II that we were to use tanks in operations.

While Deon was waiting for his troops and equipment, he conducted other operations. *Inter alia* they continually bombarded the Cuito Cuanavale Airfield with G5s. By the middle of October it was unusable. It was a hard blow to the Soviet, Cuban and Angolan pilots. Now they had to operate from Menongue and consequently could not cause much damage. Although altogether they had flown more than a thousand sorties over the South Africans at this stage, they had hit only one G5, one supply vehicle and one water lorry. They had caused no loss of life.

It was an open secret that South Africa was involved in something with Unita in the south-east of Angola, but we could still not yet release information to the press about the operation. It caused some embarrassment because I had had to announce on 2 November 1987 that eleven soldiers of the SA Defence Force and the SWATF had been killed in encounters with Plan three days earlier. Few people believed me. The suspicion that the report had something to do with the Unita-South African Cuban-Fapla fighting was too strong.

I told the truth. The men were killed when a Plan base was attacked just across the border from central Ovambo. Most of them died as a result of a single mortar bomb explosion. One hundred and fifty insurgents were killed. It was an unrelated operation initiated by the SWATF that took place hundreds of kilometres west of the Cuito River.

As soon as our fresh troops were in position, they started to drive back the Cuban and Fapla forces who were still east of Cuito. Successful battles took place on 9, 11, 13 and 17 November. Altogether 525 enemy troops died in action and 33 tanks were destroyed or seized. The result was that all the elements that took part in the offensive against Jamba and still found themselves east of the Cuito, had been driven back to within 24 km east of the river.

By mid-December 1987 Fapla were still receiving reinforcements including Cuban soldiers and T-62 tanks, which were placed in the general Cuito Cuanavale area. So they too came under the fire of G5 guns.

The South African gunners with their G5s and later G6 guns were a decisive factor throughout the campaign. The G6 is a self-propelled version of the towed G5.

Unita provided the foot and motorized infantry for most of the operations. Their forces also protected the objectives we had seized and our artillery positions. Their protection of our supply lines was likewise of the utmost importance. Unita also kept the enemy aircraft at a safe altitude with their Stinger missiles. (They got them from the Americans after the Clark Amendment had been repealed.)

I announced on 5 December 1987 that we would start to withdraw our troops as they had completed their tasks. I stressed that it was a tactical withdrawal executed under operational conditions and that fighting could still take place.

The troops scheduled to withdraw first, were the elements that were not needed for safeguarding the area or assisting to form Unita's tank force.

There was another period of regrouping and maintenance of equipment because those national servicemen due to be discharged on 15 December 1987 had to be replaced.

Towards the end of the month a Unita force took Munhango, the birthplace of Savimbi. They did this with the use of four T55 tanks which had earlier been seized from the enemy.

The campaign entered its last phase with successful attacks by the Unita-RSA forces on 13 January, and 14 and 25 February 1988. The result was that all the forces that had participated in the enemy offensive were driven to the west of the Cuito River. However, it still left a Fapla presence in the Tumpo area immediately east of the river.

At this point the setting of my story changes to a completely different scene. On Wednesday 10 February 1988 Cpl Arrie Jacobs and I were driving in Cape Town from Wynberg to my office in the HF Verwoerd Building. In the car we listened to the morning news. There had been a *coup d'état* in Bophuthatswana. Pres Lucas Mangope had been detained.

At the underground parking area I entered the lift on the -2 level with another passenger. The lift stopped at the +3 floor and another person joined us. My two fellow passengers happened to know one another. They exchanged small talk.

The one asked: 'How are you?'

The other one answered: 'Ag man, mercifully spared to keep on suffering!'

It made me think of something my daughter, Annamarié had told me. In her version the answer was: 'By this time of day I have already come to accept my fate.' It was nine o'clock in the morning.

When the doors of the elevator opened at +14 the oppressing atmosphere immediately lifted. The minister wanted to see me. Straight away. From that time onwards I was in and out of his and Mr Pik Botha's offices.

What was important is that nobody actually knew what was really going on.

So I issued the customary Warning Order as a result of which the following events took place:

- I flew to Waterkloof Air Base where other Defence Force officers and I met with out colleagues of the Police, National Intelligence, Foreign Affairs and others. We exchanged information and jointly planned what had to be done. If we could reach the South African ambassador, we could probaby find out exactly what was happening in Bophuthatswana. Or we could try to contact the rebel leader and start a discussion. The best would be to go and look for ourselves.
- Gen Johan van der Merwe of the SA Police, Mr Derek Auret of Foreign Affairs, I and a few staff officers therefore took off for Zeerust by Puma helicopter. There we exchanged information with our senior local representatives.
- We continued our flight and landed again some distance beyond Zeerust at the command element of the troops headed for Mmabatho. Brig Du Preez Coetzee of Potchefstroom was in command of the army troops. Again we pooled information and discussed possible courses of action.

We travelled ahead by helicopter. We circled Mmabatho. It looked safe and we landed at the South African ambassador's residence. He put us fully into the picture. Concluding our discussions the first troops arrived.

The actions to set the president free and restore authority began. First Mr Mangope was freed at the sports stadium.

The situation was a bit confusing. There were Ratels and armoured cars. They paid no heed to the rebel guards that were literally standing about among the vehicles. In the meantime the police task force had already arrived. And the press. All mixed up.

Keeping in mind that it could be useful to make contact with the rebel leader, I took a chance and walked up to one of the rebel guards. I asked him where his commander was. But he was about as bewildered as Old Smokey whom Chris Serfontein had captured during Operation Sceptic. Only less dangerous. So I advised him to hand his rifle over to me. While still talking to him, I removed the rifle from his shoulder and told him the rebellion was probably over for him. All this was of no avail. The troops forced the stadium gates open and entered. Mr Mangope was freed. Brig Jack Turner, the Chief of the Bophuthatswana Defence Force, who was with him, had been wounded in the foot.

After that the cleaning up of the other important buildings started. The army arrived on the scene with Eland armoured cars and Ratels. The rebels lost their enthusiasm. The police entered and cleaned up. Everybody reported to the ambassador's residence. Derek Auret was also there. He reported to the two ministers.

Mr P W Botha, accompanied by Gen Malan, and Mr Pik Botha arrived. Mr Mangope made a speech and Mr P W Botha made a speech. There were drinks and snacks.

The people who had come with me from Pretoria went back there and I got a lift back to Cape Town in the President's aircraft.

I was in bed by about 01:30 that night. Later that morning on my way to the office, I thought, just let somebody today say again: 'Mercifully spared to keep on suffering.'

Back to the war in Angola. I confirmed in a press statement on 20 February 1988 that a tactical withdrawal was in progress, but explained once again that it was being done under operational conditions and proceeding slowly.

In the meantime, as we had expected, the international politics over Angola had begun to generate momentum. Both Chester Crocker and Pik Botha exploited their opportunities. In March 1988 they agreed on a package for a new peace initiative for the region. From this one could deduce that the time available to us for operational actions were nearly at an end, but that it would also be advisable to maintain a military presence east of the Cuito. However small, the possibility still existed that Fapla forces could grab one last chance to break out and improve their military position before the negotiations began. The Citizen Force, 82 Brigade, established such a presence. The last battle took place at Tumpo on 23 March 1988 without changing the situation. Fapla suffered considerable losses and we none, apart from three tanks which got stuck in the mine field. This was Fapla's 'success' of the war. But still, one cannot score a try in your own half of the field!

On 30 April 1988 a small combat group replaced 82 Brigade. Their task was to support the Sappers who were still laying mine fields on the opposite side of the crossing points over the Cuito. In this fashion we continued to reduce our force levels to 1 500 men and less, sharp end and support elements, to keep the occupied area safe together with Unita.

The existing Fapla forces were concentrated at Cuito Cuanavale and Tumpo.

The results of the fighting between September 1987 and April 1988 were as follows:

Cuban-Fapla forces		**SA Defence Force**	
(Damage done by SADF and Unita)		(Damage done by Soviets, Cubans and Fapla)	
Tanks	94	Tanks	3
Armoured troop and combat vehicles	100	Ratels infantry fighting vehicles	5
BM21/BM14 MRLs	34	Casspirs	3
D30/M-46 guns	9	Rinkhals	1
TMM mobile bridges	7	Wit hings	1
Logistic vehicles	389	Kwêvoël	1
		(Last five all vehicles)	
Artillery, rocket and missile systems	15	Radars	5
23 mm anti-aircraft guns	22		
MiG 21/23 combat aircraft	9	Mirage F1 fighter aircraft (one as a result of enemy action, one as a result of an accident)	2
Helicopters	9	Bosbok light reconnaisance aircraft	1

On the Cuban-Fapla side 4 785 men were killed in action. These are confirmed figures and do not include the deserters, the wounded and those who died of their wounds later. The real figure is probably a few thousand more. On South African side 31 men were killed in action. This is the real figure. Six more of our troops died of malaria.

Many inferences can be drawn from this 'scoreboard' of cold statistics, but it does not tell of the frictions behind the scenes which are unavoidable in war. The Unita-RSA alliance functioned as (well and better) as could have been expected. But just as tension can arise between different elements of one force in peace time, so much easier can it do so between allies in wartime. It did not, but I showed signs of frustration which I regretted later on.

I did argue that we were working under time pressure. Mr P W Botha had already seriously warned me at least twice to finish the job and get out. Gen Malan and I once had to go and see him in his office just before a meeting of the State Security Council; on another occasion he stopped me in the passage after such a meeting.

He was serious and firm, but civil. When Mr Botha had finished talking, you had no doubt over what he wanted. He did not want a 'Vietnam'. We had to accomplish our mission and withdraw from Angola. To put the discussion into perspective, I have to add that the perception existed that we had already successfully completed our mission. I can understand that, because we had indeed achieved our aim; but we still had to defend it against possible follow-up attacks.

While time was running out, we had not yet progressed anywhere near to my expectations in establishing Unita's tank force. On a few occasions I used harsh words and those I regretted later.

With his deep insigth, Savimbi stayed calm. I was in too much of a hurry. Looking back, I realize that I overlooked *friction de guerre*. As I said in the first chapter, everything in war is simple, but the simplest action is difficult to perform. To walk is simple. To walk in water is difficult.

An entrepreneur who wants to start a new business with many heavy-duty vehicles will find it difficult to move his stock to his place of business, even in South Africa. But we were fighting a war in the bush. What now? How does one collect in a short space of time serviceable and semi-serviceable seized tanks over an area of thousands of square kilometres? This was the African bush with no infrastructure; in an area which the Portuguese used to call the *terras do fim do mundo* – the end of the earth. There is no readily available tow-away service for tanks. How does one assemble people in this totally undeveloped region with the necessary aptitude to become tank drivers?

It was done somehow. I was being too impatient. As you will see, the Unita tanks later showed their worth.

At this stage it is necessary to look in a wider context at the war in the bush at the end of the earth. There were in fact five 'wars' in progress: Operation Moduler, Hooper and Packer, which I have just described; propaganda war; the international diplomatic exchanges; the 'normal' war against Plan and the Unita-MPLA struggle in the rest of Angola.

The propaganda and international diplomatic encounters moved at such a hectic pace that it made one's head spin. For that reason I will give only a few flashes from which one could form a general impression of what was happening in these fields. First the propaganda:

- On 15 January 1988 the Angolan Minister of Defence alleged that 6 000 South African troops had attacked Cuito Cuanavale. The intention, according to him, was to capture Cuito Cuanavale to facilitate Unita's penetration to the central highlands in order to prevent the reconstruction of the Benguela railway line.
- Unita declared in Lisbon that they had encircled Cuito Cuanavale. (This statement possibly caused some people to think that the South Africans were making for Cuito Cuanavale.)
- The official Angolan news agency, Angop, claimed on 22 January 1988 that they had shot down 40 SA Air Force aircraft.
- Two days later an Angolan spokesman, Maj Plaçido, said that there had been a concentrated South African attack on Cuito Cuanavale.
- Pres Dos Santos of Angola declared on 15 February that the South African Forces in southern Angola had been increased during the previous three days by 6 000 troops.
- A few days later Angop announced that the South African troops now numbered 7 000.
- Pres Dos Santos added on 19 February that South Africa had lost 140 men, 6 aircraft, 47 tanks and diverse armoured cars during the previous 45 days.
- The Angolan Foreign Minister, Afonso von Dunem, declared on 17 April that more than 6 000 South African troops were preparing for another attack on Cuito Cuanavale. He said that they were only part of a larger South African force of 9 000 soldiers, 600 artillery field guns, and 500 tanks and armoured cars in Angola.

However, the truth is:

- We did not attack Cuito Cuanavale. We never even thought of the central highlands and the Benguela railway line, at any time whatsoever.
- We had no more than 3 000 troops – not three times that number claimed by them.
- We lost only the number of aircraft that I mentioned – not twelve times more as claimed by Angola.
- The other allegations about our quantities of armament is likewise ridiculously out of proportion. Six hundred field guns!

How the Angolans, at such a late stage as April 1988, could still think or claim that we wanted to attack Cuito Cuanavale is puzzling. It was practically impossible. It reminds me of a story that Gen Jan van Loggerenberg, the Chief of the South African Air Force, once told me.

It was about a motorist who entered, if I remember correctly, the town of Brits. He was trying to find the Post Office. He stopped and addressed an old man in the street:

> 'Good morning, Oom.'
>
> 'Morning.'
>
> 'Can you tell me how to get to the Post Office?'
>
> 'Okay, Son, now you take this street and you cross the first robot. You cross the second robot and at the third robot you turn this way, left. Then, when you get to the stream ... no, that's wrong. Come back. Let us start at the beginning: You take this road and you cross the first robot, then you turn left at the second robot, and then when you get to the stream ... No, that's wrong. Come back. Son, now you take this street, then you come to the first robot and you turn left, and then uh ... uh ... No Sonny Boy, here, from this place where we are now, you can't get over the stream to get to the Post Office!'

We also had a stream to cross. A very big stream – the Cuito River. We lacked the wading capability of the Russian tanks. And we did not have the necessary bridges readily available. If we had wanted to reach Cuito Cuanavale during those last few weeks, we would have had to have positioned a sufficiently strong force west of the river before the time.

This was propaganda in action. In the same style, mentioning only a few international political events, I will try here to sketch a general idea of the diplomatic activity:

- On 28 and 29 January 1988 Chester Crocker conferred with the Angolan government.
- Charles Redman, spokesman for the State Department, announced in Washington DC that Cuban and Angolan officials had affirmed for the first time that they accepted the plan to withdraw all Cuban troops from Angola. George Schultz, the United States Minister of State, described it as an important development holding promise of a settlement in the region.
- Mr Pik Botha, Minister of Foreign Affairs, was not very optimistic, but said on 11 February that South Africa would welcome progress made by Crocker on the deadlock.
- Afonso von Dunem stated on 14 February that the schedule for Cuban withdrawal would depend on the United States, South Africa and other countries ceasing their support of Unita.
- Pik Botha announced on 14 March, after having conferred with Chester Crocker in Genève, that the Angolan government accepted in principle that Cuban withdrawal from Angola should be linked to the independence of South West Africa. (The South African government had always maintained that the SA Defence Force could not withdraw from South West Africa in accordance with UN Security Council Resolution 435, if the Cubans did not also leave Angola.)
- Boutros Boutros-Ghali stated on 24 March that Dos Santos and Savimbi had declared themselves ready for personal discussions. (Boutros-Ghali became the Secretary General of the UN during the early 1990s.)

As I have indicated previously, there are much less identifiable dividing lines nowadays than before between phases of hostilities and phases of diplomacy, between peace and war.

During recent years it was difficult to tell whether we had peace mixed with war, or war mixed with peace. It was no problem to describe the war of 1987–1988, as the hostilities were more prominent than the peace initiatives. However, since November 1987, and especially during the first quarter of 1988, the peace efforts gathered so much momentum that they often became more prominent than the war.

The focus started moving continually like a pendulum from war to peace and back, and I will describe it in that way.

War. From the battle of words I return to the 'end of the earth' to describe the conclusion of the battle of guns.

The war in the south-east of Angola had been decided. The offensive against Jamba had failed. The campaign did not end on a spectacular note. There was no final knock-out, in the same way that the Gulf War did not end on a knock-out.

The drama of the conflict in Angola in terms of the Cuban and South African involvement had not yet ended. In fact, in western Angola a new drama was already building up.

Before telling that story, I expect that I had better give my answer to the frequently asked question: Who won the war over Jamba?

It is easy to answer this unnecessary question: We did – Unita and we. By far. All the facts have now become available and anyone claiming to speak with authority who gives a different judgement, does so with ulterior motives.

The mission of the MPLA, Cubans and Russians was to capture Jamba. They did not. They never even reached Jamba. They did not even reach Mavinga. They never crossed the Lomba River.

The mission of Unita and ourselves was to destroy the offensive against Jamba. We did just that; indeed, even before the attackers could scale the first hurdle – the Lomba River. As a bonus we also pushed them back to west of the Cuito River, with the exception of one isolated spot, Tumpo, east of the river.

This is the unquestionable truth.

After this the Soviets lost their appetite for war in Angola. Only a few months later they told us that nobody could win the war in Angola – the answer was negotiations.

Our longstanding conviction that the Soviets would have to abandon their military involvement in Angola sooner or later, began to be proved true.

The Cubans were also fed-up with the war. They told us that later. During 1975–1976 they thought that they were going to Angola for a year or two. In 1988, thirteen years later, they were still there, with no end in sight. The answer was negotiations.

The negotiations started in all seriousness. The end result was the signing of the, now well-known, tripartite agreement on 22 December

1988 in New York. Our men had made it possible.

The agreement did not bring total peace to the region. The war between the Angolan government and Unita continued unabated. Something still had to happen to force them to the conference table. It did happen.

The hardliners of the MPLA wanted yet another last go at conquering Jamba. During March 1989 Fapla launched an offensive on Mavinga with a total of six brigades – without Cuban support.

They used the same routes and doctrines as during 1987. We had found many years earlier that Soviet-oriented forces used the same routes and tactics over and over again. They succeeded in crossing the Lomba and progressed with one brigade to within seven kilometres north of Mavinga. There they got bogged down. Unita now reaped the results of the preparations which had started as early as 1988. The Unita tanks also proved their worth. They used 23 captured T54 and T55 tanks with great success. They received absolutely no South African support. At that stage the South Africans had long before executed a formal and monitored withdrawal.

Unita cut Fapla's supply lines to their forward troops and forced them to a standstill. They dug in and stayed in their trenches for 92 days while being harassed daily by Unita artillery bombardments. They did not get any back-up and on the 92nd day of this hell they took flight back to Cuito Cuanavale.

The brief high media profile of Unita's successful solo defence of Mavinga, and the extensive high media profile of Fapla's 92 days 'siege of Mavinga' brought the general reader and TV viewer under the impression that Unita had been overrun. And the media dust settled.

Although Unita's success passed quietly they demonstrated undeniably that our long-term strategy for the 1987–1988 campaign had worked by enabling Unita to successfully defend the area without assistance, as we had planned.

Fapla's failure caused even the MPLA hardliners to reconsider their position. Our sustained opinion that one day one of Fapla's 'annual offensives' would be its last, was proved correct.

Peace. The MPLA's failed attack on Mavinga was a major factor in bringing them and Unita together round the conference table for serious negotiations. This resulted, two years later, in the signing of an agreement on 31 May 1991 at Estoril, Portugal. In the meantime the Angolans and especially the Cubans still continued a sustained and large-scale propaganda campaign according to which they had humbled the South Africans at Cuito Cuanavale.

Not everybody fell for the Cuban propaganda. Sharp and knowledgeable observers of the war knew better. For example, I had a talk once with overseas generals and one of them remarked that it was very clear that the Marxist alliance had lost, because the Cubans were nagging too long and too loud that they had won. 'To quote Shakespeare,' he said, 'it is a matter of, "the lady doth protest too much, methinks".'

Even so, many people believed the Cuban propaganda. The same thing happened with the allies' war against Iraq. In fact, the Gulf War serves as a very good and recent example as to how perceptions are being formed and how people can argue over who won or lost a war.

We all saw Iraq biting the dust. But immediately after the cessation of hostilities, the media carried reports of statements by Saddam Hussein and others that Iraq had won the war. Amazing. During TV interviews Iraqis very sincerely said they thought Iraq had won. Thanks to the overwhelming international support for the allies and the domination of the Western media through CNN and the likes, this misperception was corrected within two days.

After that, however, certain perceptions continued to persist, especially in some parts of the Arab world where impressions are not formed exclusively by the Western media. I still hear the following argument:

First person: 'Saddam Hussein lost the war in cowardly fashion. He didn't offer any visible resistance to the missile and air attacks. Before the land war really got going and before they really started to hurt one another, he chucked in the towel and yielded faintheartedly – without firing a shot.'

Second person: 'The mightiest power in the world, the USA, assembled allies from the other big powers in the world, the United Kingdom and France, with the best armament they had at their disposal; it mobilized others – 27 countries in all; it secured the financial support of West Germany and Japan. And all of them together took the field against one single country, Saddam Hussein's Iraq – and they couldn't destroy him! He still rules Iraq and his defence force is still intact. Saddam won.'

This dialogue is a clear illustration that contradicting perceptions can be formed and that they can be sustained for a long time. Long after the war, on 29 September 1991, *Rapport* wrote: 'Since (the war)

Saddam has turned on the propaganda to make his population believe that Iraq really scored the victory "by remaining standing against thirty nations".'

We were hit by propaganda in exactly the same way. There were contributing factors: Our government's viewpoint was that the war was really an Angolan issue; that it was a war between Savimbi and his Unita against the MPLA and its allies – the Soviets, Eastern bloc countries and especially the Cubans. Although we had a real interest in the struggle, we only assisted Unita. Whether one agrees or not, this was the policy. It was Savimbi's war and we were his ally, strictly speaking, the silent partner.

Owing to this state of affairs, the initiative in handling the media was in the hands of Unita. The policy regarding liaison with the media was that Unita would release information about the operations and would use every opportunity to propagate its cause and promote its image.

This arrangement had the disadvantage for South Africa that on its part press releases could be issued only when we had to announce casualties. This created the impression that there was no good news, only bad. And this at a time when our forces were scoring one success after another.

The Cubans were another factor that contributed towards creating the wrong impressions. Through the years the overall objective was to get them out of Angola. It was a challenge which Mr P W Botha regularly presented to us. Savimbi had also stated that to drive the Cubans out of his country was the most important single motive for which he was fighting. All other activities were to be considered against the background of this overall goal.

As early as the middle to late 1970s, when South Africa entered into discussions with the Big Five of the West and the UN, we had tried to put the issue of the Cuban presence in Angola on the agenda. The reaction of all the other parties always was, as Mr Martti Ahtisaari once put it: 'It is a "non starter".' In other words, if we insisted on having the Cuban question included in the agenda, nobody would be prepared even to talk to us.

During the 1980s, however, three important developments on the international political scene had a significant impact on the SWA-Angolan situation: Reagan's election as USA President, the decision of the American Administration to support Unita, and the increased Cuban presence in Angola.

To these could later be added: the subsequent decision by the Americans to acknowledge that, in terms of Resolution 435, interdependence indeed existed between the withdrawal of the SA Defence Force from South West according to resolution 435, and Cuban withdrawal from Angola. But the most important consequence of these developments was the Americans' persuasion of the Angolans and Cubans also to accept it as a valid item for the agenda. For the first time the departure of the Cubans now became a real possibility.

This was the situation during the time leading up to the negotiations of 3 May 1988 in London. At this stage there was still no cessation of hostilities in the south of Angola. In other words, the prospect and the preparatory moves to get the Cubans out had started well before the war had officially ended.

This created a delicate situation in which public statements about the war had to be made with great circumspection.

In the first place we had to announce our successes but we had to be careful not to create the impression that Unita was playing second fiddle. Secondly we had to consider the Cubans. It may sound simple but we had already attracted criticism from Savimbi over media statements that we had made. He stated during a press conference that we were hijacking Unita's successes for ourselves.

We were compelled to publicize our successes because the Cubans embarked on a big propaganda campaign in which they claimed glorious victories, as they put it, at Cuito Cuanavale; but once again we had to be very careful with our references to them, because it would have been extremely difficult, if not impossible, to persuade them to evacuate Angola if they had to depart in disgrace as a beaten force.

The popular international picture of the typical Cuban is that of a person with a Castro type beard, in camouflaged combat dress with a rifle over the shoulder, a cigar in the mouth and a clenched fist; in short, a macho figure. It is not entirely a true reflection because I have met many charming Cubans who do not fit this picture. However, the picture does contain some elements of truth. It is to a large extent the image many Cubans have of themselves: A courageous Che Guevara figure in camo liberating countries to communism; the revolutionary who supports anti-Western revolutionary movements all over the world, leading them to victory. How do you get somebody with such a self-image out of Angola if he is being humiliated in the process? We had to provide them with an honourable exit.

Everybody agreed a few months later that this was an accurate interpretation. The Cubans insisted that they would leave Angola only if it were to be an honourable withdrawal. The motto for the negotiation should be: 'There must be no losers.' Put in a different way: 'There must only be winners.'

To them an honourable withdrawal in practice meant a steady and orderly exit, following an internationally acknowledged formal agreement, as opposed to a seemingly hasty and forced retreat as a result of the negative outcome of the war.

It was not as if there was complete and absolute silence about the Soviet and Cuban failures. During public speeches Gen Malan often described it in strong language. But the misconceptions remained stuck for a long time, and those who find support for their politics in the 'humiliating South African defeat at Cuito Cuanavale' still keep them alive.

After having told the story of the campaign and the myth of Cuito Cuanavale, I can now come to the solemn promise I made to the commanders and troops I mentioned at the beginning of the chapter. I promised them that the truth of their victories will one day become known.

Our men gained one irrefutable success after the other. They performed combat feats which will in time be recorded as unique in the history of the art of warfare.

All this they did in a manner bearing witness of a force with character; of spirited fighting commanders wise to battlecraft; of men on the ground and in the air who showed guts as one would expect of South Africans; of black, white, brown and yellow members of the South African Defence Force and the SWA Territory Force who did not flinch.

In a campaign in which altogether more than 40 000 troops on both sides participated, it is near to incredible that a handful of 3 000 South African and South West African troops could play such a decisive role in changing the international course of events.

The war is over now and I do not want to be unduly nasty toward anybody in particular. I also have full understanding for the Cubans' desire to create a positive image regarding their involvement in Angola, internationally and especially back home. It was a stated condition to making their withdrawal possible and acceptable. They were in a difficult position – but they went too far with their propaganda. They and those who liked to echo their stories, even after the beginning of negotiations when the parties were supposed to create mutual confidence and an atmosphere of only winners and no losers, continued to strum a tune to the harsh words of the 'humiliating South African defeat at Cuito Cuanavale'.

Crocker said that they and the Soviets and Angolans had tried their best to destroy Unita and instead received a proper hiding. The sketches on Map 4 put the whole matter into its proper perspective.

- If I were to describe the war in rugby terms, I could say that our opponents never came close to our goal line. That was Jamba. They could not even get over the halfway line. That was Mavinga. They barely crossed their own quarter line. That was the Lomba River. We were leading 50–0 and in the process of scoring a push-over try at the Tumpo in injury time, when the final whistle blew for the end of the game. Now our opponents brag about having beaten us because they prevented us from scoring the last try, or because they might have won some line-out or the other.
- In boxing terms, it means that you have hammered your opponent, Punchie, to pulp for twelve rounds. He stands, crouching against the ropes, his gloves tightly held against his face. He tries to cover up anything that may be hit. He barely survives to the last bell and, on buckling knees, is helped to his corner. Now, while his boxer sits there with thick swollen lips and puffed up closed eyes, his manager says: 'We wuz robbed, my Punchie was undoubtedly the toughest of the two. The other guy tried his best to put Punchie down for the count, but Punchie defended brilliantly and survived. The other guy suffered great humiliation.'

In this type of war you must not expect a knockout. You win by a technical knockout or you win on points. We won by a technical knockout.

During this war my interpretations were sometimes questioned. It disappointed me intensely.

A journalist once told me that in December 1987 I had said that we were about to begin to withdraw, but long after that we were still in Angola – I had not told the truth.

I responded that I had explained patiently from the beginning that the withdrawal would take time. Because, I said, it was an operational withdrawal as opposed to a formal withdrawal.

So I explained to him what I meant by a formal withdrawal. It is when the belligerents reach a formal agreement. In this case it is specified at what date and time a ceasefire takes effect. It also determines how the opposing forces would break contact. Each has to move back to be behind a certain geographical line at a certain date and time. One of the fundamental principles with such a formal withdrawal is that no one of the parties should gain strategic or tactical advantage from it. A mechanism is established to monitor everything.

These rules are non-existent in the case of an operational withdrawal. You must execute your withdrawal in such a way that your opponent does not gain advantage from it. He should not be allowed to undo what you have achieved. That is why an operational withdrawal is tactical by nature and not without fighting – and it takes much longer.

In any case, I added, I had issued a press release in which I explained all this. The journalist then questioned that I had in fact made such a statement.

It appeared later that I had issued the press statements on 16 and 20 February 1988. On 20 February, however, a bomb exploded at the Oshakati branch of the First National Bank, killing twenty people instantly and injuring many others, six of whom seriously. One of the wounded was the daughter of the Lutheran Bishop of Ovamboland, Cleophas Dumeni. Still on the same day, incidentally, spectacular events occurred during the flood disaster that hit the Orange Free State. All these newsworthy incidents pushed my press release off the front pages and in most cases totally out of the newspapers.

The matter was later resolved amicably between Gen Gleeson and the National Press Union.

Where I, and many South Africans, sometimes slip up, is to think that once you have released information it is the end of the story. It does not work that way. One should more often provide the information on a more repetitive basis, as Gen Malan encouraged us to do.

Perhaps it was this negligence on my part that prevented information that I had released from making a proper impact. During the campaign I said, *inter alia*, that the South African force levels from top to bottom never exceeded more than about 3 000 men. Perhaps I did not repeat that fact often enough. On the other hand the Angolans exaggerated our numbers *ad nauseam*.

My figures were not used and even the authoritative *Jane's Defence Weekly* reported that between 6 000 and 8 000 South Africans were involved, and some publications even mentioned a figure of 10 000. They fell for Angolan propaganda, or their informants collected their information of our troop strength at a time when we were in the process of changing troops, or they could not believe that 3 000 troops could manage what we did in fact achieve.

This information was then quoted by newspapers who used those sources rather than the official numbers that I had given. My facts were correct. We had to withdraw our last troops according to a formal agreement which was signed by Gen Willie Meyer (GOC SWA) and Gen Cintra Frias of the Cuban forces on 22 August 1988 at Ruacana. We did this in ten days at an easy pace. The last troops were back by 31 August 1988.

The withdrawal caused us embarrassment. We could not put up a really impressive display. We could not gather a full 1 000 troops to show. That was all we had there. We could not present the spectacle the media had hoped to see.

***

My sons also made their contribution. Martin spent 1985 and 1986 at the Military Academy. He did not make the grade in the second year and had to go back to his unit, 32 Battalion. He participated in their operations during 1987 but also continued his studies in his spare time. He was promoted to captain at the end of that year.

Bruwer started national service during August 1987. He went to the Infantry School, and performed operational duties during 1988.

Whereas I had much to tell about my immediate successors as GOC SWA Command, Charles Lloyd and Georg Meiring, and where they fit into this story, I mentioned Willie Meyer only very briefly. This casual reference to him illustrates his most outstanding characteristic of getting things done without any swagger. He was the GOC during one of the most difficult times in South West.

We have come a long way together. He was a commander in his own right. Amongst others he commanded the School of Armour and OFS Command, and he was the last GOC of South West.

Willie was completely adaptable. Although he excelled as commander, he was also a commander's dream staff officer. He was my chief of staff in South West during the earlier days. He was intelligent, diligent and devoted. But you seldom saw him or heard him.

If I could compare him with barbecue experts: one type puts up a big show with chef's cap, apron, displays of herbs and sauces and all the paraphernalia. He hustles and bustles and flamboyantly douses the flames that shoot up now and again. The other kind chats quietly, and you do not even notice that he is busy braaiing until he says the food is ready.

That was Willie Meyer. Everything is done without drama and demonstration. I always wondered how he got everything done.

Gen Dirk Marais gave me a quote that aptly sums up Willie Meyer's leadership style: 'When the best leader's work is done, the people say, "We did it ourselves".'

16

IN THE WAKE OF THE WAR
Tinfoil and phoney mines

War. The fight over Jamba was over. We had destroyed the Cuban-Fapla advance at the Lomba River and pushed them back to the Cuito. We were consolidating. We were securing our results and strengthening Unita's position in the terrain between the Cuito River and Mavinga so that they could themselves maintain the new situation that we had created.

Peace. All these events now brought us much closer to the dramatic discussion on 3 May 1988 in London. But to arrive at the diplomatic drama in London from the military crescendo between the Lomba and the Cuito we first have to look at the scene through a wide-angle lens.

War. The first facet which the wider vision brings into the picture is the other wars which were simultaneously in progress. I refer to our ongoing campaign against Plan, and the 'normal' war between Unita and the MPLA in the rest of Angola. Fapla had withdrawn many troops and armaments from elsewhere to reinforce the offensive against Jamba. With these forces now tied up at Cuito Cuanavale, Unita started to gain ground on an increasing scale in other parts of Angola, including the Cazombo block.

The next aspect of the larger picture that comes into focus is the threatening drama in the west and south-west of Angola, which I have already mentioned. The Cubans had started with the build-up in the west as early as November 1987. In the beginning it happened without drawing much attention, because it apparently did not fit in with the normal MPLA-Unita conflict, the Swapo campaign, and the fighting in the south-east on which most people focused. They were deploying forces cautiously and without aggression in the vicinity of the Namibe railway line and then gradually moving them southward.

A number of events, however, started to attract attention. Gen Arnaldo T Óchoa Sanchez had in the meantime been dispatched to Angola to take over the command. He was the Cuban commandante that I mentioned in regard to Savannah. Óchoa had an impressive military record. He was in the Castro force that had ousted the previous government in Cuba. At the coming of independence to Angola, he was involved in the planning and conduct of operations that put the MPLA into power. During 1975 he was also in command of the Cuban troops in Syria against Israel. He was the architect of the Somali defeat in Ethiopia and for two years, starting in 1983, he was in command of the Cuban forces in Nicaragua.

He also served in Afghanistan and Grenada. On 1 January 1984 the State Council conferred on him the title of Hero of the Republic of Cuba, and the order of Máximo Gómez.

Back to the build-up. It was based on 50 Division which was continuously being reinforced and they now started a southward advance in the direction of Kaokoland in the west. They lengthened the runways of the air bases at Cahama and Xangongo and greatly improved the ground facilities in a short space of time.

The first deployments were all west of the Cunene River, but when we did not react, they also started to position themselves eastward opposite Ovambo (Map 5).

By January 1988 there were 3 000 Cuban troops just north of the South West border. The southward movement continued and by the end of May the forward Cuban units were positioned on a line from Namibe through Chibemba, Cahama, Humbe, Xangongo, Cuvelai and Cassinga. By this time the force was nearly two divisions strong and equipped with the most sophisticated weapon and radar systems.

Three combined Cuban-Plan battalions supported by tanks and artillery concentrated at Cahama, Xangongo and Mupa.

We collected our information through the country's intelligence systems, but naturally also from the newspapers. The papers' information was fairly accurate, but they reported on this formidable force in a tone of alarm, as if one was supposed to read it shaking with fear and choking with anxiety. In fact, it reminded me of the story of the East Germans who were supposedly poised to invade South West during the late 1970s.

But not everything was mere show. This was not chess, it was war. On 18 April 1988 a Cuban force made contact with elements of our forces which were following a Plan group, south of Xangongo. In the subsequent battle we lost a major and a medical corporal.

I kept the minister, Gen Malan, informed, and he in turn briefed the president, Mr Botha.

One should bear in mind that Castro and the Cuban generals had already taken command of all operations since January. And Pres Fidel Castro gave the orders. From that time onward one always had to take the Castro factor into account when assessing future Cuban intentions and actions. Months later, when the Joint Commission to which I have already referred, met in Havana, Gen Rosales showed me around the planning room, complete with clay models and maps, where the president made his decisions.

While this build-up was in progress, we naturally had to ask ourselves what the Cubans were up to. What was Óchoa thinking and what were his instructions from Castro?

Military Intelligence presented me with a useful staff paper on Óchoa. He was a shrewd man and a good strategist. I remember that he had a liking for special operations, operations behind the forward line of enemy troops. He had a predilection for unorthodox actions. The paper regarded his master, Castro, as unpredictable.

As regards Cuban intentions, there were a few alternative possibilities. One was that they wanted to split our attention and forces between south-east and south-west Angola to give them the opportunity to resume the offensive against Jamba.

Another possibility was that they had accepted their defeat at the Lomba as a historical fact and were now searching victory at another place even if it were inside South West. Information from overseas tended to support this hypothesis. It indicated that the least South African offensive action would be used by the Cubans as provocation to attack targets on South West African soil. Swapo could then capitalize on these attacks with Cuban support.

Thirdly, I and a few others began more and more to believe that the Cubans had accepted that their allies had suffered a decisive defeat in the south-east. They regarded the defeat as the turning point not only of the campaign, but in fact of the whole long drawn-out war, and that they would have to start negotiating.

However, negotiations often lead to troop withdrawals, something which one does not like to do while looking like a loser. Therefore they had to change the impression created by their defeat at the Lomba.

Round the conference table one would also like to negotiate from a position of strength. A threatening posture in the south-west would support this stategy and, as a bonus, draw the limelight away from the south-east.

I told people close to me that although I agreed that we could not completely ignore other possibilities, my experience and gut feeling told me that this was probably the real alternative.

Certain events supported this way of thinking. The Cubans had already started intensive propaganda that they had achieved a heroic victory over the South Africans and Unita at Cuito Cuanavale. At the same time, during late November 1987, they put out feelers at the South African mission at the UN in New York regarding the possibility of negotiations.

At this stage Gen Malan had issued instructions which Pres Botha repeated to me later in his presence. According to him we had accomplished our mission and we had done it well. He said he stuck to his point of view that we should not allow ourselves to be sucked into Angola to end up in a Vietnam situation. In the Unita area we had valid reasons to become involved, but in the south-west of Angola we had an interest only in the hydro-electric scheme and the water supply to South West. The Cuban venture in Angola, opposite Kaokoland and Ovambo, was a new situation. We were not interested in picking a fight with the Angolans. Let the Cubans do what they like, watch them closely, stay in contact, but do not start a new war. Maintain your aggressiveness but do not be arrogant and cheeky. Keep cool and exercise selfrestraint.

But, Mr Botha said, if they put one foot across the border, you hit them with everything you have. If that happens, then Ovamboland becomes the new battlefield.

As usual, one knew precisely what P W Botha wanted. The Defence Force had always been very successful with operations in Angola; we kept the war out of South West; but if war were to come to Ovambo, we would be fighting on our home turf. What a great inspiration and motivation that would be – not to speak of the other advantages!

But this discussion did not send me off on another military excursion. I ended up involved in peace negotiations. I did not pack my pistol and go to war, I packed my paisley tie and went to London. We were still assessing the Cuban intentions when I received orders in April 1988 to go to London. As a member of the delegation headed by Neil van Heerden, who had been DG of Foreign Affairs for only twelve months, I had to prepare myself for negotiations with the

Cubans and Angolans. Chester Crocker would be the facilitator.

Peace. Thorough and systematic as always, Neil arranged a meeting or two in his office before our departure to exchange ideas in preparation of the negotiations on 3 May in London. During the last meeting, I remember that I seriously stressed the point that we should not be unduly influenced by Cuban propaganda. We had won the war. The heroic victories of Fapla and its Cuban allies at Cuito Cuanavale were pure and simple propaganda. We must not allow ourselves to be intimidated by the Cubans.

All these thoughts kept crossing my mind. What is Castro up to? I believed that the Cubans wanted to advertise themselves out of their quandary of the Lomba River and advertise themselves into the glory of Cuito Cuanavale. They wanted to scare us across the South West border and talk fear into us around the conference table. They wanted an international agreement and withdrawal from Angola with honour. But who knows? There was still the Castro factor. A real military victory would mean much to him. The possibility of a Cuban raid cannot be completely discarded. People told me in the lobbies of Brown's Hotel in London that we should not dare to clash with the Cubans. They would welcome it and hit across the border with all their might. We could then expect air attacks on Ruacana, Ondangwa and Oshakati as well as Rundu.

I now resume the story which I interrupted in chapter one. It was during these negotiations on 4 May 1988 that my Cuban counterpart, Gen Ulises Rosales del Toro, threatened me: If we did not watch our step a destructive war would overcome us.

One can keep your options open, but sooner or later you arrive at the moment of truth. Then you have to make up your mind. That moment had now come for me. Was Rosales serious? Would they strike across the border? Did Castro want to have a go at the South Africans to beat them decisively and so bring an end to the war? Or was it all a bluff? It was then that I pulled a Pik Botha on him and confronted him with the Boer War.

But for him it was also the moment of truth. After this we never glared at each other in exactly the same way as before.

It was not all that easy. Operational events started to complicate matters on that very day.

Although I called our discussions the moment of truth, we still did not really know exactly what they were up to.

War. Operational activities now had a direct influence on the negotiations. The big Cuban presence in the south-west of Angola with the integrated Cuban-Fapla-Plan battalions caused more frequent and bigger clashes between Plan and the security forces. And the Cubans and Fapla did not stand aside when it happened. The clashes with the Cubans which I have mentioned, had already taken place on 18 April 1988.

On 4 May 1988, the day of my discussions with Rosales, a Cuban force attacked elements of 101 Battalion, the Ovambo Battalion, which were conducting operations against Plan south of Humbe.

We lost six soldiers and four Casspirs. One of our men was wounded and taken prisoner. He eventually landed up in a hospital in Havana where he was treated for a serious wound to his leg. He was Johan Papenfus whom I later got to know better.

The Cubans also suffered losses. Some of them were crushed by Casspirs in shallow trenches. After the war a Cuban told Brig Chris Serfontein that we were crazy to make war like that.

A few days later there was another clash between Cubans and elements of 101 Battalion. It can well be imagined that these incidents created an awkward situation between Rosales and myself; a situation which I had no option but to manage.

Peace. The negotiations of 3–4 May 1988 were not the end of the international political wrestling. It was the beginning of increased propaganda and diplomatic activity behind the scenes, in addition to military positioning. But one could already have forecast that the peace initiatives generated a momentum which would never again be stopped.

Perez de Cuellar talked with the OAU at Addis Ababa on 27 May 1988. He placated.

- Reagan and Gorbachev conferred on 30 May. They said that a peace plan for Angola-Namibia must be drawn up before 29 September 1988 – the tenth commemoration of Resolution 435, and shortly before the American presidential elections. (We arranged it for them. This story unfolds towards the end of this book.)
- Pres Fidel Castro addressed a conference of the non-aligned states on 2 June 1988. He threatened us.

War. Back to the increasing tension and drama of the operational situation.

The two kinds of operations, the 'normal' operations against Plan, and the Cuban advance southward, and our counteractions now began to converge. It produced the last dramatic climax of our operations against the Cubans on 26–27 June 1988. The run-up to this point took ten days. On 16 May Cmdt Jan Hougaard, with his tactical headquarters at Ruacana, began reconnaissance operations with men from 32 Battalion. There was also a small force guarding the installations at Calueque. A while later Jan's force was reinforced with three more companies of 32 Battalion which would also be used to play a delaying role. A combat team of 61 Mechanized Infantry Battalion Group was deployed south of Calueque as a mobile reserve. The normal military infrastructure and force levels of Sector 10 with its headquarters at Oshakati were in place as well.

To face this situation I had naturally issued the necessary directives to the Chief of the Army, the Chief of the Air Force and the Surgeon General. In turn they had given their own orders further down. The exact wording of my instructions I can no longer remember. But I have always tried to give clear orders leaving the minimum room for doubt.

Orders usually work well in paper wars, but in practice we now found ourselves in a very complex situation. The operations against Plan, now integrated with Fapla and the Cubans, had taken a new turn. I have already fully described the arguments around the Cuban intentions and the tit-for-tat threats. Posturing, to adopt a position that carries a certain message, was used in this situation to a greater extent than usual. But you cannot tell commanders to posture and pose. They must get clear orders. You have to give your orders and then discuss them with those who will be responsible for their execution. In this way a commander knows what he has to do, but he also knows what the intention behind the orders is. He can therefore also use his own initiative with more confidence.

Brig Serfontein, now the commander of Sector 10, was still not sure what the Cuban intentions were. He experienced a tense period. His mission was *inter alia* to delay for as long as possible the Cuban southward push and to report their progress. He had to try to make contact with the Cubans and to test their reaction so that the intelligence picture could develop. At this stage we were still pumping water uninterruptedly from the Cunene at Calueque. There was no water in Ovambo. It was important to keep the water flowing for as long as possible. At this stage Chris had no additional troops and had to make use of 101 Battalion for offensive patrolling and 102 Battalion, the Kaokoland battalion, to develop a strong point at Calueque.

A Cuban brigade was dug in at Techipa in the west, about 40 to 50 km north-west of Calueque. This was their secure base from which they threatened the water works at Calueque. A second Cuban brigade took up a similar posture at Xangongo. It was here that the ingenuity of South Africans was demonstrated.

The textbook contains many doctrines and methods of deception, including the use of phoney mine fields, but they are not always easily applied in practice, and sometimes only possible if you improvise. That is what Chris and his men did. They laid a 'mine field' without mines, but with all the customary wire fencing and markers. They also provided a lane through the mine field. They dug holes in the ground according to the book, in which they buried cans. Behind the mine field they prepared tank positions with earth-moving equipment into which they put three plastic tanks.

Members of the local population who had reason to cross the mine field, were escorted through the lane. The usual control points at the entrances regulated the traffic. All these activities ensured that the 'existence' of our mine field became known.

Much later, after our withdrawal from Angola, it took the Angolans three months to clear Calueque and to reoccupy it. They requested our assistance with the mine-clearing operations and were suspicious about the short time in which we did it.

The South African forces in the area were very sparse. So we decided to deploy additional troops for the protection of Calueque and to deny the Cubans access to South West Africa through Ruacana. Task force Zulu was formed and put under command of Col Mieg Delport. It consisted of a 32 Battalion battle group, three companies of 101 Battalion, 61 Mechanized Battalion group, a battery of Valkyrie 127 mm multiple rocket launchers, a battery of 155 mm G5 guns, a troop of G2 guns and a troop of 120 mm mortars.

Skirmishes took place. I have already mentioned the clashes of 18 April and 4 May 1988. In another battle E-Company commander, Capt Maurice Devenish, with troops from 32 Battalion, shot five Cuban sappers and a number of infantrymen, as well as the commander of four BRDM-2 armoured vehicles south of Techipa. Devenish also lost a few Unimogs, but suffered no personnel casualties.

This single paragraph is a cryptic description of what could be excellent material for a movie. They were a very small force. They set an ambush and then found themselves facing an overwhelming force of infantry, tanks and artillery. At one stage twelve men were missing for longer than 24 hours, but by 16:00 the next day they had all returned. Thorough training and experience brought them back safely.

With all the threats, counterthreats, positioning and posturing in mind, we issued early warning for a mobilisation to the commanders of Citizen Force units of the conventional force at home. I announced on 8 June that elements of the Citizen Force were being called up for service in South West Africa. The call-up had to provide for the necessary force levels in the event of an attack into South West Africa, but it was also meant to convey a message to the Cubans of what they could expect if indeed it should happen.

Operational intelligence available to Chris Serfontein indicated that the Cubans were on the point of resuming their southward movement. Whether they intended to frighten us away from Calueque or indeed to attack us was uncertain.

Mieg in the meantime had decided to seriously disrupt the Cubans at Techipa with artillery bombardment before they started their advance. He decided furthermore to deploy 61 Mech to delay them if need be and to protect our artillery.

While I was on my way to talk peace in Egypt, where my father had also served for a while during World War II, Maj Hannes Nortmann joined 61 Mech with a small combat team, including four of his own Missile Ratels.

These developments brought us to 25 June 1988 – the eve of the last big armed encounter in which we would be involved in Angola. It would be the biggest clash since 1976. The following two days would produce one of the most brilliant operations of our military history. But at this critical point of the story the limelight shifts to the diplomatic scene once again.

Peace. At the Hyatt el Salaam Hotel in Cairo the next round of negotiations was about to begin.

The various delegations followed a meandering route through the hordes of newspeople with their flashing click-clack cameras, TV lights and occupational impertinence. The scene reminded me of professional boxers moving down the aisle with their entourages, on their way to the ring for a world championship fight. Or rugby: I bring up the rear, the last to take the field like fullback Gerbrand Grobler; Pik Botha like the Free State captain, Pote Human, is right up in front, and between us jostling journalists close up so tightly that I arrive in the negotiation arena with serious claustrophobia.

By means of his oratorical skill and superb acting Risquet launched a biting attack on the South Africans. Pik Botha could hardly wait. He responded with alternating cool logic and transparent viciousness.

We adjourned without any further ado, wondering what the next act would be like.

To the student of conflict and conflict management analysing the situation in terms of certain models, this debate would not appear to reflect a decrease of conflict, but rather a phase of conflict intensification:

- You attack the person of the other party to weaken his intellectual position.
- You bring emotional pressure to bear on the other side (play the man and you'll get the ball) while pretending strictly to conform to the rules of fair play.
- You subtly bend the rules of logic to deceive the other party.
- You elevate the other party's position to something big and then you attack that position as exorbitant and unrealistic.[1]

Such a debate is by nature a kind of intellectual violence. But the parties still believe that they can in fact settle their differences through discussion.

This debate replayed itself in my mind's eye a few years later while following Codesa speeches on TV, watching Mr Mandela gunning for Mr de Klerk.

The first day of the conference came close to being a failure. Its only usefulness was the momentum it gave the negotiation process. Everyone let off steam, but got to know each other better.

The next day, suddenly, things improved. Those were still the days when we talked in hushed tones of the Soviets who were also active somewhere close by. We were given to believe that they had something to do with the clearing of the foul air. The leaders of the delegations probably knew what was happening behind the scenes. I was told later that Crocker's counterpart, Anatoliy Adamishin, had intervened.

Rosales and I again had a session on the first evening. He delivered the same cautionary sermon as before, but in a more collegial tone than in London. It could be no other way, he had to act in step with Risquet's approach. I suppose it was planned that way. He was doing his duty.

During this meeting Gen Neels van Tonder, Brig Johann Sonnekus and I discussed the release of Johann Papenfus with Rosales and his officers. It was the beginning of a long, tedious and taxing process in which Neels and Sonnie displayed tremendous stamina. We got Papenfus back eventually.

We were also given the opportunity to visit South African war graves.

I think Cairo was the place where 'negotiation by means of a step by step approach' started. It was also here where the idea caught on that the next step should be to reach agreement on a set of principles upon which a total settlement could be based. Before we dispersed, all the parties decided to meet again.

War. Again we see the South Africans' battlecraft and inventiveness at work.

Sunday afternoon, 26 June 1988, after the South African delegation had departed from Cairo, Jan Hougaard and a few of his men sent a number of meteorological balloons carrying tin foil up into the air from a koppie north of Calueque. This happened just before last light while the Air Force Impalas executed some mock manoeuvres.

As expected, the reflections of the tin foil on the Cuban radar convinced them that an air attack was under way.

Our commanders and staffs planned well. They knew that on a Sunday afternoon at 17:00 all soldiers' preparedness is about zero. They knew that the Angolan air force needed at least 60 minutes to react if they had not been placed on Red Alert. They had not. During wintertime the light fades so fast that flying sorties is no longer possible after 18:00. Thus we had one hour in which to identify targets, and this we did extremely well.

The Cubans activated their air defence system and launched six SA-6 ground to air missiles at the balloons. This enabled our radar operators, artillery observation officers, and members of a recce regiment who had been prepositioned, to observe the launchings from Techipa and to plot their positions.

We engaged these targets for a period of four hours after dark. The first salvo destroyed the Cuban artillery command post, so we continued shooting without fear of counterbombardment. Only one Cuban battery fired about ten shots and then also became silent.

Perfect.

However, the Cubans started their advance on Calueque in spite of their heavy losses. Cmdt Mike Muller's 61 Mech Battalion group was deployed to stop them. Early the next morning Hannes Nortmann and his force met up with one of Mike's companies under command of Maj André Vermeulen. Vermeulen took command of the combined combat team.

At about 08:00 tanks and infantry of the Cuban advance guard engaged Vermeulen's force. They shot out two of our Ratel 90s killing the Platoon Commander, Lt Meiring. Vermeulen's men knocked out a Cuban BTR 60 and a number of vehicles and caused heavy losses among the enemy infantry.

Hannes knocked out a tank and became involved with enemy infantry and RPG teams, which he held at bay with his tank's machine gun. During the intense fighting he sustained injuries to his neck and hand.

Two Olifant tanks of other subelements of Mike Muller's 61 Mech simultaneously hit another T55 tank carrying a platoon of infantry, destroying the tank and its passengers. The South African tanks destroyed another BTR 60. After about half an hour the Cubans broke contact and fell back northward.

Mike Muller read the battle brilliantly and handled the different elements of his force calmly and systematically.

The Cubans withdrew.

They never resumed the advance and retreated to Techipa. The losses among the columns which clashed with 61 Mech was 302 men, two T 55 tanks and eight vehicles. The South Africans and South Westers now also withdrew.

Several South Africans distinguished themselves. In this battle all of them did, commanders, staffs and troops. Kat Liebenberg told me how everybody participating in this operation had remained calm. They were aggressive, but calculated. They manoeuvred tactically and step by step. They did everything that one would like to expect of commanders, staffs and troops on the field of battle. Outwitting the Cuban artillery, as I have described, was only one of many examples of deception and other combat techniques that were used. In anybody's book this means top battlecraft.

Then something happened which really hit me very hard.

Seven MiG-23s attacked the bank of the Calueque dam at about 14:00 on 27 June 1988. The eighth MiG veered off and attacked the water pipeline to Ovambo. One of the bombs damaged the line and another, which missed the target, exploded between a Buffel and an Eland-90 armoured car. It killed eight men of 8 SA Infantry Battalion and three men of 2 SSB.

The anti-aircraft troop of 32 Battalion with its 20 mm guns hit two MiGs of which one crashed on its way back to Lubango.

The Cubans exploited our loss during the air attack for propaganda purposes claiming an important military victory.

Our operations on the ground effectively stopped the Cuban southward advance. They had given up any intentions that they might have had of achieving military victories. Further losses and a repetition of the operations in the south-east might have made it impossible for them to withdraw from Angola with honour.

Friction de guerre was good to us on this day, but it had also dealt us a bitter blow.

The general situation on 27 June 1988 was, of course, not yet as clear as I have described it with the advantage of hindsight. We had to continue to take the necessary precautionary measures. The mobilized Citizen Force contingent became part of 10 Division, the conventional force in the area as opposed to the anti-insurgency forces which continued with their operations.

The tenth Division consisted of three mechanized battalion groups, a tank regiment, three armoured car squadrons, and an artillery brigade under the command of Col Jean Lausberg. These forces remained deployed until the last South African forces were withdrawn from Angola on 1 September 1988.

My son, Bruwer, was among those who pulled out during August 1988.

Peace. No major battles took place after 27 June 1988. The Cubans made no further aggressive moves.

This was the turning point.

Negotiations would now continue on a serious note and at a hectic pace. But we still had to see it as something that was happening during the aftermath of the war in the south-west of Angola. Strangely enough the Cubans did not make anywhere near as much propaganda of this war as they did of the war in the south-east. One reason was:

In the south-east it was the Cuban-Fapla forces who were on the offensive. But they turned this around. The Unita-RSA forces crushed the offensive and cleared the area up to the Cuito River. But the Cubans propagandistically presented the mopping-up operation as if it were a pucka offensive per se which they had gloriously repelled. They pretended that this facet was what the whole war had been all about. In this way they camouflaged their total failure in not accomplishing their mission.

Crocker described it as follows: 'The Soviets and Angolans had labored strenuously to smash Unita, and had instead been thoroughly defeated.' And 'How, then, did the fighting at Cuito become a heroic Cuban legend? By proclaiming to a credulous world that the town of Cuito Cuanavale – a town under MPLA control since 1976 – was the 'prize' over which the entire campaign was fought, and then by crowing when you have managed not to lose it.'[2]

In the south-west, however, there was no question this time of anybody else but the Cubans pushing southwards. And in the absence of anything resembling any real counteroffensive on our part, there was no opportunity for them propagandawise to paint a picture of a South African 'offensive' which had 'gone wrong'.

Rather than focusing on a South African offensive, they concentrated their propaganda on the strength and formidable nature of their force projecting its 'big push' southward as an approaching monster.

In the south-east they had to use propaganda to cover up a defeat. Now, in the south-west, they had to use propaganda to instill fear and to threaten us out of the war. For public consumption they depicted their manoeuvres as a brilliant strategic move which ended the war and forced negotiations.

It is not true that their 'big push' forced negotiations. They had already tested the climate for initiating negotiations several months earlier, during November of the previous year in New York. Crocker said Castro had told him afterwards that the plan to extricate himself from the bad military situation had already been made on 7 November 1987. In fact the first formal negotiations of the series were already started on 3 May 1988 in London, while the fighting in the south-west only ended on 27 June 1988.

The dramatically announced Cuban advance to the south ended on an anti-climax. It came to a halt and petered out. Rather than providing something to boast about, it caused a certain measure of embarrassment. We made no concessions in exchange for discussions.

If you objectively assess these clouded events, and once you penetrate through the mist of propaganda, if you are willing to do so, you will discover the true picture clearly showing the real crux of it all, 'linkage' – the link between the implementation of Resolution 435 and the withdrawal of Cubans from Angola.

The South African government would not agree to the implementation of the resolution, along with the withdrawal of South African troops from South West, until such time as a satisfactory agreement could be reached on the withdrawal of Cuban forces from Angola.

Previously the linkage received little or no recognition from the Western powers, and even less from the African states. The resultant international political deadlock over South West and Angola dragged on into the 1980s.

When Reagan appeared on the scene he acknowledged the interdependence between these two proposed actions, reopening the checkmate situation. During his systematic and extensive diplomatic campaign concerning the Western powers, Africa, the Soviet Union, Cuba and Angola linkage was a key point.

It was Chet Crocker's task to win them over. But they gave him a hard time.

The battle of 3 October 1987 at the Lomba, which had turned the war, had an almost invisible but decisive effect on the negotiations. Towards the end of January 1988 Cubans joined the Angolan delegation at Luanda for discussions with the US. They had already confirmed that they were prepared to negotiate their total withdrawal in exchange for the independence of South West Africa. Linkage had been accepted even if initially it was expressed in well-chosen camouflaging diplomatic jargon.

What the Cubans did achieve in the south-west of Angola, was to save their allies from further humiliation in the south-east – from a campaign which apparently they had not wanted to join in the first place.

With London and Cairo behind us, we faced the next three rounds of negotiations – New York, Sal Island and Geneva which, for me, would be the most crucial and exciting of all.

17

THE UNITED STATES – A COMMON ENEMY

Nuances and finesse

The negotiations and politicking that now followed meant a lot of travelling. We became sick and tired of taxis, luggage, airports and aircraft; the inside of hotel rooms, limousines and conference halls; of waiting and strolling around, packing and unpacking; of becoming hot under the collar and cooling down; taking notes and doodling; of late nights and red eyes.

To pass the time I took refuge in playing cards – bridge. I played with Neels van Tonder, Johann Sonnekus and Derek Auret. Niel Barnard sometimes joined us but his intelligence was better than his bridge.

I take up the story of our diplomatic journey in New York.

We met at Governor's Island, New York, on 11 June 1988. The parties had reached agreement on the set of principles on which a complete settlement could be based, as envisaged at Cairo – the New York Principles.

These discussions inspired me to develop, what seemed to me, a useful line of thinking. I had already experienced the way in which the Cubans and Angolans misinterpreted our intentions whenever we had launched an operation in Angola. They believed that our efforts were not directed at Plan but mainly at Angola itself. On each occasion they were convinced that our intention was to penetrate deeply into Angola. They told me themselves once that, during Operation Protea, they thought that we were heading for a much longer-range objective – right up to Lubango! Also during Operation Moduler they publicly announced that we had our sights on the central highlands and the Benguela railway line.

They always vociferously exaggerated the size of our invading force into Angola. After every operation they would accuse us of having stayed there longer than in fact we had. I do not know if they truthfully believed it themselves. It might have been propaganda to make us the 'bad guys' and to arouse international sympathy for themselves, the 'good guys'. And perhaps they were starting to believe their own propaganda. Indeed, on a few occasions we had to negotiate our withdrawal from Angola while we were in any event on our way out, or actually already outside, as was the case after Operation Askari.

In New York their tactics were suspiciously similar. It became clear to me that, as before, they believed, or pretended to believe, that we had stronger force levels than we actually had; also that we were not already in the process of withdrawing, or at the very least, scaling down. During the conferences they called on us every now and again to get out. To tell the truth, if they had not made it a point of discussion, we would have withdrawn on our own account and probably sooner. In fact, Gen Malan had told me to withdraw in harsher tones than they did; not to mention Pres Botha. He had more authority than they had. I was more scared of him than of them.

To withdraw or not was not the question, the question was how and when to complete it. We had never even considered a counterperformance from the Cubans and Angolans.

At Governor's Island the Cubans once again told us that they were not afraid of the G5 gun. it was inaccurate and did not really hurt them. But silence it, please.

So I started to think along these lines: From what they said one could conclude that they thought that we intended to continue fighting and to extend our presence in Angola, and that it was up to them to persuade us to cease fire and leave.

In other words, we did not have to stop firing for nothing and get out for nothing; if they wanted to achieve this through negotiation, then it was a matter of give and take, then surely we could be rewarded for our ceasefire and withdrawal performances. I discussed the matter with our leader, Neil van Heerden, who agreed that I could enter into separate discussions with Rosales.

Thus it happened that Neels van Tonder, Johann Sonnekus and I had a brief conference with Rosales and his staff in my room at the NY Plaza Hotel. We had to cut it short to join the rest of the delegations at Governor's Island. Here Rosales and I continued the discussion in an anteroom.

During these military conferences I could make Rosales certain offers. We suggested a cease-fire, a gradual disengagement of the opposing fighting forces, and a South African withdrawal. Neels and Sonnie worked it out for me. But, based on the principle that we had had to fight to get where we were and that they should not exploit our withdrawal to gain strategic and tactical advantage, they had to undertake to perform reciprocal actions. For example, the battle area east of the Cuito was to be cleared of South African and Cuban forces.

I got the impression that they were surprised by such a sudden proposal. They were also a bit suspicious, probably because it had not been made in the mainstream of the negotiations and presented by Neil van Heerden himself. They were cautious and would not commit themselves.

There was not enough time to take the matter any further but all the parties agreed that the military components of the delegations would take it further during special future meetings. This would happen soon at Sal Island.

New York had also produced some lighter moments. I suppose the Hudson River inspired my Angolan counterpart, Ndalu (Gen Antonio dos Santos Franca) to tell us this story: An Angolan, an American and a Cuban were standing on a river bank. Let us say they were himself, Crocker and Risquet. He described how Crocker opens his briefcase and produces a long hot-dog with mustard, peeling the paper wrapper away and taking a tasteful bite. And all of a sudden he chucks the rest into the river and it drifts away with the stream. The other two shout at him: 'What the hell are you doing now?!'

He replies calmly: 'What are you screaming about? Here in the States we have millions of hot-dogs – it's no loss at all.'

So they continue talking. And suddenly Risquet produces a long Cohiba cigar from his briefcase. He unwraps it carefully, goes through the whole customary rigmarole and eventually puts it into his mouth. He lights it, turns it around with the burning end upwards, inspects it and exhales with great satisfaction. Unexpectedly he flicks the cigar into the water. The other two grab him by his jacket, 'What are you doing now, are you mad?'

'Listen, chaps, in Cuba we have thousands and thousands of cigars, we won't miss this one in the least.' He looks at Crocker and starts talking again as if nothing has happened.

Like a bolt out of the blue Ndalu kicks Risquet in the pants right into the water and there the Cuban drifts downstream, sprawling and shouting.

Crocker gets the fright of his life. He grabs Ndalu by the shoulders and shouts at the top of his voice: 'Are you out of your mind?! The poor man will drown!'

'Ah well, what does it matter? In Angola we still have thousands of Cubans. This is no loss.'

I thought that Ndalu was taking a bit of a chance telling such stories, but I found later that he was a very well-balanced person and that there was a very good understanding between him and the Cubans, and that they were not over-sensitive. They are full of jokes themselves.

Unlike some of his colleagues, Ndalu was not full of rhetoric, propaganda and pretentions. He was natural, soft-spoken and pragmatic. A gentleman. I cannot believe that there was any person who could not get along with him.

In New York I sensed that a better understanding had developed between the Cubans and ourselves. In Angola and South West we were enemies. Here we were still negotiating 'opponents'. But we could talk better sense.

On one occasion a Cuban asked me if we had flown to New York by South African Airways (SAA). I told him no, and described the long route via Europe where we had to change over at various places and how we had to make use of different airlines. So he wanted to know why we did not use SAA. I told him that SAA did not have landing rights in the States.

He was surprised: 'Neither have we!'

Then he said that he supposed I come to the States quite often. I told him that I had neither the money nor the motive to visit the USA. This visit was an exception and in any case being an officer in the SA Defence Force I was not entitled to an American visa.

He got very excited: 'Neither are we!'

He said that it was exactly the same with them. They had no landing rights and were not allowed visas. And he carried on about all the other things that the Americans denied them and did to them. So the Cubans and we had a common enemy – the United States of America. Just imagine.

The same type of discussions apparently also took place between other South Africans and Cubans. All of a sudden there was more mutual appreciation.

It was an upside down world. It was difficult to know whether you should glare at a Cuban, smile at him ... or shed a tear with him.

The New York Principles formulated at Governor's Island was an important milestone on the negotiation track. The talks among the military in New York naturally did not draw much attention as they were conducted on the sidelines. The follow-up military discussions at Sal, likewise, took place without trumpets and floodlights. I noticed later that books and articles on this period and subject did not even mention the military conferences; but they were meaningful and did not take place without drama. Crocker gave it considerable coverage in his book.

The special discussions at Sal took place in July only a week or so after our return from the States. We were going to follow up the proposals that we had initiated 'out of the blue' at New York. The agenda would therefore contain subject matter such as cease-fire, northward redeployment of Cuban forces and withdrawal of South African forces.

As this conference was to deal with practical aspects, I decided to select more junior officers to accompany me as advisers. I do not believe in the tendency always to involve only senior officers. I prefer the people who are practically involved and know most about a particular matter, irrespective of rank. I therefore took Col Eddie Viljoen, who was an operations staff officer, and Col Freddie Oelschig, an intelligence staff officer.

Eddie still sported a lush bushwar moustache and Freddie a savage bush beard.

As is the custom during the opening of a conference, I introduced the members of our delegation to the other parties. If it was a strange experience for Eddie and Freddie to meet the enemy face to face, they did not show it.

On the third day at Sal, I had the feeling that something funny was brewing amongst the Cubans. Then suddenly Gen Rosales came up with a surprising move. As we were about to take our seats for another session, we were called to another room where he and his delegation were formed up in a semi-formal type of formation. Gen Rosales del Toro was first in the line-up. In a friendly but stately style, which had clearly been worked out before the time, he introduced us to the second officer in the row, whom he had in the meantime ordered to report for conference duty. He presented him as a National Hero of the Republic of Cuba. It is a formal title in Cuba, something majestic.

Operating through interpreters and the often accompanying confusion, I did not immediately realize what exactly was happening, but I did meet the officer – Gen Arnaldo Óchoa Sanchez.

But Óchoa left as suddenly and inconspicuously as he had arrived.

I later heard the rumour that, when I had arrived there with Viljoen and Oelschig, the Cubans suspected me of trying to impress, or even intimidate them, with our hairy bushfighters. That caused them to decide on a counter for Eddie and Freddie – their own top fighter. This story gives one an indication of the extent of the clever tricks and suspicion that still existed. It should therefore not come as a surprise that, in spite of the long discussions and hours of mental wrestling, we could not reach an agreement on cease-fires and disengagement, redeployment and withdrawal of forces.

I suppose that is why the discussions at Sal Island did not make the books and articles. But I was quietly content with the meeting. I felt that we had planted a seed in New York that now sprouted at Sal and that the time would come to pick the fruit. By the way, this meeting at Sal was not the alleged debauched affair with which Crocker later created a sensation.

I am quite certain that if it were not for this link in the chain of negotiations we would never have achieved success at Geneva.

Months later a wooden box was delivered to my home in Pretoria. It was filled with tinned fruit juices and rum – a small gift from Gen Arnaldo Óchoa Sanchez.

A day or so after our return from Sal, we were off again to Geneva.

For me this was without doubt the turning point in the negotiations. Here the discussions of the preceding sessions reached a high point. Knowing that the fate of countries and peoples was at stake tested one's moral courage.

The formal discussions took place between 2 and 5 August 1988.

Before every round of negotiations Neil van Heerden would gather his team for preparations. We called them in-house meetings. I like his methods and style.

Chet Crocker on his part, usually arranged informal discussions with each of the parties before, during and after the formal negotiations. More often than not he involved only the leader groups of the delegations.

These informal talks usually took place during mealtimes. With mock seriousness I told Neil that he should use his influence to have the pattern changed so that we would not have to talk serious business over meals. I pointed out that when saying grace we ask the Lord's blessing and that my mother used to caution us that if we were not cheerful and on our best behaviour at table, He would refrain from blessing the food; and this was probably why we sometimes suffered from indigestion! To my utter surprise he actually tried to change the arrangement. He is sensitive to the small things in life.

This time, however, he did not succeed. It was now 31 July 1988 and before the negotiations were to begin we had to have a working meal with Crocker. During the eating and talking and in view of our 'failed' attempt at Sal I asked Crocker how long it would take the UN to begin implementing Resolution 435, from the time that the word go is given. Crocker replied that if one credited the UN with speed, they should be able to do it within approximately three months.

So I therefore did the following sum in my head: tomorrow is 1 August 1988, add three months and the answer is 1 November 1988.

Later in the day Sonnie asked me, why don't we propose tomorrow at the first plenary session, the full formal session of all parties, a specific date for the implementation of Resolution 435? I said yes, brilliant – 1 November 1988. We would then work backwards to arrive at the other dates: South African troop withdrawal, Cuban redeployment and withdrawal, disengagement of forces, and ceasefire. That evening we put it to Neil van Heerden, Derek Auret and Niel Barnard.

Probably more than a year later Neil invited all the members of his team, together with their wives or girlfriends, to an 'in-house' dinner at the State Guest House in Pretoria. That evening he delivered a short intimate speech and thanked everyone for his contribution. He recalled some of our experiences:

> The negotiations around a settlement in Namibia and Angola proceeded through many phases and alternated between moods of optimism that a solution was close and stages of deep mistrust between the respective delegations.
>
> Gen Geldenhuys and Brig Sonnekus came up with the suggestion, at the end of July 1988, in my hotel room during one of our countless late-night preparatory discussions, that we should simply propose a date for the implementation of the settlement plan to the other parties.
>
> It would allay the mistrust on the part of mainly the Cubans and the Angolans and give direction to the negotiations which at that

particular point had reached a state of near checkmate.

This proposal was submitted to the government and approved, and the next morning when we proposed in plenary that 1 November 1988 be the starting date for the implementation of the settlement plan, it had a dramatic effect on the whole meeting. There was an immediate request for an adjournment of the meeting. Our 'opponents' were clearly caught off-sides.

In the end this decision made an important contribution to an agreement being reached and which resulted in the independence of Namibia and the withdrawal of Cubans from Angola.

During this round, agreement was reached on the Geneva Protocol. From a purely personal point of view this success was to a great extent the result of the wearisome work we had done in the side-halls at New York and especially at Sal Island. It included:

- A recommendation to the Secretary General of the United Nations that 1 November 1988 be earmarked as a date for the implementation of Resolution 435.
- Fixing 10 September 1988 as the target date for signing a trilateral agreement.
- Fixing 1 September 1988 as the deadline for Angola and Cuba to reach agreement acceptable to all three parties on a schedule for the northward redeployment and the total withdrawal, in stages, of the Cuban troops from Angola.
- South Africa's assent that all its troops would be withdrawn from Angola by 1 September 1988.
- Angola and Cuba would use their good offices to restrict Swapo to the north of the 16th parallel after the withdrawal of the South African troops (the latter was completed before 1 September 1988).
- An undertaking by Cuba not to deploy its forces within specified geographical boundaries described in the protocol. (This excluded Cuban forces from an area in the south-east of Angola.)
- The establishing of a Joint Commission (JC) to develop additional practical measures to build confidence and to reduce the risk of unintentional incidents.

It became clear later that it was impossible in practice to keep to all these target dates. The delay of only a few months, however, made no material difference to the content of the eventual agreement. This round put us, in Niel Barnard's words, in command of the 'moral high ground'.

On the road of war the last major battle with Fapla and the Cubans took place on 27 June 1988 on the border in the south-west of Angola. The path of negotiations towards peace had been clearly demarcated by the end of July and the beginning of August 1988 at Geneva.

In this book it is to be expected that I will write about the people with whom I have travelled along the road of war, but as the roads of war and peace crossed, I also travelled some distance along the road to peace with other people. One of them was the Cuban, Jorges Risquet.

He was a bearded man who in some respects projected the same type of image as Fidel Castro. But not quite the same. He was of shorter and sturdier build. We called him Oom Kaspaas. Around the conference table he was all rhetoric and fiery emotion from beginning to end. It is quite amazing that a person can present a public image that is commanding and confident but at the same time be almost timid and socially comfortable in private.

Señor Aldana, who took over from him, was an almost unobtrusive person. He was cultured, with a keen sense of humour and impressive intellect, but he stood with his feet firmly on the ground. One cannot but have respect for his professionalism. According to Neil van Heerden, he is an expert in the field of labour relations; and that is why we found him such a proficient negotiator.

The Joint Commission once met in Havana. The next meeting was scheduled to take place in Cape Town. So, just before the adjournment of the Havana meeting, Aldana asked Neil van Heerden: 'How does one get to Cape Town?'

Neil jokingly replied: 'You fly east and then you turn right.'

Aldana: 'Mr van Heerden, are you sure – Cubans ... turn right?'

During the same meeting Chet Crocker quoted the American Admiral, Dick Walters, as having said: 'A person who does not recognize the value of flattery is one who does not get any.'

I am not sure whether Aldana then tried to flatter Crocker, albeit ambiguously, but he said: 'I was always one of Crocker's most loyal opponents.'

I once sent Aldana a small South African national flag with explanatory notes. Our national flag was hoisted officially for the first time ever on 30 March 1928 in Havana, Cuba. This was two months before it was hoisted for the first time in South Africa and elsewhere on 31 May 1928. Mr Eric Louw, South African Trade commissioner in

New York at the time, had had the flag manufactured in time to fly at Havana during the international conference on immigration and emigration.

Another Cuban, Gen Ulises Rosales del Toro, was spartan in his eating and drinking habits. He kept himself neat and healthy as becomes a soldier. He was loyal, courteous and quiet. He did not seek the limelight. He did not deviate from the rulings of the politicians. His appearance was that of a professional soldier and not that of the poster image of the bearded Cuban soldier in combat dress with a rifle slung over the shoulder. I got along well with him.

Once before our departure from an airport in Europe, a few of the South Africans were singled out for special attention by the airport security staff. A woman, an airport official, asked me whether my luggage included any parcels given to me by anybody. I said no. Innocently.

I was already in the air when it struck me that the Cubans had given some of us a few packets of coffee. I still wonder what the woman's reaction would have been if I had said, yes, a Cuban gave me a parcel.

If she had reacted with suspicion, she would have been wrong. We flew without mishaps and the coffee has been consumed long since.

I had met our facilitator, Dr Chester A Crocker, some years before, on 20 September 1981 at the Zurich airport. I had been a member of the team under diplomat Brand Fourie that was involved in one of the first rounds of discussions in the new series. Crocker and I were both waiting for our luggage. He did not make any particular impression on me at first sight; it was when he spoke that the hidden talent showed. I saw him only a few times after that but I got to know him better after May 1988.

I have heard him being described in a variety of ways: 'Oh, that bloody conservative'; 'Oh, he's a dangerous liberal'; and by a number of congressmen, 'He's arrogant.'

Perhaps he was just an American and a man for realism; not the type of realism that necessarily suits you, but true realism. Later, when all was over, many conservatives resented him for what he had achieved in southern Africa and some of his liberal opponents regarded him with malicious envy for the same reason.

I cannot think how anybody else could have played this role better, if at all. He was very practical for an academic; purposeful and systematic – good qualities for this type of negotiation, because we travelled many tricky roads and saw much beating about the bush.

Fortunately I had already retired from the service when he wrote: 'He (Geldenhuys) also had the disconcerting habit of doing crossword puzzles or falling asleep during Pik Botha's windier monologues.'

The other milestones in the series of formal negotiations were the discussions at Brazzaville: 24–27 August 1988, 6–9 September and 26–28 September; New York: 6–8 October; Geneva: 11–13 October.

All these dealt with the northward redeployment, and the phased total withdrawal of Cuban troops from Angola. Agreement regarding the time-scale was reached at Geneva and afterwards confirmed in the formal bilateral agreement between Angola and Cuba on 22 December 1988. It contained: the redeployment of all Cuban troops to north of the 15th parallel by 1 August 1989 and the 13th parallel by 31 October 1989. The Cuban troops concurrently had to withdraw from Angola: by 1 April 1989, in other words before the implementation of Resolution 435, 3 000 troops; by 1 November 1989, in other words the election date in Southwest, 25 000 troops (50%); and so on until they were all out by 1 July 1991.

The linkage between the various steps foreseen in Resolution 435 and the Namibian settlement plan, and the schedule for the redeployment and withdrawal of Cuban troops was now clearly confirmed. It was an exceptional achievement, especially considering the near universal rejection of such a linkage in the past.

This series was again followed by formal negotiations at New York: 22–24 November 1988, and Brazzaville: 1–3 December 1988. They concluded a new date for the implementation of Resolution 435: 1 April 1989; provided for the signing of the trilateral agreement between South Africa, Cuba and Angola; and for the bilateral agreement between Angola and Cuba concerning the end of the Cuban military presence in Angola, as well as a mechanism for its monitoring by the UN.

The trilateral agreement was finally signed on 22 December 1988 in New York.

However, this was not the end of the talks. The parties had to make the trilateral agreement work. The Joint Commission established by virtue of the agreement was assigned this function.

Somebody asked me one day what I had learnt from all the politicing and diplomacy. I responded by quoting a piece that I invented as a means to tease my diplomat friends and colleagues:

> It is more difficult to make peace than to make war. In war you try to

> deceive and outwit your opponent and he knows it; he tries to deceive and outwit you and you know it – which I think is quite an honourable arrangement.
>
> When you talk peace, the first thing that the parties do around the negotiation table is to establish mutual trust and confidence. Having done so, everybody starts to lie to everybody else – and you're not supposed to know it.

This is of course just a little joke that has no bearing on reality.

Then situations arise when the parties must agree because their masters insist that the talks will not be derailed and that a favourable press statement will be issued. In the meantime, however, one party says that the glass is blue and the other insists that it is green. Then they decide to agree that the glass is not yellow. They release a report to the press stating that the negotiations are still on track; there are aspects on which they agree, and although many problems still remain to be solved, they are cautiously optimistic; they have agreed to meet again. Whether the glass is yellow or not, to me it sounds much like the same language that one was hearing in South Africa during the early 1990s.

Neil van Heerden can talk straight, but he can also play this game of nuances with finesse.

The military are internationally renowned for being at ease with their foes, or war opponents if you like. I have already related the story of Maj Edwards and Gen Manie Maritz who considered a cease-fire during the Anglo-Boer War so that they could play a game of rugby against one another at O'Kiep.

The SA Defence Force was likewise never blood-thirstily hateful towards their enemies. With very little and definitely no meaningful exceptions, its approach was always professional, scientific and businesslike. I sometimes even got the impression that military enemies find it easier to make contact with each other than political opponents. It surprised me to read that Crocker wrote: '... but getting these men (Rosales and me) to communicate openly was a struggle.' Bridgland described our first meeting with the Cubans on 3 May 1988 in London as follows: 'The atmosphere was stilted and thick with suspicion. it took the military men to break the ice.'

The *Sunday Star Review Special* of 9 April 1989 wrote:

> General Geldenhuys, described by an American diplomat as

> 'somewhat quiet, taciturn and reserved', took the initiative. Dressed in a blue-grey business suit, he walked over and introduced himself to his Cuban counterpart. He broke the ice. After that there were small, informal, and initially rather stilted meetings over drinks, dinner and coffee, the diplomat noted.

I visited Windhoek after Namibia's independence. The permanent Secretary for Defence, Mr Frans Kapofi, received me in his office. The Chief of Staff of the Namibian Defence Force, Gen Dimo Hamaambo, was also present. He was my opposing commander many years ago.

Mr Kapofi arranged a small informal reception for me. Some of my officers and I swopped war stories with ex-Plan commanders. A good spirit prevailed. I really appreciated his gesture.

Some of my erstwhile colleagues, South Westers who had previously served in the SWATF, were also present. I could sense that some of them were slightly uncomfortable. They possibly thought that I had an unfavourable view of their decision to stay on in the Namibian Defence Force.

I told them clearly that I never even remotely felt such emotions. In fact, I told them that I supported them whole-heartedly. There is no question of resentment. They must unreservedly serve their country.

18

A TRAGIC FIASCO
Flagrant violation of the Geneva Protocol

I was now approaching the end of a long road. My contract as the Chief of the Defence Force and DG of the Department of Defence would expire on 31 October 1990. There was less than two years to go.

The war was over and the most difficult negotiations over South West and Angola were also a thing of the past. But the road was still not running downhill. It had not even levelled out. Some of the biggest ever intrigues were lurking ahead.

UN Security Council Resolution 435 still had to be implemented. South West had to become Namibia. The peace syndrome caught up with the war and overtook it. The scaling down of the SA Defence Force had to begin even before the Cubans had withdrawn from Angola. And scaling down, which also includes cutting back your people, is an ugly thing that taxes one's emotions to the extreme.

The implementation of Resolution 435 provided its own drama. I have said that it is difficult enough to conclude an agreement between warring parties, but to make it work – that is the big test. Just recall the story of the Lusaka Agreement.

How does one make a peace settlement plan work? I aired my opinion in this regard with reference to another peace agreement which still had to be implemented, that between the Angolan government and Unita. It had to end the 17-year war between them. I told the editor of *Politica Internaçional*:

> The overall Angolan peace agreement and the documents in the ambit thereof make for heavy and formidable reading. They include the ceasefire agreement, including all its annexes, the

Fundamental Principles for the Establishment of Peace in Angola ... (etc) ...

The contents of the package spell one word, namely complexity – for the simple reason that it attempts to bring peace to a very complicated situtation. Now, let me tell you, the multitude of papers will not make the agreement work. Success will depend on three equally important factors. First is the political will of the main parties, the Angolan government and Unita, to make the agreement work. Second is the effective functioning of the Joint Political and Military Commission and third, the continued involvement of their principal and, very important, the top echelon of the mediating country and observer-participants to the agreement, ie Portugal, the USA, the USSR and the UN.

This opinion was just as valid for the pre-implementation stage of Resolution 435. But it would soon become apparent that not all the parties' *bona fides*, at least in the beginning, were above suspicion: '... they (and others) expected false moves on the part of South Africa.'[1]

Our fears were the exact opposite. As a result of previous experiences we feared that Swapo would turn up with tricks.

Our troop withdrawal cut the flow of information, making it more difficult at that stage than before for military intelligence to keep track of Plan activities. But they quickly adapted to the new situtation and succeeded.

Information was soon received of Plan manoeuvres in contravention of the agreements. According to the Geneva Protocol of August 1988 the South African troop withdrawal from Angola had to happen concurrently with an evacuation of all Plan members in the border area to the north of the sixteenth parallel. This Plan withdrawal had to be completed by 1 September 1988.

It did not happen.

Other spokesmen for the Defence Force and I reported this threat to the successful unfolding of the peace process, along the prescribed channels and at the committees and forums on which we served. But the situation continued unchanged. In fact, it worsened as D-day, 1 April 1989, approached. I thus not only kept to the normal routine, I created opportunities to focus attention on the dangerous situation that had developed. But no corrective action was taken.

I also informed to Neil van Heerden. He took it further. It seemed as if nobody would listen to us. As I have already mentioned I often got the impression that most people were always only too eager to believe Swapo propaganda because it provided them with ammunition to have a go at South Africa. But if we had problems with Swapo, I always felt our accusations were being rejected as unnecessarily alarmist, probably in the hope of derailing some peace policy or other.

Neil van Heerden presented our case in very strong terms at the Joint Commission, but it made no difference.

Esterhuysen writes:

> ... Plan-guerrillas continued to roam the area between the border and parallel 16. South Africa's complaints were disregarded in the 5-power Joint commission and, presumably, perceived as alarmist ... The loopholes exploited by Swapo and the laissez-faire approach towards this irregularity had been plain for months, even before the signing of the New York Accord. These mistakes were to be paid for in human lives ...[2]

What Esterhuysen said, proves the correctness of my intelligence, concerns and actions at that stage. But he wrote it only very much later; while it was actually happening, I felt very much alone.

I had also instructed the South African component of the Joint Military Monitoring Commission to take the matter up with their Angolan and Cuban counterparts. This was yet another monitoring mechanism that had been established by agreement. The other parties did not react and refused to investigate the information such as was provided for in the Geneva Protocol.

Every time I addressed the accredited military correspondents during the monthly conferences, or whenever I had contact with the media, I informed them of the violations and the dangerous situation that had developed.

At the last monthly meeting that I conducted before the implementation date, in which Glen Babb of the Department of Foreign Affairs also participated, I told them out of desperation that if they wanted to make a positive contribution, they could publish the information to put pressure on the parties to stick to the rules. The media reported as follows:

- Swapo is cheating, says Gen Jannie' – Headline, *Die Transvaler*, 17/2/89.
- 'Angolans not keeping pact: Defence Chief' – Headline, *The Citizen*, 17/2/89.

- 'Angola and Cuba are allowing several thousand Swapo fighters to operate ... in violation of the cease-fire agreement,' the Chief of the South African Defence Force, General Jannie Geldenhuys, said in Pretoria yesterday.
- The Angolan government's apparent unwillingness to move Swapo will be one of the hottest items on the agenda when the Joint Military Monitoring Commission (JMMC) meets in Luanda next week.
- The Deputy Director of Foreign Affairs, Mr Glen Babb, said the Cuban-backed Angolan government had not honoured an undertaking to urge Swapo to withdraw from southern Angola by September 1 1988. Mr Babb warned this put Swapo in a position to interfere with the Namibian elections and could 'affect independence'. – *Pretoria News*, 17/2/89.
- 'Angola must say now if it does not want to, or cannot oversee Swapo's withdrawal.' *Beeld* quoting me on 17/2/89.

It is a pity that the press was not taken seriously. Why not, I could only guess. I was actually very worried about what I had told them. It could have been interpreted that I was exceeding the boundaries of my responsibilities as a soldier. I could have been taken to task. But I was not called to account. In fact, there was no visible reaction at all.

It still puzzles me until today that Swapo's invasion, when it happened, was described by everybody as a surprise. The whole world expressed its shock over the invasion that came 'out of the blue'. How could it possibly be? I ask you!

During the early hours of 1 April 1989 the first wave of 1 600 heavily armed insurgents crossed the border at various places.

The rest is history. A handful of South African Police and air force crews, together with elements of the SWATF and the SA Defence Force which were reactivated, saved the situation.

Bruwer was one of those who became involved again. With others he went to Ondangwa on his twenty-first birthday on 6 April.

The security forces wrote a chapter of courage and glory which make Rambo's adventures look like child's play, but also a chapter dripping with blood. Under the UN flag they shot more than 300 Plan members but also sacrificed 26 men of their own.

> ... Swapo had suffered one of their worst blows of a long war – after agreeing to a cease-fire![3]

In the meantime South Africa suspended the implementation of Resolution 435. A meeting of the Joint Commission was hastily convened to work non-stop through the night discussing alternative appropriate actions to get the peace process back on track again. We met at Mount Etjo in South West and other places. There was also a considerable flow of correspondence from the South African government to the UN.

> While Secretary-General Perez de Cuellar, under immense pressure from Swapo's friends, began to show signs of vacillating and wanting to compromise, the US State Department issued a hard-hitting legal analysis which left no doubt that Swapo was the transgressor. The document also concluded that if Angola and Cuba had permitted the infiltration of insurgents into Namibia, they too were guilty of 'flagrant violation' of the Geneva Protocol.[4] (Neil van Heerden had warned Angola and Cuba at the Joint Commission before the event.)

The implementation of the settlement plan was recontinued on 19 May 1989.

Various commentators offered different explanations for this tragic fiasco. Amongst others:

> As was to be expected, the trilateral monitoring mechanism created by the Protocol (the JMMC) failed like its predecessor in 1984.

I do not agree with this. No sort of monitoring commission such as those about which I am writing can prevent war, not to mention make war. Unless the governments in whose hands the commission is an instrument, have the political will to maintain the peace and take the commission seriously, you can forget about it. This is the big lesson.

Plan's incursion was just part of a bigger scheme. But even by itself it had meaningful influence on the subsequent events.

Many people told me that it was to the advantage of Swapo's opponents that the invasion happened, because, they said, Swapo damaged its image in London, Washington, Paris, Bonn and other places. That was true. But the Londoners, Washingtonians, Parisians and citizens of Bonn were not going to vote in the elections.

People who want to intimidate for effect, must threaten, and then they have to demonstrate that they have the capability and the will to go through with their threats. This is exactly what Swapo achieved *vis-à-vis* the bush voters of South West. For many people the results of the election in Ovamboland remain a mystery.

Among the people that I had forewarned of the danger of possible disruptions to the process were Mr Ahtisaari and General Prem Chand.

Prem is a loveable person. He will do nobody any harm. He appreciates the beautiful things in life. He is brimful of memories. He says things happen to him. He calls it 'happenstance'.

He took over command from the British of the first Gurkha Rifles Regimental Centre at Dharamsala Cantonment in the northern Himalayas in January 1948. On 29 January he attended a regimental centre commander's conference in New Delhi. On 31 January 1948 he was with his father in the city when he heard that Mahatma Gandhi had been assassinated. He and his Gurkha driver travelled by jeep to the house where Gandhi had been living. In the confusion nobody stopped him and he went into the house. Thus it happened that he spent half an hour with the deceased in his room.

He has many other recollections. During his first visit to Pretoria he was looking down a jacaranda-lined street at the Union Buildings when he got a strange feeling of *dèja vu*. Then he realized that he was thinking of another Herbert Baker building – the bigger brother of the Union Buildings: their main secretariat close to the presidential residence on a hill in the centre of New Delhi.

He is British, more so than the British of today. He makes ample use of strings of English army jargon of a few decades ago. He executes his political masters' policy to the letter.

He is a gentleman.

The Swapo incursion was, strangely enough, still not the end of the irregularities. Even with it still fresh in the mind, our information of another threatening Swapo violation was not believed.

And now I come back to Operation Sceptic which had taken place in 1980, as I promised to do in chapter 9 when, with Cmdt Chris Serfontein in the lead, we clashed with Plan's mechanized force. Now, in 1989, after 1 April, we received reliable information that Swapo were enjoying freedom of movement in Angola and that they were not being monitored according to the settlement plan and agreements. They had not even handed in their weapons and armaments, including the armoured vehicles of their mechanized force still under their own control. We lodged complaints. Swapo and the Angolan government, as before, rejected our allegations with contempt. They denied indignantly that Plan had ever had such a force. Neil van Heerden received notes from governments of other countries, including major powers, in which our accusations were shot down as being absurd as Plan in no way whatsoever had used such types of weaponry. Either these countries were partial to Swapo, or they had fallen for Swapo's propaganda, hook, line and sinker, and believed along popular lines that we had cooked up the information to wreck the peace process.

I therefore submitted a summarized dossier containing sufficient detail about the history of their mechanized force, including an inventory of their armaments, training programmes, names of commanders, and much more. I was also in the fortunate position of being able to confirm that I had seen their mechanized force in the field myself, BTRs, 76 mm field guns, and so forth. That enabled Neil to reply to the notes and to the best of my knowledge we never heard from them again.

Plan members never entered South West at predetermined entry points as prescribed in the resolution and the settlement plan. But there was still more to come.

The Chief of the Army, Gen Kat Liebenberg, one day brought me intercepts made on the radio net of the Kenian battalion of Untag.

Most of the countries of the world practise radio and electronic interception. Those who don't, do not regard it as necessary, or do not have the capability. And those who do it, don't talk about it. The secrecy around this method of collecting intelligence has often caused embarrassment to ourselves and other countries. We regularly received military intelligence collected in this manner, which would have had to be released some time or another and in some format or other. But if enquiries were made of how we had obtained such information, we had to answer evasively or we had to pretend that we had collected it by other means. And should somebody ask what evidence you have, you've had it!

Even people with reasonable knowledge tell you that these methods are being used all over the world and everybody knows it; why are you so secretive about it? The answer is: although the enemy suspects you of doing it, they do not know when you do it, for how long and on what nets, frequencies and call signs. As soon as they determine that, they change their frequencies, call signs, and the worst of all, their codes. Then it may take you a few hours or maybe six months to break their new codes. Or, and this can be more dangerous, they plant false messages for you to intercept. The secrecy, as we all know, had fallen flat in respect of the Kenian intercepts. It was in all the papers, which is why I feel free to write about it. The intercepts boiled down to this: the Kenian battalion were to close its eyes to certain dubious Plan activities.

Kat Liebenberg and I went to see Neil van Heerden and Niel Barnard and together we went to Gen Magnus Malan and Mr Pik Botha. Mr Botha released the information and the other parties immediately rejected it as fictitious.

The last word about this saga in the news media is that I or somebody else in the Defence Force was allegedly producing false intercepts to wreck Resolution 435, or that somebody else outside the Defence Force did it for the same purpose. This is not only untrue, it is practically impossible. The standing objection against my explanations was that I had failed to prove my case from the files of the accused, the Kenian battalion, and secondly the question was asked: Why had the tapes on which the intercepts were made been 'destroyed'?

The tapes were never destroyed. Anybody who has a typist will know that dictation tapes are used over and over again. After she has transcribed the day before yesterday's dictation of your letter to the bank manager, it will serve no purpose to ask her for that tape tomorrow. By then she has already used it for your letter to the municipality. This is exactly what happened to us in this case. The tapes were already in use again. The poor signaller did not have the foggiest notion that those particular intercepts would cause such a sensation. Any person who wanted to produce such a volume of false intercepts with a ring of authenticity to it would have had to have the apparatus, the people able to operate it and detailed intimate knowledge of the Kenian battalion's daily activities and transmission patterns. They would have had to be special people, because furthermore they would have had to be conversant in Swahili, speaking African English with a Swahili accent and be proficient in the use of morse code. Forget it.

Until today there is still not the slightest indication of any kind whatsoever that anybody had done such a thing or could have done it. And until today nobody can negate the possibility that there was another irregularity in the offing. In fact, I had forecast in an Austrian magazine, *Zeitspiegel*, after the 1 April fiasco, that other breaches could still take place: 'In my opinion more problems may arise and the further implementation of Resolution 435 will not proceed without hiccups but it will in all probability go the whole way to independence.' Nobody can deny that Mr Botha's disclosure did prevent another 1 April trick.

Just as we had hoped to prevent the 'shocking' and 'surprising' incursion of 1 April 1989 by disclosing Swapo's violations, this time too by reporting and exposing yet another irregularity our only intention was to avoid a repetition of the disruption of the peace process. That is all we had in mind. Take it or leave it.

Our operational involvement in South West had come to an end. Precisely a week after Gorbachev became President of the Soviet Union, South West became independent on 21 March 1990 – Namibia. And now one can see the nature and characteristics of our military actions in better perspective.

The war in South West was often depicted as child's play. On other occasions it was portrayed as a war of extreme dimensions coupled with extensive destruction and sorrow.

I regard it as accurate to describe the war inside the borders of South West as a low-intensity insurgency war. Willem Steenkamp wrote:

> It is an indication of the low intensity of the border war that during its course the population increased rather than declined and no part of the territory was laid to waste. It is remarkable, in fact, how little the struggle impinged on daily life in SWA/Namibia.
>
> South of the black tribal areas it was always barely noticeable except for the occasional urban bomb blast and a couple of small-scale Swapo raids on white owned farms in the midlands, and in places such as Ovamboland the regional economies actually benefited from the conflict; ironically, probably the greatest consequence of the war was the accelerated abolition of most segregational laws and the inclusion of blacks in the previously all-white administration, so that by 1988 the territory's internal government was mainly non-white.

However, if one limits the analysis of the war to South West, one is left with a distorted perspective of what was actually happening. You have to see it as part of a bigger conflict.

Plan infiltrated South West mainly from Angola and Zambia. In Angola itself there was a much bigger and more intense conflict than can ever be compared with the one in South West.

In Angola the whole of the Benguela railway line from the Atlantic Ocean to Zambia was permanently put out of action. Angola's economy collapsed completely. Unita operated from within Angola and for all practical intents and purposes controlled areas as big as some European countries and provinces of the RSA. At the border between Angola and Zambia they even issued visas. The International Red Cross liaised with Unita at their seat in Jamba.

The Soviets, East Bloc countries and Cubans were involved on a large scale by any standard. The Cuban presence towards the end of 1988 exceeded 52 000. The situation in Angola was not by the wildest stretch of the imagination comparable with the situation in South West Africa.

Swapo also became involved with the MPLA-Unita struggle and South Africa also clashed with Angolans during cross border operations with Plan and for strategic reasons became involved with the MPLA-Unita war.

The truth therefore is that the war alternated from a low-intensity insurgency war in South West Africa to a prolonged regional conflict with international involvement in Angola. Here it was of much wider dimensions and periodically reached peaks of very high intensity.

Plan was good. We kept them running. Sometimes fifty kilometres a day. They escaped and evaded extremely well. They lived in desperate circumstances, but they knew well how to survive. And if they were in trouble, they fought bravely and well.

During the 1970s and early 1980s commentators regularly made statements to the effect that after World War II all the revolutionary organizations had won their wars. Furthermore they declared that if such movements had the support of Soviet Russia and Cuba, nobody could stop them. In our case it did not happen. We effectively reduced and isolated the insurgent activated area to only a part of Ovamboland.

We, the security forces, won the struggle on the field of combat.

19

OFFICE POLITICIANS AND SENIOR GENERALS
So much information and so little knowledge

The war in South West was over. In Angola the government and Unita still continued fighting. But with our withdrawal this war was something of the past for us. We had entered a new era.

Just as I had reviewed our actions in South West, our military performance in Angola could also now be placed in perspective – and journalists were doing so; they now had much better access to information than before. One of the changed approaches in the new era was that it was no longer necessary for us to apply the same degree of restriction on the release of information about the operations of the previous years. Classified information was thrown open on a large scale.

All over the world the supply of information on military matters to the media had been a point of dispute for many many years. I do not believe that the different parties will ever really make peace. Conflicting interests do exist. The media will always say they do not get enough information and the military will always say the media is insensitive to their security problems.

I would like to mention briefly a few aspects of the problem as I experienced it in the past. The first basic truth is: To threaten or to make war means conflict. Therefore, one has to consider the elements of conflict when you analyse the flow of information to the media during war.

In the case of armed conflict 'secrecy' is actually an old and proven principle for successful campaigning. But secrecy can also relate to other principles such as 'surprise'. You will not be able to surprise your opponent if he can read in the morning paper what your intentions are.

Many experts also list 'deception' as a principle of warfare. The well-read Brig Blackie Swart, the task force commander during Operation Savannah often said: 'War is deception.' Your opponent must be so informed as to guide him to draw incorrect inferences. In a basic sense it could mean, if you are strong, to your opponent you must appear to be weak; if you are weak, you must appear to be strong.

It is in this atmosphere that journalists insist on getting the news on the one hand, and the military being reluctant to give it on the other hand, that the media more often than not complain they do not know what is happening. They said so again during the Gulf War. In this case they were flooded with information, but there were still complaints.

After giving the war correspondents due recognition, Lord Deedes said: 'The fact remains that the ceaseless sound, the plethora of voices round the clock sheds extraordinarily little light on what is actually going on.'

Then he quoted the well-known Malcolm Muggeridge: 'There is so much information, and so little knowledge.'[1] In other words, the information contains facts and images, but they do not tell a story; there is a gap between the facts and the interpretation of the facts.

Sensitivity about the release of information is not peculiar to the military. One also finds it during other forms of conflict. I noticed that there is normally a free flow of information in the field of finance, economy and trade. But the moment boycotts and disinvestment start in all seriousness, the situation changes dramatically. When South Africa moved into an 'economic and trade war', it had to be managed as a conflict situation, especially in regard to imports and exports. People to whom military secrecy previously probably did not make much sense, suddenly changed their views.

Raymond Parsons, Director General of the South African Chamber of Business, suddenly, on more occasion than one, said that the less information we released about our imports and exports the better.

But one must always bear in mind that the journalists are also professional. They also have principles, such as 'it is in the public interest'. They will always try to get their stories. It is their job and you cannot blame them if they ask questions that you find difficult to answer.

By way of reflection I must say that I cannot complain about the questions the media asked me. In fact, what really caused me embarrassment were not the questions related to the Defence Force. I suffered when questions of a non-military nature, especially political, were put to me. I tried my best, but I made mistakes.

Once during 1978 in Windhoek, my old diplomat friend from the AG's office, John Viall, phoned me. He was a veteran of the South West International High Court days and the senior civil servant in South West. He told me about a news report, in which I was quoted, and said: 'Pik was looking for you all day long. So, now I will give you his message. He wants to know who the hell do you think the Minister of Foreign Affairs is, he or you?!'

Now to get back to our military actions in Angola: with all the information made available after the war many books, as well as magazine and newspaper articles were published about the operations of the past years. Helmoed-Römer Heitman wrote the book, *War in Angola, the final South African phase*. He is a correspondent for the authoritative *Jane's Defence Weekly*. Fred Bridgland wrote *The war for Africa, twelve months that transformed a continent*. He is a correspondent for the *Sunday Telegraph* (London) and *The Scotsman* of Edinburgh, in southern Africa.

These and other publications are useful aids for evaluating our involvement in Angola and especially the military aspects. However, one should read these books and articles against the background of that time. Until the beginning of 1990 South Africa had a very bad image in the international world. Internally, too, a section of the reading public often had a poor impression of the government and its instruments. With regard to the Defence Force there was a great deal of negative talk about the 'securocrats' and the destabilization of southern Africa.

Any writer who made a living from journalism would have had to take this into account, especially when writing in English for the international market. A writer could not really come out in praise of the South African Defence Force because 'the business of every business is to remain in business'. The worst accusation that could be brought against a journalist was to be accused of being partial to South Africa or of relaying 'Defence Force propaganda'.

I believe that they were very much aware of it. They tried to protect their credibility in various ways. For example, in his foreword Bridgland says his publisher told him before he tackled the book, that:

> I (Bridgland) would be free to interview as many men as time, energy and money would allow. There would be no interference from top levels of the military or the government ... My own stipulation and that of my publisher was that there should be no question of the book being subjected to censorship by Pretoria ... These did not prove to be obstacles ...

The advertising pamphlet for his book describes it as 'the unofficial story of the war through the eyes of the men who fought it, not those of generals and politicians hundreds of kilometres from the blood, sweat and dust.'

Bridgland continues to explain:

> ... I subsequently pieced together the course of the war for Africa through scores of interviews with the fighting men. The only officer I interviewed above the rank of colonel was the Chief of the South African Defence Force (SADF), Gen Jannie Geldenhuys, who retired in November 1990.

Seen against this background, it came as a surprise to me that both Bridgland and Heitman expressed themselves so strongly about who had won the war. Heitman says:

> The defeat inflicted on the Fapla forces ... was so crushing that it changed the strategic situation beyond recognition.

These and other writers, although describing Unita and its allies as the undisputed victors, also take them to task in no uncertain terms. They lash out at the Defence Force, 'the generals' and 'policitians'.

Well now, one should always take criticism seriously. The writers offer valid arguments for their views. However, there are a few aspects with which I do not quite agree. The first is that some other overall strategy might have delivered better results and that the campaign could have been handled in a different way.

Well, I suppose, especially with the benefit of hindsight, one can always say that things could have been done better, but I would like to query the approach of some writers. If they do not want to restructure the tactical run of operations on the versions of generals far away from the battlefield, they should also not try to analyse the strategic course of a campaign based on the opinions of the fighters in the bush far away from the strategic world.

As a result of discussions that journalists had had with junior members of the force about the 'bigger picture', they created certain debatable impressions. One is that if the ideas of the junior commanders had been put into practice, our victory would have been even greater. Possibly those field commanders were right, possibly not. It is their right to express their views. It is a good approach, it is part of our culture. We encourage people to air their views fearlessly, especially during debriefing conferences. Criticism from the bottom upwards is good, especially if you have won. If you have lost, it is bad. But the worst of all is when there is criticism from the top downwards. I have no such criticism.

One should appreciate the position of the field commanders. Some of them might only have participated in one part of the campaign and then gone back to the Republic with their troops.

During the campaign, of course, the junior commander regarded himself responsible for achieving only his mission, at the place that he found himself and during the time that he was there. How to do it successfully was his only concern – and so it should be. But there was also a new commander and his troops, possibly from the Republic, who had to take over the situation as the previous commander had left it and proceed from there.

The subordinate commanders were not relieved between specific operational phases of the campaign. Somebody had to be responsible for the continuity in order to ensure that the operations to follow could be executed and that they would still fit in with the planned overall operational design. And that is the task of the higher commander.

Montgomery said:

> This firm grip (of the senior commander) does not mean interference or cramping the initiative of subordinates; indeed, it is by the initiative of subordintes that the battle is finally won. The firm grip is essential in order that the master plan will not be undermined by the independent ideas of individual subordinate commanders at particular moments in the battle.

Another hint was that political interference with operations occurred. It is not true. Of course, from an overall perspective, politics did by its nature play a dominant role. To make war is a commitment of the political will. But I can personally bear witness that I received no political orders which meant interference with tactical decisions in the field. Perhaps some critics became confused with the grey area between tactical and strategic decisions, because political guidelines did have, as usual, an influence on strategic considerations.

The criticism is actually ironic, because the best examples of political interference could be found in this war – on Cuban-MPLA side! The most outstanding illustration of political intervention was of course, Castro's handling of operations in Angola from Havana. But it goes further.

I promised earlier to tell why, in September 1987, the Fapla forces very unwisely, much like the proverbial donkey, thumped their heads against the fatal defensive wall of the Lomba time and time again. This was due to politics.

On the eve of President dos Santos's visit to Europe, he wanted to have a military victory to his credit when he arrived there. That was why the troops had to try and try again to cross the Lomba – with tragic consequences.

Another theme of criticism found in the world of books, political commentators and the news media, was that of the stupid office politician or the senior general restraining the brave combat general or commandant from destroying the enemy. It is an old and popular theme which is usually successful in arousing sensation. The most recent case is that of President Bush, who according to critics, stopped General Schwartzkopf during the Gulf War from destroying Saddam. I don't agree with that.

Bush had done as well as anybody in his position possibly could. Since governments make war without declaring war, it has lost much of its effectiveness in solving international disputes.

War can be declared only if there is a strong political will plus a sound resolution by the government of a state to commit itself. It requires sincerity, openness, courage and integrity.

When one country declares war against another, it goes flat out to destroy the other country and its capability to resist. Having done that, it subjects its enemy to its will and authority, and the dispute is settled. Then its publicly announced objective has been achieved.

When a country formally and openly declares war it must, however, realise that it can bring upon itself the mistrust, violent disapproval and possibly even action by the international community. It must therefore have a good case for which international sympathy exists or it must be so powerful that it does not have to worry about international opposition. But it will always be a momentous decision taken with circumspection and integrity.

Nowadays, however, wars are being waged without prior formal declarations, to achieve so-called limited objectives. In other words, where the 'aggressor' does not aim totally to subject another country to its authority, but only to attain certain vitally important political goals, or temporarily to safeguard its own national security.

What frustrates the critics so much is that these wars come to an end without all the international disputes having been settled in full, which often leads to further acts of violence.

The war comes to an end when the limited objectives have been accomplished or when regional or international political pressure leads to cease-fires and politically concluded peace settlements.

From the sidelines I got the impression that Bush's political management of the military terrain was accompanied by insight and understanding. He handled the Gulf conflict brilliantly. He mobilized the whole American nation behind the war effort. In fact, he mobilized the whole international world that mattered to stand behind him. And, what is very important, he secured a legal base – a mandate to make war – from the Security Council, namely, take note, to eject the Iraqis from Kuwait and to reinstate the former government. Bush internationally and openly committed himself to this mission, to nothing less and to nothing more.

If Bush did make any mistake at all it was that he had formulated the wrong political objective and not because he held Schwartzkopf back. His mistake then was that he did not obtain a resolution from the Security Council that would have authorized the allies to knock out Saddam Hussein completely and to subject Iraq to their authority. Whether he had any chance of securing such a resolution, even had he wanted to, is highly improbable.

As soon as the Iraqis had been ejected from Kuwait, and the mission as described in the resolution successfully accomplished, the war had come to an end. Bush simply had to honour his word. It was unthinkable that he could, on his own authority, act outside the mandate with the aim of totally overpowering Iraq and subjecting Saddam to his will. There was never even such a possibility. I do not argue that the war did not settle all the real long-term political disputes of the region. It left a situation still full of problems which could lead to renewed armed conflict within a few years. But this is a different matter.

The opinion of some of the Western media on this subject is well reflected in *The Citizen* of 18 March 1991: 'We are beginning to wonder whether the United States and its allies went far enough in their battle against President Saddam Hussein.'

How far the operation went, is irrelevant. What is important, is how far the political decision went before the war started.

Rapport of 29 September 1991 stated:

> REGRETS OVER SADDAM TOO LATE. The American president, Mr George Bush, at this stage would probably like to tear out his hair because he forced Gen Stormin' Norman Schwartzkopf to abort his onslaught on the Iraqi capital Baghdad, a few hours before they would really have been in a position to overthrow President Saddam Hussein's régime.

Bush did not constrain Schwartzkopf at the end of the war. He restricted his freedom of action long before the war started.

Our aim in Angola was not to overthrow the authority. We did not want to capture Cuito Cuanavale and get involved with Menongue and then create a Vietnam situation. We wanted to help Unita to repel the onslaught against them and to enable them afterwards to defend themselves. Once we had achieved this objective, we had accomplished our military task.

Heitman read the situation well:

> The 1987/88 campaign thus achieved its immediate aim and brought about a situation that offered interesting additional strategic diplomatic opportunities. These were recognised and followed up, finally bringing about a settlement in south-western Africa that suited almost everyone. Quite apart from its tactical successes, therefore, the campaign of 1987/88 was a good example of how to use the carefully directed application of military force to achieve a political end – without so overcontrolling the operation that it fails. The South Africans had come a long way since 1976.

What more could we, and should we have wanted to achieve, than we actually did in 1987–1988? Bridgland wrote:

> Castro's dream of a Marxist revolution spreading from Angola to encompass the whole of southern Africa has become a poor

> music-hall joke except perhaps in South Africa itself, where the ANC-South African Communist Party alliance had become by late 1990, along with Fidel Castro, among the last serious defenders of Marxist politics and economics in the world ...
>
> It was the South African and Angolan men who fought the war for Africa against the Cubans and the MPLA who made it possible for Chester Crocker to secure his regional peace agreement.

Heitman said that the key factor was the disaster that hit Fapla late in 1987, early 1988. This persuaded Moscow and Havana to reconsider their roles in this theatre. The campaign delivered conclusive proof that Fapla could not stand against the South African forces on their own. The successes achieved by a very small South African force furthermore indicated that even Cuban intervention would not be able to stand up to them, unless their forces in Angola were reinforced. It would not only require additional troops and equipment but also need creation of the necessary technical infrastructure to support a bigger force in a country such as Angola.

Notwithstanding the successful result of the campaign, commentators exercised their good right to query leadership styles.

Another writer, the Englishman Thomas Pakenham, in his precise account of the Anglo-Boer War, reflected on the styles of the two Generals, Redvers Buller and Louis Botha:

> What a contrast between the styles of the two Commanders-in-Chief. A British C-in-C was a grand seigneur, withdrawn behind a ring of ADCs, isolated even from his brigadiers. Botha's tent was open to the humblest burgher. It was an ordinary bell-tent, captured from Symon's camp at Dundee and furnished with a packing-case and a stretcher chair. When an elderly burgher entered, Botha would give up the chair to him and sit on the ground. There he sat, as a procession of visitors tramped through the tent. He ate, drank, slept and wrote his official dispatches under their gaze. It won everybody's heart. Botha valued his privacy, but valued the confidence of his burghers still more. He took trouble with everything and everybody. He trusted in God – which of the Boers did not? – but left nothing to chance.

Let us forget the two personalities for a moment and concentrate on the general styles. On the one hand we find the absolute maintenance of status and formalities in the field and on the other hand a good-natured openness.

From what I have been told, the Israelis probably lean towards the latter style. To them the task at hand is the most important thing. They do not go in for unnecessary ritual and show of discipline, they are not interested in mere pomp and ceremony. To them it is taboo – they call it 'bullshit'.

I would say that nowadays the South African leadership style lies more or less between the two. It does, however, attract criticism to the effect that the presence of senior officers with battle groups during operations is unwise and unacceptable.

In rcent decades it was Gen Viljoen who initiated the culture of senior officers, one way or another, being present during operations with task forces, battle groups or combat teams.

I did not lead troops from the front. I never fired my rifle, shoulder to shoulder with the troops in the forward trenches, amid all the smoke, sweat, blood and flying shrapnel.

I would not argue that Gen Viljoen in his dauntlessness perhaps went too far in certain situations; but rather this way than the other way round.

The army has a sound doctrine governing where a commander positions himself during operations. He must place himself at a point from which he can best perform his duties. In other words, it depends on the officer's appointment, the function he has to perform, and the nature of the operation.

However, the few times I was present during operations, I did not necessarily go there to do a specific task. I went there merely to be present and to observe. There are many reasons, in my opinion, why generals, or certain generals, depending on their appointments, should be present to observe.

In the first place one should bear in mind that to make war with volunteers is one thing; to fight with part-time soldiers, including national servicemen, is another. The public interest in the part-time soldiers is understandably much greater than in the volunteers. I believe that the nature of the South African culture is such that it would be unforgivable, as the critics would put it, for generals to bide their time in their luxurious offices and to enjoy themselves after hours at cocktail parties in pretty uniforms, while the fathers, brothers, and sons of the people back home struggle and sweat in the bush getting wounded and perhaps even killed.

The nature of operations differ from place to place and from time to time. During the Second World War one could have served in the same regiment throughout the whole war, and the commanding officer of the regiment gets to know every man. A strong bond developed between the commander, his staff and troops. The same was true for much more senior commanders. Generals often had the opportunity to address all their troops on parade. With the relief system in use in the South African army for the last few decades this type of continuity never existed. One had no hope of getting to know all your men or even talking to them, because they were continually being replaced. It denied a senior commander the possibility of presenting himself and of demonstrating sympathy with his men and to foster a sound spirit of togetherness between him, his commanders, staffs and troops. The most and the least that he can do, is to tag along during operations. Then he can talk to the men. He can live under the same circumstances and experience what makes life difficult for them. He shares the success of victories and sweats blood with them when the going gets tough.

A leader must be seen. A military leader is not like the normal business manager. He is responsible for the weal and woe of his men 24 hours a day. In an operational situation his decisions could mean life or death. In any case who wants a factory manager who does not know what the production line looks like and all that happens there? The duty of a commander and especially a senior commander also is to inspire his troops. He still has to promote that unique atmosphere and culture with the special values he wants to see in the military organization. And he cannot do that from a distance for too long.

I have experienced that the field commanders sometimes tactfully try to keep one out of potentially dangerous situations and in this respect one is probably a nuisance. It can also happen that you have an inhibiting influence on a commander. He may think that you are there to evaluate or criticize him or that you might want to interfere. The overwhelming majority of our commanders, however, have so much self-confidence that they are not in the least put out.

I have always been careful not to interfere with subordinate commanders' responsibilities. Although, on the other hand, it has happened that commanders have told me straight out that it was comforting for them to know that I was in the vicinity. It does happen occasionally that they welcome the opportunity to ask for an opinion.

A high-level commander must beware of *fiction de guerre*, not to be confused with *friction de guerre*; it means having a fictitious impression of what really is happening during war. He relies on the information that he receives. Much of the operational information he gets by radio or telex; or by staff officers putting him in the picture by means of verbal briefings or written operational reports. But papers do not answer questions and the cryptic style of operational reporting does not adequately describe the general atmosphere. It does not properly explain the influence of wind, weather and well-being on the practical execution of operations. Perception gaps and distorted impressions can be created in this way.

Remote and paper information can cause one to make the wrong decisions. But if you are prepared to take the trouble to join an operation, even if it's only to observe and experience, then the same type of reports will mean much more to you later – you can then interpret them against the real background. You can put them into their true perspective and make better decisions in the office if necessary.

Let us move the scene away from Angola for a while: You are at Defence Headquarters Pretoria, or at the HF Verwoerd Building, Cape Town. You receive reports and briefings on the unrest situation in Natal and the Rand. You form an impression of what is happening there. Now you go and visit those places. You talk with the senior commander, and together you talk to his junior commanders and troops. Perhaps there is an opportunity to see them in action. Now you get a different impression.

Back in Pretoria or Cape Town you get more reports, but if you have to make decisions now, your judgement is greatly improved. Then you are not suffering from *fiction de guerre*.

Gen Malan regularly visited subordinate headquarters. Another outstanding example was the Minister of Law and Order, Mr Adriaan Vlok. If an unrest incident occurred and it was only half humanly possible, he was there. He talked to the police and to those disturbing the peace. He could make certain decisions in his office. His mind was not clouded by *fiction de guerre*.

If there is a degree of danger present during visits, you just have to use your good discretion and be prepared to take calculated risks. Likewise, in a situation such as south-east Angola, where a sophisticated war was being waged, any general who has a role to play must not have distorted impressions.

One such misconception I observed for the first time during Operation Savannah in 1975. The phenomenon recurred now and then until 1988. It had become a pattern: On a few occasions a sombre picture was painted in Pretoria of developments in the war. Then you go to Windhoek. You are briefed and the situation does not look quite so dark. Now you go closer, say to Oshakati, and then the situation looks almost good. And when you arrive at the forward bases, you find that everything is under control.

It happened a few times that worried staff officers would bring something to my attention. Then I would tell them that I didn't think the situation was quite as bad as it seemed and that we should first have a look. Usually the situation turned out to be much better than expected and we could make quick contributions to improve it. I am not trying to pretend that we never had serious problems – problems that caused a great deal of stress.

This brings me to the next point of criticism against our high-level leaders – that our decisions had been unduly affected by the fear of losing human lives.

When you are a leader of men in an armed conflict, a unique factor distinguishes you from leaders in other fields: decisions you make can result in loss of life. This factor has a tremendous psychological influence on the decision-making process and the people concerned in it, and especially the leaders who carry the responsibility.

Before the armed conflict in the Falkland Islands the United Kingdom mobilized the biggest fleet and air force since the Second World War for the operation. They set out with a formidable force to tackle the Argentinians on the Falkland Islands.

It appeared to me, however, as if they had procrastinated for a long time before the eventual decision was taken to give the command that really got the land battle going. This was only given on 20 May 1982 after the Argentinian invasion had taken place on 2 April.

One explanation could be that there was nobody in the British cabinet or high command with much experience in taking decisions about sending people off to war and taking the responsibility for the consequences.

The Gulf War was characterized by the same pattern of reluctance. Newspaper headlines and extracts dealing with the period before the land war started, tell the story:

- 'Officially, Bush had not even decided when he will decide ...'
- 'Bush dispatched Cheney and Powell to the Gulf to talk with Schwartzkopf and other allied commanders ... and they will give

Bush their recommendations on whether the ground war should be launched and when' (*Time*, 18 February 1991).

- 'I don't want my men to die – US General Norman Schwartzkopf "Agony of fatal decisions"' (*Sunday Times*, 10 February 1991).
- 'Delay Gulf land attack plea' (*Citizen*, 11 February 1991).
- 'Tearful Bush tells of war order' (*Citizen*, 7 June 1991).

I believe that in similar situations the Israelis, for example, make such decisions more quickly. They attach the highest value to the life of a soldier, but they already have experience of the psychological torment.

When James Ambrose Brown's book *Retreat to victory* was published, it also started a controversy over the question, was Gen Dan Pienaar's decision-making during the Second World War unduly influenced by the high price he set on the lives of his men? His son denied such assertions.

After the war in the south-east of Angola during 1987–1988 there were also hints to the effect that South African generals had become over-sensitive to the possibility of losing lives during operations.

The insinuations unsettled me. A person defending himself against such statements can easily be tagged as someone who is not sensitive to the loss of human life. It is an emotional matter and you are easily placed at one of two poles: Either you are sensitive to loss of life, or you are careless about it. Why cannot one place the highest price on every life and still have the moral courage of your conviction to take real decisions? Experience of this kind of psychological wrestling helps you to develop this frame of mind and mood which I believe the senior South African officers have.

It may perhaps seem noble to delay taking a decision in the hope that something that will change the situation may happen, but the time that elapses can ultimately cause more lives to be lost. You give the other side more time to prepare, and the possibility of surprising and misleading the enemy becomes less as time goes by.

Montgomery says in his memoirs:

> The matter of decision is vital. The modern tendency is to avoid taking decisions, and to procrastinate in the hope that things will come out all right in the wash. The only policy for the military leader is decision in action and calmness in crisis: no bad doctrine for the political leader either.

After now having given this free and openminded review of the war, especially in Angola – I have still left unanswered one question: What had the Cubans' real intentions been, especially with their campaign in the south-west of Angola?

A dramatic incident provided the answer: The man I met at Sal Island, who sent me a box of canned fruit, fruit juice and rum, Gen Arnaldo Óchoa Sanchez, was sentenced to death in Havana.

When the sentence was confirmed by the State Council on 9 July 1989 Castro delivered an address in which he gave his version of what had happened during the war. It confirmed what we always suspected.

Suddenly, as a result of these events and Castro's speech, sensational headlines appeared in the newspapers.

- Castro tells how his tactics ended Angolan war – *The Pretoria News*, 28 July 1989.
- Cuba executions spark suspicions about Castro – *The Star*, 28 July 1989.
- Why Cuba's scapegoat general died at dawn – Fidel's fight not to lose face – Castro explains why Angola lost battle against the SADF – *Business Day*, 27 July 1989.

Simon Barber wrote for *Business Day* from Washington:

> ... (Óchoa) was to preside over Cuba's last hurrah in Angola and the 'heroic' defence of Cuito was therefore a vainglorious fraud, designed to cover a retreat that had already been decided. The 15 000 new troops who followed Óchoa came to save Cuban face, not the MPLA.

Bridgland says:

> Nothing illustrated the Cuban crisis more aptly than the decision of a 47-man revolutionary military tribunal to shoot Gen Arnaldo Óchoa Sanchez, the soldier chosen by Castro to pull his chestnuts out of the fire in the War for Africa. For his efforts in Angola and elsewhere over the years Óchoa was one of only five officers to have been made a Hero of the Republic of Cuba. But scarcely a year after the Cubans and the South Africans fought their last battle on Angola Óchoa was put to death in 1989, by a firing squad,

ostensibly for drug smuggling offences of which he was found guilty at a bogus show trial.

Barber, a professional analyst who reports authoritatively on the American-Caribbean sphere, gave his comments on Castro's speech:

> It is popular style to allege that Pretoria agreed to withdraw from Angola and Namibia as a spent force with its tail between the legs ...
>
> This is not the analysis that emerges from Castro's version of events in his speech ...
>
> In contrast it is clear that Castro had already decided towards the end of 1987 that the MPLA was militarily and economically over the wall, defeated in the field and four years in the red with the insignificant 20 million dollars per year the Cubans apparently charged for their services. South Africa and Unita had won effectively. For Castro there was only one way out – a unilaterally staged demonstration of military prowess and go home ...
>
> The immediate aim with his address on 9 July was to denigrade Óchoa's role during the last year of the war by portraying him as lazy, incompetent, insubordinate and venal ... When Óchoa arrived in Luanda in November 1987, the Angolan army and its Soviet advisers were in head-long retreat after their rout at Mavinga ... On 15 November Cuba began to land the first of 15 000 reinforcements, amongst others 'our best pilots'.
>
> 'Everybody was asking us to do something,' Castro explained, adding, with thinly concealed contempt for his allies, 'we understood that even though we were in no way responsible for the errors that had led to that situation, we could not sit still and allow a military and political catastrophe.'
>
> In the meantime there was panic and mutual recrimination at the Soviet-Angolan-Cuban operational centre in Luanda. 'Many problems had to be solved.'
>
> Óchoa, judging from remarks last month by Cuba's Minister of Defence, Mr Raul Castro, Fidel's brother, during June 1989, was appalled by what he had found and apparently remarked: 'I had been sent to a lost war so that I will be blamed for the defeat ...'
>
> The Angolans were no longer a factor in the war. On the other hand, the Cubans had secured their flank for the next move.
>
> It was the time for Castro's grand, solo stroke – the gesture that

would save Cuban honour without the nuisance of Angolan incompetence.

On 10 March a new reinforced Cuban main force under Generals Cintra Frias and Miguel Lorente Leon was ordered to move from Lubango southward towards the Namibian border. 'The most important of all strategic operations had begun ...'

His major concern was that the South Africans would spoil his gesture by giving battle ...

Castro merely informed President Eduardo dos Santos by telex that he had ordered his generals to 'place all forces on a state of maximum alert ...'

Although he did not play open cards with dos Santos, Castro was adamant that all other parties knew about his plans. 'We notified the Soviets ... we were warning everyone of the danger of the possibility that we might have to launch a strong attack in northern Namibia ...'

He cabled Óchoa: 'The first step must be a strong air attack against the camp, military installations and South African personnel in Calueque and its environs ... if the enemy's artillery can be located, strike it harshly.'

Twelve South Africans were killed in the air attack, the dam was hit and Pretoria 'raised a big fuss'. But the South Africans also 'restrained themselves militarily', just as Castro had hoped they would. 'We have given them our initial response. Now it is up to them to decide what to do and if they should continue the escalation ...'

It is not the story of a South African defeat. It is the story of an Angolan defeat and how, with considerable nerve and panache, the Cubans extricated themselves from it.[2]

Crocker confirmed Barber's assessment.

***

I definitely do not agree with Crocker on everything, but he still is one of the best, if not the best, who can write with authority about this important period of wars and diplomacy in the history of south-western Africa, 1980 to 1990.

He was the man who listened to all sides, talked, cautioned and coaxed. He practised a great deal of restraint not to have taken sides.

He demonstrates this to an extent in his book: not by the fact that he is equally generous in handing out bouquets and backhanders, but rather because he gives everybody the same dressing down.

He took a few digs at me. And he says our knowledge of Cubans is 'the stuff of comic books'.

As I have said many times, interpretations of these events depend largely upon the person's political convictions. I have given my version, but we have also had others with regular intervals.

First there were the Cubans and Angolans who announced to the world that they had won the war. Then came the professional journalists, who claimed the opposite. Then Castro came and qualified the earlier Cuban position virtually beyond recognition. Then I came with my account of the war.

As I was completing my manuscript, the magazine, *Insig*, of November 1992 came with its version. On the outside cover is a sketch map of Angola with a drawing of a tombstone and a wreath. The words on the gravestone read: 'Here lies the pride of the SA soldier (and the broken back of our economy)'. Inside is an article by Mr Jan Mellet under the heading 'ANGOLA – SA still licking its wounds'. Next to it is another article under the title, 'Agony of a parent'.

By this time it is not difficult to know exactly what position *Insig* would adopt and how Mellet's version would be coloured. It is in my opinion well summarized by his choice of a quote of what Stephen Ellis wrote four years before, in May 1988 – before the war had ended and long before Castro and all the others had disclosed meaningful and illuminative information and findings on the war:

> More than 6 000 South African and South West troops are dug in about forty kilometres south of Cuito Cuanavale and 400 kilometres from their base after they couldn't capture this strategic southern town.
>
> What the SADF had lost, is the initiative and the belief that it could beat any black army.

Amazing.

Then came the next version: the *Sunday Times* of 25 October 1992 placed a story on Crocker's book about the same events, and presented a very different picture to the one presented in *Insig*, as if replying to it, under the heading, 'Crocker: the big lie of Angolan war'.

* * *

Just about weekly more and more of the truth came through, but up to March-beginning of April 1993 I still came across people who would ask me: 'Now, what has 'really' happened at the Lomba ('Cuito Cuanavale')?' When I told them; they would ask: 'But what has really happened?' And they would ask more questions, such as why did we withdraw? The answer is: We never wanted to and never tried to keep a fighting force of any consequence in Angola on a permanent basis. It is a historical fact that we withdrew after every crossborder operation and there was absolutely no reason why Moduler-Hooper-Packer should have been an exception.

It illustrates the problem of creating perceptions by means of propaganda. Once a perception had been established one tends, even unconsciously, to take account only of the information which confirms your impression or fits into it. If the information does not suit you, you ask questions and if the answers do not fit into your perception you search for more questions to ask.

Anybody who does not want to accept that the Cubans launched a crafty and extensive propaganda scheme and who wants to believe that the Fapla alliance had clinched a victory and keeps on asking questions to have these views confirmed, will never accept my answers.

Such people will keep on asking questions such as: 'Why did you stop at the Tumpo?' Answer: We had accomplished our mission, we had already started to withdraw, the official clock on the scoreboard had long ago indicated that the game was over and the political whistle had already announced the end of injury time – exactly as had happened so many times before.

They will keep on asking: 'What about our fighter aircraft's 'technical deficiencies'?' Answer: Unlike sport, the playing field in war is never completely 'level' and the opposing parties never use the same standard equipment. In the armament technology race there is always a horse that pushes its nose ahead of the others, and then another one, and another and then again perhaps the first horse and so on. It is usually at any given point in time a temporary arrangement.

In addition, cometh the weapon, cometh the countermeasures, then the counter-countermeasures, and the counter-counter-countermeasures, and so on. In my experience there was never a need to worry about a technology problem that could have put the result of the campaign in the balance.

But we did suffer a certain disadvantage that caused me conscious irritation and about which few people talk. This drawback was the result of geographical chance, misfortune, *friction de guerre*.

The airfields at Cuito Cuanavale and Menongue from where the Soviet pilots, the Cubans and Angolans operated, were very close to the battle area. By contrast we had to operate from much further, from Rundu and Grootfontein. (Map no 2)

The disadvantages are obvious. To name a few: In practice it took our ground attack fighters such as the F1AZs 42 minutes from Grootfontein to the target area which gave them three minutes fighting time. From Rundu it took our air to air fighters like the F1CZs 18 minutes, which gave them 17–20 minutes over the combat area. Our enemies, on the other hand, needed only 11 minutes over the much shorter distance from Menongue, which gave them approximately 45 minutes over the battle field. If the geography had been the other way round, or if it had only been neutral, it would have been a horse, or rather a course, of a different colour. Then we would have exceeded our proven excellence.

Whatever other questions still may be asked and answers given – it will not change the scoreboard nor the result.

20

REVOLUTIONARY POLITICS
Perceptions and false perceptions – 'The pig in the middle'

At the end of the road through Angola and South West I could now shake the dust of war and peace from my feet. But in South Africa the thunderstorms and clouds of unrest were pouring scattered political violence.

The use of violence in the form of terror to achieve political aims follows a pattern.

It was a phenomenon in Africa after World War II that many political parties, of which some were also resistance movements, had their own 'armed wing'. Everyone calls it by a different name to suit his politics.

In South West only one of the political organizations, Swapo, had its own armed wing – Plan. In South Africa we were in much the same position as in South West. Only the ANC's *Umkhonto we Sizwe* (MK) was worth mentioning.

However, one cannot in any way compare MK with military wings such as Fapla of the MPLA, Fala of Unita and Plan of Swapo; not in respect of numbers, capability, history, military achievement and armament. Be that as it may, as a psychological factor and an implement to aid political efforts, MK could not be ignored.

As a result of its armed capability Swapo decidedly had a political edge over the other parties in Namibia. Swapo supported its politics to the end with the use of weapons, or the threat to do so. The same could happen in South Africa.

But here the situation has become more confused. The PAC's Apla has become more prominent on the news front. Whether it really now possesses a bigger capability that it had in the past, I cannot say. In the meantime armed organizations are also emerging on the right of the political spectrum. If you allow one party to have its own 'defence force' you cannot deny it to another.

If only one party has its own military capability, the chances are good that when arms are laid down you could have a bloodless period of transition following it – as in Namibia. If two parties have the capability, the possibility of civil war of a kind in the transitionary phase cannot be excluded – as in Angola. If more than two parties possess armed capabilities, it can lead to anarchy. Perhaps one should try to ignore them into insignificance. If you cannot do that, it is already a sign that their intimidation is successful and then you have to constrain that.

I am not altogether sure who is going to shoot who but if this lot breaks loose, we will certainly reach the point where the Defence Force will again have to assist the police. Therefore it is of vital importance that the Defence Force remain neutral.

It is definitely no longer the time for revolutionary movements and take-over strategies. It is the time for political parties and settlement politics. It would nevertheless seem during 1992 and the beginning of 1993 as if the PAC, ANC and the SACP are showing some reluctance to wave goodbye to armed wings. For decades they had lived in the atmosphere which prevailed in the Soviet Union, its satellite states and allies, such as Cuba and Libya – the atmosphere created by dictators, one-party states and communism. The doctrines they had practised for years were those of revolution and other violent forms of seizing power.

It is certainly not good for the extremely important politics of today still incessantly to hear of maintenance of underground structures, forming of defence units, mass action and the 'struggle continues'. This language belongs to revolutionary models. It creates suspicion exactly at a time when one wants to foster mutual trust. It makes me think of what sovietologist, Dr Jan du Plessis, said many years ago: The Soviet top leaders used to talk of peaceful co-existence or whatever the nice 'in'-words of the time were; in the meantime, however, instructions were going out to the Communist Party or the KGB to divide, to cause friction, to start revolutions – to incite violence.

The same pattern has also occurred in Africa. The top figure says the nice things. Meanwhile the party, the military wing or the youth movement receives orders to commit violence. Even after this phase and when peace negotiations begin, the problem does not cease to exist.

After Angola and South West an officer told Fred Bridgland, 'We have won the war, but can we manage the negotiations?' It is difficult. Diplomacy is not the only alternative to war, there is also politics. But there are politics and politics. Communist schooled revolutionary movements conduct a revolution through revolutionary politics and revolutionary warfare. But when the revolutionary war comes to an end, the revolutionary politics continue. Call it what you like, political warfare, psychological warfare, street politics, propaganda, or whatever; it is on this field of revolutionary politics where politicians, used to the Westminster kind of democratic politics, normally find themselves awkwardly off-sides.

It is the politics of mobilization of the masses, control of the masses, enforcing stay-away actions, boycotts and strikes. It is the politics of ultimatums, demands, claims and threats. It is the politics of creating perceptions through uninterrupted repetitions of accusations.

You do not have to like revolutionary street politics, but one thing is sure, you cannot ignore it; and you do not have to. It can be countered. If you do not do it, the non-stop allegations create suspicion, and the suspicion creates impressions, and they become firm public perceptions which later cannot be changed.

However, in South Africa we have to cope with violence erupting from politically related unrest as well. Unrest also forms a pattern.

In 1984, 1985 and 1986 unrest followed on the inception of the tricamaral parliament. The unrest was revolutionary by nature and aimed at the authority. The unrest that started in 1990, and which at the writing of this book is still in full swing, similarly followed on political change. It was to be expected that we would experience a renewed wave of unrest after the coming to power of the new president, the release of political prisoners and the unbanning of political organizations. In the beginning it was not of a revolutionary kind and not aimed against the authority.

This wave of unrest was also politically inspired, but of a different nature.

The unity among black people which was based on a common cause, namely to acquire political power, has crumbled. In the new dispensation accomplishing their aspirations became possible – without having to fight for it. As a consequence the black parties and politics-related organizations in their endeavours to obtain political power became fierce political opponents. This has given rise to polarization, friction and violence. Political conflict between factions began to include armed clashes.

The problem now was not so much that of national security but rather that of public safety. Not so? Most of the analysts use sociopolitical and socio-economic models with which to analyse the situation and make forecasts. They are valid, but other models should not yet be discarded. The unrest of 1984, 1985 and 1986 neatly fitted more than one revolutionary model. After political reform, revolutionary incitement of unrest should go out of fashion.

But we can expect that unrest-related violence will spill over into the reforming transitionary period. It may continually increase or decrease in intensity and frequency, but it will be there. Every political peak, referendum, election or whatever, brings its own friction. It does not matter if it is a success or a failure. What is heartening for one is a serious disappointment to the other.

After the transitionary phase of political reform we can expect a new wave of violence and indeed of a socio-economic and criminal nature. It will also probably be manipulated for political gain. Sociologists claim that the population growth cannot meaningfully and timeously be checked. Economists say that we will not be able to reach the economic growth necessary to provide jobs for our population. Over a few years, consequently, we shall have to face the prospects of thousands of young people, many of whom have only scanty education and training, without the moral support of the family unit, and unable to find jobs. Those who cannot be upgraded will probably have to be suppressed.

I am optimistic. Dr Wim de Villiers assured me that the economy will be able to provide enough work. I believe him. And Prof Laurie Schlemmer says that something can be done about the searching jobless youth. I believe him. One consolation is that if extraordinary measures are necessary to suppress violence, they will be much more acceptable than before because the new government will be more popularly regarded as legitimate.

The entry of rightwing radicals to the arena of violence became a serious problem during 1992. It can be contained on a manageable level, or it can break loose and become a serious threat to the negotiation process. But sooner or later the negotiators will have to return to the conference room. Through all this the role of the security forces remains vitally important.

I agree with those who say that sorting out unrest incidents is not the primary task of the Defence Force. But there are other angles to the problem. I would like to put the matter into perspective.

Those who were opposed to the use of the Defence Force in unrest situations, propagated their cause very actively and emotionally through the mass media. Thus it happened that a general impression was created that it was negative and evil. Anybody who wanted to say anything positive about it, did not count. Then you were out of step. You were promoting immoral doctrines. The emotions mobilized against the employment of the military seriously damaged neutral and objective approaches to the problem. I would like to plead for fairness and rational thinking, because the public opinion of this matter can greatly assist in solving the future problems of our country, or it can do a lot of harm.

I still agree that the use of troops in internal unrest situations should be limited to the minimum, but it is also true that virtually all countries of the world provide for it in their legislation. And they make use of it.

The Defence Force, like most other government departments, does not have only one primary task. And in this respect our Defence Act is in line with international customs.

The National Guard of the US has state and federal functions to protect life and property and to maintain peace, order and public safety under conditions determined by law. And it is regularly called up for such duties.

In South Africa too troops have been used in unrest situations over many decades and by governments of different parties.

We should never regard the use of troops in unrest situations as completely taboo. The insistence on not employing troops has boomeranged on us before. At one stage during 1990 a variety of people and organisations almost pleaded for deploying troops in unrest stricken residential areas. For example, newspapers reported that the Black Sash had come out in support of deploying troops in Natal. Troops were used and they received praise for their actions. I received letters of appreciation.

Just as I had done during previous waves of unrest, on this occasion too, I formulated a personal message printed on a card which was issued to each and every soldier performing unrest duties. By doing so I had made public my approach to the situation and the orders to the troops. It read as follows:

Fellow Soldier

Hundreds of people have already lost their lives in the renewed conflict in the black townships. Property, freedom and the right to a peaceful existence has been destroyed.

The people have the right to protection. We have been asked to assist in providing it.

During 1984 and the years thereafter you have been asked to deliver this service amid violence and chaos similar to what is at present happening in some areas.

This time, however, there are important differences – some of the people who previously insisted on your withdrawal from those areas, today plead for your presence – it is a tribute to you, the soldiers of this country.

Nowadays violence is often aimed not so much against the state to achieve political goals, but it is used rather to settle disputes amongst groups of the population.

Justice and good order is essential for stability and for the future of our country and all its people.

Be firm but friendly, determined but impartial; and above all, fair.

Respect the person and property of other people!

I appreciate your valuable contribution.

Gen Jannie Geldenhuys.

My sons also received these cards.

Martin, in the meantime, through war and all, had studied privately and passed the Military Academy's second-year exams at the end of 1987. He was now qualified to go back to the Academy in 1988 full-time to complete the final year. And in 1989 he was back at 32 Battalion.

I coincidentally bumped into him a few times. Once was in Angola when I had work to do there at the JMC after the Lusaka Agreement. He was involved with the joint South African-Angolan patrolling. Another time was when he was doing unrest duty in Natal.

Bruwer voluntarily signed up for eighteen months' 'short service' after completing his national service. He cleared out as a lieutenant from the Defence Force in December 1990. He too did unrest duty in Natal.

I had undergone training in unrest duties during the early years of my military career, in the 1950s, while still smelling of quartermaster stores. And we should continue to do so. We must not emotionally cut our nose to politically spite our face. Take care.

The problem is that propaganda is being used during times of conflict to create false perceptions for political gain. However, in the following phase of reconciliation, they are being kept alive and obstructing the peace process.

But I still believe in the basic ideal that it should not be necessary to use the Defence Force for such service. We must give the police the opportunity to increase their numbers. As far as possible they should be able to manage unrest themselves, at least for normal, and even short-lived abnormal, situations. During the early 1990s the police force is indeed far below strength in comparison with the police forces of other countries of the world.

But the police need our sympathy and co-operation. They have to be neutral and treat all political parties alike. But there are parties and parties. They are not all like the Democratic Party of South Africa, the Conservative Party of the UK or the Republican Party of the US. Some parties have their own armed wings, their own intelligence departments and what have you – such as 'undergrounds'. What now? Should the intelligence community demonstrate the same lack of interest in them as in the others?

If the police turn up at a place of unrest before violence starts, they are accused of having caused the violence; if they arrive after the violence had begun, the accusation is that they purposely arrived late and could have prevented the violence through timeous action; if they arrive there just at the 'right time', their mere presence created the climate for violence, or they erred in some way or another.

In the Western world the security forces called upon to serve during situations of internal conflict are always the target of propagandists. It follows a pattern. In future we can expect that again there will be real objectors, pretentious objectors and supposed objectors from many quarters which will agitate against the 'unholy' and 'unjust war'. It is always the same. Indeed, the book by Desmond Hamill on the British security forces in Northern Ireland is titled:

PIG IN THE MIDDLE, The army in northern Ireland 1969–1984.

21

THE END OF THE STORY
Ancient history and peace syndromes

Owing to politics, propaganda and suspicion, different attitudes exist towards the role and image of the Defence Force.

It is unfair, in my opinion, to accuse the Defence Force of wittingly having gone all out to protect evil practices. Impressions have and are being created which do not reflect the true characteristics of the Defence Force. I do not believe that a single soldier ever joined the Defence Force with the purpose, or even the vaguest notion, of becoming a champion of evil.

The single most important theme of Gen Pop Fraser's study, completed and officially accepted as far back as 1960–1961, was that the prevention or winning of a revolutionary war required 80% political effort and only 20% military activity.

In fact, the 20% military action was meant to prevent violent revolutionary take-over, maintaining stability and public safety while political and constitutional solutions were being sought. Military solutions were not regarded as real solutions.

Gen Malan, indeed, publicly supported this eighty-twenty principle over a period of 25 years, such as on 20 October 1981 at a banquet in Johannesburg: '... the solution to a revolutionary terrorist war is only 20% military. The main burden, that is 80%, rests with the politicians.' His stated point of view was, in fact, used by many of his political opponents as ammunition with which to blast him, for example during the parliamentary debates of 23 April, 12 May and 16 May 1986.

My successors and I likewise publicly declared that it was our task in South West to create sufficient order, stability and safety so that the internal constitutional development and international politics could follow its course to democracy and independence. And significant progress had been made in this direction during that time.

To tell the truth, there is no bigger single group of South Africans with more experience of living in a country in such an advanced stage of total democracy as our defence people in South West. They served with cheerful devotion. As from 1978 South West was way ahead of South Africa in terms of political reform. The Turnhalle Conference was already constituted during 1977, fourteen years before Codesa, even if not according to the exact same blueprint.

The biggest and toughest battles we ever fought together with the SWA Territory Force, happened after the corner stones of apartheid in South West had already been destroyed. As far back as December 1978 one-person-one-vote elections took place. The free democratic process was well on track. Swapo had been invited to participate in the process. One can but wonder whether they would have done better or worse than during 1989 if they had accepted the invitation.

Some political commentators, usually apathetic towards the Defence Force, for a long time promoted the idea that the army should be a professional, in other words, a voluntary organization. Okay, let us hypothetically assume that we had had a purely voluntary army since 1948. Then for decades we would not have had national servicemen representative of the whole range of the white political spectrum. Then also we would not have had the Citizen Force and Commandos equally representative of all the white political persuasions. If through the years we only had volunteers, we would probably have ended up in the 1990s with a purely Malan, Strijdom, Verwoerd and Vorster army. Would we not then have had a type of party-political army? Or what am I saying?

No, if the Defence Force was evil, it was no more evil than the government. And if the government is now good, the Defence Force is now no less good.

War is an activity involving violence and passion.

War is subject to the vagaries of human behaviour.

War is essentially subordinated to politics.[1]

The most fundamental element of Clausewitz's philosophy is that war is subject to politics, and should be. He says it many times and in many ways. But politicians are not always the best people to assist the military with their war problems, which they would not have had if it had not been for the politicians.

The Defence Force would have served the government if Gen Smuts had tried to realise his idea of incorporating South West into the Union of South Africa. The Defence Force did serve the government when the Odendaal Commission divided South West into subterritories representing different population groups – only there was no military duty to perform. The Defence Force did serve the government when there was a 'majority government' in South West during the 1980s. The Defence Force is serving the government in times of reform and transition.

During a joint sitting of parliament on 1 March 1992 Mr F W de Klerk said:

> The government and I are proud of our security forces and their achievements. They saved the lives of many innocent people and bought time for South Africa through their successful counterrevolutionary actions over the years against conflict and terror. That is why we can now work full-steam to get the new South Africa politically and economically going.

He said that he looked upon the security forces as an indispensable element of a safe and stable future.

The employment and control of the Defence Force in future, besides the government of the day, will probably be prescribed by a law such as a constitution, which would in turn probably be maintained by an independent judiciary.

The country still needs the Defence Force. And it will need it again in future. It does not seem as if much is coming of the 'new order' for the world. The question, whether the present Africa culture can support a democratic Africa, has yet to be answered. While the new arrangement of blocs, the new Europe, the Americas, and the Pacific Rim, draws much attention, we also cannot totally ignore the many forecasts that the overwhelming majority of Africa is dying. Many reasons are offered. One is its inability to use new technology in order to increase its well-being.

As a result of European and other countries needing all their time and money to solve their own problems, Africa runs the risk of returning form its present prominent position in the international floodlights to its former proverbial state of darkness. How long will it take them before they once again turn the spotlight on Africa to take a renewed closer look at its many unexploited assets – and in the process causing clashes of interests: And will such possible disputes be settled without the use of violence? In such a case, one should always bear in mind that a defence force is not there to protect your interests only by waging war. It is there to serve your interests by preventing war giving you a seat around the conference table.

Although after every war there are people who think that war serves no purpose and will never occur again, this is not how it has worked out until now. Before a war people are often enthusiastic over the idea. After a war people are often caught up in the syndrome that war is futile. It becomes a recurring cycle.

Somebody once told Gen Denis Earp, former Chief of the Air Force: 'It served absolutely no purpose to have made war in Korea.'

Now, before I describe his reaction, one should remember Denis does not talk lightly on the subject of armed conflict. During the same war, on 27 September 1951, his aircraft's cooling system was shot to pieces. He had to eject and was caught near Kaesong. For 23 months and three days he was a guest of Red Chia. He was released only towards the end of August 1953, after peace had been concluded on 27 July. And on the fifth of January 1982 Puma pilot, Lt Michael John Earp, was killed in action shortly after his twenty-sixth birthday during South Africa's border war. He was Denis and Beth's only son.

However, he replied:

> How can you say that? After all, we saved a country, South Korea and its people, from communist domination which in other countries had caused so much grief and misery to so many people over so many decades. And look where South Korea is today – one of the most dynamic and prosperous industrial countries of the world. North Korea, its neighbour, by way of contrast is one of the most miserable, cruelest and suppressive of all the Stalinistic countries. It is also one of the poorest.

Every year the South Koreans still express their thanks and pay tribute to South Africa and to our air force.

What did we achieve in South West and Angola?

I have no doubt that Swapo's goal was to seize power in South West by force. In fact they said so themselves and on many occasions. And they also tried to do it. Furthermore I have no doubt that they would then seriously have been tempted to establish a one-party Marxist government – on the style of Mozambique and Angola of the 1970s and 1980s.

Our military countermeasures prevented that. The mission of the Defence Force and the SWATF, as publicly stated, was to make its contribution towards giving South West its independence in the form of a democracy. It was to have happened by means of constitutional change as opposed to violent revolutionary takeover. That is what we achieved.

Still there are people who say that nothing was achieved by the war. Commentators' interpretations of the war depend on where they position themselves politically in respect of the war effort. Naturally I will be inclined to correct the 'distorted picture', as I see it. It was meaningful that we had kept the security situation stable up to 1988.

Although the intensity of the conflict increased, the security forces remained on the winning path while Plan was losing ground. In the meantime Fapla, on which Plan depended heavily, were steadily losing ground against Unita. We won time until 1988, creating a favourable situation for a political solution.

One would unconsciously be inclined to analyse the war years against the background and thought patterns of the present situation. We took such a quantum leap during the early 1990s that only with great difficulty can we a few years later properly think ourselves into the forgotten ancient history of the 1970s and 1980s.

But we have to place ourselves back into the circumstances of that time. Cuba, which played a big role, still believed in a military victory in Angola. Until 1989 the MPLA still bargained on it. Within South Africa itself the ANC and the SACP believed that they were going to destroy the structures of the administration by December 1986 – with matches and necklaces. The so-called frontline states reached the peak of their political aggressiveness against South Africa during the same year. If a settlement had to be negotiated under military pressure during the middle 1980s you can imagine how one-sided and excessive the revolutionaries' demands would have been.

During a conference on 3 November 1989 Dr Wim de Villiers said:

> In 1975 South Africa stood almost alone in an environment where Marxism and one-party states were being established. But we won this third colonial war in Africa.
>
> We gained time for the rest of the communist system to fall to pieces all over the world.

If it was not our strategy to gain a quick overall military victory, it certainly was to fight over a period in order to create a situation inducive to the favourable settling of political disputes. And that we did. If anybody finds fault with this approach I have to shoulder at least part of the blame.

There are also those who say that the war only foiled our diplomacy; that we caused South Africa's isolation; and that the war impoverished us.

I always believed, and it has now been proved by recent history, that South Africa absolutely had no hope in any way whatsoever, war or no war, to be accepted by the international community of states while its domestic policy remained what it was.

During 1989 we did get a new government with a new policy. Political prisoners were released, banned organizations were unbanned, including the SACP. Even so, it takes years to get back, and it will never be complete until a new constitution and a new government are in place.

We would have been in a much worse position if we had not held the front. The mere cessation of the war would not have brought us back into the international world while apartheid was still in force.

It is also clear now that the war did not cause disinvestment and trade boycotts. Even if the war ended, those problems would have remained. The problem was politics. We did in fact conclude peace in 1988 and it made no difference to any boycott. Hopeful signs only appeared during 1990 when the politics were changed. It takes years.

And still people say the war was unnecessary. Swapo won the elections, not so? Swapo did – it is true. But Namibia is a multi-party democracy with a sound constitution that only needs to be maintained. The representative distribution of parties in parliament is a good start. Friends tell me things are going well there.

Swapo collected 57% of the votes and the moderate parties 43%.

The *Sunday Times* of 24 September 1989 reported that the Arnold Bergstraesser Institute had found in June 1989, after a three-month opinion poll, shortly before the eflections, 'if an election had been held in June the South West African's People's Organisation would have won easily with two thirds of the votes.'

The authoritative South African Institute for International Affairs in a forecast gave Swapo something like 60% to 70% of the votes.

Many commentators' predictions on the election result were hopelessly wrong. To them the result came as a shock. Swapo drew substantially less votes than they expected. Analysts should have asked themselves where their information went wrong, or where their judgement left them in the lurch. However, they made a big mistake.

I would say that they were the victims of excellent Swapo propaganda, and they suffered from *fiction de guerre*. And they ignored the influence of the successes of the security forces.

I always said that if the Swapo fighters were to return to South West from the bush proud, neat and triumphant they would clinch a large majority. First they came back through flagrant violation of the settlement plan and thereafter mainly as refugees. They never even returned according to the directions of the settlement plan.

Our endeavours enabled us to keep the war on the winning path until South West, Angola and South Africa were in the best position over the past ten years for constitutional transition to democracy. South Africa's bush and border war must be rated among the most successful wars of its kind since World War II.

In future South Africa will be cited as a good example of a country that waged war at low cost, even during an arms boycott. Indeed the war was almost entirely financed from a normal defence budget which could be favourably compared with other budgets internationally.

An analysis of the total amount of money allocated to the defence force during the ten completed financial years for which audited appropriation balance sheets were submitted to parliament by the auditor general (1977–1978 to 1986–1987) shows the following:

During these ten years the defence allocation in real terms was an average of R7 173 million per year, which is slightly less than the R7 232 million for 1977–1978. In real terms the 1986–1987 defence allocation was 7,6% higher than the 1977–1978 allocation as opposed to the 37,6% increase for the country as a whole.

Defence expenditure as a percentage of state expenditure decreased from 18,4% in 1977–1978 to 14,4% in 1986–1987. Defence expenditure as a percentage of the gross national product decreased from 4,8% for 1977–1978 to 4,2% for 1986–1987.

In real terms, at 1988 rand values, the amount budgeted by the Department of Public Works for the Defence Force decreased from R272 million for 1977–1978 to R197 million for 1986–1987 – a decrease of 28%. Figures which I released on 1 April 1989 showed that the costs of our involvement in South West ran into R580 million per year, plus limited assistance to Unita. The defence budget was less than 5% of the gross national product. It compares favourably with countries such as the USA (6,5%), the UK (5,4%), Israel (14,8%), and Mozambique (10,8%).

The Defence Force provided SWATF with equipment and other stores against repayment. During the six years before independence the Department of Finance provided for additional budgetary assistance in respect of defence to South West; during the 1988–1989 book year it amounted to R80 million.

We were definitely not insensitive to financial matters. While I am on the subject of finance and while one had to endure so many taunts of the 'rich' senior civil servants enjoying such a 'good life', I cannot help but use this opportunity to mention that during my last few years an Airways Boeing captain received a larger income than the Chief of the South African Air Force. There were about a hundred Boeing captains.

Towards the end of 1986 we formalized our productivity improvement programme and already during 1988 received a gold award in the competition run by the National Productivity Institute.

I now conclude my review of the war with the final bit on the Soviet factor. We believed that the Soviets' military involvement in Angola, together with other factors, would have exhausted them so much that eventually they would have had to give it up.

During the late 1980s a certain aspect drew more and more attention: it is one thing to have the technological capability to manufacture armaments, such as the Soviet Union did; but it is another thing to use those armaments; and it is a totally different kettle of fish to use those armaments thousands of kilometres away, while having to maintain them technically. With every technological advance it becomes more difficult.

In contrast we could use our new technology armaments in Angola straight away while also being able to provide the necessary logistic and technical support and so forth. In fact we even operationally tested weapon systems in Angola which were still in the project stage, for example the G6 and the Rooikat. Nobody else was in the position to do the same. We won the race in the use of new technology in Angola in 1987–1988.

I have said earlier that I publicly stated that the Soviet Union could burn its fingers in Angola – and that my statement had been reported by the media. I want to turn to that now, but let us look first at what Crocker's man, Chas W Freeman Jr, said on the same topic. He was Principal Deputy Assistant Secretary of State for African Affairs from

April 1986 till May 1989. He made this statement with the benefit of hindsight during 1989:

> As the Soviets embraced perestroika and looked afresh at southwestern Africa, they came to see their escalating exposure as more expensive in both economic and political terms than their interests could justify. They sought to cut their losses, and to do so in a way that would gain them a reputation as responsible international actors with the United States and the West more generally.

With the same benefit of hindsight Heitman said in 1990:

> They (Moscow) were already badly embarrassed by Afghanistan and really did not need another endless insurgency in their empire. They also had clear memories of what happens to armies that overreach themselves logistically – that very error by an enemy had twice saved Russia from defeat.

One of the times I commented on the matter was during a public address at the Windhoek showgrounds. It was during 1979, ten years before Freeman and Heitman. I quote from *Die Suidwester* of September 1979:

> Turning to the international world he said that Soviet Russia has moved so far out of its sphere of influence and its area of interest, that it was now running the risk of burning its fingers in Angola such as happened to the United States in Vietnam.
>
> Soviet Russia is also now unpopular with the international community as a result of its intervention in Afghanistan, Geldenhuys said.

***

During the early 1990s it became a general intellectual exercise, political discourse and speculation game to ask what the ultimate political end of the military result of the 1987–1988 war in Angola would be. Who were and would be the political winners and losers?

I am often pressurized to give my opinion. As a soldier it makes me feel as if I were in a minefield with barbed wire obstacles, vehicle mines, personnel mines and booby traps – too scared to make a move.

What was the influence of the Cold War on events in our region and what will the influence of its end be on our future? When did the Cold War begin to end and why? Can we already now answer these questions? The question is being asked: Is the result of the 1987–1988 war and the negotiations that followed the cause of democracy in Namibia, or was the end of the Cold War the reason?

I do not know why it must be the one or the other. I do not believe that the result of the war caused the end of the Cold War. However, I do believe that the Soviet Union's involvement in the war as a whole, considered together with its involvement with armed conflict elsewhere in the world, decidedly contributed towards its crumbling. At the very least the conclusion and result of the war represented some of the last convulsions of the Cold War. Fact is that the end of the 1987–1988 war, which ended favourably for us, happened in the same time slot as the fall of the Berlin wall in 1989 and they jointly played major roles in establishing Namibia's democracy.

I find it difficult, in a fast changing world and region, to make forecasts. War is still raging in Angola; Mozambique is preparing itself for elections and multiparty politics; there is a new government in Zambia; the future of Zaire is unsure and reform is taking place in South Africa.

I find it just as difficult to forecast backwards what the course of our region would have been if the South African government had followed a different policy in regard to South West Africa after the end of World War II. What would Namibia have looked like today if it had been an independence baby, born of the Cold War in 1950 or in 1960, or during the middle 1970s when Angola and Mozambique became independent, or in 1980 when Zimbabwe became independent? I do not know. We know what Namibia looks like now. Given the historical fact that armed conflict started during the Cold War, we could barely have done better.

The future may tell us that Pres de Klerk's speech of 2 February 1990, whether you are for or against it, was a more fateful event for South Africa. But once again it is difficult to say what would have happened if it had been delivered at any other time during the Cold War.

Winners? South Africa and Unita won the war. The MPLA and Unita continue to fight. South Africa can work out its future in a climate free of the Cold War. The United States won the Cold War and got the Cubans out of Angola. The people of Namibia got peace, peacefulness and democracy – a rare phenomenon in this subcontinent.

***

My last glance at the war, however, is still not the end of the Angolan story. And it is a story with a moral. Elections took place during September 1992 under UN supervision after the peace agreement was signed between the Angolan government and Unita.

In the presidential election Pres dos Santos led by a head; and in the general elections the MPLA won by quite a few lengths. Savimbi refused to accept the results and the long war recommenced. It was the same old story all over again – propaganda, propaganda, propaganda. South Africa again became the target. The Angolans alleged that they had shot down a South African aircraft giving support to Unita. The last I heard was that South Africa requested Angola to provide substantiating evidence – and never another word.

Another accusation was that South Africa assisted Unita from Rundu in Namibia. Namibia was an independent country in full control of Rundu and probably one of Angola's best friends. The next allegation was that South Africans were fighting on the side of Unita and that more were being recruited.

As had happened earlier in the case of Mozambique, Angolans in Luanda told South African confidants not to bother about the accusations, 'because we have to say these things for political reasons'. The problem is that so many people believed them.

But then, in any case, reports reached the newspapers telling quite a different story: South Africans being killed and wounded, while fighting against Unita, defending government controlled oil installations in Angola's war zone!

This brother versus brother peace-time war in Angola after an agreement had been reached, is the bloodiest in the history of the country. I tend to think that the sponsors and overseers of the agreement should bear part of the blame.

One of the defects probably was that South Africa played no visible role in the negotiations. I hope that the peace process in our other neighbouring country, Mozambique, will not suffer from the same defect. Many people look upon Namibia's transition as a model and I believe the success was due particularly to South Africa's involvement, rather than in spite of it. Min Pik Botha once went to Angola to try to assist in saving the situation, but it was too late and he was sent back.

While the war dragged on, the government and Unita were playing the good-guy, bad-guy game. The government won.

For South Africa there are important lessons to be learned. It involves the planning and managing of peace and election processes.

Sapa Reuter and Sapa AP reported in the *Pretoria News* of 8 October 1992:

> ... Angolan Foreign Minister, Pedro de Castro von Dunem, conceded that 500 000 ballot papers – 12% to 13% of the votes – were invalid, but he said, his government was 'trying to identify the irregularities that had taken place'.

A news bulletin of the SABC read:

> Portuguese observers who monitored the elections during December, meanwhile allege that large-scale fraud had been committed. The spokesman of the group, Mrs Maria Antonia Paula, says the MPLA government was responsible for the wangling that took place before, during and after the elections. She says irregularities occurred with the registration of voters and numbers of ballot boxes were transported without the observers of all the parties being present. Mrs Paula says the truth never came out because most of the international observers had left Angola before the results of the elections had been announced.

With a view to the future one should take note of these reports. According to another report, from UP, Lisbon, 26 November 1992, internal documents of the UN show that, 24 hours before the UN representative, Margaret Anstee, declared the elections as 'generally free and fair', she had been advised by her staff that there was proof of election fraud. The key document of 16 October 1992 states:

> It may generally be concluded that there were irregularities discovered in the electoral process which could have affected the overall outcome of the voting. In some cases, the volume of votes lost or gained by each candidate could, taken nationally, be so significant as to distort the final results.

The same report alleges that Anstee took her decision with trepidation because the investigations of Unavem, the UN's group, generally supported the opposition parties' accusations. The deciding factor apparently was an expedient political decision, made in the office of the Secretary General in view of the costs of a second round of elections should this one be annulled, and to avoid international embarrassment.

At one stage Mr Pik Botha, speaking in Gaborone, expressed his concern that the election problems could put a question mark behind the legitimacy of the results. He requested the UN to provide additional personnel for the monitoring of the second round of elections. It never happened.

What really bothered me was that during this time the news media carried reports to the effect that various persons propagated that the election results should be accepted 'whether they were free and fair or not' – in the interest of peace. I hope that 'elections and peace as soon as possible and at all costs' does not become a widely held view. It is too costly. It did not require special insight to forecast that war would again have erupted – the most destructive ever. Elections can promote, or even be essential for peace, but they are not a guarantee for it. In practice peace needs a sound base to take form. While I was listening to Margaret Anstee, early 1994, delivering a paper on 'Angola, what went wrong?', I realized that my warning against 'elections and peace at all costs' was not far off the mark. She asserted that the 'inelasticity' of the election date, which she had been unable to change, was one of the biggest problems.

During negotiations it is essential, sooner or later, to fix certain deadlines. These, however, should be set with great circumspection as deadlines often lead to deadlocks.

Was lack of time perhaps a major cause for the widely condemned *coup d'état* which was regarded as essential to get Bophuthatswana to toe the line? Or perhaps for the deadlock over KwaZulu?

Then there were elections in Kenya that came under suspicion.

Mozambique and South Africa are also preparing for elections, and it would be irresponsible not to learn from the lessons of previous elections. South Africa cannot be compared to Angola, but the aspects that should receive attention during the planning and preparation are obvious. I have no reason to suspect that it is not being done. One can only imagine how the South African parties would react if a 12% acknowledged irregularity occurred during the election without having provided for a mechanism to deal with such a contingency in a satisfying manner. The media can play a vital role.

***

My story ends in an era of the most intensive flood of democracy and philanthropy that the world has ever experienced.

The world of dictators and one-party states is crumbling. The Soviet Union is being democratized; most of Eastern Europe is being democratized, the US are using the threat of sanctions to get Argentina and Chile to abandon the road of military government and to turn onto the road of democracy. One-party states in Africa are being squeezed into the multi-party and democratic crush-pen.

My story ends with the highest springtide ever of humanitarianism, righteousness and human dignity.

The most extensive operations ever to feed the hungry of the world have been launched: Ethiopia, Somalia and Mozambique.

The rights of the individual are being extended to the rights of the elderly, children, unborn babies and animals.

Protection of the environment is the order of the day. Trade in ivory has been banned. The green rivulet of Green Peace is becoming a global flood with increasing momentum.

The warm war was replaced by the Cold War; and the Cold War has been replaced by peaceful co-existence. The USA and USSR have become negotiation partners. The uncontrolled arms race has been turned round into controlled arms reduction.

And yet?

Yet the Gulf War broke out – in many respects the most destructive violence the world has ever seen!

It is only war and peace again.

And yet the Yugoslavian war broke out.

It is only peace and war again.

South Africa banned its bomb.

We pray for peace and preach against war.

But in the meantime violence rages.

But it does not stop the peace syndrome. Now is the time for peace. That is the way the world wants it.

Although one should be fighting fit and employ combat craftiness when there is a war to be waged, one should not obstinately pursue battle when peace is being sought. The soldier who resists will find it hard to kick with his military boots against the political pricks. Just as certain syndromes come into play when nations decide to take up arms and make war, particular syndromes emerge when nations decide to engage in negotiations to make peace. The prospects of peace bring into play dynamics that have their own impetus.

A soldier must fall in with the political decisions taken in this atmosphere – with enthusiasm. His responsibility is to make war: then he needs maximum freedom of movement. The political leaders carry the responsibility when it comes to making peace: then they want maximum freedom of movement. When I had to make war, I did my best. And when I had to make peace, I did my best. But I was not wrong when I said it is easier to make war than peace.

Patterns and models are sometimes used to study the transition from war to peace. One of these, in its crudest form, is: the victor disarms the defeated, he dictates the conditions for peace, he smells out the war criminals and writes a history.

If this model is used in the case of the South Africa of the early 1990s, it would almost seem as if it is being applied the wrong way round. Ironically it was the ANC themselves who publicly told their militants that their claims should not be exorbitant, as the security forces had not been defeated in the field.

But the wrong model is being used. We are not so much in a transitionary stage from war to peace, as we are in transition from an old political era to a new political dispensation. For the study of such a situation, other models should be used, even if it is common practice to blame war for everything and to find fault with those who were held responsible for waging it. The real problem to be solved is not so much to make peace between military enemies, as to make peace between quarrelling political opponents.

It does not serve much purpose to look back. This is one lesson that we can learn from the new Namibian government. They did not yield to *Vergangenheitsbewältigung*. Because, if you are obsessed with managing the past, you become blind to the favourable opportunities of the present and you can end up with an unpredictable history and an uncertain future.

While the fault-seeking focus in South Africa falls on the war and warriors of the past, I would now like to take a look at the current peace and peace makers, whoever they may be, from a special angle, just to get another perspective. Making war is a way of settling clashes of interest. Making peace and negotiating, likewise, are processes for settling disputes. To make war is costly. What is the price of making peace?

During 1991–1993 we lost on average three times more policemen during peace while they were containing political violence than the members of the Security Forces lost in South West and Angola while they were waging war with aircraft and artillery. And it is just as costly.

According to various economists who were quoted in the press, one day's mass action stayaway costs the country R300 million to R500 million and even more. It could have financed one year of making war in South West and Angola. Likewise the amount of damage caused by currency fraud is being expressed in figures of hundred millions and billions of rand.

In its report of 18 March 1993 on violence during 1992, as published in *The Pretoria News* of the next day, the Human Rights Commission stated that the death toll as a result of politically related violence during 1992 had increased to 3 499. It means an average of 9,6 deaths per day and 35% more than during 1991. The worst period of violence, as one could have expected, was just before the referendum of 17 March 1992.

During the war we anxiously held our breath every time we saw the SADF flash coming up on the TV screen preceding the announcement of a war casualty during the news bulletin. Death through political violence has now become so bad, but generally accepted, that *The Pretoria News* keeps a routine scoreboard of the violence, like that of a weekly market report. I mention a few examples at random:

- **This is too much – Deaths in political violence:** midnight Thursday 26/11/92 to midnight Thursday 3/12/92 – 54; 12-week total since midnight Thursday 10/9/92 – **493**.
- **This is too much – Deaths in political violence:** midnight Thursday 11/3/93 to midnight Thursday 18/03/93 – 14; 27-week total since midnight Thursday 10/9/92 – **898**.
- **Deaths in unrest**: recorded from midnight Wednesday 30/03/94 to midnight Thursday 07/04/94 – 149; 82-week total since midnight Thursday 10/09/92 – 4 867.

According to *The Pretoria News* of 5 December 1992 the commissioner of police announced the previous day that more policemen had been killed during the year than during the wars in Namibia and Zimbabwe in any single year.

The Citizen of 25 January 1993 quoted a spokesman for the police who said it was the most in one year since the establishment of the police force in 1913.

To kill a policeman in the United States is a serious issue. In Israel they are prepared to cause grave international problems and to take military revenge if a member of the security forces is killed.

I spent a considerable part of this book on military leaders being supposedly reluctant to take decisions as they suffer so much emotional stress over loss of life, such as the 36 men we lost with grief during the big war in the south-east of Angola from mid-1987 to mid-1988.

The Defence Force accepted the responsibility for the war-time losses. Who is responsible for the peace-time losses?

The Citizen of 24 February 1993 quoted the psychiatrist, Dr Merryl Vorster, claiming that the daily bombardment of reports of crime during transit to a 'new' South Africa had caused the public to become insensitive, and to develop a general disregard for the value of human life.

Yes, she is right. It is possible that these figures do not shock, but only bore you.

The figures did not shock me either, but for a different reason than that mentioned by Dr Vorster. I had anticipated the violence because it was predictable. In fact, I forecast the violence during 1991 during at least three public seminars held under the auspices of one of our big banking groups.

I do not say this with any feeling of self-satisfaction. I mention it because when you anticipate something, and it happens, you do not get panicky. Now is not the time to lose your head. Now is not the time to begin thinking with your heart. Now is not the time to arouse suspicion between people. Now is not the time to point fingers.

Once again it is time to be strong in your belief, in your head and in your heart. Then we may walk the road of South Africa together.

* * *

As my story draws to an end and while reflecting on the past years I cannot help but be proud of the people of the Defence Force. Never since the Second World War has anybody got close to facing the full hitting power of the SA Defence Force. During the civil war in Angola of 1975–1976 our force level was about 3 000 men and again during the campaign of 1987–1988 in the south-east of Angola. With the unrest in South Africa between 1984 and 1987 our highest monthly average force level was 5 500. But this was a peace force.

When I look back I am proud of them all. From the generals at the top to the drivers at the bottom.

One of the most pleasant moments of my military career was when a big contingent of my drivers of the last number of years attended my Forty Days party on very short notice. They had organized the occasion with the help of my personal staff shortly before my retirement.

The people of the Defence Force stood firm and worked hard to create a situation with opportunities. Many of them lived for it and some of them gave their lives. I have come a long road with them. I will remember them.

Remember, war is war.

Peace is peace.

When it is war and you reflect on the past, remember that it was peace then.

When it is peace and you reflect on the past, remember that it was war then.

It is not easy.

But that is how we remember our soldiers of World War II. It was war.

Now we must remember our new veterans as follows:

War is not only war. There is also peace.

Peace is not only peace. There is also war.

If you reflect on the past, remember that it was war and peace, peace and war.

This is difficult.

I will remember our new veterans for walking together the road of peace and conflict, of joy and stress – the friction of war. Everything in war is difficult. If you want to repair your vehicles you have to drag a garage along with you in the battlefield. If you want to work during the night, you have to do so without light; or if you are allowed to have light, you have to supply your own power. Then you have to pack up and go and get it started again at some other place. That is how things go in war.

And on the journey through war, a multitude of unforeseen incidents can happen as a result of chance. And they accumulatively cause friction that makes everything in war difficult. As a result one never reaches peak performance. Everyone who participates in war is subject to such chance and it may mean bad luck. Everyone has the potential to make excusable mistakes and the least of these incidents can make things go wrong for many people – and cause us to lose the war.

Like they often say in rugby, cricket and other types of sport: we lost because we made too many mistakes. That is so, but one must take care. If you are only intent on not making mistakes, you do not try to score points yourself, you try to prevent your opponent from scoring points. Eventually you do not play to win any more, you play not to lose. Then you will lose.

One must be prepared to take calculated risks. Luck is on the side of the audacious.

But everything does not depend on your making few mistakes, or on your playing to win; it does not depend on fortune and misfortune. There is also another side. Clausewitz did not only write about *friction de guerre*, he also argued other factors – the quality of your people and the standard of their training. One does not only lose because you make too many mistakes; you win because you do the right things right.

If you do the right things right it can greatly compensate for the unforeseen misfortunes. That is why we won all our campaigns. Our people were top quality and they were well trained. Their tread was true, their fist was firm and their aim secure. Everyone played his part.

As a result of the standard of their training they caused less stress. As a result of their muscle and bone they could handle the stress. 'In their resistance to stress, in their ability to carry on when things go wrong, good officers are more easily distinguished from poor ones.' (Joint Staff Course Association Newsletter). That is how our people distinguished themselves; not only the officers – all of them.

I have heard speakers say 'everyone in the organization is important' at so many occasions, that I do not use such words myself. It has become such a common expression that to me it began to sound too much like superficial motivation and cheap encouragement, as if it was merely a matter of good manners and something nice to say. But if I now use those words, I know what I am talking about and I mean it. I have no need to motivate or flatter anybody. If I say that I thank every man and woman and pay tribute to them, I say it because I know it is the contributions of all of them which caused us to win. Arnold Glasow said: 'It doesn't take great men to do things, but it is doing things that makes men great.'

There were also those who did more than merely doing the right things right. Certain persons and groups of persons were genial and brave. Heroes. But they did not perform in stadiums in front of spectators like a Springbok rugby hero who scored a decisive three points for South Africa, or the cricketer who scored a matchwinning century. Yes, we had them in the Defence Force too, and I want to praise them. The value of their contributions was immeasurable. But even they could not have applied their courage, genius and utmost devotion without the others.

Some courageous and excellent people were publicly acclaimed. But there is a multitude of others who enabled us to win wars, each and everyone who did his bit, and of whom we did not hear, including those who are not mentioned in this book. I also think of Elizabeth Albrecht of the Southern Cross Fund and others like her and the thousands who assisted them to make life for the troops a little more pleasant. This book belongs to all of them and to all who believe in South Africa.

I see myself as one of the many. Referring to the many generals with whom and against whom Napoleon had campaigned, someone once asked him who the best generals were. He replied: 'The lucky ones.'

There are people who are known as 'being smiled upon by the goddess of fortune'. Others are described as 'being haunted by the bird of ill omen'.

People have told me too that I was lucky. But there are those who argue that luck does not only follow on chance. You can create your own luck. The formula is: You must know what you will; you must believe that you can; you must be enterprising and take the initiative; you must take calculated risks; and you must work hard and cleverly.

But there are others who say that if you try to harness luck it evades you like quicksilver.

On the other hand, Frank Clark said: 'It's hard to detect good luck – it looks so much like something you've earned.'[1]

Yes, I was lucky.

But bad luck struck me too.

There is a truth which is bigger than the chance, fortune and misfortune about which I wrote so much – fate. God rules all destinies.

I had two sons who were two of the many thousands of people I am talking about. Bruwer did his national service plus eighteen months voluntary duty. Martin did national service and then joined the Permanent Force. Both served in 32 Battalion.

Maj Harper Martin Geldenhuys was killed on 17 August 1991 in an air-craft incident at his unit at Pomfret. Chaplain Sidney Middlemost buried him there.

Thus, once again, I dedicate this book to all the thousands who served in the South African Defence Force and the South West African Territory Force – those who were injured or wounded, those who are already dead and those who are still alive.

Napoleon, having fought with many nations and against many nations, inspired Madame Montholon to ask him which were the best soldiers. He said:

'Those who are victorious.'

NOTES

Notes to chapter 1

1 'Boers' was what Angolans and Swapo called South Africans.
2 T N Dupuy

Notes to chapter 3

1 A J Brookes

Notes to chapter 5

1 Director General
2 S du Preez
3 W Steenkamp
4 The term security forces refers to members of the Army, Air Force, Navy, Medical Services, Permanent Force, Auxiliary Service, Citizen Force, Commandos and National Servicemen including South Africans and South West Africans of all ethnic groupings; Railway police, Police and Tribal police.

Notes to chapter 6

1 Nothing to report

Notes to chapter 7

1 *Militaria*
2 W Steenkamp
3 H Heitman (a)
4 P H R Snyman

Notes to chapter 8

1 B Retief
2 B Retief

Notes to chapter 9

1 W Steenkamp

[2] *Militaria*
[3] Contraction of 'Artificers'.

Notes to chapter 10

[1] *Windhoek Observer*, 12 July 1980
[2] *Conduct of War*
[3] *To the Point*, 23 September 1977
[4] H Heitman, 1990(a)

Notes to chapter 11

[1] *Militaria*
[2] Sgt-Maj Koos Kruger. He was once attacked by a crocodile which unsportingly removed parts of his upper leg.
[3] J Breytenbach

Notes to chapter 12

[1] S Armstrong

Notes to chapter 13

[1] Botswana, Angola, Mozambique, Tanzania, Zambia, Zimbabwe
[2] *The Citizen*, 2 November 1982

Notes to chapter 14

[1] A pack of dry rations.
[2] Ambassador to Switzerland since 1991.

Notes to chapter 15

[1] Goat ragout with chillies.

Notes to chapter 16

[1] Instituut voor Organisatie Ontwikkeling.
[2] Chester Crocker.

Notes for chapter 18

[1] *Politica International*
[2] P Esterhuysen
[3] P Esterhuysen
[4] P Esterhuysen

Notes to chapter 19

[1] *Sunday Times*
[2] S Barber *Business Day*; W Steenkamp

Notes to chapter 21

[1] Al Smith Feature Service.

REFERENCES AND ACKNOWLEDGEMENTS

Allen, Roy. 1980. *Sungong*. Windhoek: Gamsberg.

Armstrong, Sue. 1989. *In Search of Freedom: The Andreas Shipanga Story as Told to Sue Armstrong*, Gilbraltar: Ashanti.

Breytenbach, Jan. 1990. *They Live by the Sword: 32 "Buffalo" Battalion – South Africa's Foreign Legion*. Alberton: Lemur Books.

Bridgland, Fred. 1990. *The War for Africa: Twelve Months that Transformed a Continent*. Gilbraltar: Ashanti.

Brookes, Andrew J. 1975. *Photo Reconnaisance*. London: Ian Allen.

Brown, James Ambrose. 1991. *Retreat to Victory; A Springbok's Diary in North Africa, Gazala to Alamein 1942*. Johannesburg: Ashanti.

Conduct of War. 1950. British Army Pamphlet for Senior Officers.

Collyer, J.J. 1939. *Die Veldtog in Duits Suidwes-Afrika*. Pretoria: Die Staatsdrukker.

Crocker, Chester, A. 1993. *High Noon in Southern Africa: Making Peace in a Rough Neighborhood*. Johannesburg: Jonathan Ball Publishers.

Du Preez, Sophia. 1989. *Avontuur in Angola: Die Verhaal van Suid-Afrika se Soldate in Angola 1975-1976*. Pretoria: J.L. van Schaik.

Dupuy, T.N. 1987. *Understanding War: History and Theory of Combat*. New York: Paragon House Publishers.

Esterhuysen, Pieter and Leistner Erich. (Eds). 1991. *Namibia 1990: An Africa Institute Survey*. Africa Institute of South Africa.

Freeman. 1989. *The Angolan/Namibia Accords*. Foreign Affairs, Spring Edition.

Heitman, Helmoed-Römer. 1990(a). *South African Armed Forces*. Cape Town: Buffalo Publications.

Heitman, Helmoed-Römer. 1990(b). *War in Angola: The Final South African Phase*. Gilbraltar: Ashanti.

Instituut Voor Organisatie Ontwikkeling. *"Process of Escalation of Conflicts and Roles of Third Parties". Militaria*. 19 Februarie 1989, pp. 8, 9, 11.

Montgomery, F.M. 1958. *The Viscount Bernard Law of Alamein, K.G.; The Memoirs*. London: Collins.

Pakenham, Thomas. 1981. *Die Boere-Oorlog. (Vertaal deur Leon Rosseau.)* Johannesburg: Jonathan Ball.

Politica Internaçional. Accordos de Paz Para Angola. No. 4 (Verao, 91 Trimestral), p. 65.

Raw, Wyatt Vause. 1988. *Flares: Fragments in Discord.* Durban North: 54 Gleneagles Drive.

Retief, Bertrand. 1990. *Humour in S.A. Uniform.* Johannesburg: Perskor.

Sellars, Duncan W. *International Freedom Review.* 1989. Vol. 2, No. 2, p. 47.

Snyman, P.H.R. 1989. *Beeld van die SWA Gebiedsmag.* Pretoria: Public Relations, SADF.

Steenkamp, Willem. 1990. *Suid-Afrika se Grensoorlog 1966-1989.* Rivonia: Ashanti.

Tabois, Geneviève. 1938. *Blackmail or War.* 5th Ed. London: Wyman & Sons.

Westmoreland, William C. 1980. *A Soldier Reports.* Dell Publishing.

Zeitspiegel, Magazin für Entscheidungsträger No 5/4 JHG/89. "War and Peace, The Caribbean-African Way". Malek Druckerei Gesellschaft mbH.

SELECTED INDEX OF NAMES

As the history in this book takes place over a considerable timespan, military ranks have been omitted from this index as many of them changed over that period.

ICELAND
Brazzaville
Kinshasa
ZAIRE
Cabinda
Ambrizete
Luanda
NORWAY
Oslo
ANGOLA
Lobito
SCOTLAND
Namibe
IRELAND
ENGLAND
London
The Hague
GERMANY
BELGIUM
Bonn
BOTSWANA
Prague
ATLANTIC OCEAN
Paris
Walvis Bay
Windhoek
SWA/NAMIBIA
SWITZERLAND
Gaborone
Vienna
FRANCE
Mmabatho
Lüderitz
PORTUGAL
Madrid
ITALY
Barcelona
SPAIN
Rome
SOUTH AFRICA
Port Elizabeth
Cape Town